AMERICA
MADE IN BRITAIN

AMERICA
MADE IN BRITAIN

TOM ARMS

AMBERLEY

For my Family

First published 2021

Amberley Publishing
The Hill, Stroud
Gloucestershire, GL5 4EP

www.amberley-books.com

British Library Cataloguing in Publication Data.
A catalogue record for this book is available from the British Library.

ISBN 978 1 4456 9901 1 (hardback)
ISBN 978 1 4456 9902 8 (ebook)

1 2 3 4 5 6 7 8 9 10

Typeset in 10.5pt on 14pt Sabon.
Typesetting by SJmagic DESIGN SERVICES, India.
Printed in Great Britain.

Contents

Acknowledgements 6

Introduction: The Manor of Man 7

1 Prisoners of Geography 13

2 Liberty's Foundations 27

3 Liberty Takes Off 61

4 Liberty Matures 88

5 Liberty and Free Speech in the Modern World 118

6 The Slave Trade 133

7 I Believe 152

8 British Disasters That Made America 179

9 Money, Money, Money 202

10 Gun Control: Militia *vs* Tyranny 232

11 High Brow, Low Brow 250

12 War and Diplomacy 283

13 Role Reversal 313

Bibliography 343

Index of People 350

Acknowledgements

At the very top of the list of those who need to be thanked for help with this book is my son Christopher. He played a major role in determining the book's basic structure, read every word and provided valuable suggestions. He is proof that wise heads can be found on young shoulders.

In fact, I am blessed with a family that has always provided me with valuable support, help and advice including my wife Eileen, my other son Simon, our daughter Kimberly, her partner Liam Garrett and my brother Bob.

I have also received invaluable assistance from a number of people. Father Stuart Dunnan, headmaster of Saint James School, my alma mater, provided help on the religion chapter along with Rick Sullivan and Kenneth Ray.

Ray Cox, QC and David Coleman helped with chapters on the law. Colleagues from my days at Thomson Newspapers – John Marquis, Stuart Birch, John Tylee and David Cripps – came riding to my rescue with information and help on several occasions; as did one of India's better journalists, Ramananda Sengupta.

My weekly radio broadcasts with Lockwood Phillips at North Carolina's WTKF helped me to refine my thinking, as did regular political discussions with good friend, neighbour and former diplomat Tim Holmes.

Others who deserve thanks are Helgi Agustsson, Jean-Michel Gaussot, Chris Severs, David Graham, Carla Rapoport, David Raikes and George Rhyne. Finally, there is the team at Amberley Publishing, especially Connor Stait and Shaun Barrington. Apologies to anyone left off the list. I can assure you that all help, advice and support was appreciated.

INTRODUCTION

The Manor of Man

An architectural metaphor can be used to suggest that our present world can only be understood, and our futures planned, in the context of an understanding of our past. The edifice that mankind has built is not a simple building with four walls, a door and a few windows. It is a vast and growing structure with turrets, towers, arches, philosophical flying buttresses and the occasional folly. There are bricked-up windows, and then there are windows with awe-inspiring views. Some doors open into a filthy broom closet and others reveal rooms filled with beautiful art. In some rooms the doors have been blocked and walls bricked up to hide a terrible family secret; others proudly display vast libraries and achievements. But no matter how beautiful, indifferent, ugly or frightening a particular chamber, corridor or wall appears, they all share one common bond: the foundations. The most beautifully constructed edifice will collapse, or at least subside, without a firm knowledge of the bedrock that underpins this vast Manor of Man.

There is a myth that America is different. There is even a term for it: American exceptionalism. America, argue its adherents, is unique. It is the political equivalent of Venus who rose fully formed from the political ether. To a certain degree this is true. Every nation has its own history and culture, which differentiates it from others and helps to form the national identity that becomes an integral part of every individual citizen. But in most cases, that history extends back into the mists of time. American children are taught that their historical experience starts with the 1607 Jamestown settlement. There is little reference to the country from which the settlers came, or the political, social and economic conditions in England which drove the first colonials to risk (and in many cases lose) their lives in an unknown New World. Nor is there much consideration of the contributions that Britain made in the succeeding years to American society in the fields of religion, law, philosophy, culture, music, sport and politics.

It is perhaps in the field of law that English history has had the greatest impact on the United States. Magna Carta (the Great Charter) is the recognised cornerstone for legal systems on both sides of the Atlantic. It was written more than 400 years before the Puritans landed at Plymouth Rock. The principles of habeas corpus, the right of trial by jury, innocence until proven guilty and the right of defendants not to self-incriminate themselves (known in the US as 'taking the Fifth') were fought for over centuries by a succession of English jurists. English common law is the legal foundation for forty-nine out of the fifty states. (Louisiana pays legal homage to its French roots.) In the twenty-first century there are still court rulings that refer to medieval English law in their judgements.

When people refer to the Bill of Rights they generally mean the first ten amendments to the US Constitution penned by James Madison. That was the second Bill of Rights. The first was written in 1689 in England to establish once and for all the constitutional supremacy of Parliament over the executive or, in the case of seventeenth-century England, the monarchy. Parliamentary sovereignty and the relationship between the legislative and executive branches are at the heart of America's revered system of checks and balances. Gun control was also part of the English Bill of Rights which said that Protestants 'may have arms suitable for their defence'. A principle enshrined in the controversial second amendment of the United States is largely the result of the tumultuous seventeenth-century English civil wars and fear of Catholic coups and invasions.

The oft-cited first amendment on free speech, freedom of religion and freedom of assembly also has its origins in England. The principles and values of a free press were laid down by the poet John Milton at the height of the English Civil Wars. They were later reiterated by English philosopher John Locke and fought for by English parliamentarians such as John Wilkes. The first American newspapers were modelled on their English equivalents and printed on presses imported from the Mother Country. Freedom of religion was not so much borrowed from the English as a reaction against its absence in England, where a State Protestant religion (the Church of England) was established in the sixteenth century in opposition to the Roman Catholic Church and quickly became as obstinate and politically powerful as its Catholic predecessor. Anglican intransigence combined with the religious zeal of intolerant Puritans led to the founding of New England's Quaker-inspired Pennsylvania and Catholic Maryland. It also made America fertile ground for a wide variety of Protestant groups, most of whom have English roots.

Fourteen per cent of the American population are African Americans, and most of them can trace their ancestry back to the slaves uprooted from their African homes and transported across the Atlantic to the New World in English ships. From the end of the seventeenth century the English dominated the transatlantic slave trade. The highly profitable business in human flesh helped to finance Britain's industrial revolution. Slavery also provided cheap labour for the agrarian economy of the American South as well as leading to the American Civil War, Jim Crow laws, segregation and the civil rights movement. The British not only brought the slaves, but in one of the all-time historical about-turns, they became the major force for the suppression of the trade and the practice of slavery in the British Empire and America.

Everything starts with an idea. Before you can build a house or construct a new nation, you have to logically determine what you want. And before that you have to know why you want it and, finally, how you will get it. These were essential elements in the creation of America. The formation of the United States was the ultimate political expression of Britain's Age of Enlightenment. Thomas Jefferson, one of the intellectual engines of the American Revolution, said his political beliefs were formed by the English philosophers Thomas Hobbes, Sir Isaac Newton and John Locke. Jefferson's stirring phrase 'life, liberty and the pursuit of happiness' is almost a direct lift from Locke's *Two Treatises of Government*. Sir Isaac Newton's 'natural laws' also found their echo in the Declaration of Independence with the assertion that it had become necessary for the peoples of the United States to assume 'the separate and equal station to which the laws of nature, and of nature's God, entitle them'.

British involvement in the United States did not end at Yorktown. The focus of most American history teaching is on the realisation of its 'Manifest Destiny' to establish a coast-to-coast continental nation. Little regard is paid to the role of nineteenth-century Britain in helping to achieve that goal. The Louisiana Purchase was the consequence of Napoleon's need to finance a war with Britain. Nineteenth-century Britain provided the markets for American agricultural products. British banks provided the capital that built the Erie Canal and opened the American West to those markets. The British invention and development of the railways linked the Atlantic and Pacific coasts and ushered in an American transport revolution. The British steam engine powered an American industrial revolution. Concepts such as Adam's Smith's laissez-faire economics, free trade and the dreaded income tax originated in Britain. And finally, the Royal Navy's Atlantic Squadron ensured that Britain's investment in a fast-growing America was protected from interference from other European powers. Until recently, Britain and America were the two biggest investors in each other's economies. (Japan now invests more in the US.)

The links are as much cultural as economic and political. Television is a British invention. America's actors owe a huge debt to Shakespeare and Britain's rich theatrical tradition. America's Ivy League colleges were closely modelled on Oxford and Cambridge and the one-room schoolhouses of the American West were based on a British system. The absence of copyright laws meant that British authors dominated the American literary scene until the start of the twentieth century, ensuring that the stories of Charles Dickens and others are as much a part of American as British culture. A common language guarantees that British authors remain a major force in the US market. Baseball – 'America's favourite pastime' – is a variation of the British schoolchildren's game of rounders with a bit of cricket for good measure. An estimated 29 million American golfers play their game according to rules compiled by a club on the windswept Scottish east coast. The home of tennis is in a London suburb and American football started as a combination of British rugby and soccer.

All of the above leads neatly to the question of whether a 'Special Relationship' exists today between the United States and the United Kingdom. The term is used to refer to the political bond between the two countries. It certainly existed during the Second World War, when Anglo-American military and political collaboration exceeded any cooperation achieved by any alliance at any time in history. The forging of the Special Relationship is one of Winston Churchill's greatest achievements. He took the initiative in pursuing friendship with President Franklin D. Roosevelt before and during the war. During the course of the conflict the two men were together for 120 days during the course of eleven meetings and their correspondence extended to 1,700 letters and telegrams. Churchill knew that British wartime survival depended on American military support and that the Soviet threat meant American help would be required after the fighting. In his famous 1946 Iron Curtain speech in Fulton, Missouri, he said:

Neither the sure prevention of war, nor the continuous rise of world organisation will be gained without what I have called the fraternal association of the English-speaking peoples ... a special relationship between the British Commonwealth and Empire and the United States. Fraternal association requires not only the growing friendship and mutual understanding between our two vast but kindred systems of society, but the continuance of the intimate relationship between our military advisers, leading to common study of potential dangers, the similarity of weapons and manuals of instructions, and to the interchange of officers and cadets at technical colleges. It should carry with it the continuance of the present facilities for mutual security by the joint use of all Naval and Air Force bases in the possession of either country all over the world. There is, however, an important question we must ask ourselves. Would a special relationship between the United States and the British Commonwealth be inconsistent with our over-riding loyalties to the world organisation? I reply that, on the contrary, it is probably the only means by which that organisation will achieve its full stature and strength.

The upshot has been that Britain and America became the two main pillars of the North Atlantic Treaty Organisation. The electronic intelligence agencies of Britain's GCHQ Cheltenham and America's National Security Agency have worked hand in glove since 1947 and became the nucleus of today's Five Eyes Intelligence Network, which also includes the Commonwealth countries Canada, Australia and New Zealand. Almost every British officer has a tour of duty in America and MI5 and SIS work closely with their American equivalents. The CIA's London representative sits in on meetings of Britain's Joint Intelligence Committee and the first foreign leader every newly elected US President phones is almost always the British Prime Minister and vice versa.

In the immediate aftermath of the Second World War and throughout most of the Cold War there was close military, security and political cooperation. America needed Britain's global contacts from its imperial days and Britain needed America's military and economic muscle. But gradually America developed its own global structures. Britain's worldwide contacts shrank as its empire disappeared and its economic and military position weakened. America's need for a special relationship with the UK diminished. In almost inverse proportion, the UK's need for a special relationship with the US increased. This has led many political analysts to dismiss it as a thing of the past, or at best a one-sided, insubstantial policy designed to keep Britain punching above her weight on the world stage. The problem with this offhand dismissal is that it fails to take into account the value of the foundations of the Special Relationship. It did not start with the bromance between Churchill and

Roosevelt; that was only the flowering of a seed which had been planted long before. The politics that dominate the Special Relationship are built on English history that predates the first settlement of North America by centuries and the fact that Britain continued to be a dominant force in every facet of American life long after independence. It fails to take into account that America's foundation stones were laid on the other side of the Atlantic on an island off the coast of Europe. In short, America was made in Britain.

1

Prisoners of Geography

A Cold Start

We are stuck with our geography. Our histories and our economic, social and political structures are largely determined by our country's natural resources, climate, rivers and physical position in the world. Well, maybe not completely. We can dig tunnels, build bridges, roads, railways, airports and ports to overcome the obstacles that nature has put in our path. The digital age allows us to send information and even three-dimensional products from one end of the planet to the other. But even as we achieve those modern-day miracles, the fact that we have to expend trillions to overcome such restrictions demonstrates in itself the impact that geography continues to have on our lives.

There are geographic advantages as well as obstacles. The well-watered forests and fields of northern temperate climates compare favourably to the deserts and jungles of much of the southern hemisphere. Mineral resources, trade winds and warming or cooling ocean currents are major factors determining the success or failure of a nation. There are also considerations such as access to the sea and trade enjoyed by nations with long coastlines as opposed to those that are landlocked, or a country's position on the planet in relation to trade and manufacturing centres. We are, as Tim Marshall pointed out in the book of the same name, 'Prisoners of Geography'.

Both Britain and America are blessed with natural advantages on which their populations have built prosperous nations. Britain should be a frozen wasteland. It is further north than Canada's Calgary, where the temperature regularly drops to -22°C. It is saved by the warming currents of the Gulf Stream that originate in the Gulf of Mexico, cross the Atlantic and keep not only Britain but most of Northern Europe from freezing over. Then there is the undeniable fact that Britain is an island. The English Channel and the North Sea are the moats which – except for the Romans, Vikings, Anglo-Saxons and Normans – have kept out invaders and allowed the development of a political and social culture distinct from its Continental neighbours a mere 20 miles away. The boundaries across the Channel in Europe constantly shifted with marriages, wars and treaties; not so in Britain. Since 1066 and William the Conqueror there was Scotland, Wales, Ireland and England and the borders then are more or less the same now.

Britain's island status straddling the North Atlantic sea lanes between Europe and the rest of the world also meant that it has always had a semi-detached relationship with the Continent. The main thrust of its foreign policy has historically been to maintain a balance of power across the English Channel (La Manche or 'the Sleeve' in French) so that no single European power rises to threaten British-dominated trade routes. The Napoleonic Wars and the First and Second World Wars occurred because first France and then Germany rose to dominant positions in Europe. This semi-detached relationship was one of the underlining – but little discussed – reasons for British departure from the Europe Union.

Britain is an island because 425,000 years ago a massive ice dam broke. It stretched from Scotland to Scandinavia and held back what we now call the North Sea. Exactly how and why it broke remains a mystery. It could have been a slow and gradual leak or a dramatic flood with the ice splintering and trillions of tons of freezing water bursting through a plughole where the White Cliffs of Dover now tower. Britain's being an island is a determining factor in the weather, and the weather has been a major factor in shaping Britain. Water-filled clouds gathered from the Atlantic make their first landfall at the British Isles. The result is grey skies and a rich, varied and fertile landscape capable of supporting both arable and grazing farms. The country's mineral resources drew Roman settlement, attracted the Normans, helped to finance the settlement of America and spurred the industrial revolution. In recent modern times Britain became an oil-exporting nation, which financed a shift from a manufacturing to a service economy. Oil, coal, natural gas, tin, gold, iron, silver, lead, limestone, chalk, slate and granite reserves all contributed. In the future, its island status gives it an edge in exploiting the future technologies of wind and tidal power.

The first humans are believed to have arrived in Britain 950,000 years ago. That is 500,000 years before the North Sea broke through its ice dam to form the English Channel, which meant that Palaeolithic man was able to stroll across a swamp area to the Norfolk coast where archaeologists have uncovered their stone tools. They didn't stay. When the ice returned they fled south. Of course, there were several ice ages and each time the glaciers crept south over Northern Europe they performed the role of frozen sponges, soaking up the water and exposing patches of dry land. One of these was a land bridge called Doggerland, which stretched from eastern England to the modern-day Dutch coast. About 10,000 years ago men crossed the bridge to southern England, which was the only part free of ice. Then about 6,500 years ago the ice receded. Doggerland disappeared beneath the waves and the first Britons were trapped on their island. Archaeologists have discovered Stone Age settlements in the middle of the North Sea, which confirm the existence of Doggerland.

Because Britain is an island off the edge of western Europe, thousands of miles away from the traditional centres of civilisation in first the Middle East, then Greece and later Rome, it was for most of its history considered a poor piece of real estate. The Roman soldiers and administrators based in Britannia from the first to the fifth centuries described the island as grimly isolated. The Roman general Agricola, who conquered Britain, said it was 'a savage place, as are the fierce inhospitable Britons who live there'. But at least it was not as bad as Ireland, which Agricola reported as inhabited by cannibals who 'eat their fathers and sleep with their mothers and sisters'.

Being so distant from the centre of imperial power in ancient times meant that Britain benefitted little, if at all, from the opening of the Silk Road at the end of the second century BC. It was dubbed the Silk Road because silk was just about the only non-perishable commodity that could survive the 5,000-mile journey across mountains, deserts and sea, as well as through bandit country and the taxable territories of dozens of warlords. The one-way trip itself could easily take a year, but the transport problems did not put a dampener on demand from Roman women, and before long Roman prudes were complaining that the clingy silk togas were revealing too many female curves. Nonetheless, the dangers involved in the trip could explain why the Romans only ever sent one diplomatic mission to China and the Chinese sent none to Rome.

In fact, there was little direct trade or contact between China and Rome. The Silk Road was more of a loosely linked chain of trading centres rather than a continuous road. Both sides, however, had extensive political and economic ties with India, Afghanistan, Persia, Egypt, Yemen and the tribes of the Russian steppe. Of course with the collapse of the Western Roman Empire and the onset of the Dark Ages, Cathay, silk and the spices of the East became the vaguest of vague memories within northern Europe as the Orient and Occident became separated once more. The Crusades revived both knowledge and interest in the Far East. The eastern edge of the Mediterranean was a final stepping stone for Asian merchants seeking to reach Constantinople, and European knights quickly developed a taste for spices which enlivened boiled meat and cabbage, and cotton and silk as opposed to coarse flannel. The trade links were extended to Italian city states such as Genoa and Venice and financed the Italian Renaissance. From there, goods and the accompanying wealth spread in diminishing circles north and west, so that the countries who benefitted least were those – like Britain – on the outer fringes of Europe.

This imbalance started to shift in the fifteenth century with Portugal's Prince Henry the Navigator. At the time, Islamic civilisations controlled the trade routes with the East. Prince Henry was determined to circumvent the Ottoman Empire, which during his lifetime conquered Constantinople and rose to become the dominant naval power in the Mediterranean. To do that he sailed into uncharted southern waters. The vehicle he used was a new kind of ship called the caravel. Ever since Roman times ships had been built to travel short distances either within the Mediterranean lake, up and down rivers or from port to port along the northern European coast. They were not designed for long voyages of exploration.

Prince Henry's caravel revolutionised maritime travel. It was built to cover vast distances at faster speeds. It was also highly manoeuvrable and could perform the hitherto impossible task of sailing into the wind. Overnight, the Atlantic Ocean was transformed from a frightening watery barrier filled with imaginary demons into a maritime highway. Henry's initial aim was to outflank the Muslim-controlled territories in North Africa and reach the fabled African gold coast. He did it in a series of leapfrogging voyages that also established profit-making sugar plantations in the Azores and the Canary Islands. In 1441 Portuguese ships landed at Cape Blanco; in 1443 the Bay of Arguia; and in 1448 the Senegal River. Finally in 1452 they were south of the tenth parallel, which marked the southernmost extent of Islamic influence.

They were also into African gold country, and began shipping the treasure back to Lisbon. Also shipped back were the first African slaves to reach Europe since Roman times. The Portuguese were the first modern Europeans to trade in human cargo. Eventually, Portugal carried nine million Africans to slavery in Brazil – three million more than went to the US. But the ultimate prize was still to be discovered – the route to India. On 12 March 1488 Bartholomew Dias opened the door to the Orient when he landed at the Cape of Good Hope and realised that there was a southern tip of Africa, that it could be rounded and that beyond lay the treasures of the East. In 1497, Vasco Da Gama set off to find them and returned two years later with ships laden with Eastern spices and goods worth sixty times the cost of the expedition.

While the Portuguese were busy establishing the route east, Genoan explorer Christopher Columbus had secured the backing of the Spanish court and sailed west in search of exactly the same destination. On 15 October 1492, Columbus landed in the Bahamas and the world changed. Until his dying day, Christopher Columbus believed that he had landed in the Orient. He was wrong. He had done even better. His discoveries provided his Spanish backers with access to unheard-of wealth in gold and silver and lifted Spain from a backward country only just rid of its nearly 800 years of Moorish occupation to the role of global superpower. Columbus was followed by the Conquistadores. Men such as Hernan Cortes and Francisco Pizarro in the first half of the sixteenth century raped and pillaged their way across Mexico, Central and South America and what is now the southern United States. In 1533 Pizarro captured the Incan Emperor Atahualpa and demanded that his subjects fill a 374-foot-square and 9-foot-high room from floor to ceiling with gold and silver artefacts. They complied. Pizarro killed Atahualpa and his followers anyway.

Almost all of the beautifully wrought treasures of the Aztecs and Incas were melted down and cast into easily transportable gold and silver bars, which filled the holds of Spanish treasure galleons. But the richest prize was a practically solid silver mountain in Bolivia called Potosi. Two-thirds of the 50,000 tons of silver which found its way across the Atlantic between 1540 and 1700 came from this single source.

Most of the gold and silver went to pay for the grandiose European ambitions of Spain's ruling Hapsburg family who also controlled the Holy Roman Empire of central and eastern Europe and the modern-day countries of Belgium and the Netherlands. Large chunks also went to merchants of Venice and Genoa and from there to China, where it caused a glut in the silver market and a subsequent drop in the price of silver bullion. This was especially damaging to the Chinese economy because its currency was based on the price of silver. But not all of the gold and silver made its way from South America to Spain. Some of it was, shall we say, 'diverted'. Men such as England's Sir Francis Drake – backed by Queen Elizabeth I – started attacking the Spanish treasure ships. They then expanded operations to raid treasure houses on the South American coast. In 1578 Sir Francis sailed about the tip of South America and spent a year terrorising Spanish settlements and treasure ships along the Peruvian coast. He finally went home, sailing west to reach England by circumnavigating the globe. He brought with him more than 25,000 tons of gold and silver. The queen's share of the booty was used to clear England's entire foreign debt and lay the financial foundations for the Royal Navy and the British Empire.

The English tried to enter the colonial game early. In 1497, Henry VII signed up another Genoan, Giovanni Cabot (aka John Cabot), to find a northern route to China. Cabot came up with the interesting idea that as the world was a sphere, the shortest distance from west to east (and vice versa) would be at the northern and southernmost points of the globe. Therefore, if he set off across the North Atlantic he would reach the riches of China much faster than the Portuguese had reached India. The theory was sound, but Cabot and Columbus had both failed to take into account the unknown North America. Cabot did, however, bump into Nova Scotia and Newfoundland and laid the foundations for the British claim to Canada. But it was not until Sir Humphrey Gilbert set foot on Newfoundland in 1583 that Britain had its first overseas colony. Henry Hudson managed to expand both the British and the Dutch empires. In 1607, under a British flag, he set off in search of the elusive Northwest Passage to China. He found ice. In 1609 he returned under a Dutch flag, discovered the Hudson River and founded the colony of New Holland, which later became New York. Then in 1610 the intrepid explorer returned to British protection and made a third attempt at the route to China. He thought he had made it when his ship entered Hudson Bay. No such luck. In fact, his luck very quickly ran out. The crew mutinied, threw Hudson, his son and a handful of loyal crew members into a skiff, and sailed back to England without him.

The Scots made their own attempt to grab a slice of the colonial pie at the end of the seventeenth century. In 1697 a group of Edinburgh investors made an attempt to establish a colony at the Gulf of Darien on the Isthmus of Panama. The Scottish settlers encountered stiff opposition from the Spanish, the English, local Native Americans and, most of all, the malaria and yellow fever carried by the mosquitoes. In 1698, the Scots abandoned the settlement at the cost of about 2,000 lives and £40,000. The money was equivalent of a fifth of the entire wealth of Scotland. The failure of the Darien adventure was a major factor in the decision of Edinburgh merchants to opt for union with England in 1707, partly because of their financial loss and partly because they wanted a slice of the growing British Empire in America.

Back to the Other Side of the Pond

Almost at the same time as humans were arriving in Britain, their Asian counterparts were trudging across the Bering Strait which connects Alaska and Siberia. Not attracted to the Alaskan climate, they quickly headed south and spread across the Americas. In South America they created civilisations such as the Mayans, Toltecs, Aztecs, Olmecs, Zapotec, Huatec and Incas. North America is credited with a less civilised settlement, but archaeology tells a different story. In the lower reaches of the Mississippi there emerged a culture who built huge earthen works more than 100 feet high. The Mound Builders, as they were known, are believed to have established an extensive trading network which encompassed the Mississippi River basin area between the Appalachian and Rocky Mountains. Remnants of these civilisations were still in the region when the Spanish explorer Hernando De Soto arrived in 1520, but, like the rest of the Native American population, they quickly succumbed to European diseases.

Although they didn't build cities or giant mounds, the Native American civilisations of the eastern seaboard were often a far cry from the savages depicted by early British settlers. The Iroquois Confederacy dates back to the twelfth century when the five nations were united under one council with distinct laws, political structures, courts and customs. Most of the tribes of the eastern seaboard didn't require the trappings of civilisation. They lived in an Arcadian paradise. There was plenty of wood, land to grow crops, water in wide rivers filled with fish and surrounded by plentiful game. For them it was a life of low-hanging fruit with no need to build cities or pyramids, or develop compensatory trading networks and the political and military structures to offset what nature failed to provide.

The inhabitants of the eastern seaboard enjoyed the benefits accrued from living on the edge of the world's oldest mountain range. The Appalachians were formed 480 million years ago. It took roughly another 300 million years for continental drift to form the Atlantic Ocean. Wind, rain and ice have had more time to work on the East Coast mountains than any other mountains in the world. They have ground rock into topsoil, which has been washed and blown down the eastern slopes, which led to the development of a well-watered alluvial plain rich in wildlife, timber, edible plants and cultivable land. The ancient mountains are also home to some of the world's largest coal deposits, which later played a major part in America's industrial revolution, overtaking that of the mother country. Later, oil was discovered on its western slopes and turned John D. Rockefeller into the richest man in the world.

The continental United States is framed by two mountain ranges. Opposite the Appalachians are the Rocky Mountains, a relative youngster at a mere 100 million years. The aptly named Great Plains which fill the gap between the two mountain ranges are bisected by the mighty Mississippi and its main tributaries, the Ohio and Missouri rivers, neither of which are riverine afterthoughts themselves. The Great Plains were the perfect environment for the great herds of American bison that were followed by the nomadic Native American tribes. The Native Americans on the west coast clung to a narrow strip of land between the sea and the mountains and developed a society supported mainly by fishing. At the northern end are the Great Lakes – Superior, Michigan, Erie, Ontario and Huron. They were formed 14,000 years ago along with the Hudson Bay and a string of smaller lakes when retreating ice floes dug out huge holes and then filled them by conveniently melting.

The early colonial settlers almost from the start were divided into southern and middle America and New England. The southern and middle American colonies enjoyed the rich alluvial soil of the Piedmont or Tidewater region. Linked to England, they developed the cash crops of cotton and tobacco to feed the textile mills of Britain's nascent industrial revolution and the smoking addiction of the growing middle class. Both crops required large numbers of field hands and back-breaking work. The settlers tried enslaving the Native Americans, but they either died of disease or fled back to their nearby villages. They tried indentured Englishmen, but they died. Then in 1619 a ship arrived at Jamestown, Virginia, with twenty indentured African labourers. They succeeded, and by the end of the seventeenth century slavery and the slave trade were an established fact of southern American life and the seeds of centuries of racism, abuse, war and civil discord were planted. In New England the mountains stretched out to meet the sea. This is where the Iroquois Confederacy was based. The colonials tried farming but their efforts were rewarded with crops of stone and a few meagre grains and vegetables. So they turned to fishing, timber, trade, shipbuilding and, eventually, manufacturing.

The Native Americans initially tried to live with the European settlers, who brought goods which made their lives easier. But this was when there was a mere trickle of colonials. Within a decade the trickle had become a stream and within another decade it had become a flood imbued with an overwhelming sense of entitlement. Their communal societies were replaced with foreign laws, customs and property deeds. They fought back. They failed against a superior technology. But they failed even more against European disease. It is estimated that in 1492, 15 million Native Americans lived in what is now the continental United States. By

1880 there were 306,000. More than 90 per cent are believed to have been killed by European diseases.

During the colonial period the Native Americans were used by the competing French and British to fight their proxy battles. Treaties were negotiated, signed, broken and re-negotiated. The British sense of commitment to their Native American allies was one of the factors that led to the American Revolution. After the Seven Years War (which was waged from 1756 to 1763 and was called the French and Indian War in America), King George III issued a proclamation reserving all lands west of the Appalachians for Native American settlement. This angered the colonials who had for some years been greedily eyeing up the future western states. George Washington had already bought land in Kentucky, Ohio, western Pennsylvania, West Virginia and upstate New York. As the lands to the west were settled, the Ohio and Mississippi rivers and the Great Lakes grew in political and commercial importance. Louisiana was purchased by Thomas Jefferson not because he wanted a large chunk of land but because he wanted control of the Mississippi and the port of New Orleans, which was a major outlet to the sea and to European markets. When the Erie Canal was completed in 1825 the American West found another connection through the Great Lakes to the Hudson River and New York.

Man's next technological triumph over American geography was the railways. Invented and largely financed by the British, the railway linked the Pacific and Atlantic Oceans, opened America's trade with Asia and transformed the United States into a continental power. Before the railways, the roads were a muddy, pothole-infested network of over-ambitious footpaths. If you wanted to travel from New York to Boston, Baltimore, Washington or Charleston you were best advised to sail along the coast by ship. Most of the early plantations were situated on a river before the land rose into the Appalachian foothills because that was as far as the English ships could sail to bring goods and collect cotton and tobacco. The railways linked the coasts and everything in between. The vast arable and grazing lands found markets on either side of the continent. The new territories on the Pacific coast ranged from the sunny, fruit-bearing south to the timber-rich north-west. Rich deposits of gold and silver were found in the Rockies. But most important of all, the creation and linking of the continental United States completed the dream of a two-ocean contiguous empire, transforming America from a solely European-focussed nation to one that was oriented to both the European and Asian continents. The dream of reaching the fabled East by sailing west was finally realised.

Geography is much more than the study of the land. Roughly seventy per cent of the Earth's surface is covered by water and a big chunk of that water is the Atlantic Ocean that separates the British Isles and America's eastern seaboard by 3,058 miles (the distance from Galway Bay to New York). For most of history its size kept the two landmasses apart. The seafaring technology of the ancient Celts, Romans, Anglo-Saxons, Normans and medieval British meant that sailors were loath to sail too far out of sight of land. Leif Erikson's Vikings were the exception that proved the rule, but their own position on the periphery of Europe and the absence of a printing press meant that the Viking discoveries in North America failed to be publicised properly.

It took the *Mayflower* sixty-six days to cross the Atlantic in 1620. Two centuries later, British mail-carrying packet ships were making the journey from Boston to Falmouth in twenty-one days. The great divide had become a great highway linking the two sides of the 'the pond'. The winds and currents which carried the sailing ships were a major factor in migration and trading patterns. The *Mayflower* took so long because it was battling against the dominant 'Westerlies' and the Gulfstream currents. If it had first sailed south towards the coast of Africa, the ship would have picked up the currents and trade winds that would have carried it to its intended destination, the coast of Virginia. This circular pattern of Atlantic currents meant that ships would sail south with manufactured goods from England, sell or trade them for sugar or rum in the Caribbean or tobacco and cotton in the southern American colonies and then head north for timber and possible repairs before picking up the Gulf Stream back to England. Sometimes they would sail to the west coast of Africa for slaves and sell those in South America, the American south or Caribbean and buy rum, tobacco or cotton before heading home.

The Atlantic Ocean – along with an alliance with the French – played a vital role in the American War of Independence. In 1781 Lord Cornwallis was camped in Yorktown, Virginia, with vital reinforcements for the British fight against the American rebels. A combined Franco-American force under George Washington surrounded Cornwallis' forces from the land with their backs to the York River and Chesapeake Bay. Under normal circumstances, the British would have simply used their naval superiority to escape by sea and reposition themselves on a more salubrious section of America's long eastern seaboard. But on this occasion the French fleet arrived first and cut off any chance of escape by the British. Cornwallis was forced to surrender and the American War of Independence was won.

In the years following independence the Atlantic acted as a protective barrier – this time with help from the British – against encroachment by the European powers. The British invested heavily in America's western expansion in the nineteenth century and thus had a vested interest in keeping other European powers out of North America. One of the consequences of this investment was that the Royal Navy's Atlantic Squadron was tasked with the job of protecting the trade routes across the North Atlantic. This meant that the US could devote its resources to fighting the Native Americans and Spanish as part of expansion to the Pacific coast and the establishment of a contiguous land-based empire that would rival and eventually surpass the British Empire. The move west opened up the American plains to cattle and wheat production, which quickly dominated world agricultural markets and fed the growing urban population back in Britain. The discovery of gold and silver was another consequence of the western shift. The discovery of gold in California in 1848 helped to end dependence on British banks for American industrial expansion and ended an economic depression. The discovery of oil in Pennsylvania in 1859 and later in Texas, Louisiana, California and the Gulf of Mexico provided fuel for American industry, along with rich deposits of coal in Appalachia and hydroelectricity from its network of powerful rivers. Iron deposits in Northern Minnesota's Mesabi range provided the raw material for the world's greatest steel industry. By the end of the nineteenth century, American geography had helped the United States knock Britain off its pedestal as the world's number one industrial nation.

Geography also helped to drag America into the two world wars of the twentieth century and helped simultaneously to threaten and defend Britain. It also played a vital role in defence planning and the strengthening of Anglo-American relations during the Cold War. The ocean between the two countries is a highway in peacetime and barrier during war.

The most striking example of the wartime barrier came during the First and Second World Wars. In the years before 1914, the Imperial German Navy had taken the lead in the development of submarine warfare. The result was that German U-boats systematically savaged American and British ships carrying weapons and stores to the beleaguered British Isles. Then in May 1915 a U-boat sank RMS *Lusitania*. In all, 128 American lives were lost and the Wilson Administration threatened to sever diplomatic relations with Germany. Berlin realised this would quickly tilt the balance of power in favour of the Allies, so it promised to steer clear of neutral merchant ships and passenger vessels. But by 1917 the Imperial High Command reckoned that Britain was on the verge of collapse. It just needed a tightening of the U-boat blockade to push it over the edge. Unrestricted U-boat attacks were resumed. In March 1917 three American ships were sunk and in April America declared war on Germany. During the Second World War, the Germans made a second attempt to close the North Atlantic lifeline. This time the British and American navies were better equipped with sonar, radar, depth charges and a convoy system. However, the Kriegsmarine U-boats still managed to sink 3,000 Allied ships.

The Second World War also saw the emergence of Britain's key role as 'the unsinkable aircraft carrier' off the coast of Europe. British bombers flew a total of 365,513 operational sorties during the war. The US Air Force had 500,000 personnel – 100,000 of whom were aircrew – scattered across 200 airfields. Another 2 million American soldiers used Britain as a springboard for the D-Day invasion in June 1944 and the succeeding months. The Americans withdrew in 1945 but were back in 1948 for the Anglo-American Berlin Airlift and the start of the Cold War. Up until 1990 there were 100 American air bases in Britain including the controversial intermediate-range nuclear missile base at Greenham Common. As of 2021, a total of thirteen US airbases remain as Britain is still a key forward deployment area for the United States military.

Britain and America are the two most important members of the western alliance appropriately named the North Atlantic Treaty Organisation. NATO was set up to counter the threat to western Europe by the Soviet Union, which was seen as a danger to both British and American interests. The Soviet access to the North Atlantic sea lanes was through the Baltic, and the watery gap between Greenland, Iceland and the UK (GIUK gap). The Royal Navy was tasked with patrolling the waters while the United States based reconnaissance planes and radar stations in Iceland and Greenland. Every detail of Soviet shipping was monitored and logged. In the eighteenth and nineteenth century the Royal Navy had patrolled the Atlantic; after the Second World War it became the responsibility of the US Navy from its base at Norfolk, Virginia, only a few miles from the site of the Yorktown battlefield.

Up until 1957 the main vehicle for delivering weapons across distance was the strategic bomber, which reinforced Britain's role within NATO as the unsinkable aircraft carrier. It also meant that Britain was a prime target for Soviet bomber attacks from the opposite direction. Then on 21 August 1957 the United States launched its first intercontinental ballistic missile (ICBM) and the need for a British base diminished rapidly. Now the missiles could be launched from fixed or mobile launch pads in the American Midwest, which made them less vulnerable to Soviet attack. In 1968 the introduction of Polaris submarine-launched missiles meant that the ICBMs could be launched from submarines anywhere in the world. Trident II missile systems were first deployed in 1990. In 2019 the United States had 6,185 nuclear warheads creating a nuclear umbrella under which Britain and the rest of the NATO alliance shelters. Britain has 215 submarine-launched Trident missiles.

A man-made 'geographic' feature has played a major part in world history and continues to be a determining factor. The Prime Meridian, which runs through the London suburb of Greenwich, is the longitudinal North–South line dividing the world into eastern and western hemispheres and from which all time and distances are measured. The Prime Meridian could be anywhere in the world. It is at Greenwich because in 1851 Britain's Royal Astronomer, Sir George Airey, decided he wanted it in Britain and outside his office at the Greenwich Royal Observatory where he could regularly walk across the invisible time marker. Before Sir George, every country had their own prime meridians, which usually ran through a national landmark. The French, for instance, continued to claim that the international prime meridian ran through the centre of Paris for decades after an 1884 international conference in Washington decided to go along with Sir George's totally arbitrary decision. The position of the Prime Meridian has been vital in establishing London as a world financial and transport hub and helped to link the American and British financial markets.

In 2017, airlines around the world moved over a billion passengers. London's six international airports were head and shoulders above every other city in the world in moving the greatest amount of that traffic. Heathrow alone carried 78 million passengers and 1.7 million metric tonnes of cargo. Planes from Heathrow have 72,000 possible international connections. London is an international air hub because of its position and its time, which also contribute to the city's success as a financial centre.

On the financial side, London's Square Mile, the City (the old walled Roman city) and New York's Wall Street take turns in the number one spot, further strengthening the ties between the two countries. The London Stock Exchange, however, is the more international of the top two financial centres. Seventy-five per cent of the Fortune 500 companies are headquartered in London along with nearly a quarter of Europe's top 500 companies. London is the largest financial exporter in the world. The City of London is also a world centre for insurance and shipping through Lloyd's of London and the Baltic Exchange. (Some or all of this may be under threat post-Brexit.)

Britain's geographic location has also attracted the world's largest and most diverse group of media organisations, which in turn have acted as additional bait for finance houses. As the former UN Secretary General Kofi Annan and others have noted: 'Knowledge is power.' One of the reasons for the rise of London as a financial centre was the development of the news and financial wire service Reuters, from 1851. Thomson Reuters (as it is now known) and its American competitor Bloomberg supply all of the world's financial news and trading systems. Reuters also provides most of the world's news outlets with their international news coverage. The transport links, time zone, geographic location and proximity of so many international companies and organisations has turned London into the world capital of foreign correspondents. In 2018 there were 1,700 accredited foreign correspondents in the British capital. The next nearest was Paris with 945. The BBC is the world's largest news organisation and its World Service reaches an audience of 426 million. Major British newspaper titles such as *The Financial Times*, *The Economist*, *The Times*, *The Guardian* and *Daily Mail* are known for their international reach in print and online.

For thousands of years, geography meant that Britain and America were ignorant of each other's existence. From the seventeenth century the Atlantic barrier became an oceanic highway. Today, jet aircraft, a web of transatlantic cables and a fleet of geostationary communications satellites mean that the barriers of distance have all but disappeared, and the consequent world shrinkage has bound the two countries closer together.

2

Liberty's Foundations

An Englishman's Rights

The famous orator and attorney Patrick Henry stirred the fires of the American Revolution when he stood before the Second Virginia Convention in Richmond, dramatically pointed an ivory letter opener at his breast and declared: 'Give me Liberty or Give me Death.' Henry's words of March 1775 were soon repeated throughout the Thirteen Colonies as a rallying cry for rebellion against British tranny. Liberty became synonymous with independence and freedom. All this is a well-known and accepted matter of American historic folklore. Not so well known is that Henry (a slaveholder) was not demanding anything new. He was in fact maintaining the right of rebellion because the British government had broken its promises to ensure that the colonists were guaranteed the liberties and rights of Englishmen.

This pledge had been enshrined in the charters of each colony; first by the London investors who established the initial settlements and later by the British government when the colonies became Crown dependencies. Without such a guarantee it is unlikely that the colonies would have attracted more than a handful of settlers at the start of the seventeenth century. The English were justifiably proud of their political rights. Compared to the twenty-first century they still had a long way to go. The next two centuries saw dramatic changes during England's Age of Enlightenment, with political freedoms introduced and changes in parliamentary government, philosophy, the law and the media on both sides of the Atlantic; changes undreamt of by men such as Captain John Smith. At the start of the seventeenth century, however, Britain was way ahead of its autocratic Continental neighbours and on the cusp of dramatic reform.

As is typical of so many British legal declarations, the pledge to guarantee the liberties and rights of the colonists was suitably vague. It failed to specify what those rights were and, in doing so, opened the door to a whole raft of freedoms that emerged in seventeenth- and eighteenth-century England. A degree of religious tolerance (by no means universal), natural rights of life, liberty and the pursuit of happiness, a decapitated king, an overthrown king, the supremacy of Parliament, freedom of speech and press, the right not to incriminate oneself – all these things emerged from the English political and social cauldron and found their way across the Atlantic to water the seeds of American rebellion. Freedom and liberty were the catchwords of the day in England and its American colonies. The rule of law was required to both protect hard-won freedoms and restrict the abuse of those freedoms.

The Rule of Law

The law, we are told, is an ass. It is also blind. But the rule of law underpins our entire society. Without the rule of law at local, national and international level the structures of our society would collapse into an anarchic free-for-all. Basically, the law is a set of rules by which a group of people agree to abide. Increasingly, in both Britain and America, the law today is coming into conflict with the concepts of liberty and freedom as a growing number of people argue that these treasured ideals are being restricted by laws imposed by an overbearing Big Brother government. The latest and one of the most dramatic examples was prompted by the coronavirus pandemic. Strict lockdown laws were imposed to prevent the spread of the disease. This had a major negative impact on the global economy. Governments were forced to treading the thinnest of lines between saving lives and saving the economy and, in the opinion of many, they impinged on people's freedom to earn a living and support their families. The pandemic underscored one of the conundrums of the law: how to protect the ultimate freedom of the right to life while at the same time safeguarding liberty and property.

The first known set of laws dates back to the twenty-second century BCE and the Sumerian ruler Ur-Nammu. But probably the best known of the ancient lawmakers was Babylonia's King Hammurabi, who literally set in stone 282 laws on subjects ranging from divorce to murder. It was Hammurabi who first decreed 'an eye for an eye and a tooth for a tooth', 350 years before Moses borrowed the draconian measure for his oft-quoted Old Testament law.

Hammurabi and co. made their contributions to the legal system, but the biggest single influence on the world legal system was Rome. Roman law is the basis for English common law which in turn is the foundation stone for the legal systems in every English-speaking country in the world, including the US. It is also the legal root of civil law, which is the legal system of Europe, Latin America and all of the former French and Italian colonies. Most British and European universities advise undergraduates to study Roman civilisation and language (the Classics) as preparation for a law degree. Legal textbooks and court language are peppered with Latin phrases. It was the Romans who introduced courts and judges. Trial by jury was a Roman legal concept before it was adopted by the Anglo-Saxon world, as was the law of habeas corpus. Possibly most important of all, the Romans established a legal system based on historical precedents and judgements, which links the rule of law to the wisdom of the ages.

When the Romans abandoned Britannia in AD 410 they took their laws with them. When the Angles and Saxons arrived they brought a new system for administering justice: trial by ordeal. This system was based on the belief that God would protect the innocent and punish the guilty. Therefore, the accused were subject to horrific punishments. If they survived unscathed they were innocent; if they didn't they were guilty. These included ordeal by fire in which the accused would walk nine feet across red hot ploughshares, or ordeal by boiling water, which involved plunging your hand into a pot of boiling water to retrieve a stone. Trial by ordeal was officially abolished in England by Henry II in 1219 when he replaced it with trial by jury. Variations, however, continued to linger. Suspected witches, for instance, were subjected to trial by water up until the eighteenth century in both Britain and America. The unfortunate accused would be bound and thrown into a pond. They were innocent if they sank and guilty if they floated. This would have been a no-win situation if a rope was not tied to the would-be witch. An associated justice system was trial by combat. Once again, the thinking behind it was that God would give strength and victory to the innocent party. Trial by combat was usually the preserve of the English upper classes and remained on the statute books until 1819.

The shift in the judicial system started with the Norman invasion of 1066. One of William the Conqueror's closest and most loyal advisers was the Italian monk and jurist Lanfranc, whom he named Archbishop of Canterbury. Before setting up a school in Normandy, Lanfranc studied law in Pavia just as the basic tenets of Roman law were being rediscovered. However, it took another 160 years, a baron's rebellion and a Great Charter before principles such as trial by jury and habeas corpus were accepted and the foundation stone of English – and American – common law was laid.

Bad King John Does a Good Thing (Reluctantly)

King John was a bad king and a bad man. But because he was so bad, the Magna Carta was drawn up and signed, and the foundations were laid for the British and American legal system. John seduced and on at least one occasion raped the wives and daughters of his barons. He took their land. He overtaxed them and largely ignored their ambitions, aspirations and needs. He was also a coward in the days when kings were expected to lead their troops from the front. Some have described him as an atheist, which was as low as you could sink in thirteenth-century Britain. It is not surprising that he is one of the chief villains in the Robin Hood stories. In mitigation, it should be said that John Plantagenet was king of England at a time when Europe was fishing about for a political philosophy to fit the role of feudal king. From the time of William the Conqueror it had been the principle of *vis et voluntas* – force and will – or might is right. But this hard view of life was tempered by the rules of chivalry, which decreed, among other things, that captured nobles were treated with compassion. King John was noted for tossing captured nobles into dungeons, throwing away the key and allowing them to starve to death. Magna Carta was the reaction to John's misuse of *vis et voluntas*. It was the first real attempt to curtail monarchical powers and introduce the element of right over might into English and, later, American law.

When John succeeded his brother Richard the Lionheart to the English throne, England controlled an empire which encompassed two-thirds of Wales, half of Ireland and two-thirds of France, including its entire Atlantic coastline. It was called the Angevin Empire and had been built up in the previous 100 years by expanding William the Conqueror's Norman roots through war, treaties, alliances and marriages. Within a dozen years John had lost all of England's land in France except Gascony, which abuts the Spanish border.

The reason for the loss was a series of military disasters which were exacerbated by the fact that his treatment of the knights and barons in his French holdings managed to alienate almost all of them. But John was not the sort to give up. He was going to fight back and to do so he needed money so he started raising taxes. In those days, contrary to the tales of Robin Hood, taxes were not raised from the peasants. They were raised from the aristocracy because they were the only ones who had any possessions worth taxing.

This had negative repercussions for King John. The barons renounced their feudal ties to the king, raised an army, marched and occupied Exeter, Lincoln and, most important of all, London. They then made noises about overthrowing the king. John appealed to the Pope for help. He was sympathetic, but before he could offer any practical help, the king was backed into a corner and forced into conciliation. His concessions were the Magna Carta. For ten days the two sides negotiated in a water meadow at Runnymede halfway between King John's Windsor Castle and the rebel camp at Staines. It was a bog, and it was chosen as a negotiating venue because the ground was too swamp-like to fight in for either army. The Archbishop of Canterbury, Stephen Langton, acted as honest broker. The rebels were led by Robert Fitzwalter, Baron of Little Dunow. Lord Fitzwalter had a particularly strong grievance: his daughter had been raped and then, according to some sources, poisoned by King John.

No one bothered to produce any eyewitness accounts of the historic moment, at least none that have survived. The closest is a report in Scotland's thirteenth-century Melrose Chronicle, discovered in 2014. Written in Latin, it said:

> A new state of things begun in England; such a strange affair as had never been heard; for the body wishes to rule the head, and the people desired to be masters over the king. The king, it is true, had perverted the excellent institutions of the realm, and had mismanaged its laws and customs, and misgoverned his subjects. His inclination became his law; he oppressed his own subjects; he placed over them foreign mercenary soldiers, and he put to death the lawful heirs, of whom he had obtained possession as his hostages, while an alien seized their lands.

The charter was signed on 19 June; but that was by no means the end of the matter. Pope Innocent III declared the Magna Carta null and void because the king had been coerced into signing it. The barons whose signatures appeared at the bottom of the document were excommunicated. The Pope also denounced Magna Carta as 'shameful and demeaning'. It was clear that the Vicar of Rome saw the charter as a threat to the underlying principles of monarchy and as such also undermined the authority of the Roman Catholic Church. His intervention led to another war between the barons and King John just three months later. This ended with the death of John in October. But the issue was still unresolved. John was succeeded by his nine-year-old son who became King Henry III. The fighting between the barons and the throne continued sporadically and for a while it looked as if France's King Louis VIII might take the English throne with the support of the barons. The charter was rejected, accepted, ignored, amended and enforced, dependent on who held the upper hand at any given time – until Henry III decided to regain the French territories that his father had lost.

To fight these new wars Henry III needed a lot of money and the best source of that cash was the barons. The only way they would agree to pay the taxes required was if Henry renewed his support for Magna Carta with the addition of the line that he was doing so of his own 'spontaneous free will', and he then had to affix the royal seal. This dealt with the papal objections and gave the charter new authority. Of course, the king still wanted to be kingly and keep as much power as possible, especially as it seems he was concerned about protecting his father's reputation. He had a constant need for taxes to fight his wars in France. The result was that Henry III's final affirmation of the Magna Carta did not come until 1253 and it was not until 1297 that it became an official part of English law.

What exactly did Magna Carta say? There were a number of clauses which related to specific medieval grievances and have been superseded by subsequent legislation. For instance, there are laws about Jews and moneylending. Then all the fish weirs were to be removed from the River Thames and the relatives and descendants of Gerard de Athee were banned from holding any public office. In the last case, the de Athees changed their name to Athy, moved to the west of Ireland and by the end of the fourteenth century were prominent public figures once again. But hidden among the medieval detritus was truly ground-breaking material starting with the first clause, which established the freedom of the English Church from monarchical control. Although Pope Innocent III supported King John in repudiating the Magna Carta, an ongoing dispute between John and the Vatican was one of the causes that led to the war between the barons and the king.

Clause 13 guarantees the 'ancient liberties and free customs' of the City of London in perpetuity. One of the money-raising schemes hatched by King John was the sale of rights to towns and cities, such things as the right to hold a market or elect its own officials. The barons feared that John, or future monarchs, would remove those rights if only to raise more money by auctioning them again. Because of Magna Carta, London was one of the few major medieval centres with an elected mayor and a strong element of self-government. With that political foundation, London evolved as a major trading capital able to pass laws and regulations which ensured that it retained its leading position first in England, then Europe, then the British Empire, and finally the world. It also established a model for other city governments.

Clause 39 established trial by jury: 'No free man shall be seized or imprisoned, or stripped of his rights or possessions, or outlawed or exiled, or deprived of his standing in any way, nor will we proceed with force against him, or send others to do so, except by the lawful judgment of his equals or by the law of the land.' Clause 40 is probably one of the shortest and most important clauses in the English legal canon: 'To no one will we sell, to no one deny or delay right or justice.' These two clauses firmly established that the king – or the government that represents the king or head of state – has no right to deny justice to any individual. It means that the rule of law applies to everyone regardless of their standing in society and everyone is protected by it. This was radical back in 1215 and is still radical in many parts of the world today. It is the foundation of the British and American legal systems.

Magna Carta has been pulled out of the dusty archives many times throughout the centuries. It was repeatedly cited in the seventeenth century in the battle between Parliament and King James I and Charles I over the vexed question of the divine right of kings. And right from the beginning, Magna Carta was cited time and time again in American history. In 1606 it was incorporated into the Virginia Charter with the phrase that all colonists would 'enjoy all liberties, franchises and immunities' as people born in England. The colonial Massachusetts General Court specifically said that the Magna Carta was 'the chief embodiment of English law' and therefore the cornerstone of the colony's law.

William Penn in 1687 published the first copy of the Magna Carta on American soil in his pamphlet *The Excellent Privilege of Liberty and Property: being the birth right of the free-born subjects of England*. When Benjamin Franklin was hauled before Parliament to justify colonial opposition to the Stamp Act he responded that the colonists could be taxed only with their consent 'as declared by Magna Carta'. The Declaration of Independence is infused with the language of Magna Carta, which is unsurprising because a young Thomas Jefferson complained about how much of his legal studies were taken up with reading the document and all of its seventeenth- and eighteenth-century interpretations.

During the revolution Massachusetts chose for its symbol a militiaman with a sword in one hand and a copy of the Magna Carta in the other.

The founding fathers justified their rebellion on the grounds that King George III was denying them their liberties in the same way that the barons had been denied theirs in 1215. The fifth amendment of the Bill of Rights is best known for its frequent citing in the avoidance of self-incrimination, but it also makes a clear link back to the Magna Carta when it says that no person shall 'deprived of life, liberty or property without due process of law'. There are also references to Magna Carta in the sixth, seventh and eighth amendments to the Constitution.

The contribution of Magna Carta to American law is literally cast in bronze on the 13-ton doors of the US Supreme Court. Sculpted in bas-relief in a panel on one of the doors is the signing of the Magna Carta. In 1957, the American Bar Association built a pillared memorial at Runnymede and the American delegation was one of the largest at the 800th anniversary celebrations in 2015.

The Grandmother of Parliaments?

Magna Carta set the legal foundation. What was now required was a political structure that would act as a continuing check on unbridled monarchical (executive) power and approve new laws to reflect changing social norms. Hence the strengthening of a legislative system which had its roots in the distant past. The British Parliament is often referred to as 'The Mother of Parliaments'. True enough, but who was responsible for the birth of the mother?

They came after the Romans left Britain. The Angles and Saxons who sailed across the Channel from modern-day northern Germany, the Netherlands, Belgium and Denmark had a long-established tradition of *folkmoot*. The tradition also became part of Viking society and many historians argue that the true 'Mother of Parliaments' was the Icelandic Althing, which held its first assembly in AD 930. The Althing is the first known attempt to establish a fairly representative legislative body which agreed rules for society. In that respect, the British were light years behind the Icelanders. The English equivalent was the Witan, or Witenagemot. Each of the seven Saxon kingdoms that eventually became England had a Witan, which was composed of the leading aristocrats and ecclesiastical personalities. They had no legislative powers. There were no formal rules or schedule. The Witan had no fixed meeting place. They assembled when and where the king summoned them and the king decided the membership. He could take their advice or leave it as he saw fit. They did, however, have one key arrow in the Saxon political quiver: they elected the king. But once elected, the king was deemed to have absolute power. Normally, election was a formality, with the throne going to the eldest son of the incumbent, but not always, as was the case with Harold Godwinson, who was elected king by the Witenagemot in 1066 and then was promptly overthrown by rival claimant William the Conqueror. William wound up the Witan and its elective powers and replaced it with the Curia Regis, or King's Council. William's dismissal of the Witan gave rise to what was known as the 'Saxon Myth', which was advanced by Thomas Jefferson and other leading American revolutionaries, wrongly claiming that the Witan was an elected body of Saxon landholders which was overthrown by Norman conquerors and that American patriots were going back to their ancient Saxon roots.

While the Witan's powers were heavily circumscribed, that was not the case for Saxon local government. Every county or shire had a shire moot which met at least twice a year. As with the Witan, the key figures were the local aristocrats and clergymen. But also attending were representatives from each of the villages within the shire. The moots were presided over by a representative of the king known as the king's reeve and usually took the form of a court to settle outstanding disputes. It was the beginnings of English representative democracy, albeit at a local level, involving commoners as well as the local lords, and it continued up until 1889 when the shire moots were replaced by the county councils. Gradually, the king's council and the shire moots started to work in tandem as the monarch needed political input and grassroots intelligence. However, the Norman kings ruled as absolute monarchs – as long as they were able to deliver the goods. And in those days, delivering the goods meant continually enriching the supporting power base of barons, knights and clergy.

When William the Conqueror crossed the Channel in 1066 to conquer England, he did not relinquish his lands in Normandy to do so. In fact, during his reign over England he spent more time on the Continent expanding or defending his holdings than he did in England. His descendants followed his example and by the start of the thirteenth century, the king of England also controlled nearly two-thirds of modern-day France. Then, by 1214, it was almost all gone. As previously noted, King John had managed to lose virtually all of his French territory through a combination of misuse of his authority, brutality, disastrous wars and poor financial management. Out of money, he went to his barons and asked for a cash injection. They not only refused, but rebelled in what became known as the First Barons' War, which resulted in Magna Carta, establishing the right of the barons to serve as consultants – or a parliament – to the king. Furthermore, it founded the then revolutionary idea that the power to tax was limited by general consent exercised by the barons. Thus this Parliament managed to secure its first tenuous hold on the purse strings and started its long up and down journey to political power. The new Parliament's first opportunity to flex its political muscle came in 1258 when Henry III reluctantly summoned the legislature of barons to ask for money to regain his French inheritance. The barons responded by demanding a reaffirmation of Magna Carta and political reform in the shape of a parliament that would consist of fifteen members, only three of whom would be chosen by the monarch. It would appoint the king's ministers and be empowered to raise and spend money. The Parliament would also choose an independent judge to rule on grievances, would not require a royal summons to gather and would meet at least three times a year. But Henry had no intention of abiding with what became known as 'the Provisions of Oxford', and with the help of the Vatican spent the next four years clawing back political power. At this point the barons – and parliamentary democracy – found a champion in the form of the Earl of Leicester, Simon de Montfort, who is recognised on both sides of the Atlantic as the 'Father of Parliamentary government'.

Simon de Montfort was a deeply religious French aristocrat with an English title and a reputation for virulent anti-Semitism. He had made himself popular with England's cash-strapped barons by calling for the expulsion of the Jews and the cancellation of all debts owed to the Jewish community. In 1263 he returned to England from the Crusades to find the barons on the brink of war with their king. The politically astute de Montfort spotted the opportunity and invited the English aristocracy to join him in rebellion against the king, which led to the Second Barons' War, the de facto overthrow of the king, the installation of de Montfort as the true ruler of England, yet another reaffirmation of Magna Carta, and England's first representative Parliament in 1265. De Montfort's Parliament was radical in that it was composed not only of the barons (later the House of Lords) but also elected 'knights'. Each county and selected boroughs sent two knights to the new Parliament. The local county courts elected the representatives. Henry III was captive and remained king in name only. The true ruler of England was de Montfort through Parliament. Unfortunately, the barons broke into warring factions almost as soon as de Montfort assumed power, with the result that de Montfort came to a sticky end in August 1265 at the Battle of Evesham at the hands of forces loyal to the king. But by this time, Henry III had come to realise that the only way he could avoid another barons' war was by reluctantly accepting that he needed to rule with the help of, or rather interference from, some form of representative government if he was to rule at all. It had cost him his life, but de Montfort had established the principles of parliamentary power.

Parliament gradually consolidated its power during the reign of the three Edwards from 1272 to 1377. The reign of Edward I is especially noteworthy for the three Statutes of Westminster (1275, 1288 and 1290), which established many of England's basic laws, including the principle that 'elections ought to be free'. Of course, that did not mean that everyone should be free to participate in the voting process. From the start, the franchise was limited to males with fairly substantial property holdings. Serfs, slaves and peasants, who made up an estimated 88 per cent of the population of medieval England, were deemed to be either incapable of making political decisions or it was thought that giving them a voice would represent too great a threat to the rigid social order. To ensure that politics remained the exclusive reserve of the elite, parliamentary debates were conducted in secret.

The relationship between the monarchy and Parliament was not stabilised even by the English Civil Wars. But by the end of the eighteenth century the principles of a constitutional monarchy were finally put into practice. Until then, the monarch acted pretty much as a twenty-first-century prime minister or executive president with bells and whistles. Arguably, Parliament lost the fight. It was used to provide a veneer of national unity to the absolute rule of the occupant of the throne. All matters related to foreign affairs and defence were the exclusive reserve of the monarch. Parliament only became involved when extra money was required. The throne also had the exclusive right to ennoble, and (after the Reformation) to appoint all bishops who sat in the House of Lords. In the Commons, the king could also support the election campaigns of his hand-picked candidates. Laws had to be approved by Parliament, but most of the laws were submitted by the monarchs or ministers who were chosen by the king. The judges responsible for implementing and interpreting the law were appointed by the monarch, as were the sheriffs and constables who enforced it. The throne decided when Parliament would sit and for how long. Parliament met only seven times during the reign of Henry VIII from 1509 to 1547. It fared just as badly under his daughter Elizabeth I, meeting only thirteen times during her forty-five-year rule.

One of the bones of contention which was gradually settled in favour of Parliament was the right of parliamentarians to speak without the fear of retribution. It was a hard-won right and at times a parliamentarian would go too far and be sent to the Tower of London to cool his heels. The right of parliamentarians to speak freely became a major cause célèbre during the English Civil Wars and their aftermath. It was eventually enshrined in law in Article Nine of the 1689 Bill of Rights. MPs and Lords now have legal immunity from prosecution for anything they say or do during proceedings in Parliament. They can, if they wish, slander, libel, commit contempt of court or breach the Official Secrets Act as long as they do so within the precincts of the Palace of Westminster. If they repeat the action outside the grounds of Parliament they can be arrested and prosecuted. The British position is mirrored in the US Constitution, which says that both Houses of Congress 'shall in all cases, except treason, felony and breach of the peace, be privileged from arrest during attendance at the session of their respective houses, and in going to and from the same; and for any speech or debate...'

One of the main reasons the MPs secured the right of parliamentary immunity was their agreement to hold meetings in secret, an agreement which dates back to 1347. The general public was kept completely in the dark about the activities of their representatives in the Commons. Even the Crown, its ministers and the House of Lords were not meant to know details. Instead, the Speaker of the House would brief them on proceedings, being careful to omit references to the views of individual members. Guarding the rights of Parliament became the key duty of the Speaker and remains so to this day. His role as official spokesperson was partly designed to protect parliamentarians from royal retribution, but it was also born from the feudal and arrogant belief that it was best that the common folk be kept in the dark about the debates that led to decisions being made on their behalf. It was not until 1774, following the efforts of campaigning journalist MP John Wilkes, that the ban on reporting parliamentary proceedings ended – just in time for the American Revolution.

Freedom of Speech

There's a good reason that the first amendment is number one in the US Bill of Rights. Without freedom of speech and its associated freedoms regarding religion, assembly, the press and the right to petition the government, democracy would quickly fall apart. What is the point of having elected representatives if they can't represent you? If they can't speak freely on the floor of the Senate or Congress or, in the case of Britain, Parliament? What is the point of you – or your elected representatives – speaking freely if what is said cannot be freely reported to a wider audience? Thus the need for freedom of the press.

Freedom of speech protects the general population against special interest groups whether they are businesses, lobbyists or government. It gives minorities a voice. The free exchange of ideas encourages growth in science, business and academia, as well as encouraging competing political factions to move towards workable compromise. Free speech combats the hatred and bigotry by allowing people to put forward ideas backed by ethics and reason rather than bans and censorship. If effectively wielded, tolerance defeats intolerance in an arena governed by free speech. And finally, freedom of speech is an ultimate check on the abuse of power.

The ancient Greeks are generally credited with giving the world free speech and its handmaiden, democracy. Greek democracy had its roots in sixth-century BCE Athens. Its development was at times rocky and there were periods when it disappeared and then reappeared. But during the Age of Enlightenment the British turned towards the classical Greeks for political guidance, rediscovered democracy and free speech, adapted it to their modern world and shipped a version to America where it was further enhanced.

Of course Athenian democracy was circumscribed. Out of an estimated adult population of 250,000 only about 30,000 were entitled to participate in the main assembly known as the Ecclesia. Banned were women, slaves and foreign merchants who were not citizens of Athens. The format was similar to the direct democracy of a modern-day town hall meeting and must have at times appeared chaotic. The participants in the Ecclesia were not elected, instead every qualified male was expected to participate as a civic duty and a quorum of 6,000 was required for every session. Everyone who attended the Ecclesia was allowed total freedom of speech in debates. Freedom of the press meant nothing because there was, of course, no press. Possibly the closest ancient Greek medium to the press was the theatre, and playwrights such as Aeschylus, Sophocles, Aristophanes and Euripides were adept at producing political satires.

Inevitably, the vested interests and Athenian oligarchs became frustrated by the necessity of long-drawn-out debates and successive compromises. Any possibility of reviving Athenian democracy ended in 338 BCE when Philip of Macedonia, father of Alexander the Great, conquered Athens and united the Greek city states. A further blow was delivered by the Roman defeat of the Macedonians in 168 BCE at the Battle of Pydna.

Greek ideas became the philosophical foundation stone of Rome, although Roman government was a long way from a democracy. In the days of the Republic there were elected members of the Senate but the ruling body was controlled by a coterie of hereditary patrician families who used patronage to cement family-based political ties. Any potential political discord was squashed with bread, circuses and an expanding economy financed by military conquests which brought tributes, slaves and trade to the citizens of Rome. The people were prosperous without the complications of democracy. When imperial rule succeeded the Republic in 49 BCE, any vestiges of representative government disappeared. There was, however, an element of free speech concerning religious practices. Ancient Romans realised the importance of maintaining the peace by allowing local religions to continue. Rome even helped local religions to flourish by adding key regional deities to the Roman pantheon of gods. All they asked in return was that the local religions add the worship of the emperor to their beliefs.

This did not sit well with the first of the Ten Commandments of the Judaeo-Christians: 'You shall have no other Gods but me. You shall not make for yourself any idol, nor bow down to it or worship it. You shall not misuse the name of the Lord your God.' The exclusive monotheistic nature of Christianity was one of the main reasons for Roman persecution after initial attempts at accommodation. It also meant that when the Emperor Constantine decriminalised Christianity in AD 313 it was inevitable that Christ's teachings would quickly become the official religion of the Roman Empire. And because of its inbuilt intolerance, other religions were banned and the Roman Empire – and Europe – embarked upon more than a millennium of religious intolerance. And because freedom of speech threatens the tenets of a proscriptive religion, that right was also lost. From the time that Christianity was declared Rome's state religion in AD 380, the Church refused to allow any criticism, political discourse or scientific discussion that ran counter to the teachings of the Bible. It maintained an iron grip on the levers of power which would have been seriously envied by George Orwell's Big Brother. To enforce its will, the Church condemned free thinkers to hell with an order of excommunication, or created hellish conditions by declaring them heretics and burning them alive. All aspects of life were viewed with the biases of the Catholic Church, which supported and was supported by an oligarchical feudal power structure. And it worked – until the arrival of Johannes Guttenberg and his printing press.

One of the main reasons that the Church and the nobility were able to suppress freedom of speech for so long was because there was no press, free or otherwise. New ideas were available only through word of mouth or in laboriously handwritten manuscripts confined to abbeys and universities controlled by religious scholars. The population was illiterate because there was no literature. Then in 1439 Johannes Gutenberg invented the movable type printing press. The initial reaction to the challenge of Gutenberg's invention was to suppress its products. In 1559 the Vatican created the *Index Librorum Prohibitorum*, or Index of Prohibited Books. Any published works on the list were forbidden to all Catholics without written permission. The index was not formally abolished until 1966 and contained publications by Galileo, Copernicus, Jean-Jacques Rousseau, Baruch Spinoza, Immanuel Kant, David Hume, René Descartes, Francis Bacon, John Milton, John Locke, Simone de Beauvoir and Jean-Paul Sartre.

The secular and religious authorities operated a sort of mutual support system, so that it was no surprise that the Catholic Church's restrictions on the new invention were mirrored by Europe's kings and queens. In England the sudden appearance of pamphlets led to a 1538 ruling from Henry VIII that all printed publications had to be approved by the Privy Council. In 1557 the Stationer's Company was formed to license all publications. In 1581 the publication of seditious or libellous material was made a capital offence.

Before Gutenberg's invention every book had to be laboriously copied by hand. This was usually the job of monks who also produced the parchment, made the ink and bound the sheets inside heavy leather covers. Across Europe an estimated 20,000 books were produced, mainly Bibles, between AD 1000 and 1400. Only 2,000 have survived. This compares to 184,000 different titles published in the UK in 2019 alone. Because of the printing press, ideas, stories, news, scientific achievements and political philosophies could be mass produced and sold at a (relatively) affordable price. People made the effort to learn to read because there was now something to read, and the natural law of supply and demand meant that they could afford it. Johannes Gutenberg's invention was the engine that drove the Age of Enlightenment, produced the ideas that brought Europe into the modern age, and helped to create America.

The first printing press arrived in England in 1476 courtesy of one William Caxton who had seen in it action in Cologne while touring the Continent on business. He immediately realised its potential and set up operations in Westminster around the corner from Westminster Abbey and the seat of government. Gutenberg concentrated on printing Bibles and indulgences, which priests controversially sold to sinners. Caxton went for the popular market. His first work was Chaucer's *Canterbury Tales*. He also published Aesop's Fables, some histories and romance stories. But also on his print list were Plato and Aristotle.

William Caxton not only brought the first printing press to England, he also brought the first printer to run it. The appropriately named Wynkyn de Worde was a German who took over Caxton's business in 1491. Wynkyn moved the presses to London's Fleet Street, which became the global centre of the news publishing industry. The first printing press to reach America most likely came from Fleet Street. It was brought across the Atlantic in 1638 by the Revd and Mrs Jose Glover to print religious texts for the students and faculty at the newly opened Harvard University. The Revd Glover died on board a ship en route, and so it was left to his widow to look after their five children and start the business. She did so admirably, producing innumerable religious tracts, the Bay Psalm Book, an almanac and the Freeman's Oath – a loyalty pledge to the Massachusetts Bay Company which all newly arrived settlers had to make. Unfortunately, all copies of the oath have been lost to time.

America's most famous printer was Benjamin Franklin. It was his primary career. At the age of twelve he was apprenticed to his older brother James to learn the business. In 1726, he sailed to England to find his own printing press to bring back to America. He failed to raise the necessary finance but did find jobs in Fleet Street that enabled him to hone his printing and journalistic skills. That in turn helped him to establish a printing and publishing empire which stretched throughout the thirteen colonies and became a vital vehicle for spreading the ideals of the American Revolution. His print empire also turned Franklin into a wealthy man who could afford to focus his energies on science, politics and chasing women.

I Think

Everything starts with an idea. It begins with a hope, a thought, a belief, a dream or a new way of looking at an old problem. Before you can build a house, plough a field or construct a new nation, you have to logically determine what you want. Most of us take the thought processes required to answer these basic questions for granted. They were essential elements in the creation of America.

The formation of the United States was the ultimate political expression of Britain's Age of Enlightenment, which was in turn drawn from over the millennia of European culture stretching back to the Greek Golden Age and the philosophical triumvirate of Socrates, his student Plato and his student Aristotle. These three men laid the foundations of philosophy. They taught the world to question, debate, observe and reason. And then everything they taught was lost to western Europe. More than half of the continent was plunged into the Dark Ages and philosophy was replaced by survivalism.

The works of the ancient thinkers were kept alive and nurtured in the eastern half of the old Roman Empire and the Islamic-controlled territories. When the West began to crawl back towards the light around the tenth century, Plato and friends were in the East, Spain and North Africa waiting to be rediscovered. But in the meantime, western Europe had to fight its way out of the double straitjacket of the Catholic Church and feudalism. That is not to say that the Church and the feudal lords did not play a vital transitional role. Their unbending rules based on total obedience, a rigid social structure, hierarchical obligations and a thin veneer of civilisation prevented the West from sliding back into the mindless, unenlightened pit of ignorance. But at the same time, religious and feudal rulers worked largely in tandem to protect their own interests rather than those of society as a whole. In fact, they *were* society. Everyone else – the peasants, serfs and merchants – were supporting actors, discouraged from thinking for themselves and prohibited from advancing through the social hierarchy.

Feudalism has never entirely left Western society. Britain still has a monarchy, although it has evolved, arguably, into a protective pillar of democracy. A third of Britain's land is still owned by the aristocracy. One of the reasons for the longevity of the British upper classes is the rule of primogeniture – the rule that the first-born inherits the entire estate of his parents. In continental Europe the estates were divided between all the surviving children, which meant that as the generations progressed, the wealth of the individual aristocrats shrank. The rule of primogeniture crossed the Atlantic to colonial America where it was especially prevalent in the South among the plantation owners, who saw themselves as the American branch of the English aristocracy.

Feudalism was a sort of socio-economic and political chain of command. It was a pragmatic solution to the problem of imposing a semblance of order without adequate transportation or communication links. The serfs swore loyalty to the lord of the manor who might be a baronet or baron who often held scattered lands across the country. Each section of territory was called a manor. Because they couldn't be everywhere, the manorial lords appointed vassals to administer their lands. They were either low-level barons or knights or, on occasion, a rich merchant or even a well-off peasant. The vassals swore an oath of loyalty to the lord of the manor, paid him a slice of the revenues and promised to provide him with soldiers. The lords made a similar deal with the king. Everyone was born to their position in this hierarchy. The serfs could not change jobs or move to another part of the country. Almost all serfs worked the land and were allowed to keep some of the fruits of their labour for themselves. Ten per cent went to the Church and most of the rest went to the lord of the manor or his vassal in return for protection. All of this sounds like an extremely bad deal for the serfs, except when you consider that this was the age of rape and pillage and security was a rare and vital commodity.

At its best, the system created a sense of stability led by men with a strong paternal sense of duty and responsibility. Freed from manual labour, they could focus their efforts on creating social and political structures for the benefit of the whole of society. At its worst, the system encouraged arrogance, entitlement, exploitation and greed. The latter course was the one most often followed.

The feudal structure was dealt a severe blow in the fourteenth and fifteenth centuries by successive waves of the bubonic plague. It suffered another setback when the Protestant Reformation undermined the power of the Church which supported it. However, in the seventeenth and eighteenth centuries it was still very much the norm, although concepts such as 'natural rights' and the equality of men were marching to the front. This could be seen in colonial America where the competition between feudalism and the Age of Enlightenment created an almost schizoid political philosophy, especially in the South, home to four of the first five American presidents.

On the one hand the 1776 Declaration of Independence pronounced that 'all men were created equal' and a gifted cadre of philosopher kings was produced with a selfless sense of duty and obligation. On the other, millions of Africans were being kidnapped, transported across the Atlantic in overcrowded ships and sold into a life of slavery for themselves and their descendants. The Washingtons, Jeffersons, Madisons and Monroes were the American equivalents of feudal lords. The Africans were the serfs; except in the case of the American South, the Africans were owned and few of their owners believed that they owed the Africans anything. As in Britain, remnants of feudal philosophies of entitlement based on birth remain, largely related to the country's racial history.

People didn't have time to think in medieval England. The serfs and peasants were too busy ploughing, sowing and harvesting. The nobility were fully occupied preparing for war or actually fighting. Even if they did have the time, they were illiterate. The only ones who could read and write in any number were the clergy, and they used their skill primarily for reading the Bible and writing religious works. There were a handful of philosophers – among them Anselm of Canterbury, Roger Bacon, Duns

Scotus and William of Ockham – but most of their work was within the parameters of the teachings of the Church. When it occasionally strayed beyond the acceptable boundaries towards the realm of individual liberties, wrists were firmly slapped – sometimes worse.

The first medieval English thinker arrived with William the Conqueror. Anselm of Canterbury was actually an Italian who as a young Benedictine monk made his way across Europe to Normandy where he became friendly with William before the duke conquered England. William put Anselm in charge of the monks at the French monastery at Bec, which under the Italian monk quickly became a centre for European learning. Shortly after William conquered England, he brought Anselm across the Channel and appointed him Archbishop of Canterbury. Anselm continued teaching and his followers laid the foundations for Oxford in 1106, then the second oldest university in Europe after Bologna.

There is some dispute as to whether Anselm was a theologian or a philosopher, but most agree that because he used logic to prove the existence of God, he was first and foremost a philosopher. Anselm thought faith important – in fact, he believed it should precede reason – but felt that rational thinking would inevitably expand faith. He has been called the 'father of scholasticism' and an early proponent of what is called the ontological argument, which used reason to argue the existence of God. Anselm's favourite starting point was a definition of God as a being that 'than which no greater can be conceived'. Anselm preceded by half a millennium the French philosopher Descartes' famous 'I think, therefore I am,' when he argued that, if the greatest possible being exists in the mind, it must also exist in reality: 'If it exists only in the mind, then an even greater being must be possible – one which exists both in the mind and in reality. Therefore, this greatest possible being must exist in reality.'

Scholasticism is not a philosophy. It is a method for teaching philosophy, or, in Anselm's day, rationalised theology. In many respects it was the forerunner to modern debating methods. Anselm started using the method at his monastic school at Bec and when Oxford was founded it became the primary method of learning. From there it spread throughout medieval Europe and dominated teaching methods right up to 1700. The system works like this: a proposal is put forward and opponents respond with a counter-proposal. This is rebutted and the two sides argue back and forth within an agreed formal framework. The idea is that eventually a consensus is agreed. When Harvard was founded in 1636, scholasticism dominated the young college's teaching methods. The same was true of Yale, Princeton, Columbia, the University of Pennsylvania, William & Mary, and Dartmouth.

John Duns Scotus was a medieval friar and philosopher with the dubious distinction of having his name used as the origin of the word 'dunce'. In fact, Scotus was anything but. In the seventeenth and eighteenth centuries his teachings were popular in Europe's Catholic universities. This made him unpopular in Protestant England and Scotland where his name became mocked. During medieval times he was revered on both sides of the English Channel. Born in the town of Duns on the Anglo-Scottish border country, Scotus took holy orders before studying at Oxford. He then studied and taught in Paris before heading off to Germany. His memorial reads: 'Scotland brought me forth. England sustained me. France taught me. Cologne holds me.'

John Duns Scotus is known for formal distinction, the univocity of being, and haecceity. Formal distinction is simply a way of distinguishing different aspects of the same thing. For instance, the writer of this book could be described as an old, wrinkled, bald, slightly deaf, partially blind, overweight man who walks with a limp. He could also be described as a well-read, young-for-his-years, well-groomed raconteur. Both are true, although the second might be slightly exaggerated. Univocity of being arose from a slight difference of theological/philosophical opinion between Scotus and the greater Italian medieval philosopher Thomas Aquinas. The latter argued that God was on a different plane from man and the two beings could not be compared. Scotus accepted this but qualified it by saying that the terms used to describe God would have the same meaning when describing humans. For instance, there was no distinction between goodness, greatness and kindness when describing the qualities in God and humans. Finally, there was haecceity, which, as with most medieval philosophical terms, was drawn from Latin, the language of the educated. The loose translation of haecceity is 'thisness' and John Duns Scotus invented the word to argue that every living thing – person, animal and plant – was a distinct individual being with distinct individual characteristics. In 1776, a Scotist (as the followers of John Duns Scotus are called) would have argued that all men are created equal individuals.

William of Ockham (or Occam) is famous for 'Occam's razor'. Boiled down to its barest bones, it argues that 'simple is best'. The simplest solution is most likely to be the correct one and if you are presented with two opposing propositions to a problem then you should select the simpler of the two. It sounds so basic, but in a fourteenth century dominated by convoluted faith-based arguments to defend Church teachings, it was radical. So much so that William was summoned to the papal court at Avignon to answer charges of heresy. While there it became clear that things were not going his way so he fled to the court of Holy Roman Emperor Louis IV and was promptly excommunicated.

William and the Pope clashed over the issues of poverty, property rights and the relationship between the secular and religious worlds. William of Ockham took his Franciscan vow of poverty seriously and thought that it should be extended to the rest of the Church. Furthermore, to ensure that this was the case he argued in favour of a strict separation between Church and State. This brought him into conflict with Pope John XII whose princely lifestyle in Avignon prompted the Holy Roman Emperor (William's friend and protector) to invade Italy and set up an anti-Pope, Nicholas V. William's row with the Pope turned him into one of the first political philosophers and led him to develop such outrageous ideas as the right to personal property and the right to choose your own ruler – concepts which found their ultimate expression in the election of an American president.

Ironically, William of Ockham was also probably one of the most deeply religious of the medieval philosophers. Unlike Anselm and John Duns Scotus, he was opposed to using logic and reason to argue in favour of the existence of God. He emphatically declared: 'The ways of God are not open to reason, for God has freely chosen to create a world and establish a way of salvation within it apart from any necessary laws that human logic or rationality can uncover.'

Roger Bacon revelled in the posthumous accolade of 'Doctor Mirabilis'. This, however, is more because of his fictional work than his philosophical insights. He is alleged to have invented a talking brass head and a philosopher's stone that could turn lead into gold or silver as well as giving its owner immortality. As Bacon died in 1292, the latter is obviously untrue. Bacon's dabblings in alchemy did not, however, detract from his genuine achievements in setting down some basic philosophical and scientific precepts. He was an early proponent of the study of nature through the senses. Basically, he argued that if it looked like a duck, talked like a duck and walked like a duck, then it was a duck. This basic assumption led him to further early developments in scientific methodology and he set down some of the first rules of careful observation accompanied by rigorous scepticism, careful observation, constant challenging, measurement, experimentation and then a repetition of the process.

The greatest achievement of the medieval English philosophers was founding the first universities and rediscovering and promoting the

Greek philosophers, especially Plato and Aristotle. In doing so, they guaranteed that those philosophical foundation stones were available to build upon in the modern age. That is not to say that they did not make their own contributions to political and social philosophy that can be traced on both sides of the Atlantic. Anselm's scholasticism developed into modern debating methods and parliamentary procedures. John Duns Scotus's focus on the individual found an echo in the determination of British and American law to treat each person as subject to the same rights, responsibilities and liberties as other individuals. And Roger Bacon's emphasis on scientific observation led subsequent generations to question social and political conventions, as well as what they thought they knew of the natural physical world.

One of those to question the social and political conventions of his day was the English cleric John Wycliffe. The Church preached that the bubonic plague was God's punishment for the sins of man. Wycliffe turned that on its head and claimed in his 1356 treatise *The Last Age of the Church* that the plague was the result of a sinful and corrupt Roman Catholic Church. Wycliffe was a man well before his time, possibly because he did not have the advantage of the printing press that Martin Luther had 160 years later. But his stand established a strong Protestant strand in English religion which eventually found its expression in the sixteenth-century Reformation. And if one challenges the divine wisdom of the Church, it is but a small step to questioning the divine right of kings.

The pieces were now fitting together for the start of the launch of the English Age of Enlightenment which would eventually spark the American Revolution. All that was required was a few more pieces in the legal and free speech fields; a break with the Roman Catholic Church; a series of civil wars; the death of a king; and the overthrow of another. The break with Rome is discussed in chapter 7 and the death and overthrow of kings is dealt with in chapter 8. The additional foundation stones for the English (and American) legal system and freedom of speech are dealt with here.

After the introduction of the printing press, defining exactly what constituted seditious and libellous material became one of the key jobs of the infamous Star Chamber. The words 'Star Chamber' are synonymous with injustice. They conjure up images of secret court hearings, extorted confessions and politically motivated judgements. All this is true and the infamy of the Star Chamber is well deserved. But it started life as a tool for correcting and speeding up justice. It was launched in 1487 by Henry VII two years after the end of the War of the Roses and his accession to the

English throne. The impetus for the formation of the court was political. After the disastrous civil war between Plantagenets and Lancastrians, Henry needed to stamp his authority on the kingdom. He also needed to curry favour with the common man whose influence was growing in the wake of the Black Death. The common law courts were slow and cumbersome and they were weighted in favour of the aristocracy who played the major role in administering them. The other legal forum was the Church courts, which heard cases involving blasphemy, heresy, defamation, incest, adultery, divorce, probate issues and the misdeeds of the clergy.

One of the main reasons for the slowness of the courts was the right to trial by jury as enshrined in the Magna Carta. The other was the promise of a fair hearing. It was politically impossible for Henry to abolish the common law courts and bordering on heresy to dissolve the Church courts. So, he set up another court which he called the Court of the Star Chamber after the heavenly decorations on the ceiling of the court's chamber in the Palace of Westminster. The cases covered by the Star Chamber involved public disorder, riots, corruption of juries and officials, sedition, libel, robbery, illegal hunting, forcible entry, murder, witchcraft, fraud, trade disputes, and land enclosures. The Star Chamber could not pass the death sentence and, contrary to legend, the claims of torture in the chamber are wildly exaggerated. The court could, however, order tortures. Not that the courts needed to resort to the rack or thumb screw; the format of the hearings was such that if you appeared in the Star Chamber you almost always walked out a guilty person with a heavy fine and/or prison sentence. The defendant was banned from speaking or giving evidence. Everything had to be channelled through court officials. Neither could the defendants hear any of the evidence against them or even know who was giving the evidence. The cases were heard by privy councillors and senior judges from the common law courts, all of whom were appointed by the king.

The Star Chamber had the desired effect. The threat of a renewed civil war was suppressed. Justice – if that was the correct word – was swifter. Using the Star Chamber as a base, Henry VII established a system of justices of the peace independent of the aristocracy. By the time Henry VIII ascended to the throne in 1509 they were England's chief enforcers of law and order. During the reign of Henry VIII, the Star Chamber became the chief tool of Chancellor Thomas Wolsey and Archbishop Thomas Cranmer for rooting out, punishing and silencing the king's enemies. The politically astute Cranmer and Wolsey liked using the chamber because the court allowed them to impose punishments which the judges (whom they controlled) deemed morally reprehensible, even though they were allowed under English common law. In the 1530s, at the height of the king's dispute with Rome, the number of cases heard by the Star Chamber reached 150 a year.

Rushed judgements through the Star Chamber became a hallmark of the Tudor period. As a result there were many instances of miscarriages of justice. But the Tudor Star Chamber did have one redeeming characteristic: its hearings were held in public. This changed with the 1603 accession of James I and the start of the troubled Stuart dynasty. The number of cases heard also changed. It jumped to 700 a year. It was during the reigns of James I and Charles I that the Star Chamber became notorious for its secret hearings, arbitrary rulings and extreme injustice.

The abuses of the Star Chamber were one of the causes of the English Civil Wars. During the eleven years when King Charles refused to call Parliament, he used the Star Chamber as a substitute for the legislature. The increasingly oppressive nature of the court was a major factor in encouraging migration to America and left the colonials determined not to repeat its abuses in the New World. The Puritans, in fact, were a particular target of the Star Chamber and the Stuart kings. But Charles bit off more than he could chew when he took on Puritan John Lilburne.

Freeborn John, to use the moniker bestowed on him by the London mob, was a hero of freedom of the press. He also established the right of a defendant to protect himself against against self-incrimination, more commonly known as 'taking the Fifth' after its inclusion in the US Constitution as the fifth amendment of the Bill of Rights. Freeborn John was protecting his right against self-incrimination before the infamous Star Chamber on a charge of distributing seditious and libellous material. Lilburne himself was no great writer. He was distributing the work of the Puritan firebrand William Prynne, who during the Civil Wars became notorious as one of the leaders of the Levellers who advocated the then outrageous idea of a universal franchise (excepting women, of course). Lilburne was flogged, pilloried and imprisoned, but refused to compromise his principles and continued to distribute anti-government leaflets. Prynne suffered the same fate with the addition of having his ears chopped off and being branded on both cheeks with the initials SL for seditious libeller. Both men lived to see their tormentors either condemned to death or imprisoned, and in 1641 the Star Chamber was abolished.

The end of the Star Chamber, the civil wars and the collapse of royal authority created a political vacuum which was quickly filled by pamphlets representing every conceivable political and religious perspective. Between 1643 and the conclusive Battle of Naseby in 1645, a total of 722 politically inspired pamphlets were published. Among the most famous was *Areopagitica*, written by poet/philosopher/politician John Milton.

Milton was a devout Puritan and the Protestant cause was central to his thoughts and actions. He firmly believed that his religious beliefs were superior to any others and that if people were allowed freely and openly to debate the issues involved, Puritanism would emerge as the clear winner. Milton's primary target was the same laws that bounced Freeborn John in and out of prison: those relating to seditious libel. They were based on a variation of the belief in the divine right kings. The king was deemed to be above criticism. Therefore any public criticism of the king or any of his advisers or ministers was against the law. Truth was no defence because – to use the convoluted argument of the day – such criticism could not possibly be true because the king was above reproach.

Milton went on to extend his attack to censorship in general. As a good Puritan, he believed it stood in the way of the triumph of his religion. Over the years, Milton's religious views have been sidelined as philosophers and historians have focused on what is regarded as the first and possibly the most cogent argument for a free press that set the foundations for all subsequent debates and actions on both sides of the Atlantic and elsewhere in the world. The targets of his censorship attack were the licensing laws, which Milton described as a 'dishonour and derogation to the author, to the book, to the privilege and dignity of Learning'. Licensing, argued Milton, hinders discovery of the truth, 'because there will always be more truth to be found that we do not yet know of'.

Areopagitica was not widely read at the time. It is believed that only 300 copies were printed. But it emerged again at the end of the seventeenth century with a delayed bang. In the meantime, England was more absorbed with the English Civil Wars and their consequences. The period between the beheading of King Charles I and the restoration of the monarchy in 1660 is known as the Interregnum. It involved rule by the army, a puritan-dominated Parliament and the dictatorship of Oliver Cromwell at various and at times overlapping periods. In many ways it was a period which allowed the flowering of radical political ideas whose time would not come until centuries afterwards. The Levellers advocated a universal franchise, the Diggers pushed for a government more akin to communism and the Quakers were in the forefront of the cause of feminism. All of these views were expressed in a growing flood of pamphlets. Printers were still required to be licensed but the Star Chamber was abolished and the Stationers' Guild was made to take a back seat to the views of the New Model Army, which was controlled by Cromwell. If a political group was in favour with the army ranks – as was the case with the Levellers – then their pamphlets were spread far and wide. If they fell out of favour – as was also the case with the Levellers – then their writings were suppressed. The politicians of the Interregnum led the way in establishing the principle that freedom of speech served the interests of those seeking power and censorship benefitted those in power.

An influential contemporary of Milton's was Thomas Hobbes. He differed with Milton over a Republican versus monarchical government. His ideal world was one in which the citizens enjoyed liberty and freedom but within the context of a strong monarchy. In this respect the differences between Milton and Hobbes preceded the debate between Edmund Burke and Thomas Paine and their adherents, Thomas Jefferson and strong government federalist Alexander Hamilton, over a century later. Hobbes's most famous work, *Leviathan*, was published in 1651. It set out the principle of a social contract between the governed and the government. And that if the government failed to govern fairly and adequately, then the governed had a right to seek a different contract with a different government. Although the term social contract did not become commonly deployed until the French philosopher Jean-Jacques Rousseau used it in the pamphlet by the same name. Hobbes, however, was the first to explain the concept in print. The colonists' assertion that Britain had broken the contract between governed and governed was at the heart of the Declaration of Independence.

Things Go Better With Coke

One of the leading legal opponents of the Star Chamber was Sir Edward Coke, who has been called the most influential jurist in the English-speaking world. His rulings and writings not only provided the foundations for common law in Britain and America, but also Australia, New Zealand, Canada and throughout the British Empire. The legal musings at the root of his work can even be said to extend to international law.

Edward Coke did not have much choice about a career. He was born into a well-established middle-class family of legal eagles and after three years of at Trinity College, Cambridge, joined the London Bar. He started as a big fan of the monarchy. His career began with a few high-profile cases which led to a seat in Parliament in 1589, just a year after the defeat of the Spanish Armada. In 1592, the job of Solicitor General fell vacant. Queen Elizabeth I summoned him to the Throne Room and in no uncertain terms told him off for his successes in defending men whom she regarded as enemies of the Crown. According to legend, Coke was reduced to tears. At the end of the audience the Queen offered him the job of Solicitor General. The first Queen Elizabeth was as political an animal as any monarch, but finding and hiring the best possible legal talent was her priority. Coke developed a good relationship with the Queen as first her Solicitor General and then, after 1594, with the higher rank of Attorney General. In Parliament, he rose to become Speaker of the House, which gave him additional influence. At that time there was no prime minister or cabinet. It fell to the Speaker to represent the view of the Commons to the monarch as well as scheduling debates and bills.

Coke's relationship with James I was more fraught. It started off well enough. Edward Coke and his wife headed north as soon as they heard that Scotland's James VI was to become England's James I. His grovelling was rewarded within weeks when the king knighted Coke. He also confirmed Coke in the post of Attorney General. But relations quickly unravelled when James I insisted that Sir Edward prosecute the English hero Sir Walter Raleigh on trumped-up treason charges. Sir Edward did his job and conducted a ruthless prosecution of Raleigh. The result was that the man who laid the foundations for the colonisation of Virginia spent ten years imprisoned in the Tower of London before finally being executed. Coke emerged from the trial with a tarnished reputation and a feeling of distaste for the new monarch. Queen Elizabeth I had been firm, she had reduced him to tears, but she was fair. She used the throne to pursue and protect the national interest. James I equated the throne and the national interest with his personal interests and wrapped them in the cloak of the theory of the divine right of kings. Sir Edward's opposition to the king grew in almost direct proportion to James's assertion of his God-appointed rights.

This was not immediately apparent in the wake of the Raleigh treason trial, which was followed by Sir Edward's successful prosecution of the conspirators who attempted to blow up Parliament in the Guy Fawkes Gunpowder Plot. In 1606 Coke was rewarded by the king for his prosecutorial efforts with the appointment of Chief Justice of the Court of Common Pleas. Almost overnight he turned from ruthless prosecutor to venerated jurist. His first target was the *ex officio* oath, in particular the one administered by the Court of High Commission, a monarch-appointed ecclesiastical court. In 1607 Parliament asked for Coke's opinion on the High Commission's practices; he replied that 'no man ecclesiastical or temporal shall be examined upon secret thoughts of his heart or of his secret opinion', thus clearing the way for Freeborn John Lilburne's campaign against self-incrimination and the later fifth amendment.

Coke's battle for the independence of the judiciary continued with what is known as 'Fuller's case' and the corresponding 'Case of Prohibitions'. Barrister Nicholas Fuller was charged with contempt of court for charging that the ecclesiastical court was 'under jurisdiction not of Christ, but of anti-Christ'. At the time there were several courts: Coke's Court of Common Pleas, the ecclesiastical courts, the Star Chamber, the King's Bench and the Exchequer Court. A large proportion of the courts' proceedings were wasted arguing over jurisdiction. In Fuller's case the Court of Common Pleas claimed that they had jurisdiction while the ecclesiastical court said it fell in their bailiwick. Coke became the unofficial mediator with a bias towards his own Court of Common Pleas. He lost, Fuller was convicted and Coke appealed for a review. Both sets of judges were summoned to appear before James who told them he would decide jurisdiction based on their arguments. But did the king have the authority to decide? No, argued Coke, in what became known as the 'Case of Prohibitions'. James said that 'in cases where there is not express authority in law, the King may himself decide in his royal person; the Judges are but delegates of the King'. Coke challenged this, asserting that 'the King in his own person cannot adjudge any case, either criminal – as treason, felony etc., or betwixt party and party; but this ought to be determined and adjudged in some court of justice, according to the Law and Custom of England'.

Coke further stated, 'The common law protecteth the King.' James replied, 'The King protecteth the law, and not the law the King! The King maketh judges and bishops. If the judges interpret the laws themselves and suffer none else to interpret.' Coke rejected this. He said that the monarch was not subject to any individual, but he was subject to the law. This very public dispute nearly landed Sir Edward in the Tower of London.

Next on the list was Dr Bonham's case, which involved a dispute over who had the right to issue licences to practise medicine. This led to a ruling that common sense as interpreted by judges responsible for administering the law took precedence over Acts of Parliament. Or, as Coke put it:

In many cases, the common law will control Acts of Parliament, and sometimes adjudge them to be utterly void: for when an Act of Parliament is against common right and reason, or repugnant, or impossible to be performed, the common law will control it, and adjudge such Act to be void.

The ruling has since been dismissed by Britain where it is now accepted that Parliament is sovereign. But in America Dr Bonham's case was used to justify opposition to the writs of assistance and the 1765 Stamp Act, two of the precursors of the War of Independence. It also provided the intellectual foundation for the establishment of the US Supreme Court, which has the right to review congressional legislation and presidential actions. The big difference is that they are reviewed and interpreted in relation to the written Constitution rather than common law or common sense.

By this time, Sir Edward Coke had become a major thorn in the king's side. So James decided to promote him to Chief Justice of the King's Bench, where he thought he could be more easily controlled. The king was wrong. Since the Crown had taken over as head of the Church in England, it had used the position for patronage purposes by appointing political allies and friends to bishoprics that produced handsome incomes for the officeholders. In 1616, James appointed Richard Niele to his seventh bishopric. Coke persuaded his fellow judges on the King's Bench that the appointment was illegal and blocked it. The king ordered the judges to reverse their ruling. All but one – Coke – complied. In a statement which established the importance of an independent judiciary, Sir Edward Coke said: 'When the case happens I shall do that which shall be fit for a judge to do.' James's response was swift and sure. Sir Edward was suspended from the Privy Council, his judicial rulings were expunged from the record and he was dismissed from his judicial post. But Coke soldiered on. In 1620 he returned to Parliament where he quickly emerged as leader of the opposition to the king.

The independence of the judiciary did not become entrenched in the British legal system until the Victorian era. Despite Coke's efforts, judgeships continued to be appointed either by the king or politicians for many years to come. The practice was common in Britain when the US Constitution was written, which could explain why the US Supreme Court justices are appointed by the president and confirmed by the Senate rather than by an independent commission, as is the case in contemporary Britain. The electorate, however, supplanted the monarch as the ultimate source of authority, which explains why 87 per cent of all American judges are elected.

There is another major divergence between the American and British jury systems. Jury trials were introduced in Britain in the twelfth century and the jurors were chosen because they knew the defendant and the facts of the case. They were tasked with the job of using this knowledge plus their own questioning to determine guilt or innocence. There was no legal representation in twelfth-century British courts. Gradually, as a legal profession grew, the role of the juries evolved into considering the facts of the case and delivering a verdict. But it was still thought to be an advantage to have prior knowledge and this led to some biased juries and miscarriages of justice which America's Founding Fathers were determined to avoid. They did this with the sixth amendment, which specifies the impartiality of all juries. This has led to courtroom dramas where jury selection is almost as important as the trial itself. The British now choose their juries completely at random, except that prior knowledge of the defendant obliges a member of the jury to stand down.

The grand jury is another legal custom which started in twelfth-century Britain and made its way across the pond. The purpose of the grand jury is to determine whether or not a *prima facie* case has been established. It started dying out at the end of the nineteenth century in Britain and most of its work is now done by local government authorities and the Crown Prosecution Service. Grand juries still operate in half of the American states.

Sir Edward Coke is regarded as having had a direct effect on several amendments to the US Constitution. One is the fourth amendment, which is based on the famous phrase 'An Englishman's home is his castle'. This in turn is an abbreviated version of Sir Edward's statement that 'the house of every one is to him as his castle fortress, as well for his defence against injury and violence as for his repose'. Because of Coke's work it was ruled that the king could only search an English person's home after a search warrant had been obtained. This prohibition, however, did not apply to colonial America. There the law was specifically rewritten to allow customs officials to search without a warrant. Opposition to the Writs of Assistance (as these searches were called) was one of the sparks that lit the revolutionary powder keg. The Founding Fathers made certain that warrantless searches became a thing of the past with the fourth amendment:

> The right of the people to be secure in their persons, houses, papers, and effects, against unreasonable searches and seizures, shall not be violated, and no Warrants shall issue, but upon probable cause, supported by Oath or affirmation, and particularly describing the place to be searched, and the persons or things to be seized.

Habeas corpus, or the right not to be held without charge, was first mentioned in Magna Carta but in the intervening years was honoured as much in the breach as in the observance. As the conflict between

Parliament and king grew in the first half of the seventeenth century, Charles I would use it to imprison those who refused to pay taxes that Parliament had failed or declined to approve. At the time, Coke's opposition meant he was off the bench, but that did not stop the jurist from continuing to forcefully express his opinion. Because of his standing, Coke's opinions were treated with deference on or off the bench. So people sat up and took notice when he wrote in 1627:

> No freeman is to be committed or detained in prison, or otherwise restrained by command of the King or the Privy Council or any other, unless some lawful cause be shown ... the writ of habeas corpus cannot be denied, but should be granted to every man who is committed or detained in prison or otherwise restrained by the command of the King, the Privy Council or any other... Any freeman so committed or detained in prison without cause being stated should be entitled to bail or be freed.

Coke's words did not bear legal fruit until the 1640 Habeas Corpus Act, which provided additional protection to the rights enshrined in Magna Carta. The American version of this is found in Clause One of the Constitution, which says, 'The Privilege of the Writ of Habeas Corpus shall not be suspended, unless when in Cases of Rebellion or Invasion the public Safety may require it.' The get-out clause related to suspension has been used twice, the first time by Abraham Lincoln during the US Civil War and the second time by George W. Bush to justify Guantanamo Bay and other activities in his 'War Against Terror'.

Petition, Petition, Petition

Sir Edward Coke also had a key role in writing Britain's Petition of Rights, which is considered one of the pillars of British law along with Magna Carta and the 1689 Bill of Rights. James I died in 1625. He passed on his staunch belief in the divine right of kings to his son Charles I, who firmly grasped the baton and ran even further and faster. It was a race which brought him increasingly into conflict with Sir Edward and Parliament, and eventually ended with the English Civil Wars, the beheading of the king and Oliver Cromwell's joyless dictatorship. Coke had already made clear his position on the divine right of kings when he said the king was subject to the law.

The power of Parliament grew quickly in the seventeenth century, but it was still without the power to make laws. It could make suggestions, but the signature of the monarch – the royal assent – was required for a parliamentary proposal to become the law of the land. This is still technically the case, but it is now a constitutional formality. In the seventeenth century the royal assent was regularly withheld at the whim of the monarch, and Charles made a regular habit of it. Parliament did have one major trump card which it had used repeatedly over the centuries in dealing with difficult monarchs, however: control of the purse strings. It started to use that power again and to tie it to wider issues such as the cause of Protestantism and protection for the rights enshrined in Magna Carta.

Charles's problems with Parliament started when he was still Prince of Wales. His father was keen to use his son as a marriage pawn to restore the European balance of power and prevent the spread of the Thirty Years War beyond Bohemian borders. To do that he proposed marrying Charles to Catholic Spain's Maria Anna. Protestant public opinion and Parliament vehemently opposed the marriage, but this did not stop Charles and his confidant the Duke of Buckingham travelling to Madrid to try to secure the match. Parliament, however, need not have worried. Maria Anna refused to marry an infidel unless he converted to Catholicism and England's penal laws imposed against Catholics were repealed. Charles knew that Parliament would not stomach this, and so a crestfallen Prince of Wales returned to England. The nation rejoiced. Charles did eventually achieve a Catholic marriage; he was wed in 1625 to France's fifteen-year-old Henrietta Maria and quickly consummated the union before an opposition Parliament was called.

Parliamentary opposition to a Catholic marriage was understandable. Memories of the Spanish Armada and the Gunpowder Plot were still fresh in people's minds. On the Continent the Hapsburg Holy Roman Emperor Ferdinand II was attempting to forcibly impose Roman Catholicism on all of his subjects. And finally, Protestantism was increasingly seen as an integral part of a rising English national identity. Besides, Parliament had good reason to suspect Charles's actions. He had promised the denizens of Westminster that he would maintain the anti-Catholic religious restrictions. Then he struck a secret treaty with his new brother-in-law, France's King Louis XIII, to relax the religious laws and send English ships to fight against France's Protestant Huguenots.

The one thing that Parliament and the king could agree on was support for the Protestant side in the Thirty Years War. This was mainly because the religious war quickly metamorphosed into a war over who should govern Europe. Parliament and the king disagreed, however, on how to conduct the war. Charles I wanted a major say in any subsequent peace treaty and knew that such a role was dependent on sending a large land army to the Continent, so he asked Parliament for the staggering sum of £7 million. Parliament responded with approval for £140,000 and the suggestion that British involvement be restricted to capturing Spain's transatlantic treasure galleons in order to enrich the British treasury. The English Parliament also stuck on the added proviso that any taxes levied to pay for the war would be reviewed every twelve months. Furthermore, Parliament demanded the dismissal from office of King Charles's much despised and distrusted close confidant Buckingham. Charles responded by dismissing Parliament instead. He also went about raising the money he needed without parliamentary approval and threw into prison those who refused to pay it.

Five men in particular contested their imprisonment for refusing to pay: Thomas Darnell, John Corbet, Walter Erle, John Heveningham and Edmund Hampden. They fought back with a writ of habeas corpus demanding that the king properly charge them or set them free. The subsequent court case became known as the 'Five Knights Case' and led to the Petition of Rights. The king was the initial victor as the court decided that he had the power to imprison whomever he wanted, wherever and whenever he wished, but the legal ruling spurred Parliament on to force a change in the law, which was no easy task given the king's role as the ultimate lawmaker.

Sir Edward Coke took the central role in Parliament's fightback. He convinced the House of Lords to meet with the Commons in April 1628 to discuss the drafting of a petition to the king that would confirm the rights and liberties of his subjects. The Lords were reluctant, but eventually agreed that a committee chaired by Coke should draft a document. When the king heard about this he sent a message to Parliament forbidding them to discuss the issue under threat of parliamentary destruction. Coke responded with a speech filled with legal precedents which established the principle that parliamentarians could say whatever they wanted within the confines of the Palace of Westminster. This was the basis for parliamentary privilege which protects legislators in both Britain and America, in the latter under article one, section six of the Constitution.

With the issue of parliamentary privilege out of the way, the two houses got on with the job of drawing up their petition. On 7 June an angry king agreed to terms which reaffirmed Magna Carta, habeas corpus, trial by jury, due process of law, parliamentary approval for taxes, prohibition on the imposition of martial law on civilians, and prohibition of soldiers being billeted in private homes without the owner's agreement. The petition was greeted with church bells and bonfires throughout

England. The public was clearly on the side of Sir Edward and Parliament in their dispute with the king. But Charles almost immediately went back on his word. In 1629 he dismissed Parliament and reasserted his right to collect taxes and rule as he saw fit. Parliament remained dismissed for eleven long years, until the king's lack of money forced him to recall it. By this time, it was apparent that only a civil war could decide the issue of monarchical or parliamentary supremacy.

The Petition of Rights is generally regarded as the beginning of constitutional monarchy in Britain. Its provisions are mirrored in the US Constitution. The third amendment of the Constitution states that 'no soldier shall, in time of peace, be quartered in any house without the consent of the owner, nor in time of war, but in a manner to be prescribed by law'. The British government's flouting of the petition's prohibition on the billeting of troops in the years just before the American Revolution was one of the causes of the War of Independence. The Petition of Right also influenced the fourth, fifth, sixth, seventh and eighth amendments of the Constitution.

As England's turbulent seventeenth century drew to a close, the foundations of liberal thought in philosophy, speech, politics and law had been firmly laid. They had yet to find a truly practical expression on the other side of the Atlantic. That was to come with the Age of Enlightenment.

3

Liberty Takes Off

The Apple Falls

Some historians have given a specific date for the start of the Age of Enlightenment: 5 July 1687. This was the year of the publication of Sir Isaac Newton's *Philosophiae Naturalis Principia Mathematica*. In his three-volume work Newton shifted the balance of society. After *Principia* the political, philosophical, societal and economic structure of the world was no longer based on faith and belief but on scientific observation and logically determined mathematical formulae. Newton had predecessors, most notably Sir Francis Bacon, who a century before had advanced the pursuit of knowledge through scientific observation, but Bacon's time was split between his roles as barrister, politician, jurist, courtier, scientist and philosopher. He observed. He advocated scientific observation. But Newton turned his observations into 'natural laws'.

Sir Isaac Newton is best known as the world's greatest mathematician, astronomer, physicist and scientist upon whose head an apple fell. The last bit is false. The apple did not fall on Newton's head. It fell while the great thinker was observing an apple tree in his Cambridge University garden. The university has kept the memory of the tree alive by planting seeds from the tree's descendants. It recently cashed in on this foresight by marketing a gin infused with apples from the descendants of Newton's tree.

Newton did not regard himself as a scientist, even though he is regarded as a towering figure in the scientific world. This is partly because the word scientist was not used until 1833 (and even then it was slightly pejorative). Newton thought of himself as a 'natural philosopher' who studied the laws of nature to better understand man's position in it and his relationship with God, and God's relationship to nature. In the course of this study he had a profound influence on political philosophy. Consider Newton's Third Law from his *Principia*. It states that for every action there is an equal and corresponding reaction. This became a keystone upon which scientists have been building ever since. But the physics law also has a role in the world of human relations. A human action elicits a reaction or consequence in much the same way as a jet engine propels a Boeing 747 by pushing against air molecules. If you punch someone in the nose you will suffer a consequence. If you are a monarch who unreasonably raises taxes (a la King George III) you will also suffer consequences. Monarchs are part of the natural world, argued Newton, and, as such, were subject to Newton's 'natural laws'. It was pure Newtonian logic when the Declaration of Independence stated that it had become necessary for the people of the United States to assume 'the separate and equal station to which the laws of nature, and of nature's God, entitle them'.

Newton's greatest contribution to both the physical and metaphysical worlds was the establishment of logically determined laws that governed behaviour. This was a core element of the Age of Enlightenment. In the seventeenth and eighteenth centuries reason became a substitute for other forms of authority that had previously governed human action such as religion, superstition, or authority based on hereditary principle. Newton imposed a set of unalterable scientific laws based on observation and mathematical certainties on which future generations could build. Political philosophers applied the same logic and methodology to their world so that previously nebulous rights such as 'life, liberty and the pursuit of happiness' moved from the conceptual stage to – as the Declaration of Independence stated – the level of 'inalienable rights'. It is one of history's greatest ironies that England's Age of Enlightenment found its ultimate expression in a successful rebellion against English authority: the American Revolution that created the United States, which eventually went on to supplant Great Britain as the world's greatest power.

Less scientific and much more political was John Locke, who took it upon himself to expand on Hobbes's social contract and Newton's natural laws. The son of a West Country lawyer, Locke was also instrumental in the final abolition of the licensing print laws and has been dubbed the 'Father of Liberalism'. In his *Two Treatises of Government*, Locke argued that under 'natural law' all people have the right to 'life, liberty and property'. The last word referred to private property, which Locke asserted was a natural right and the source of individual security and happiness. He further maintained that under the terms of the social contract the people had the right to rebel against a government when it acted in opposition to the interest of its citizens.

Locke's pamphlet was first published in 1698 but for the next sixty years it was overshadowed by Hobbes's *Leviathan*. In 1760 it was reprinted and was a second-time success. It was an even bigger success in America, where it was published in 1762. Among the fans of Hobbes, Locke and Bacon was Thomas Jefferson, who used almost identical language to that of his seventeenth-century English forefathers when he wrote in the Declaration of Independence:

> We hold these truths to be self-evident, that all men are created equal, that they are endowed by their Creator with certain unalienable Rights, that among these are Life, Liberty and the pursuit of Happiness. – That to secure these rights, Governments are instituted among Men, deriving their just powers from the consent of the governed, – That whenever any Form of Government becomes destructive of these ends, it is the Right of the People to alter or to abolish it, and to institute new Government, laying its foundation on such principles and organizing its powers in such form, as to them shall seem most likely to affect their Safety and Happiness. Prudence, indeed, will dictate that Governments long established should not be changed for light and transient causes; and accordingly all experience hath shewn, that mankind are more disposed to suffer, while evils are sufferable, than to right themselves by abolishing the forms to which they are accustomed. But when a long train of abuses and usurpations, pursuing invariably the same Object evinces a design to reduce them under absolute Despotism, it is their right, it is their duty, to throw off such Government, and to provide new Guards for their future security.

John Locke also enjoyed a direct hand in determining the physical structure of America. He was secretary to Anthony Ashley Cooper, the first Earl of Shaftesbury and one of the investors in the settlement of North and South Carolina. Shaftesbury tasked Locke with drafting the 'Fundamental Constitutions of Carolina'. This involved town planning as well as the basics of government. Locke's planning system was a simple street grid that became the template for American towns from the Atlantic to the Pacific.

Locke's governmental structures for the Carolinas were more controversial. The man who wrote about respect for freedom and liberty devised a constitution that entrenched slavery and the principles of a hereditary landed aristocracy up until the end of the American Civil War. This, plus Locke's personal investment in the slave trade, exposed him to charges of hypocrisy and was one of the reasons that in Britain his works were denied the prominence they deserved until half a century after his death. It also helps to explain why Locke was an overnight success when he was published in America in 1772. He was particularly popular in the South.

One of Locke's major goals was the abolition of the licensing laws that had survived Cromwell's republic and the restoration of the monarchy. The problem was that as the seventeenth century drew to a close, the print industry and the ideas they promulgated had assumed the characteristics of Cnut's waves. But that did not prevent the Crown from fighting against the tide. The king's censor-in-chief, Roger L'Estrange, reduced the number of licensed printers to twenty and cut the number of foundries allowed to cast lead type to a mere four. All printers had to post a £300 bond (the modern-day equivalent of roughly £30,000) as surety against any transgressions. However, the unlicensed – or black market – print industry continued to grow at the rate of about 1,000 publications a year, feeding the growing appetite of coffeehouse news junkies.

One of L'Estrange's targets was John Locke who was at the forefront of the pro-free speech argument following the restoration of the monarchy in 1660. In 1679 the censor's men raided Locke's home but, fortunately for Locke and subsequent generations, failed to find his manuscript, *Two Treatises of Government*, which endorsed the right to rebel against an abusive monarch. Under surveillance for sedition, Locke fled to Holland where he wrote the next chapters in the annals of free speech and press: *An Essay Concerning Human Understanding* and *A Letter on Toleration*.

Like Milton before him, Locke approached the free speech debate from a religious perspective. He convincingly argued that tolerant debate was required to reach an agreement between the various dissenting religious groups and that debate could only take place with a free press. In the climate of the time, it was a short step to apply Locke's views on religious debate to secular matters.

By 1688 the British public and Parliament had tired of the restored Stuart monarchy. Pro-Catholic James II was forced to abdicate and his niece Mary and her Dutch husband William of Orange were invited to cross the English Channel and assume the throne as co-monarchs. John Locke accompanied the 'invasion force' and quickly emerged as one of the new court's philosophical giants. Censorship was quickly becoming assigned to the dustbin of British history, but it still had its adherents in government and Parliament, so a way had to be found to abandon official censorship without angering the vested interests. In the end a typical British solution was found to the problem – they ignored it. Parliament required that the licensing laws be renewed every few years. In 1695 the laws were simply not brought before Parliament for renewal and lapsed. Freedom of speech and press in England came into existence by the absence of any law governing those rights, rather than the entry of any written legal statutes. Freedom of speech did not officially become part of British law until October 2000 when membership of the EU forced Britain to adopt the European Convention on Human Rights as part of UK law. This convention guarantees everyone's right to freedom of expression, to hold opinions, and receive and impart information and ideas without interference. For over three centuries the lack of a formal statute protecting British freedom of speech was regarded as both a strength and a weakness. Its absence allowed the courts the widest possible interpretation in the support of free speech. It also led to widespread suppression during times of war and the imposition of laws such as the Official Secrets Act.

The King Can Do No Wrong

Developing in tandem with freedom of speech was the gradual move towards a constitutional monarchy that started in Tudor times. Probably Henry VIII's greatest contribution to history was to catapult religious debate into the political realm. That is not to say that it did not already play a significant role before the English Reformation, however. In many ways the Church was the most powerful political instrument in medieval Europe. But it was a role that was largely controlled by the Church on behalf of the Church. Henry's decision to dissolve the monasteries and declare himself the head of the Church in England combined religion and politics as never before and opened the gate to following century's English Civil Wars, the Age of Enlightenment, the establishment of the sovereignty of Parliament, the 1689 Bill of Rights and many of the influences that shaped the thinking of America's founding fathers.

There had been a strong undercurrent of English religious dissenters long before the German friar Martin Luther nailed his ninety-five theses to the door of All Saints Church in Wittenberg. But fear of retribution meant that they kept their beliefs largely to themselves. Parliament's 1534 Act of Supremacy, which named the English monarch the head of the Catholic Church in England and Wales, encouraged the Protestants to publicly emerge and seize the reins of power. Henry VIII was not himself a true Protestant. His break with Rome was based on practical politics spiced with lust rather than religious ideals. Even after the Act of Supremacy, Henry remained Catholic in his basic beliefs and practices. But there was a small but growing band of Protestants in Parliament and at court, and Henry's decision to seek parliamentary approval for his break with Rome allowed religion to become as much a concern of Parliament as it was of the king and the clergy. Throughout the Tudor years Parliament conducted endless debates on a new Book of Common Prayer, the marriage of priests and the appointment of bishops. In 1559, the Puritans had their first electoral breakthrough when fifteen of them were sent to the House of Commons in elections that year.

Elizabeth I managed to check the growing power of the Puritans by simply summoning Parliament for the absolute minimum of sittings. She was also helped by her own Protestant inclinations and repeated threats by Catholic countries – especially Spain – to overthrow the Tudors and reinstate the True Faith in England. Unfortunately, Good Queen Bess's battles with Spain also left her successor (James VI of Scotland and James I of England) with a pile of debts. These were added to by the first Stuart's rapidly acquired taste for the English high life after the rigours of the spartan Scottish court. This meant he needed cash and the past way to acquire it was through taxation. This required the approval of Parliament, which, as usual, demanded concessions from the Crown in return for a settlement of the king's debt and a generous annual stipend. The negotiations between James I and Parliament over what became known as 'The Great Contract' broke down amid mutual distrust. Parliament was concerned that if it granted him a large stipend then the king would never again have to summon the legislators for their approval. The king was of the firm belief that Parliament's job was to rubber-stamp the demands of the Crown. The outcome was that the king dissolved Parliament in 1610 before trying again in 1614 to resolve the impasse, failing and dissolving Parliament again. It remained dissolved until 1621 when James summoned Parliament to ask for money to oppose Spanish actions in the German Palatinate. Again, the parliamentarians exploited the king's financial difficulties by demanding political concessions. This time they tied their financial support to James's assent to the 'Protestation of 1621', which asserted 'the ancient and undoubted birth right' of Englishmen to debate any subject in Parliament without 'fear of arrest or punishment'. James I promptly tore up the document and dissolved Parliament once more. It did not sit again until 1640. In the intervening years James I and his son Charles I (who ascended to the throne in 1627), managed to finance most of their needs by the sale of peerages, monopolies, trade concessions, tariffs, £40 annual knighthood fees and licences to settle the future United States, none of which required parliamentary approval.

Despite his problems with Parliament, James I was relatively popular with his subjects. He ensured a smooth transfer of power from the Tudor to the Stuart dynasty, ended the long war with Spain, and his disputes with Parliament kept taxes low. But at the same time his financial profligacy, cronyism, corrupt practices and strong belief in political absolutism meant that his son would die on the executioner's block; and the principles of parliamentary sovereignty emerged supreme on both sides of the Atlantic. James I was a firm believer in the divine right of kings. In 1598 (four years before becoming king of England) he wrote *The True Law of Free Monarchies*, in which he argued in favour of absolute monarchy according to God's will. In his view it was the right and obligation of the monarch to impose new laws by royal prerogative. He set out his views on the role of Parliament in a lengthy 1599 letter to his son, whom he advised: 'Hold no parliaments … but for the necessity of laws, which would be seldom.' James I believed that monarchs took legal precedent over all else by virtue of being first on the political scene. They existed long before parliaments and were responsible for the distribution of wealth and land on which the social order was based. Therefore the law (and Parliament) should be subject to the will of the king rather than vice versa.

Charles I bought completely into his father's beliefs and compounded the problem by shifting back towards Catholicism. His marriage to the Catholic French Bourbon Princess Henrietta Maria was clandestine. The marriage negotiations were conducted in secret, which only served to stoke the simmering fires of anti-Catholicism and anger against the king when the affair suffered the fate of all political secrets – revelation. Charles's father had managed to tread the tightrope between growing Puritanism and the still powerful Catholic English families. He was helped by the 1605 Gunpowder Plot. His Protestant credentials were cemented by his sponsorship of the 1611 King James Bible, the best-selling book in publishing history. Charles I, in contrast, swung away from Protestantism. He married a Catholic. He supported High Church Anglican ecclesiastics and he refused to aid Protestant forces during the Thirty Years War. As King of Scotland he attempted to force the Church of Scotland to adopt High Church practices known as Arminianism, which led to the Bishops' War and soon thereafter the English Civil Wars.

Wars are expensive. The sale of peerages and royal warrants fell way short of the cost of fitting out an army and navy for battle. It required proper taxes and for this Parliament had to be recalled. Parliament was angry at being prorogued for so many years and when it was summoned by the king in 1640 it demanded political concessions in return for cash. The king refused and the 'Short Parliament' was quickly dissolved. He then suffered a series of military setbacks and had to recall Parliament again in November 1640. This was the start of the 'Long Parliament', which sat all through the Civil Wars and beyond. One of its first acts was to declare all taxations not approved by Parliament illegal. Then in November 1641 it narrowly passed what became known as 'The Grand Remonstrance', which set forth 204 separate objections to the king's policies, including a parliamentary veto over Crown appointments, the expulsion of all bishops from Parliament and a purge of officials. Charles rejected it but tried to inject a moderate tone, which failed to mollify the Puritans in Parliament.

On 3 January 1642, Charles ordered Parliament to hand over five MPs who were leading the opposition to him: John Pym, John Hampden, Denzil Holles, William Strode and Sir Arthur Haselrig. They were all to face charges of high treason. Parliament refused, so Charles and his guards marched on the house to arrest them. But news of this action preceded their arrival, and the five fled before the king and his troops arrived. When they demanded that the Speaker of House, William Lenthall, reveal the whereabouts of the five men. Lenthall famously replied: 'May it please your Majesty, I have neither eyes to see nor tongue to speak in this place but as the House is pleased to direct me, whose servant I am here.' To this day, British monarchs cannot enter Parliament except by express invitation, and can only go into the House of Lords. They are barred from the Commons.

Fighting broke out immediately. Parliament seized London. The king sent his family abroad for safety and marched with his supporters to the north to bolster his army. In August 1642 the royal standard was raised and the English Civil Wars began. The fighting lasted throughout most of the 1640s and eventually ended with the king's beheading on 30 January 1649 outside the still-standing Banqueting House in London's Whitehall. At his trial Charles I was accused of treason by reason of putting his personal interest before that of England. He was effectively found guilty of war crimes and held responsible for the estimated 300,000 deaths that occurred during the Civil Wars.

Throughout his trial, Charles refused to plead, insisting that the trial was illegal:

No earthly power can justly call me in question as a delinquent ... this day's proceeding cannot be warranted by God's laws; for, on the contrary, the authority of obedience unto Kings is clearly warranted, and strictly commanded in both the Old and New Testament ... for the law of this land, I am no less confident, that no learned lawyer will affirm that an impeachment can lie against the King, they all going in his name: and one of their maxims is, that the King can do no wrong ... the higher House is totally excluded; and for the House of Commons, it is too well known that the major part of them are detained or deterred from sitting ... the arms I took up were only to defend the fundamental laws of this kingdom against those who have supposed my power hath totally changed the ancient government.

But the court ruled that 'the King of England was not a person, but an office whose every occupant was entrusted with a limited power to govern "by and according to the laws of the land and not otherwise"'.

The execution of Charles I set the Anglo-Saxon death seal on the concept of the divine right of kings and put Britain on the road to the parliamentary sovereignty, although it was not confirmed in writing until the 1689 Bill of Rights. The usual narrative is that the English Civil Wars were a conflict between the forces of Parliament and the king. They were much more than that. Parliament became both the vehicle and tool in which the new values of nationalism and the Age of Reason fought their battle with the remnants of feudalism.

Rumps and Barebones

Oliver Cromwell is one of the most controversial figures in British history, and a key and oft-ignored contributor to American history. He was a religious zealot who led the Parliamentarian forces in the Civil Wars and was one of the key signatories to the death warrant of Charles I. He established the rights of Parliament at the point of a sword. Winston Churchill called him a military dictator. John Milton labelled him 'a hero of liberty'. In Ireland his name is synonymous with the most damnable swear words. From 1649 to 1653 he waged a genocidal war against Catholics. Thousands of Irish Catholics were sold into indentured servitude in the Caribbean and North America. His eventual victory led to the 1652 Act for the Settlement of Ireland, which banned the practice of Roman Catholicism, ordered the execution of priests and confiscated all Catholic-owned lands and handed them over to Scottish and English soldiers. This established the political, social and economic foundations for centuries of Anglo-Irish enmity, the mass migration of Irish people to North America, the division of the island of Ireland and a long history of support for Irish national causes by the US. At the same time, Cromwell is credited with laying some of the foundations of the British Empire. At the height of British imperialism in the 1890s there was a move to erect a statue of Cromwell outside Parliament. The Irish nationalists who then sat in Parliament threatened a revolt and eventually the statue was paid for by the former Prime Minister Lord Rosebery. It straddles a commanding space between the Commons and Lords, staring out across the busy road to Parliament Square.

Cromwell was born into minor gentry in the east of England and led a fairly uneventful life as a yeoman farmer until he was elected to Parliament in 1628 at the age of twenty-nine. Nine years later he converted to radical puritanism. It is believed that at this time he even considered emigrating to the newly founded Puritan colony of Connecticut, but he stayed in England and represented Huntingdon in the Long Parliament, convened in 1640. As a radical Puritan he quickly sided with the anti-Royalist forces and when the First Civil War broke out in 1642 he returned home to raise a cavalry militia. Cromwell found he had a knack for leadership and military innovation. He quickly rose through the ranks of the Parliamentarian army serving under the Earl of Manchester and then Sir Thomas Fairfax. He solidified his political and military reputation by reorganising the forces under the banner of the New Model Army and soundly defeating the Royalist forces at the 1645 Battle of Naseby. By now Cromwell was the undisputed military commander and, as a war was in progress, the de facto political leader of the Parliamentarian forces.

As the head of the New Model Army and – after the King Charles's execution – 'Lord Protector of the Commonwealth of England, Scotland, Ireland and the dominions thereto belonging', he found Parliament almost as troublesome as the king had. In the political vacuum created by war all sorts of radical ideas and groups sprang forth from Cromwell's army. One of them was a group called the Fifth Monarchists, who wanted to establish a theocracy. But they were overshadowed by the Levellers and the Diggers. The latter agitated for an agrarian-based socialism in which land was communally owned and farmed. The name and the policies were adopted by several hippy groups in the 1960s and 1970s in San Francisco. The group that struck the loudest chord were the Levellers, who demanded biennial elections to Parliament, electoral reform and a free vote for every male head of household. Women were, of course, considered unqualified to vote. Servants were disregarded because it was thought they would simply vote as instructed by their masters. These radical ideas were discussed at what became known as the 'Putney Debates' in October and November 1647 at St Mary's Church in the village of Putney outside London. The purpose of the debates was to devise a new constitution for England. They never got anywhere. The debates were presided over by what were termed the army 'Grandees', led by Cromwell, who wanted a suffrage based on property qualifications. The new rulers were as frightened of mob tyranny as the monarchy had been. They were now the elite with interests to protect. When the Levellers continued to demand change with a pamphleteering campaign – and even organised mutinies in the ranks of the New Model Army – they were bloodily suppressed.

There were differences among Parliamentarians as to the fate of the imprisoned King Charles. There were many Parliamentarians who thought that a negotiated settlement could be reached with the monarchy. But the Puritans had become dead set on his trial and execution following the king's duplicitous negotiating tactics. On 6 December, Cromwell ally Colonel Thomas Pride posted himself at the entrance to Parliament with an an armed guard. In possession of a list of Parliamentarians opposed to the king's trial, he simply arrested those named on the paper. Those entitled to attend dropped from 507 to about 200. The 'Rump Parliament', as it became known, on 4 January 1649 voted for the king's trial. Two days later the House of Lords was abolished and the day after that the monarchy was abolished. The House of Commons was declared the source of all authority and it was made an offence to proclaim a new king. Fourteen days after the execution of Charles I, a Council of State was set up with Cromwell in the chair. The military leader was now the de facto ruler of England.

As the new source of all 'just power', the Rump Parliament was tasked with devising a new constitutional settlement for the country. In addition, it had to deal with the everyday business of raising taxes and debating and passing bills. The problem was that its membership continued to be comprised of individuals with conflicting motives and ideologies. Cromwell attempted to resolve the divisions by dissolving Parliament and calling fresh elections. Parliament rejected the dissolution and continued sitting. So on 20 April 1653, Cromwell attended a session. He listened stony-faced to a few speeches, rose to his feet and ranted: 'You have sat too long for any good you have been doing lately ... Depart, I say, and let us have done with you. In the name of God go!' The Commons' doors were then thrown open; a troop of armed soldiers marched in and the chamber was cleared at the point of musket and sword. The Rump Parliament was replaced with what became known as the 'Barebones Parliament', named after one of its prominent members, Praise-God Barebones, rather than for its further reduced membership of just 140. Despite the fact that the MPs were nominated by the Army Grandees, Cromwell still failed to secure the parliamentary support he demanded and after just seven months that Parliament went the way of its predecessors, to be replaced by the Protectorate Parliament, which also stubbornly refused to toe the Cromwellian line on all matters.

During his struggles with the shrinking Parliament, Cromwell became increasingly dictatorial and began to assume the monarchical trappings that he had fought so hard to remove from the English political landscape. He was offered the hereditary crown but rejected it because it would make him subject to the same parliamentary restrictions that had brought about the fall of his foe, King Charles. Much better to have himself declared Lord Protector for Life with dictatorial powers. But Cromwell did allow himself to be addressed as 'Your Highness'. He signed his name 'Oliver P', substituting the title Protector for Rex. At the ceremony to install him as Lord Protector, Cromwell sat upon the throne, wore ermine and wielded the ceremonial sword of state and orb. Later, he re-established the House of Lords and created three new peerages.

Return of the King

By the time Cromwell died on 3 September 1658, the British public and political Establishment were thoroughly fed up with his joyless dictatorship. He was succeeded as Lord Protector by his thirty-one-year-old son Richard. But this was only a stopgap measure. Richard lacked his father's authority. More importantly, he failed to secure the trust and support of the army. Within nine months he was out of power and fading away into a long exile. For a short time there was a real danger that the political vacuum would result in another civil war. But the de facto ruler of Scotland, one General William Monck, headed this off by marching south and demanding the reinstatement of the Long Parliament. The problem was that in the intervening years some 390 MPs had died. A single-issue election was called: the restoration of monarchy. The royalists won and the throne was offered to the son of the beheaded Charles I, Charles II, who had been plotting his return to England since going into Continental exile in 1646. The restoration of the Stuart dynasty was not achieved by force of arms or subterfuge. The king was invited to return by the country's elected representatives. Although it was not spelled out at the time, a tectonic shift had occurred in the relationship between Parliament and the monarchy.

Religion had played a big part in the Crown *vs* Parliament conflict, the wars that followed and the Cromwellian interregnum. It remained high on the agenda during the Restoration period. Support for the monarchy was synonymous with High Church Anglicanism. The king was restored as head of the Church of England, and the bishops were back in their palaces and in the House of Lords, whose members were fully reinstated with all their previous powers. The Anglican Book of Common Payer became compulsory and public office holders had to swear allegiance to the Church of England as well as the Crown. Unchanged, however, was a widespread antipathy to and suspicion of Catholics and the Roman Catholic Church. It was this fear and loathing of the Vatican and its followers that would bring about the final collapse of the Stuarts and further strengthen the hand of Parliament.

The last two male Stuarts to rule England, Charles II and his successor brother James II, are probably best described as crypto-Catholics. All too aware of the political dangers of emerging from the religious closet, Charles was the more circumspect of the two. However, there was little doubt of his Catholic leanings. In 1672 Charles issued the Royal Declaration of Indulgence, which in theory supported the concept of wide-ranging religious freedoms. In practice the declaration created a political clash with Parliament because it included Catholics. Throughout his reign there were rumours that the king had secretly converted to Catholicism, and in fact he did so, on his deathbed on 2 February 1685.

If there were doubts about Charles II's Catholic credentials, there were none about those of his brother James II. He formally converted to Catholicism in 1668, but this was kept secret until 1676 when he was forced to relinquish his post of Lord High Admiral rather than swear allegiance to the tenets of the Church of England. Both Charles and James fathered a large number of children. Unfortunately, none of Charles's legitimate children survived so it was left to James and his heirs to carry on the family business. Parliament, however, was terrified that because of James's religion this would mean the return to Catholicism in England. At first this was not a problem. For a long time James had only one surviving legitimate child, Mary, by his first wife Anne Hyde, who was raised Protestant and married to the Dutch Protestant William of Orange. But Anne died and James married the Italian Catholic Princess Mary of Modena who, after several miscarriages and stillborn deaths, gave birth to a male heir, James Francis Edwards, who was raised to be a Catholic. Parliament responded by attempting to pass a bill which blocked Catholics from acceding to the English throne. Backing his younger brother and dynastic legitimacy, Charles II dissolved Parliament in 1679 rather than risk passage of the Exclusion Bill. The new clash between Parliament and the Crown prompted Charles's illegitimate Protestant son, the Duke of Monmouth, to plot a coup. He failed, was forced into exile and public sympathies swung back in favour of the Stuarts. But it didn't last.

When James II acceded to the throne in 1685 it became quickly apparent that he was going to fight for the rights of his fellow Catholics. Opposition was inevitable. Within a year his nephew the Duke of Monmouth was back with an army and a full-blown rebellion, which was bloodily suppressed. James sought to protect himself by establishing a peacetime standing army. This, however, ran counter to English traditions at the time. He then compounded the problem by appointing Catholics to senior military positions. He also received the Papal Nuncio at court. Parliament objected, so James dissolved it in 1685. It never met again during his reign. By 1688 it was clear that James would never become an Anglican, and Parliament and the British public would never accept a return to Catholicism. If England was to remain a monarchy, the only alternative was to install Charles II's Protestant daughter Mary and her husband William of Orange on the throne. Seven Protestant nobles known to history as 'The Immortal Seven' wrote to William offering to rise up in his support if he invaded England. William took the bait. His fleet of 463 ships landed 14,000 troops in the West Country. As William marched to London, James's army deserted him and he was forced flee to exile in France. In the ensuing political chaos the House of Lords was summoned to form a provisional government. They in turn called a convention which confirmed the 'abdication' of James II and the installation of William and Mary as co-rulers. But before this was done the convention took to heart the advice of Anthony Cary, Viscount Falkland, who said: 'Before you fill the Throne, I would have you resolve what power you will give the King and what not.' The result was the 1689 Bill of Rights.

Parliament had invited the king's return in 1660. The king had failed. Parliament had dismissed the king and invited another king and queen to take his place. Parliament had proved it was in charge. All that was needed was to set the new order down in black and white.

The Bill of Rights was in two equal parts of twelve articles, or clauses, each. The first half focused on James's efforts 'to subvert and extirpate the Protestant religion, and the laws of this kingdom' – the justification section. The second half listed twelve 'certain ancient rights and liberties', including declaring illegal any laws not approved by Parliament; a ban on taxes without parliamentary approval; maintenance of a standing army in peacetime with the approval of Parliament; free parliamentary elections; freedom of speech; the imposition of excessive bail on persons committed in criminal cases against the laws made for the liberty of the subjects; and the end of excessive fines and illegal and cruel punishments. This was 100 years before the US Congress transmitted to the state Legislatures twelve proposed similar amendments to the Constitution which they also called the Bill of Rights.

On the Other Side of the Atlantic

The wars, debates and turmoil that infected seventeenth-century Britain were mirrored in the American colonies across the Atlantic. In fact, in many ways, the colonies were harbingers of events in the mother country. The Pilgrim Fathers who landed at Plymouth Rock in 1620–22, decades before the start of the Civil Wars, were religious dissidents who fled England because of persecution. They demanded the right to worship God as they saw fit. A group of London investors exploited their desire for freedom to send them into the wilderness to make money. The price that the Pilgrims paid was cold, starvation, disease, hostile natives and death for half of their number in the first year. The colonists in Virginia – the other big venture of the time – were not so high-minded. They were mainly adventurers in search of gold. Instead they discovered tobacco, which could be sold for gold. But the Virginians also developed a political agenda. The New Englanders supported the Parliamentary/ Puritan forces and the Virginians backed the king. When Cromwell came to power the southern colony became a refuge for exiled royalists. So, although the colonial north and south were at opposite ends of the seventeenth-century political spectrum, they had a common purpose in building upon what they saw as traditional English liberties and structures for the protection of their rights. In the Massachusetts Bay Colony this was initially demonstrated by the Mayflower Compact, which bound the signatories to the establishment of a 'civil body politic' for the purpose of passing 'just and equal laws'. The document was short and concise and was the first expression of the concept of equality and self-government in America. It remained the political guiding light of the Massachusetts Bay Colony until 1691, when it became a Crown colony. All too aware of the problems of governing across 3,000 miles of ocean, they conceded that the settlers, 'together with the governor and council, shall have the power to make acts and laws for the government plantation, correspondent as near as may be to the laws of England'.

By the start of the American Revolution, the thirteen colonies had developed political systems similar to Britain's. There was a governor wielding executive power and a bicameral legislature made up of a council and an assembly. The governor filled the monarch's role; the council was comparable to the House of Lords and the assembly to the House of Commons. These colonial bodies dealt exclusively with domestic matters. Responsibility for foreign affairs, defence (with the exception of battles with the Native Americans) and trade were reserved for London; a situation which increasingly grated with the colonials. The system did not start out that way. It evolved from three distinct political structures: charter colony, proprietary colony and royal colony. Charter colonies were run as investments with a royal licence to operate in a specific territory. Proprietary colonies were granted to specific people, men such as William Penn whose land grant basically meant he ran the territory pretty much as he wanted. Royal colonies were usually imposed when the other two models failed, or, in some cases, to end competing land claims between the different colonies.

The first American legislature was Virginia's House of Burgesses, which held its inaugural session in 1619. It started as a unicameral legislature and Governor Sir George Yeardley largely ignored the representatives and ran the colony as he saw fit. By the mid-seventeenth century the House of Burgesses had evolved into a bicameral legislature with an appointed upper house of planters that also performed the role of a cabinet chaired by the governor. The lower house was elected by property owners. Women, slaves and servants were not allowed to cast ballots. The British Parliament was the template for Virginia. The House of Burgesses became the template for the legislative assemblies of the other thirteen colonies, as well as that of the Continental Congress.

Before the 1689 Bill of Rights the governor ruled much as the medieval English monarchs had. It was he who decided when the assembly would meet and be dismissed, and he had the power to veto any bill he did not like. The governor appointed all the members of the upper house and, like the British king, could raise money by the sale of offices and licences. After 1689 the colonial assemblies began to restrict the governor's power by asserting control over money bills and even setting his salary. As the cost of the colonies grew – especially wars against France and Spain – London demanded that the governors squeeze more money out of the colonials to pay the bills. Taking a leaf from the history of the British Parliament, the price extracted by the colonial legislatures was increased political power.

The political pattern for the colonial legislatures was the English Parliament. But there was no template for governing relations between the mother Parliament and its offspring, and the poor communications over such a vast distance complicated matters further. After the Seven Years War (the French and Indian Wars in America) it became apparent that the relationship needed to be clarified. Not surprisingly, after 150 years there were differences of opinion on what the clarification would say. London took the initiative with the Declaratory Act of 1766, which followed the face-saving repeal and changes to the much-loathed Stamp Act and Sugar Act. Alright, said London, we will give in to you on these specific taxes but it should be made clear that Parliament 'hath, and of right ought to have, full power and authority to make laws and statutes of sufficient force and validity to bind the colonies and people of America ... in all cases whatsoever'. The colonials were furious. They saw the Declaratory Act as an abrogation of their rights as Englishmen to 'no taxation without representation' as set out in Magna Carta and the 1689 Bill of Rights. Because of these ancient privileges, the colonials argued, their legislatures had co-equal standing with the London Parliament and reported directly to the Crown or the Crown's representative (the governor). Westminster put forward the rather weak argument that the colonies had 'virtual representation' in London. With such incompatible interpretations of how to apply the colonial experience to the British constitution, it was inevitable that the two sides would increasingly clash.

The inevitability of revolution was at the heart of the debate between two of the leading figures before, during and after the American Revolution, both of whom helped to build the philosophical framework of the United States. Both were English, although one is usually thought of as American. Thomas Paine and Edmund Burke were both ardent pamphleteers. Burke was also a prominent member of Parliament. Thomas Paine, the author of the pamphlet *Common Sense*, is regarded as one of America's 'Founding Fathers' and, in fact, some historians refer to him as 'The Father of the American Revolution' because of the influence of his best-selling anti-British pamphlet. Later he became embroiled in the French Revolution. He was, however, politically formed in England as he did not set foot on American soil until he was thirty-seven. The two men were both practical politicians as well as political philosophers. Their philosophies, positions and policies at times overlapped and yet they were seen as polar opposites representing the political left and right of the day. They violently disagreed over the French Revolution and a London court eventually convicted Paine in absentia for criminally libelling Edmund Burke. Both had supporters on either side of the Atlantic and their feud and its spin-offs played a major role in determining political thinking in young America.

Edmund Burke was the son of a Protestant lawyer father and Catholic mother and was raised as a Protestant. After studying at Trinity College Dublin, he moved to London where he became private secretary to the Marquis of Rockingham, a Whig Prime Minister, for a year between 1765 and 1766 and then a few months again in the spring of 1782. The Whigs grew out of opposition to James II and the Glorious Revolution and Bill of Rights that followed his abdication. They were staunch advocates of the sovereignty of Parliament and the principles of a constitutional monarchy. Their opponents were the Tories, who wanted to reinforce the power of the monarch. Rockingham managed to secure Edmund Burke a seat in 1765 and at age thirty-six the Irish lawyer entered the British Parliament. Almost from the start he made a name for himself as a political philosopher, but at first his fellow Whigs were uncertain whether he was on the radical, centrist or conservative wing of the party. To many he appeared radical because he was an opponent of the Stamp Act and the Intolerable Acts, punitive laws enacted in Westminster following the Boston Tea Party, which were driving a wedge between Britain and its American colonies.

The colonies' war cry – and that of many British Whigs – was 'no taxation without representation'. Burke took the position that from a legal point of view the British government had every right to tax the colonists, but from a political point of view, the government was sowing the seeds of rebellion and shooting itself in the foot. In speech after speech he stood up in Parliament and argued the colonists' case for fair treatment. He was America's champion in Westminster.

Thomas Paine was cut from a different cloth altogether. He was fiercely anti-establishment rather than part of the establishment calling for political evolution. He was a rabid revolutionary who, as John Adams said, was 'better at tearing down than building up'. Paine had only five years of formal schooling but this was followed by decades of debates in the coffeehouses where he honed his rhetorical skills. A corset maker by trade, he turned to tax collecting after the death of his wife and daughter in childbirth and the collapse of his business. Eighteenth-century British tax collectors – or 'excisemen' – were poorly paid, often corrupt and near the bottom of the social scale. Paine took it upon himself to campaign for better pay and conditions for his occupation. He failed. But his efforts gained the attention of Benjamin Franklin who had been sent to London as representative of the Pennsylvania colonial assembly. Franklin suggested that Paine try his luck in America and wrote him a glowing reference. Paine set sail in 1774 for Philadelphia and quickly established himself as a first-class journalist.

On 18 April 1775, Boston-based British troops marched to Concord in an attempt to seize a cache of rebel arms. The colonial militia fought back with the 'shot heard round the world' and the revolution started. But American support for the rebellion was far from universal at that stage. As Paine later wrote: 'Their attachment to Britain was obstinate, and it was, at that time, a kind of treason to speak against it. Their ideas of grievance operated without resentment, and their single object was reconciliation.' Paine decided to use his journalistic skills to persuade the public otherwise. *Common Sense* was published on 10 January 1776 and was an instant success. It sold over 150,000 copies, roughly equivalent today to 6 million. Paine pulled no punches in attacking the British monarchy and constitution and calling for an independent American government. He wrote that the British constitution should be dismissed as an outdated form of government characterised by the dual tyrannies of a hereditary monarchy and aristocracy. England's much vaunted constitutional monarchy, he said, was every bit as absolutist as the absolute monarchy of France. Paine proposed that the colonies ditch the British constitution, fight for independence and form a government based on a directly elected legislature which then elects a president.

Back in London, Burke was pleading the kith and kin argument and warning that America would refuse to back down in the face of military threats. He warned that the ultimate consequence would be akin to a civil war and told the House of Commons in March 1775:

> As long as you have the wisdom to keep the sovereign authority of this country as the sanctuary of liberty, the sacred temple consecrated to our common faith, wherever the chosen race and the sons of England worship freedom, they will turn their faces towards you. The more they multiply, the more friends you will have; the more ardently they love liberty, the more perfect will be their obedience. Slavery they can have anywhere. It is a weed that grows in every soil. They may have it from Spain. They may have it from Prussia. But, until you become lost to all feeling of your true interest and your natural dignity, freedom they can have from none but you.

Burke maintained that peace was not only desirable, but the only practical course. Force, he argued, could only be a temporary solution and he was doubtful that it could even be temporarily successful given the size of the territory and Britain's total inexperience at the time of fighting colonial wars thousands of miles away. Finally, Burke contended, the British government would run afoul of the liberty-loving character and independent streak of the Americans.

Through the War of Independence, Thomas Paine was convinced that Burke was a kindred spirit and that his parliamentary tirades in support of American demands were the same as support for the cause of independence. He was wrong. Separated by an ocean for more than a decade, the two men did not finally meet until August 1788 when the Duke of Portland brought them together during a visit to London by Paine. For a couple of years the two men conducted a friendly correspondence but their basic differences were soon exposed. Paine was a revolutionary who in a later century would have happily marched with Lenin, Stalin and Trotsky. He believed in the renewing forces of rebellion and firmly maintained that the American Revolution was the start of a worldwide rebellion against entrenched authority. Burke's Whig Party had a radical wing associated with Paine's clean sweep philosophy, but Burke was not among them. He believed in reform, but his belief was rooted in a conviction that reform was necessary to preserve the monarchy and society rather than to overthrow it.

The two men were destined to become bitter foes. The confirming catalyst was the French Revolution. Paine threw himself wholeheartedly into French radical politics. He helped to draft the Declaration of the Rights of Man and then, after Burke fired a withering broadside against the cross-Channel revolutionaries he wrote his next two great works: *The Rights of Man* and *The Age of Reason*. In these two works Paine strode off the acceptable end of the political spectrum for many of his supporters in Britain and America. The straw that broke the American public's back was Paine's rejection of organised religion. In *The Age of Reason* he wrote of his hope that 'a revolution in the system of government would be followed by a revolution in the system of religion'. For a country that owed much of its existence to a religious struggle, this was unacceptable.

The French Revolution became the benchmark for public opinion on both sides of the Atlantic. At first there was widespread support for the rebellion. How could anyone argue with a clarion call for liberty, equality and fraternity? But as ideals were replaced with terror and dictatorship, the mood reversed. Paine, however, remained true to the cause, even though his political activities landed him in a French prison for some months and he nearly enjoyed the kiss of Madam Guillotine. His dwindling band of American supporters tried to persuade the government to intercede on Paine's behalf to return him to the infant

United States, But Washington refused. The hero of 1776 was shunned by the American government he helped to create. Finally, in 1802 his long-standing friend and advocate Thomas Jefferson allowed him to return. But Paine was denied access to the corridors of power and died in poverty in 1809.

Sir Billy Blackstone Writes It Down

Poet, academic, politician, mathematician, architect, writer, lawyer, judge and philosopher, Sir William Blackstone was a renaissance man and a true product of the Age of Enlightenment. He made his mark across a broad spectrum of disciplines but has gone down in history as the man who took an ocean of disparate laws and statutes, placed them in a sound philosophical context and then transformed the jumble into a coherent and interdependent whole, which became the basis of legal teaching, constitutional law and court procedures on both sides of the Atlantic for generations after.

His brilliance was evident from an early age. He won scholarships to the prestigious Charterhouse School and then Pembroke College, Oxford. Despite his genius, Blackstone initially found it difficult to scratch a living as a lawyer and Pembroke College had to come to his aid with a bookkeeping job. His big break came in 1753 when he became the first-ever professor of law. The mission statement posted at Oxford to advertise his first lecture not only set the tone for the rest of his teaching career but provided the template for future law schools throughout the English-speaking world. 'It is proposed,' he wrote, 'to lay down a general and comprehensive plan of the laws of England to deduce their history; to enforce and illustrate their leading rules and fundamental principles; and to compare them with the laws of nature and other nations.' The following year a synopsis of his lectures, *Analysis of the Laws of England*, was published. It was a runaway best-seller. An even greater commercial success was his four-volume work *Commentaries on the Laws of England*, which started publication in 1765. The book sold out in six months and eventually netted Sir William the then princely sum of £14,000. For nearly 150 years it was *the* reference book for successive generations of lawyers and judges. It was particularly popular in America where homespun lawyers and judges travelled the frontier from court to court toting Blackstone's compact, readable and concise guide to the law. Abraham Lincoln read *Commentaries* as a young store clerk. Chief Justice John Marshall, whose decisions set the foundations of the Supreme Court, was given his first copy at sixteen. He described the work as 'the poetry of law'. The *Commentaries* are still regularly cited in Supreme Court decisions. Blackstone also had a major impact on American court procedures. He noted that lawyers are 'officers of the court' and established the basics of the Bar exam when he insisted that attorneys should be subject to examination by judges and sworn to uphold the law before they are allowed to practise. He also set down the rules related to privileged conversations between client and attorney and insisted that lawyers guilty of breaching this privilege, or committing 'deceit or collusion', should be imprisoned and disbarred.

One of the main attractions of Blackstone's *Commentaries* was the way in which he gave it a philosophical foundation by linking English law to natural law, which was derived from nature or God. These natural laws were things such as individual free will and John Locke's 'life, liberty and property'. Sir Edward wrote: 'The law works within a set of values – natural law – which is a gift from God and which gives all men individual liberty. The legal system should be constructed to embrace the free will of individuals without infringing on the rights of others.'

Stemming from Sir Edward's belief in natural law was his opposition to slavery, a desire for the free elections and an end to Britain's rotten borough system, and a strong belief in democracy and the will of the people. He even advocated civil disobedience in pursuit of natural law as long as those resorting to civil disobedience were prepared to accept the consequences of breaking man-made laws.

Commentaries hit the American bookstores in 1771. From the point of view of the would-be revolutionaries, the timing could not have been better. Here was a respected jurist who at the time was Solicitor-General of Great Britain telling them that there was a natural law that was greater than the king's law and that they had the right to employ that natural law to break the king's law – as long as they were prepared to accept the consequences, which they were. Sir Edward's books sold even more copies in America than in England. The result was the most famous practical application of the supremacy of natural law over man-made law: the 1776 Declaration of Independence.

Blackstone influenced more than the Declaration of Independence. His legal hand is evident throughout the later Constitution, the Bill of Rights, subsequent amendments and the very structure of the American government. Most people think that the system of checks and balances was invented and implemented by Jefferson, Franklin, Madison, *et al*. Not so; its roots can be seen in the 1689 Bill of Rights, but it was first laid out in detail in Sir Edward Blackstone's description of the workings of the British Constitution. In volume one of *Commentaries* he wrote:

The people are a check upon the nobility, and the nobility a check upon the people, by the mutual privilege of rejecting what the other has resolved; the while the king is a check upon both; and the executive power is checked by the two houses which have the power of impeachment and punishing the conduct of the king's counsellors.

It was Blackstone who first proposed a minimum age requirement for anyone sitting in either House of Parliament of twenty-one. The US Constitution says that you have to be twenty-five to be elected to the House of Representatives, thirty to be a senator and thirty-five to be president. Under the British constitution, Blackstone wrote, foreign affairs and defence is the primary responsibility of the executive. Domestic affairs are the main responsibility of Parliament, although both branches retain the right to act as a check on the other's primary field of responsibility. These division and responsibilities are mirrored in Article One of the US Constitution. In Britain, Blackstone wrote, all taxes originate in the lower house. In America all tax matters start in the House of Representatives.

At the time that Blackstone was writing the roles of the prime minister and cabinet were still evolving. The monarch retained significant executive powers, but the acceptance of the sovereignty of Parliament meant that increasingly the king was vesting those executive powers in ministers who were able to command a majority vote in Parliament. Today, the monarch represents the executive power but that power is implemented by her government headed by a prime minister and with the support of a majority in the House of Commons. If the monarch were to personally exercise her power, it would create a constitutional crisis because she would challenge the supremacy and sovereignty of a parliament elected by the people.

The US Constitution used Blackstone's *Commentaries* as the blueprint when it simply said: 'The executive powers shall be vested in a President of the United States of America.' From that single line flows a wide river of rights, responsibilities and powers which make the American president almost as powerful as the monarch against which America rebelled. The eighteenth-century king appointed all judges. The US president appoints all federal judges and Supreme Court justices. Blackstone's king was 'the fountain of justice and general conservator of peace'. The president, says the Constitution, 'shall take care that the laws be faithfully executed and shall commission all officers of the United States'.

Blackstone regarded the independence of the judiciary as the ultimate protector of the Constitution. Article Three of the Constitution establishes the judiciary as a separate and equal branch of the government, the independence of which is protected by lifetime appointments; and its duties include acting as a third check on the other two branches of the government. The jury system was another important part of Blackstone's judicial structure. He called it 'the glory of English law' and he insisted that any conviction of a citizen required the 'unanimous consent of twelve of his neighbours'. What does the US Constitution say about juries? 'Trial of all crimes, except in case of impeachment, shall be by jury.' In most other countries, equity law and common law come under the same court system. Not so in eighteenth-century Britain, much to the disgust and disapproval of Sir William Blackstone. The US Constitution takes Blackstone's side and says that 'the judicial power shall extend in all cases, in law and equity, arising under the Constitution'.

Blackstone's *Commentaries* were full of praise for the British 1689 Bill of Rights, which probably influenced the American Founding Fathers' decision to use the same name for the Constitution's first ten amendments. The Constitution went further than the British version but did so by adopting some of Blackstone's thoughts on subjects such as freedom of the press and the freedom to petition. Although Blackstone qualified his interpretation of a free press by saying that publication of 'improper or illegal' material could adversely impact the conduct of a fair trial. America has taken a position closer to an almost absolute protection of free speech and the distinction remains to this day, with much tougher libel and contempt of court laws in the UK than in the US.

The other nine amendments include laws covering juries, the right to bear arms, grand juries, the right to silence, the right to a speedy and public trial, impartial juries, the right to legal counsel, the right to confront one's accusers, and restrictions on excessive bail. They were all discussed and set down in a comprehensive and understandable fashion by Blackstone. Some of them were his original concepts and some first appeared in Magna Carta, the Petition of Rights or the 1689 Bill of Rights.

Forty-nine of the fifty American states specifically adopted English Common Law as the basis for their state legal system. As mentioned earlier, the exception is Louisiana. US federal law is also based on English common law. This is because American jurists needed an established set of legal precedents with which to work. They had been working with English law for nearly 200 years before the US Constitution was written. It had served them reasonably well, so they kept it and gradually built upon it. In the early years of independence there was very little difference between the American and English systems. Blackstone's

Commentaries were considered the legal bible by American lawyers right through the nineteenth century. Many of the basic principles of English law can be found in the US: the adversarial system where a prosecuting and defending attorney argue their cases before a judge; jury trials; the principle that a person is deemed innocent until proven guilty and its corollary that it is the duty of the prosecution to prove the prisoner's guilty beyond a reasonable doubt.

But it was inevitable that the two systems would slowly diverge from their common base. One of the main reasons for the divergence was that Britain has an unwritten constitution based on conventions and legal precedents. More importantly, the government requires only a simple majority in the House of Commons to make the most sweeping and dramatic changes to citizens' rights under law. America's written Constitution is another matter. An amendment to the US Constitution requires the support of two-thirds of both houses of Congress and then has to be ratified by three-quarters of the state legislatures. Alternatively, two-thirds of the state legislatures can meet and propose an amendment which again has to be ratified by three-quarters of the states. The second method has never been used. But either way, changes to America's Constitution are difficult to enact, which could explain why only twenty-seven amendments (including the ten amendments in the Bill of Rights) have passed into law 230 years after the Constitution was written.

The other main difference is that Britain is a unitary legal system, with the exception of Scotland, which has retained its own legal system. Northern Ireland also has a degree of separation. The US is a federal system with states passing their own laws in addition to nationwide laws. Generally speaking, federal law overrides state law. But if there is no specific federal law then the laws passed by state legislatures apply. In the past this led to the division between slave state and free state and, after the Civil War, allowed the introduction of the Jim Crow laws, which were not repealed until 1965. In modern times, different states have different laws relating to abortion, gun control, child custody, same-sex marriages, cannabis use, business and corporate laws, tax laws, real estate, gambling and health services, to name but a few. Indiana restricts the speed of horses to 10 mph and Virginia has banned anyone over the age of twelve from trick or treating on Halloween.

Perhaps the biggest difference – other than the fact that British courts are cluttered with robes and wigs – is that the American legal system is much more politicised than the British. In the UK all of the judicial positions are appointed. In the lowest court, the magistrates are selected by a network of forty-seven local advisory committees comprised of serving magistrates and local non-magistrates. Judges for the Crown Court, County Court, High Court and Appeals Court are selected by a Judicial Appointments Commission comprised of fifteen commissioners, twelve of whom are chosen through open competition and three are selected by a Judge's Council of two senior judges. The twelve members of the UK Supreme Court are recommended to the Prime Minister by a Special Selection Committee of past and current judges. The Prime Minister always accepts their recommendation.

In contrast, the US is overtly political. For a start, almost all of the lower court – known as Superior Court – judges are elected. They require no legal training. These judges handle cases such as small claims, rent disputes, traffic violations and misdemeanours. In the larger towns and cities, the Superior Court judges are appointed by the state governor. The state governors also control appointments to all the state courts including the state Supreme Court. At a federal level, the President nominates, and the Senate confirms, the nine members of the Supreme Court, nine judges on the Court of International Trade, 179 appeals court judges and 673 District Court Judges (as of November 2019). This gives the president enormous sway over the judicial system. For instance, Donald Trump's appointment of conservatives Neil Gorsuch, Amy Comey Barrett and Brett Kavanaugh is expected to give the Supreme Court a strong conservative bent for at least a generation. In addition, President Trump nominated another 189 conservative-minded federal judges. The roots of America's politicised judicial system can be traced back to colonial days. It is a reaction to England sending judges and lawyers from England – most of them having failed in the mother country – to preside over the colonial courts. The Founding Fathers determined that the best way to avoid a repetition of this was to make the judicial system accountable to the people, either through direct elections or by appointment by elected officials.

The US courts are a key element in the country's political structure. The American system of checks and balances is well known. There are three branches of government: the executive (the president), the legislative (the Senate and the House of Representatives) and the judicial (the courts, headed by the Supreme Court). All legislation has to be introduced by Congress. The president can veto it but his veto can be overridden by a two-thirds vote of Congress. But even when a bill is passed and becomes law it is still not safe from the scrutiny of the Supreme Court, whose job it is to examine laws to determine whether or not they conflict with the written Constitution. If the court finds a conflict, the law is thrown out. Because the law is often a matter of interpretation, the political complexion of the court is often the determining factor in its decision. In Britain, the courts shy away from political involvement. They see their job as implementing and enforcing the laws passed by Parliament; although the turmoil over Brexit cast some doubt over the British courts' political independence.

There are many other differences. For instance, the Grand Jury system in the US started in Britain but died out in 1933. British lawyers never use the phrase 'I object.' They merely raise an eyebrow or deliver a hard stare. Juries are still widely used in civil cases in the US but have been rarely used in the UK for seventy years. British law is considered much more formal than its American cousin, and not just because the lawyers and judges wear robes and wigs. In the British court the law is the law as determined by Parliament. In American courts the judges have greater discretionary powers.

4

Liberty Matures

Two Democracies That Are Not Democracies

Britain is not a democracy. Neither is America. They are representative democracies supported by universal franchise. Decisions are not made by the people, but by their representatives who are elected by the people to make decisions on their behalf. This is the common political root, but the two countries diverge in the detail. Britain is what has become known as the Westminster model. The US is the presidential model. Almost every other government in the world that lays claim to a democratic legitimacy uses one or the other template.

The Westminster model is a constitutional monarchy in which Parliament is sovereign over the monarch or largely ceremonial president. The monarch is the executive head of the government but does not exercise power. Instead, the monarch's powers are vested in a prime minister who must command a majority in the House of Commons. All of the cabinet ministers are chosen by the prime minister, and the prime minister and all of the ministers must be members of Parliament. All legislation is initiated by the government except for the occasional private member's bill. Parliament can amend or vote against government-sponsored legislation. If a government consistently fails to secure the passage of important legislation then an election is generally held to resolve the impasse. There is no written constitution. Instead there is a massive body of centuries-old laws and conventions. These laws can be changed at any time by a simple majority vote of Parliament. When a government official takes their oath of office they swear allegiance to the queen. They are not giving a loyalty pledge to a person but to the physical embodiment of the unwritten constitution and centuries of accumulated laws, tradition, history and values. Since there is no written constitution, the role of the courts is generally restricted to implementing the laws passed by Parliament. But if the government breaks an existing law then it can be challenged in the courts and the government's actions overturned.

America's presidential model is much less trusting, which is unsurprising if you consider that it evolved from a distrust and then rejection of British overlords. Its structures were designed to enshrine and protect liberties as the birthright of Englishmen in America. The structure also reflected the inevitable complications of governing a large landmass divided into thirteen states (and growing), with different values, constituencies and economic models. A written constitution that established a basic federal context with certain rights reserved for the states was the obvious answer. At the time that the American colonies were rebelling and then writing their Constitution, Britain was in the midst of its long and tortuous journey from absolute to semi-constitutional to finally constitutional monarchy. The eighteenth century saw the emergence of the party system in Britain, with the Tories supporting the rights of the monarch and the Whigs working hard to curb those rights. The basics of constitutional monarchy weren't really accepted until the reign of Queen Victoria. What emerged in America was a combination of a powerful executive, legislature and judiciary underpinned by a written Constitution which states in near unequivocal terms the rights of individuals and states, and how the federal government will operate. No one branch of the federal government was to have sovereignty over the other. Each was to act as a check on the other in order to create a balance of power.

The bicameral legislature was elected by popular vote to represent the states. The number of representatives in the lower house, who were elected for two years, was determined by the population size of each state. Members of the upper house (the Senate) were elected for six years, but one third of them were replaced every two years. Each state was allocated two senators regardless of the size of its population. The president was elected for four years and could be re-elected indefinitely until 1951, when it was decided to limit the executive to two consecutive terms. The president is the commander-in-chief of the armed forces and has ultimate responsibility for seeing that the laws are obeyed and the United States and its citizens are protected. He or she can veto any legislation passed by Congress, but Congress can overturn the veto with a two-thirds majority. The judicial system is headed by the Supreme Court of nine justices nominated by the president and confirmed by the Senate.

The justices are appointed for life. Their job is to interpret any laws to make certain that they comply with the written Constitution.

Both systems have their advantages and disadvantages. The Westminster model is more fluid and enables the government to make radical political changes very quickly. All it needs is a simple majority in the House of Commons. However, such changes can be destabilising and lead to wild policy swings, as was witnessed between 1945 and 1979 when the country shifted between nationalised and privatised industries dependent on who was in power. America's presidential system operates at a more ponderous pace. Every change is measured against the written Constitution. To amend the Constitution requires the support of two-thirds of the Senate and House of Representatives, the president and support of two-thirds of the state legislatures.

The Link Continues

Despite their differences, the British and American models have one underlying characteristic in common: they are both subject to the constant shifts in public attitudes, technology, the economy and a host of other factors. The interplay of ideas between Britain and America continued to play an important role in these changes after American independence. The two countries may not have been united politically, but British actions continued to have a major impact on how Americans thought and acted and these in turn affected the conduct of the government in Washington. If anything, British influence increased. Britain was at the height of its economic and political power in the late eighteenth and nineteenth century. Its universities were heads and shoulders above any other seat of learning in the world. They attracted students and lecturers from around the world and produced some of the most influential thinkers in history. One of these was Jeremy Bentham, who started pontificating during the American Revolution. One of his first works was a 130-page tract mocking the Declaration of Independence. Despite this inauspicious start, Bentham helped to set the stage for Britain's acceptance of facets of liberalism. Among the causes he advocated were separation of Church and State, abolition of slavery and capital punishment, equal rights for women and animal rights. All of his philosophies were wrapped up in a general guiding principle he called 'utilitarianism', which decreed that 'it is the greatest happiness of the greatest number that is the measure of right and wrong'. Acceptance on both sides of the Atlantic of what was then a still radical idea strengthened support for universal suffrage, majority rule and basic democratic principles.

Perhaps Bentham's greatest contribution was the fact that he tutored John Stuart Mill, Britain's most influential liberal nineteenth-century philosopher. Mill was a child prodigy. His Scottish historian father was determined that his son would be a great philosopher. He had him studying Greek at three and reading Latin at eight. The regime worked. Mill became a philosophical force of nature. But he suffered a miserable childhood which led to an unhappy adult life. Mill should have attended Oxford or Cambridge, but his family were Unitarians and the ancient cloisters were at that time open only to members of the Church of England. So he instead attended the newly founded University College London, before heading off for a long spell in South Asia with the East India Company. Mill's first major work, *Two Letters on the Measure of Value*, was published when he was only sixteen. In all, Mill wrote forty-five books and scholarly articles over a fifty-year career. In 1856 he was elected a Foreign Honorary member of the prestigious American Academy of Arts and Sciences, whose founder members included John Adams, John Hancock and Thomas Jefferson.

Mill's greatest philosophical legacy was to expand upon and popularise Bentham's theory of utilitarianism. Bentham treated all forms of pleasure as equal; Mill classified them. For instance, there were the higher pleasures which focused on chaste intellectual and moral aspects of life, and then there were lower pleasures associated with physical joy. Bentham and Mill agreed that there were different paths to pleasure and happiness. Mill, however, added the proviso that when faced with two or more paths, the path chosen should be the one that offers the greatest happiness to the greatest number of people.

Mill was opposed to slavery and campaigned for its abolition in the United States. He supported a free market economy and was an early environmentalist. He advocated population control, improved economic productivity, universal suffrage and participatory democracy. During his short term as a member of Parliament (1865–68) he became the first MP to call for votes for women. Mill was a passionate advocate of free speech, which he outlined in *On Liberty*. The book was published in 1859 at a time when the British press was starting to win its fight against the Establishment to become a popular and political force. Mill supported the infant media by arguing that 'free discourse' was essential for intellectual and social progress as well as a political right. To Mill, all opinions were valid as long as they were openly and fairly debated so that the truth emerged victorious. In *On Liberty*, Mill called for limits on the ruler's powers through political liberties, legal protections and constitutional checks. Individuals should be free to make their own decisions, and government, said Mill, should only interfere when the individual threatens harm to the interests of the wider society. At the same time, Mill warned against a weakness in the democratic system which he termed the 'tyranny of the majority'. He argued that the majority of the electorate blindly pursues its exclusive interests at the expense of the legitimate interests of the minority. (This echoes the declaration attributed to Hamilton, almost certainly wrongly, 'Your people is a great beast.') Mill's writings became the standard work for political philosophy in universities on both sides of the Atlantic up to the 1920s and beyond, and laid the foundations of what became known as 'classic liberalism' in Britain and America.

Charles Darwin was more of a natural scientist than a philosopher, but his theories of evolution and natural selection spawned social, economic and political beliefs which had a huge impact on the direction of American society, religion and politics. When Darwin went up to Cambridge in 1828, he, in common with most of British society, accepted the literal word of the Bible as the explanation for the existence of the universe. Then in 1831 he set off on a five-year scientific journey around the world on HMS *Beagle* that set him on the path towards the eventual publication of his world-shattering book *On the Origin of Species*. Darwin was closely related to the prominent Wedgwood family and his father was a wealthy society doctor who planned for his son to follow in his footsteps. From an early age, however, Charles was more inclined to study animal rather than human biology.

Darwin was the scientific officer for HMS *Beagle* and as such spent three years and three months ashore studying geology and the plant and animal life of the many countries that the ship visited. The *Beagle* itself concentrated on mapping coastlines for the British Admiralty. The ship's most famous stopover was at the eight main islands and three smaller islands of the Galapagos. Darwin spent five weeks on the volcanic Galapagos and while there he was struck by the minor differences between the various species which enabled them to adapt to different conditions. He was particularly fascinated by the different shapes of the beaks of the finches from island to island. He began to hypothesise that the reason for the differences was that each species had evolved over time through a process of natural selection. Darwin's Galapagos observations were not so much a Eureka moment as the planting of a slowly germinating seed.

During his voyage the naturalist regularly sent journals and specimens back to Britain. By the time the ship docked at Falmouth, Charles Darwin was already famous in scientific circles. This enabled him to devote his energies full-time to the study of natural science and to water the seed that had been planted in the Galapagos. His book *The Voyage of the HMS Beagle* was published in 1839 and his fame was extended to the general public. At the age of thirty, he was regarded as one of Britain's foremost natural scientists and was well on his way to becoming world famous.

It was not until twenty years later, in 1859, that Charles Darwin's work that changed the world was published. *On the Origin of Species* was an overnight sensation. It set out the theory of evolution, natural selection and survival of the fittest. Various scientists had been skirting around the issue for some years, but Darwin's book pulled all the threads together. There was immediate opposition from the Establishment. Natural selection attacked the social order in which everyone had a pre-ordained place in society based on where they were born on the social ladder. Among British clerics, the reaction was mixed. Some welcomed it as another example of God's genius in being able to design such a beautifully complex system. Others attacked it for undermining the literal interpretation of the Bible, which decreed that Adam and Eve were the first humans. Adam was created by God from modelling clay and Eve from Adam's spare rib. By 1870 Darwin's theory of evolution had been accepted as the norm in Britain. It took a bit longer in the US, and in parts of the American Bible Belt the name Darwin still evokes ire.

Charles Darwin regarded himself as a natural scientist rather than a philosopher. But his scientific research spawned philosophies. Social Darwinism and eugenics he denounced as a bastardisation of his theories. In the US, social Darwinism was most closely associated with Yale University's William Graham Sumner, America's first professor of sociology. American social Darwinists believed that the American businessmen were the best equipped to win the struggle for existence. Humans, they argued, required the competition of natural selection to survive and prosper. Furthermore, the poor had revealed themselves as unfit for natural selection; therefore, they should be denied aid.

Eugenics was the brainchild of Darwin's half-cousin Francis Galton, who waited until a year after his famous relative's death before coining the phrase. Charles was a staunch abolitionist and anti-racist. He was originally attracted to his cousin's ideas, but when he realised how they would be applied in the social sphere he quickly turned against them. Eugenics lent support to popular racist theories by arguing that the superiority of certain races – in particular the White Anglo-Saxons – was based on breeding through natural selection. This was music to the ears of American segregationists who combined their Bible studies with eugenics to devise a religious-cum-scientific justification for the Jim Crow laws. Eugenics also argued that certain diseases and disabilities were the result of bad breeding and the best way to improve society was by preventing – or at least discouraging – inferior members of a race from having children. The United States became the first country to forcibly sterilise the insane and mentally handicapped. Between 1907 and 2010, an estimated 60,000 Americans were forcibly sterilised.

Social Darwinism and eugenics reached their evil zenith in Nazi Germany. Adolf Hitler's justification for the invasion and occupation of most of Europe was based on his belief in a science that determined that the German Aryan race was superior to all others and therefore not only destined but scientifically ordained through the process of natural selection and survival of the fittest to rule the world. This eugenic view was enshrined in law by the 1935 Nuremberg Laws, which decreed that only those of German blood were entitled to German citizenship. Germans were prohibited from intermarrying or having sexual intercourse with anyone deemed non-German. Singled out as non-Germans were the Jews, Blacks and gypsies. Other peoples, such as the Poles and Russians, were later categorised as inferior because of their Slavic ancestry. The result we know. It is known that Hitler also planned to exterminate the roughly 5,000 black and mixed-race Germans, but the war ended before he could put his plan into action. Black people, however, were prevented from intermarrying; many of them were forcibly sterilised and they were banned from higher education and government jobs. Hitler's eugenics-based policies also extended to the disabled and mentally insane. Between 1937 and 1945, 350,000 such people were killed. Hitler's actions sounded the death knell for the science of eugenics. Social Darwinism also suffered a setback, but much of its basic philosophy can still be found in conservative circles on both sides of the Atlantic.

While Darwin was cultivating scientific circles and developing his revolutionary ideas about evolution, Karl Marx was beavering away in the British Library evolving his ideas about revolution. The inclusion of Marx in a chapter on British philosophers who had an impact on America is slightly strained. He was born and educated in Germany, but the Germans deprived him of his citizenship in 1848. In Britain he researched his ground-breaking books. He used the British class system as the template for his proposed revolutionary struggle. He employed London as a base to spread his ideas to America and Continental Europe and was financed by a British textile company. He is buried in Highgate Cemetery in North London. Karl Marx may not have been born British, but he was heavily influenced by his experiences in Britain. He used those experiences to establish the philosophical foundations for the labour movement, for communist governments around the world as well as to some extent creating the political conditions for the Second World War and the Cold War that dominated American foreign policy for nearly half a century.

Karl Marx had a junior partner, Friedrich Engels, without whom he would clearly not have had the impact he had. Engels was also German. His father was a wealthy textile manufacturer with factories in Germany and England. It was money from Engels' factory in Manchester that financed Marx's work both as a writer and revolutionary. The two men met in Cologne. On his way to take over the family business in Manchester, Engels visited the newspaper *Rheinische Post* where Marx was working as a journalist. From England he wrote a number of articles about the working and living conditions in Manchester, which he sent to Marx for publication in the Cologne-based newspaper. This was the start of a close friendship and collaboration which lasted until Marx's death in 1883. In 1845 Engels and Marx moved to Brussels where they joined the Communist Revolutionary League. They were soon well-entrenched and were asked to jointly write a pamphlet outlining the League's principles. This became the Communist Manifesto. It ended with the famous line: 'Let the ruling classes tremble at a communistic revolution. The proletariat have nothing to lose but their chains... Working men of all countries unite!'

The Communist Manifesto was published in 1848, the same year that rebellion spread across Europe. The purpose of most of the revolutionaries was to sweep away the old monarchical systems and replace them with democratic, liberal nation-states. In some countries they succeeded to varying degrees. But in Germany the aristocratic establishment was too entrenched. Thousands were killed, imprisoned or forced into exile. Engels and Marx were stripped of their citizenship.

Britain in 1848 was seen as an oasis of liberal democracy. It still had a monarch, but the supreme power was vested in an elected Parliament and there was freedom of the press, speech, assembly and religion. Britain became a refuge for the far-left political revolutionaries booted out of their home countries. Marx and Engels, along with the headquarters of the Communist League, moved across the English Channel in 1849. Almost immediately, a split developed in the Communist League and Marx started work on his magnum opus: the incredibly dense three-volume *Das Kapital* – the intellectual cornerstone of succeeding generations of Marxists.

At the core of Marx's thesis was the idea the 'history of all hitherto existing society is the history of class struggle'. This struggle was pushing mankind through progressive stages: primitive communal living, slavery, feudalism, capitalism and finally communism and the 'dictatorship of the proletariat', which Marx regarded as inevitable and highly desirable. Communism required the overthrow of capitalism, which Marx justified on the grounds that labour, not property, is the actual basis of wealth. The capitalist system, however, is based on the ownership of property and the exploitation of labour to develop property and produce profits for the property owners. Furthermore, the property was acquired by plunder over the centuries and the rights of the property owners were protected by the ruling regimes, which are controlled by the property owners (capitalists). The solution was to overthrow the supporting political structures and replace them with a political and economic system controlled by the workers (the proletariat). Marx only lived to see the first volume of his work published in 1867; his friend Engels published the remaining volumes after his death.

Marxism found fertile ground among the workers in the autocratic regimes of Europe, especially Germany, the Netherlands, the Austro-Hungarian Empire and Russia. The First World War's virtual destruction of the social, political and economic structures of the feuding European powers made revolution more likely. This was especially the case in Russia where Tsar Nicholas II's secret police had for decades struggled to hold down the lid on the pressure cooker of Russian revolutionary politics. The deaths of 1.8 million soldiers and 1.5 million civilians (the latter through disease and starvation) tipped the balance against the old regime. On 16 April 1917, the Germans smuggled back into Russia the country's leading revolutionary, Marxist acolyte Vladimir Ilich Ulyanov, better known to history by his nom de guerre, Lenin. The Germans' aim was to foment a revolution that would take Russia out of the war and allow Germany to concentrate its forces on the Western Front. It succeeded. Lenin overthrew the Tsar and in March 1918 signed the Treaty of Brest-Litovsk, taking Russia out of the war. The Russian exit from the fighting was too late to save Germany from defeat, but just in time to establish a new political order bent on the overthrow of capitalism and world domination.

Politics Reformed

The Age of Enlightenment ended with the American Revolution and the head-rolling revolution in France. It had reached its apex with those two events and the world stepped back to assess the consequences, good and bad. What followed were what might be termed the Age of Parliamentary Supremacy and the Age of Liberalism, which overlapped with each other and the end of the Age of Enlightenment. The philosophical foundations for the Age of Liberalism were laid by Edmund Burke, Jeremy Bentham and John Stuart Mill and continued until at least the mid-1930s. It can be argued that we are at the tail end of the Age of Liberalism. The Age of Parliamentary Supremacy refers to a period when Parliament governed with the minimum reference to the electorate that it claimed to represent. It started with the 1689 British Bill of Rights, moved on to the US Constitution and the formation of political parties on both sides of the Atlantic, started to unravel with the 1832 Great Reform Act, and came to a stuttering halt in the UK when British women achieved full voting rights in 1928 and in America with the 1964 Civil Rights Act.

One of the truisms of politics is that factions unite against a common foe, 'the enemy of my enemy is my friend' of realpolitik. At the same time, the foe will exploit differences to divide and rule. When the foe is eliminated, the divisions reappear. There were plenty of disputes between the different colonies. They clashed on innumerable occasions over boundaries and jurisdiction. Anglicans and Puritans actually fought a pitched battle outside Annapolis as the American contribution to the English Civil Wars. Quakers clashed with Puritans. Catholics clashed with Puritans in the north and Anglicans in the south, and Puritans repeatedly argued with the Anglican heathens of Virginia. But a shared experience and Britain's blanket imposition of what the Americans regarded as unfair taxes brought most of the colonies under one banner, except for about 20 per cent who remained steadfastly loyal to Britain and paid a high price for doing so. After the revolution, the disagreements between the former colonies led to the creation of a confederation of states rather than a united federal state. When it became clear this would not work, a constitution was devised that reserved significant powers for the individual states under a federal banner. But within this federal structure parties quickly developed: the Republicans, led by Thomas Jefferson, who wanted a loose federal structure; and the Federalists, led by Alexander Hamilton and John Adams, who wanted a stronger one.

The Republicans evolved into the Democrats while the Federalists became first the Whigs and then, confusingly, the Republicans. The states' rights issue quickly came to centre on the slavery controversy, which, of course, resulted in the American Civil War. In the Reconstruction period, the northern Republicans briefly dominated the defeated Democrats of the South and forced through pro-African American legislation, which was deeply resented by Southern Democrats. When Reconstruction ended in 1877 the Democrats returned to power in the former Confederate states and introduced a variety of apartheid known as the Jim Crow laws. These remained in effect until the civil rights movement of the 1960s led by liberal Democrats. Many white southerners who sympathised at least in part with a version of white supremacy switched to the Republican Party, which also moved further to the right in other parts of the country, while the Democrats moved increasingly towards the left of the political spectrum.

In Britain, political parties emerged in the wake of the 1689 Bill of Rights. Before that the political debate was dominated by a long-standing clash between Parliament and Crown. But even after the Bill of Rights there was a significant faction in Parliament who wanted to return the country to the more autocratic monarchical rule. These were known as the Tories. The word Tory derived from the Irish Gaelic word *Toraidhe*, for a guerrilla group which sided with Royalist supporters in opposition to Cromwell. The anti-Catholic and anti-monarchical used the term Tories for the first time as a form of abuse when referring to the supporters of the Catholic James II. The Whigs were anti-Catholic, anti-James and pro-increased parliamentary powers. The term Whig came from a radical Scottish Protestant group called the Whiggamores. The political fortunes of the Whigs and Tories see-sawed back and forth up until 1715, when the deposed James II attempted what became known as the first Jacobite rebellion to regain the thrones of England, Scotland and Ireland. There was a second attempt in 1745 by James II's son, Prince Charles. The Tories were perceived to be full-throated backers of James and Charles and the invading army of Jacobites, who were stripped of all public offices, purged from the judiciary, military, appointed national offices and local government. However, they could still be elected to Parliament and because their peerages were hereditary, they remained in the House of Lords. The period from 1715 to 1760 when George III ascended the throne is known as the Whig Oligarchy. It was during those forty-five years that the first person to be called prime minister, Sir Robert Walpole, emerged. He is also Britain's longest-serving prime minister as he stayed in office from 1716 to 1742. The Tories throughout their roughly 340 years of existence have dominated the right wing of British politics ever since. They officially changed their name to the Conservatives in 1834. In 1912 the party merged with Northern Ireland's pro-Protestant, anti-United Ireland Liberal United Party which eventually led to the division of Ireland into an independent Eire in the south and a Protestant-dominated Northern Ireland in the six counties of the north. The merged party became the Conservative and Unionist Party, which remains the official name.

By the middle of the nineteenth century the reform of the electoral system, abolition of slavery and Catholic Emancipation, along with a slew of procedural changes in Parliament, meant that the old conflict between the Crown and Parliament had disappeared and there was no chance of the country slipping back towards autocratic rule. The Whigs gradually slipped from being a religiously-based anti-Catholic party to a liberal party. In fact, the Whigs took the lead in fighting for Catholic Emancipation, which reopened British public offices to Roman Catholics, as well as the abolition of slavery in the British Empire, the end of the slave trade and the first step towards widening the franchise with the Electoral Reform Act of 1832. The public started referring to the Whigs as liberal with a small 'l' and so the party made it official by changing the name in 1868. Throughout the nineteenth century the Tories were in power for fifty-seven years and the Whigs, or Liberals, for forty-three.

Successive widening of the franchise meant that by 1868 the British working class were for the first time allowed the vote. The 1884 Parliamentary Reform Act extended the franchise again so that two in three British males were now allowed inside polling booths. At the end of the First World War it became apparent to the political establishment that they could no longer deny the vote to men and expect them to die like trench fleas. The vote was thus given to all men. Many of the new voters between 1868 and 1918 were working class and affiliated to the growing trade union movement, which formed its own political wing – the Labour Party. Gradually they assumed the mantle of the left from the Liberals, whose last prime minister was the wartime leader David Lloyd George who occupied Downing Street from 1916 to 1922. From then on British politics have been dominated by a two-party conflict between Conservatives and Labour. The Liberals continued as a reduced centrist third party. A small Green Party sprang up to deal with the rising problem of climate change. Nigel Farage created first the United Kingdom Independence Party and then the Brexit Party, which failed to win a seat in the House of Commons but pushed the Conservatives into a more Euro-sceptic position, which eventually resulted in the anti-EU referendum and Britain's withdrawal from the European Union. Northern Ireland has had a separate assembly since 1922, the year before the creation of the Irish Free State on the southern two-thirds of the island. The Protestant-dominated Northern Ireland Parliament was dissolved with the start of The Troubles in 1972 and then reconstituted as the Stormont Assembly in 1998 as part of a Catholic–Protestant power-sharing arrangement in the Good Friday Agreement. The year before, certain powers were devolved by the Westminster Parliament to a Welsh Assembly and a Scottish Parliament in Scotland. The devolution was the result of decades of campaigning by Plaid Cymru, formed in 1925, and the Scottish National Party, which was formed in 1934. Both parties want independence. In 2014 there was an independence referendum in Scotland, the vote in favour of remaining part of the United Kingdom. The vote was billed as a once-in-a-generation event, but has been revived by the 2016 UK-wide referendum that led to Britain leaving the EU. The Scots were told before the 2014 referendum that if they left the UK they would also have to leave the European Union. In the Brexit referendum they voted overwhelmingly to remain in Europe.

Who Votes and How

England's infamous rotten boroughs started as political laziness and ended up as a pillar of corruption supporting vested interests that saw no benefit to themselves in democratising the system. When elections to what became the House of Commons were first held in the thirteenth century, England was an agricultural economy with its population legally tied to specific plots of land through an iron-clad feudal structure. The constituencies (then called boroughs) chosen for the first Parliaments reflected that demographic. And because that had been the socio-economic reality for centuries, they did not foresee the need for such modern political tools as electoral boundary commissions to take into account shifting population patterns. Up until the start of the Industrial Revolution (which coincided with American independence), the 500-year-old constituency boundaries were a relatively accurate reflection of the distribution of the population. But between 1760 and 1800 there was a dramatic shift as the workforce moved en masse from the countryside to work in the factories of cities that had been little more than towns or villages at the start of the eighteenth century. Manchester, for instance, had a population of 10,000 in 1717, 25,000 in 1772 and 95,000 in 1800. Its population had no representation in Parliament. At the other extreme was the constituency of Sarum. At the beginning of the thirteenth century it had been a thriving cathedral city built on the foundations of a 3,000-year-old Neolithic hill fort and boasted a royal palace. Around 1226, the inhabitants shifted to the new city of Salisbury where water was more easily accessible. Within a few decades Sarum was an abandoned ruin. But it continued to send two members to the House of Commons. By the eighteenth century there were only eleven people entitled to vote for Sarum's two MPs, and most of them were connected to the politically powerful Pitt family. William Pitt the Elder and his son William Pitt the Younger became two of the most famous prime ministers in British history. The former was a leading advocate of better treatment of the American colonies and the latter led Britain through most of the Napoleonic Wars.

By the early nineteenth century, 152 of the Commons' 406 elected members were chosen by fewer than 100 voters each and 88 by fewer than 50 each. To compound the problem, there was no such thing as a secret ballot and the right to vote was tied to property qualifications. It is believed that the first Parliament was open to all owners of a freehold property. But in 1432 King Henry III decided that gave too much power to the masses and decreed that voters had to own property worth at least 40 shillings. To further complicate matters, the monarch had the power to enfranchise and disenfranchise constituencies at will. The Tudors used this power as a means of either making money or increasing their power in Parliament and created an additional seventy new constituencies. The new seats were either used to put their puppets in parliamentary seats or were sold to wealthy aristocrats who would then select their own MPs. The Duke of Norfolk, for instance, controlled eleven boroughs, which were called 'pocket boroughs' because the holders of the seats were in the pocket of a wealthy patron. By the end of the eighteenth century the inequities of the system had led to a growing movement for electoral reform. One of the leading reforming pressure groups was the London Corresponding Society, formed in 1792 to fight for universal suffrage. The activities of the LCS put it on a collision course with one of the main beneficiaries of the Rotten Borough system, William Pitt the Younger, who attempted to try the organisers for treason. The trial collapsed, but Pitt managed to curb their activities with a 1799 Act 'for the more effectual suppression of societies established for seditions and treasonable purposes'.

But the battle for electoral reform continued, partly inspired by the success of the newly created United States and the revolution in France. In August 1819 a crowd of 90,000 gathered in Manchester to demand 'Equal Representation or Death'. Unfortunately, their second demand was met. The demonstrators were charged by mounted British troops. Eleven people were killed and hundreds were injured. The Peterloo Massacre became a turning point in the battle for electoral reform and even the right-wing Tory the Duke of Wellington swung behind the movement in order to stem a rising tide of civil strife. The result was the Great Reform Act of 1832, which effectively ended the Rotten Boroughs.

Before 1832 there were 203 borough constituencies. In all, 56 were abolished outright. Another 30 had been represented by two members. These were reduced to one each. Then 180 new seats were created to provide representation for the mushrooming industrial centres.

The Great Reform Act eliminated the rotten borough system but it did little to extend the franchise. The right to vote was still tied to property ownership the threshold raised from 40 shillings to 10 pounds. Voters also had to be male and the head of their household. The increase in those voting was only 250,000. Some 80 per cent of the male population was still denied the right to cast a ballot. But the Act whetted the public's appetite for more, especially among the new urban-centred working class. This gave rise to what was known as the Chartist Movement, named after the six-point People's Charter for further voting reform. The Chartists demanded the vote for every male aged twenty-one or older, secret ballots, no property qualifications for MP, salaries for MPs, constituencies based on the size of the electorate, and annual elections. In 1848, the rise of the Chartists coincided with a spirit of revolution that was toppling the old order across Europe. The British establishment was terrified that it would suffer the same fate. The Chartists called for a rally at Kennington Common on 10 April. They would meet and then march from south London to Parliament to present their charter for electoral reform. The royal family was spirited out of London to the Isle of Wight. Armed guards were posted around the Bank of England, on the roof of the British Museum and at key points around London. No fewer than 90,000 police – most of them temporary volunteers – surrounded Kennington Common. In the end only 30,000 Chartists turned up at Kennington. Overwhelmed by the police presence, there was no march on Parliament and the movement fizzled out. The Chartist leaders were imprisoned and/or transported to Australia. But the pragmatists in Parliament had been won over. Over the next few decades all but one of the Chartists' demands – annual elections – passed into law. In 1867 the franchise was extended again to include another million men and new boundary rules were introduced in the cities. In 1872 the secret ballot became law. In 1884 rules related to boundary changes were extended to rural communities and more men were enfranchised, although 40 per cent of the male population, and all women, were still denied the vote. It was not until 1918 that Britain had full universal suffrage without any property qualifications. The last change was in 1969, when the voting age was lowered to eighteen.

Voting, of course, extended only to the lower house, the House of Commons. The House of Lords was populated by clergy appointed first by the Vatican and, after the Reformation, the king and aristocrats who owed their political power to the accident of birth or royal appointment. Throughout most of its history, the House of Lords has been the more powerful half of Britain's bicameral Parliament. The Lords grew out a combination of the Anglo-Saxon Witan and the Norman Great Council (Magnum Concilium). They were the aristocrats, bishops, abbots and priors who advised the king. The clergy actually outnumbered the aristocrats in what became the House of Lords up until the dissolution of the monasteries by Henry VIII. Today there are twenty-six reserved seats for the Lords Temporal in the upper house, all of them Church of England bishops. Other religions are represented by life peerages. The House of Lords was the more powerful of the two houses partly because it was able to meet without the rigmarole of elections and partly because its members controlled a large proportion of the commons through the rotten/pocket borough system, but mainly because the Lords had to approve any legislation that was initiated in the Commons and had the power of veto over it. The 1832 Great Reform Act started the process of change. On paper, the Lords retained its power, but its members lost their pocket boroughs and a fairer electoral system increased the political credibility of the Commons vis a vis the hereditary peers. The turning point came in 1909–1911 during the government of H. H. Asquith. The clash between the two houses had been brewing for a few years. Asquith's predecessor, Henry Campbell-Bannerman, had on three occasions tried to pass a law prohibiting the Lords from vetoing finance bills. It was blocked by the upper house each time. In 1909, Asquith's government proposed a 'People's Budget' that included widespread social reforms presaging many of the provisions of the welfare state. The Conservative-dominated hereditary Lords rejected it. After an election which only just put Asquith back in Downing Street, the budget was again passed by the Commons and rejected by the upper house. Asquith now proposed the Parliament Act of 1910, which eliminated the House of Lords' veto over finance bills and reduced its power to delay other legislation to two years. The Lords rejected this as well. This meant yet another election and Asquith's third tenure in Downing Street. This time he persuaded George V to threaten to create up to 400 new Liberal peers who would be guaranteed to support Asquith's proposals. It worked. The Lords narrowly passed the government legislation by 131 to 114 votes. The upper house thus started its long downward spiral. In 1949 the delaying power of the peers was reduced to one year. In 1958 the position of life peers was created. Since then only one hereditary peerage has been created, that of former Prime Minister

Harold Macmillan as Earl of Stockton. Winston Churchill was offered a dukedom in 1955 but refused it. In 1963, the first women were created life peers. In 1999 a major reform of the House of Lords reduced the number of hereditary peers to just ninety-two. In 2005, the House of Lords' role as the supreme court in the land was replaced by a new body called the UK Supreme Court. Since the 1990s there have been calls for major reform of the upper house ranging from complete abolition to the creation of a largely or wholly elected chamber. The Commons now has the power to decide, but is divided on the course to take. An elected chamber is seen as a threat to the power of the Commons, but an abolished Lords would leave the lower house dangerously unchecked.

The US Congress mirrored British Parliament in that it was a bicameral legislature. Its upper house (the Senate) did not go to the British extreme of creating hereditary positions, but the six-year term was designed to free senators from the shackles of populism and increase their power over the lower house. In fact, senators were indirectly elected by state legislatures up until 1914. The comparisons between the two bodies were much closer in 1788, when the first American elections were held, than they were only a few decades later. The monarchy still retained considerable power and George III was near the start of Britain's long march to a constitutional monarchy. This was reflected in the authority given to the president, especially the role of commander-in-chief, a position still nominally held by the British monarch.

The Electoral College is a unique American electoral institution, but it has its philosophical roots in Britain. James Madison, the vertically challenged legal eagle and fourth US president, was the principal author of the US Constitution and Bill of Rights. He was a leading member of the Virginia aristocracy and a close friend and neighbour of kindred spirit Thomas Jefferson, principal author of the Declaration of Independence. The two men were probably the most cerebral of the Founding Fathers and immersed themselves in the literature and theory of the Age of Enlightenment. Madison read Hobbes and Locke at Princeton University and avidly followed British parliamentary debates and judicial rulings. Madison and Jefferson were also co-founders of the Democratic Republican Party, which later became the Democratic Party. As a product of the Enlightenment, Madison was committed to Republican principles. But he was also a leading member of the Virginia elite with a 2,000-acre plantation at Montpelier. The result was a firm belief in the value of representative democracy tempered and led by the strong hand of a political elite. 'Excessive democracy,' wrote Madison, led to social decay. A further influence on Madison was the disparate nature of the thirteen American colonies; each with their own histories, religious backgrounds, economic structures, geography and social conditions. Madison hoped that the competing interests between the states would be another check on the abuses of majority rule. James Madison's Electoral College was a reflection of this complex mix.

Under his plan, the president is not directly elected by a majority of the voters but indirectly by electors appointed by the state legislatures. The number of electors for each state is equal to the number of congressmen plus the two senators that the state sends to Washington. For instance, Montana, with a population of 1 million, has one congressman, two senators and a total of three electoral votes. At the other extreme, California has a population of 39.5 million, fifty-three congressmen, two senators and fifty-five Electoral College votes. Madison's Constitution left it to each of the individual states to decide how their electors would be chosen. At the start, more than half of the state legislatures directly chose their representatives to the Electoral College. Those states that did allow their citizens to vote did not have universal male suffrage. As in Britain, the vote was tied to property ownership and you had to be male and over twenty-one. Slaves and women were banned (more below) from the polling booths. An interesting exception was New Jersey, where both women and African Americans over twenty-one were allowed to vote up until 1817. Also, at the start of the system, the Electoral College voted only for the president. The runner-up became vice-president. It quickly became apparent that this arrangement was unworkable when Thomas Jefferson as vice president repeatedly clashed with John Adams as president. The effect of the clash was the twelfth amendment of 1804, which instructed the Electoral College to elect the president and vice president separately.

Under the terms of the Constitution, the members of the Electoral College are not required to vote according to the vote in their state. The Founding Fathers expected them to use their judgement as a further check on popular tyranny. Alexander Hamilton described the electors as 'a small number of persons, selected by their fellow citizens from the general mass, who will be most likely to possess the information and discernment requisite to such complicated tasks'. Until 1880, in most states, the names of the presidential and vice-presidential candidates did not appear on the ballot papers. Instead the voters were asked to choose electors who were pledged to support a specific candidate. And even then, they were not legally bound to vote according to their pledge. In practice, they almost always did. In the history of presidential elections, there have only been a handful of occasions when an elector refused to vote as instructed, and none of these had an effect on the final outcome. Such college members are called 'faithless electors'. There were ten 'faithless electors' in the 2016 presidential elections – the second-highest in the history of the Electoral College. Currently, in all but two states, the Electoral College works on a winner-takes-all basis. This means that if a candidate wins a plurality of the votes in California then that candidate is assigned fifty-five Electoral College votes. This has been the accepted practice since 1836. The only exceptions are Maine and Nebraska, which use something called the district plan whereby two at-large electors are assigned to support the winner of the state-wide popular vote. The members of the Electoral College from each state meet in their states on 6 December after the general election on the first Tuesday in November. Their votes are sent to Congress where they are counted and certified by a joint session of Congress on 6 January. The candidate is not officially confirmed as president until the certification process is completed. It is possible for a candidate to lose the popular vote, win the Electoral College vote and become president. In 2016 Donald Trump won 304 Electoral College votes but only 62,984,828 popular votes. Loser Hillary Clinton won only 227 electoral college votes but 65,853,514 popular votes.

Africa in America

In eighteenth- and nineteenth-century Britain, the political establishment was terrified of the working classes securing the vote. They were ill educated, poor, resentful, and so numerous that their numbers could easily overwhelm the propertied classes. In America the same fear was based on race: African American slaves (and later freed African Americans) and Native Americans. The question of extending the vote to Native Americans was not even considered. They were effectively regarded as a separate nation of savages who were inconveniently sharing a continent with civilised European settlers. But the African Americans were in a different category altogether, whether they were free or slave. Many of them were inspired by the Declaration of the Independence's stirring assertion that 'all men are created equal', and in the first years after independence things started looking up for freed Blacks who rose from one per cent of the total African American population to 13 per cent by 1800. In several states, including the southern state of North Carolina, they were allowed to vote. North Carolina rescinded that right after the 1831 Nat Turner slave revolt. But most of the northern states acted even quicker. New Jersey denied them the vote in 1807. Connecticut followed suit in 1818. Ohio was an early vote rescinder, 1802. Pennsylvania waited until 1838 but also banned them appearing as witnesses in trials and from skilled jobs. In 1821 New York removed the property qualification requirement for all white men but kept them for Blacks, which meant that only a handful of African Americans were allowed to vote. Only four northern states – New Hampshire, Maine, Massachusetts and Vermont – allowed African Americans to vote. But even that ended with the Supreme Court's 1857 Dred Scott decision that ruled that Blacks were not citizens of the United States and therefore were denied the protection and rights of American citizenship – including the right to vote.

However, the denial of the Black vote and their slave status in the South created problems for the framers of the Constitution vis a vis elections because of the large African American populations. In fact, in three southern states they were a majority of the population and constituted roughly 40 per cent of the population in four other states. The number of Congressmen sent to Washington was determined by the size of the population and the number of Electoral College votes a state had was equal to the total number of its congressmen plus two senators. Therefore, if the slave population was excluded from the population calculations for federal elections the southern states would be – southern politicians argued – under-represented in the federal government. The northern states, however, maintained that including the slave population would lead to over-representation based on large numbers of slaves who were banned from voting. The compromise solution was article one, section three, clause three of the Constitution, which counted each slave as three-fifths of a person for election purposes. But they couldn't vote. The three-fifths rule is believed to have helped Thomas Jefferson defeat John Adams in 1800 and aided Andrew Jackson in the 1826 presidential election in which he defeated Adams's son, John Quincy Adams.

The Civil War, the Emancipation Declaration and the Reconstruction period that followed completely changed the political landscape for African Americans – for twelve years. After the war three constitutional amendments extended full citizenship rights, including the right to vote, to the freed Black slaves. At the same time the vote was taken away from hundreds of thousands of whites because they had fought for the Confederacy. To enforce these changes the South was occupied by Northern troops. The consequence was the election of 1,500 African Americans to public office, including two senators and fifteen congressmen. This was too much for the white population of the South, and the newly created Ku Klux Klan and other white supremacist groups responded with violence against the Black population. Reconstruction ended in 1877 after Rutherford B. Hayes won the presidency in one of the most contentious elections in American history. He immediately withdrew the troops from the occupied South and declared that it was up to each individual state to determine its own election laws. The result – the infamous Jim Crow laws.

The Jim Crow laws were widespread segregation commandments which affected every aspect of life in the former Confederate states. Schools, hotels, restaurants, rest rooms, shops, jobs, housing and public transport facilities were organised along racial lines with the African American population consistently forced to accept decidedly inferior products and services. There were legal attempts to challenge Jim Crow but in 1896 the Supreme Court upheld segregation in *Plessy* v. *Ferguson*, which spelled out the 'separate but equal' doctrine – a phrase adopted by South Africa's apartheid regime a half a century later. The segregation would have been prevented if African Americans had retained the vote, but in 1877 their disenfranchisement started with the introduction of a poll tax in Georgia. In 1890 Mississippi added a literacy test, which was subjectively administered by white election officials. There was an initial snag with the literacy test as a large proportion of the working-class white population was illiterate. To counter this, Southern state legislatures enacted what was called the 'grandfather clause', which said that anyone who had a father or grandfather who had voted before 1 January 1867 was entitled to vote. The freed slaves did not have the vote until 1867. The poll tax, literacy test and grandfather clause were upheld by the 1898 Supreme Court ruling *Williams* v. *Mississippi*. This opened the disenfranchisement floodgates and within ten years every Southern state had adopted the 'Mississippi Plan' with dramatic consequences for the black population. In North Carolina, for instance, between 1898 and 1904 there was not a single African American on the voter rolls. In Louisiana the number of Black voters was reduced from 5,320 in 1900 to 730 ten years later, even though the population was 60 per cent African American. White supremacy was further bolstered by the fact that if you could not vote then you could not serve on juries or hold public office. Jim Crow was supported by the Democratic Party, which by the late nineteenth century enjoyed a stranglehold on Southern politics, and because they were a solid bloc vote in Washington they were able to thwart attempts by Northern Republicans to end – or even ease – segregation. It was not until 1954 that the tide began to turn when the Supreme Court declared in *Brown* v. *Board of Education* that segregation was unconstitutional. The remaining Jim Crow laws were overturned by the 1964 Civil Rights Act and the 1965 Voting Rights Act. The latter prohibits every state and local government from imposing any voting law that results in discrimination against racial or language minorities. However, Southern discrimination against Black voters continues, albeit in a more subtle manner. One of the most recent cases was in North Carolina where the boundaries for congressional districts had been redrawn in 2010 so that African American voters became minority blocs in key areas. The gerrymandered boundaries were declared unconstitutional by the courts and the North Carolina government was ordered to redraw the boundaries.

The First Americans

Not so well known is that the Jim Crow laws were applied to Native Americans just as harshly as they were to African Americans. In fact, it can be argued they were applied more harshly. It is undisputed that the Native Americans were the victims of one of the worst genocides in history. Before Christopher Columbus landed in the Bahamas in 1492, there were believed to be up to 15 million Indigenous Americans living in what is now the United States. By 1890 this number had been reduced to about 250,000. In 2019 the numbers have recovered to 6.8 million. Many of the Native Americans were killed off by land-hungry European settlers fulfilling what they regarded as their 'Manifest Destiny', but most of them died from imported diseases against which their bodies had no natural defences.

Britain played a major role in laying the foundations for the relations between the Native American tribes and the embryonic United States. From the start, the attitude of the British towards the Native Americans was mixed. From a cultural and religious point of view they were heathen savages. But they were also trading partners, political entities and important allies in the battle to wrest control of North America from the French. The British needed Native American allies to ensure success in the French and Indian War. They garnered the necessary support at the 1758 Treaty of Easton between the British and the Iroquois, Shawnee and Lenape nations. But there was a price: a British promise to ban colonial settlement in French territory west of the Appalachians should the British win the war. They won, and in 1767 King George III issued a royal proclamation calling a halt to colonial settlement in the Ohio River Valley. The Native Americans were happy, but the colonial elite were not, especially one George Washington who had started buying huge tracts of prime Ohio real estate from 1752. Eventually he ended up with about 20,000 acres. Washington was the biggest – but not the only –

American investor in the Ohio Company. Several other key members of the Virginia aristocracy stood to lose fortunes if the royal proclamation was honoured, and the prospect of financial disaster is one of the lesser known reasons for the American Revolution.

After independence, the US government continued the British example of classifying individual Native American tribes as 'separate nations' and negotiated treaties with each tribe and then broke them under the weight of westward European settlement. As separate nations, they could not be US citizens, so therefore they had no voting rights. The one exception before the Civil War was the Cherokee nation, whose members became US citizens in 1817 but were also classed as domestic dependents, a category which meant that they were citizens without political rights, including the vote. After the Civil War, the 1866 Civil Rights Act extended the franchise to African Americans, but specifically excluded Native Americans. Senator James Doolittle summed up attitudes at the time when he said that granting Native Americans US citizenship would 'degrade American citizenship' and overwhelm the white vote in western states.

In 1871 all of the Native American tribes were officially designated as 'domestic dependent nations' and the US authorities started rounding them up and restricting them to reservations. Until 1924 they were denied the right to travel off the reservations without written authorisation by the local agent of the Bureau of Indian Affairs. After 1924 a limited number of Native Americans were initially allowed to vote if they owned property off the reservation. But that soon ended in the western states, which applied to the Native Americans the same restrictions such as a literacy test and poll tax as the Southern states applied to African Americans. The western states feared that if the Native Americans were allowed to vote their numbers would overwhelm the white population, thus closely paralleling the concerns of America's Southern states towards the Black vote. Native Americans finally won the right to vote with the 1965 Voting Rights Act, but it was not until 1968 and the Indian Civil Rights Act that they were included in the basic protections of the Bill of Rights. In 2018 there were eighty court cases pending involving the continued disenfranchisement of Native Americans. Some of these result from the high incidence of homelessness among the poverty-stricken tribes and other cases simply involve continued intimidation.

The Women

History has been unkind to women. Until fairly recent times they have been largely regarded as the inferior chattels of men. The ancient

Egyptians weren't too bad; there were even powerful female pharaohs such as Cleopatra. Mosaic Law was also even-handed between the sexes relative to the rest of the ancient world. The situation started to change dramatically with the Greeks. Women were banned from appearing in the courts, engaging in business contracts and attending public meetings, and if they were divorced they lost custody of their children. Roman law was pretty much a repetition of the Greek experience with a few notable exceptions. Roman women could own their own land, write a will and appear in court. One interesting feature of Roman law was that women came under the authority of their fathers rather than their husbands (*patria potestas*). And despite all the talk of wild orgies, virginity and feminine virtue were highly prized. In fact, a woman who committed adultery could be exiled or thrown into a brothel. The rise of Christianity did nothing for the cause of medieval feminism. The Bible is riddled with passages about women's inferior status and their need to submit to their husbands. Eve, after all, was crafted from Adam's rib so that he would have a companion. And if it had not been for Eve taking a bite of the forbidden fruit, we would all still be living in the Garden of Eden. The Virgin Mary went some way towards redressing the balance, but at the expense of enforced celibacy for millions of medieval women. At least, within the convent walls, the women found protection and a greater freedom than outside. Some women, in fact, were able to use their position within the Church to achieve political power. Abbess Hilda of Whitby played host to the 664 Council of Whitby, which took England out of the orbit of the Irish-based Celtic Church and into that of the Vatican and Europe. Single women had property rights and the Magna Carta protected a widow's right to property. Married women, however, had to hand over their property to their husbands and submit to his will as decreed by the Bible. In fact, a man was entitled to beat his wife as long as he did not disturb the peace in doing so. Marital rape was legal under English law until 1991. In the US there are still states that treat marital and non-marital rape differently. The treatment of women throughout history would have been different if women had had a vote. But, of course, voting was a rare luxury until relatively recent times. Once it became an established political fact, women were quick to realise the potential and demand their rights on both sides of the Atlantic. It just took nearly a century to achieve them.

The women's suffrage movement had its start in Britain. This was for two reasons: the fight against slavery and the 1832 Electoral Reform Act. British women were a leading force behind the scenes in the anti-slavery movement even before William Wilberforce formed his Clapham

Sect. They couldn't hold elected office. They were discouraged from addressing public meetings. They could not even express their views by signing political petitions. But the women knew men who could and they had the intelligence and means to persuade them to act. Lady Margaret Middleton, for instance, persuaded Wilberforce to take up the cause. Bristol milkmaid and poet Hannah Moret won a large following with her abolitionist poetry. The feminist writer Mary Wollstonecraft was also an abolitionist who linked the treatment of women by men to the treatment of slaves in America by their white masters. She asked: 'Is one half of the human species, like the poor African slaves, to be subject to prejudices that brutalise them ... only to sweeten the cup of man?'

There was a long and acrimonious debate that preceded the 1832 Great Reform Act and several government concessions to lower the rising political temperature. One was allowing women to sign political petitions. In 1833 an anti-slavery petition contained the signatures of 298,785 women. The anti-slavery movement had politicised British women. The Reform Act energised it. Prior to 1832 there were few demands for women's suffrage. There were even some property-owning women who were allowed to vote before 1832. Ironically even these women were denied access to the ballot box after 1832 as the Reform Act specifically named 'male heads of household' as the only ones allowed to vote. Philosopher and social reformer Jeremy Bentham proposed women's suffrage in 1817 and he was backed up in 1825 by left-wing Anglo-Irish social reformer William Thompson. But before 1832 there was no serious female-led movement. What was the point of having the vote in a system dominated by rotten and pocket boroughs controlled by men? After 1832 there was a reason. If the newly won – albeit still extremely limited – voting rights could be extended to women then that would help the fight against slavery, and other causes, in Britain and around the world. Women began to join the Chartist Movement, but the core of their efforts was for the time being still focused on the slavery issue. On 28 August 1833 the Act abolishing slavery throughout the British Empire received the royal assent. It took effect on 1 August 1834. But slavery remained elsewhere in the world and Britain's past history as masters of the slave trade meant that the abolitionists felt a strong moral responsibility to stamp it out – especially in the southern American states. In 1840, the British Foreign Anti-Slavery Society (BFASS) held its first meeting in London. Among the attendees was a fifty-three-strong American delegation including six women. The presence of the women infuriated both the American and British men at the conference. At first the women were ejected; then they were reluctantly readmitted but forced to sit behind a curtain and banned from speaking. This appalling treatment in London persuaded two of the women, Elizabeth Cady Stanton and Lucretia Mott, that they had to fight for women's rights.

In 1848, Stanton and Mott were the main organisers of the Seneca Falls Convention to organise a fight for women's rights in the United States. Seneca Falls demanded equality in family rights, education, jobs and religion. It used the template of the Declaration of Independence, changing the phrase 'all men are created equal' to 'all men and women'. Article nine of the convention's Declaration of Sentiments demanded that women be given the vote. The convention was not called to fire the starting gun in the battle for suffrage for American women; it was called to fight the wider war for women's rights, and the vote to include suffrage in their cause won only a narrow majority among the 300 delegates. But within a few short years suffragettes had effectively hijacked the women's movement. It had become obvious that the best way to achieve wider rights was through the political power of the ballot box.

The American suffragette movement was given a major boost in 1851 by the meeting of Susan B. Anthony and Stanton. The close friendship between the two became the keystone for the women's movement. Stanton was the organiser, Susan B. Anthony was the intellectual, writer and speaker – the public face of the American Women's Suffrage Movement. She argued that women were American citizens and that the fourteenth amendment gave all American citizens the right to vote. It read: 'No State shall make or enforce any law which shall abridge the privileges or immunities of citizens of the United States.' Anthony persuaded local officials to allow her to vote in the 1872 presidential election. She was arrested and charged with illegally voting and appeared before a New York federal circuit judge the following year. She lost the legal battle but won a moral victory with a stirring speech that was reported in newspapers around the country. Women's suffrage was well and truly on the national agenda. In 1875 the Supreme Court ended any hope of securing the vote through the courts when it ruled in *Minor* v. *Happersett* that 'the Constitution of the United States does not confer the right of suffrage upon anyone'. With the legal channel closed, Anthony and her colleagues decided to work to enshrine votes for women as a constitutional amendment in its own right.

In comparison to their American cousins, British women were slow to embrace the cause of women's suffrage. Instead, they continued to focus on the slavery issue and wider women's rights. Suffrage was considered by many to be too radical a concept. It was a man, the philosopher John

Stuart Mill, who created the catalyst that started the British suffrage movement. He made the women's vote a major plank in his successful 1865 campaign for a parliamentary seat, and in Westminster he spoke forcefully in favour of it. Mill's support prompted the formation of the London-based Women's Suffrage Committee and two years later the Manchester Society for Women's Suffrage. In 1868 the local groups amalgamated to form the National Society for Women's Suffrage (NSWS). From this point on there were exchanges of ideas and personnel between the American and British suffragette movements, but there was not much in the way of joint campaigns. This was partly due to the differing political structures of the two countries. In America, the federal system and devolved powers of the individual states provided opportunities for the cause. By 1887, fourteen states were allowing women to vote on school matters. Women also gained a full franchise in Washington State in 1910, California in 1911, Oregon, Kansas and Arizona in 1912 and Illinois in 1913. Washington, Utah and Wyoming allowed women to vote before they became states. British suffragettes also enjoyed some successes in winning the franchise for local government elections in a series of parliamentary Acts which gradually extended the voting rights of rate-paying women. By 1900 about one million single women were registered to vote in English local government elections. The effectiveness of the British suffragette movement was until the turn of the twentieth century badly hampered by divisions among the many local splinter groups. Then in 1903 Sylvia Pankhurst arrived on the scene with her two daughters Christabel and Emmeline. They formed, and tightly controlled, the Women's Social and Political Union (WSPU) which turned increasingly to direct action. Stones were thrown, hunger strikes were held and women chained themselves to railings. Insults and rotten fruit were thrown at their opponents in the Liberal Party. Empty stately homes were burned to the ground and one suffragette died after throwing herself in front of the king's horse at the races. British historians are divided on whether the violent campaign of the Pankhursts helped or damaged the campaign for the women's vote in Britain. American women had no doubts. They opposed it. As Kathleen Burk wrote in *Old World, New World*, the American respect for private property was too strong to countenance support for the Pankhursts.

In both countries, the fortunes of the suffragettes were transformed by the First World War. With so many men at war, the women were needed in the factories to produce guns, bullets, tanks and planes as well as to keep the wheels of industry turning in order to pay for the war effort. They were no longer obedient housewives. They were vital cogs in a machine mobilised for the sole and united effort of national survival. Their contribution was so important that it became inconceivable that they would not be given the vote at war's end. Even so, in Britain, it was not a full franchise. In 1918 Parliament passed the Qualification of Women Act which granted the vote to women over thirty who were householders, the wives, university graduates and/or occupiers of property with an annual rent of at least £5. It was not until 1928 that all British women were given the same rights as men in the polling booths and allowed to vote from twenty-one. All American women twenty-one or older (unless you were African American or Native American) secured the right to vote with the nineteenth amendment, passed by Congress on 4 June 1919 and ratified by the states on 18 August 1920.

Losing Trust

As the world advances into the twenty-first century, question marks hover over the survival of political institutions born in medieval England, fought for in English civil wars and an American revolution, nineteenth-century political battles to extend the franchise, two twentieth-century world wars and a lengthy Cold War. Both the British and American political systems are now plagued with extreme partisanship; an absence of consensus, compromise, decorum and mutual respect which is spreading from the corridors of power to infect the wider populations in the world's two most prominent exponents of democratic values. The problem is exacerbated by climate change concerns, the rise of emotionally charged populism, immigration, loss of national identity, the revived spectre of racism, the financial and political benefits of globalism *versus* nationalism and a world economic slowdown that started even before the coronavirus pandemic, which has reduced opportunities for an increasingly disillusioned younger generation. All of the above has been further complicated by a digital information revolution that has simultaneously opened the political debate to a wider audience and created echo chamber politics, which hampers rational debate.

The British parliamentary experience laid the foundations for America's political structure; in some cases as a template and in others as a reaction against its eighteenth-century weaknesses and injustices. In the twenty-first century the flow is very much the other way. Most political scientists credit Newt Gingrich, former Speaker of the US House of Representatives, with laying the foundations for the current partisan nature of Anglo-Saxon politics. A staunchly conservative Republican congressman from Georgia, Gingrich was determined to break the Democrats' long stranglehold on the lower house. He succeeded by turning on its head the conventional wisdom that in the two-party system the route to political success was through the capture of the political centre ground. Gingrich argued that the Republican base could be expanded by capturing the far right of the political spectrum. To achieve this he introduced a new emotive political lexicon. Whenever discussing rival Democrats, Republican politicians would pepper their speeches with negatively charged words such as 'radical', 'sick', 'traitor', 'betray', 'lie' and 'decay'. Positively charged words such as 'courageous', 'brave', 'wise', 'principled' and 'opportunity' were used to describe anything involving the Republican Party. Gingrich's lexicon became official party policy and was circulated in 1990 by GOPAC, the Republican Party's training organisation for elected officials, under the title *Language, a Key Mechanism of Control*.

Gingrich also introduced 'wedge issues'. These are carefully selected emotive subjects which can be boiled down to a simplified sound bite that appeals to an easily identifiable demographic. The purpose of a wedge issue is to force your opponents into an opposing position, leaving the voters to choose between what are portrayed as two extremes in which just as many will vote against, as for, a policy. Successful wedge issue topics in America include race, immigration, crime, national security, abortion, gay rights and religion. In recent years in the UK they included many of the same subjects with the addition of membership of the European Union (Brexit) and the 'will of the people' *versus* Parliament.

Gingrich's strategy worked. In the 1994 mid-term elections, the Republicans ended forty years of Democrat control of the House of Representatives. Gingrich was named *Time Magazine*'s Man of the Year and his Republican colleagues in Congress elected him Speaker of the House. Newt Gingrich was forced to resign after the Republicans' poor showing in the 1998 mid-term elections, the revelation of an extramarital affair with a junior congressional employee and a reprimand from the House Ethics Committee. However, he was able to use his tenure as Speaker to place conservative allies in key committee positions to ensure the continuation of his policies. In 2012 he was one of the front-runner candidates for the 2012 Republican Party's presidential nomination but in the end lost out to Mitt Romney. He was an early supporter of and consultant to Donald Trump in the 2016 presidential race and was reported to have been on a shortlist of three as Trump's running mate. The tactics, policies and language that carried Trump into the White House were pioneered by Newt Gingrich, and Trump used them to great effect in adjusting the American system of checks and balances to the advantage of the presidency.

Gingrich's political strategy was also carefully studied in Britain and reached its fruition with the 2016 referendum campaign over continued membership of the European Union and the three-and-a-half-year-long battle to implement the referendum decision to withdraw against a strong parliamentary bloc determined to overturn the referendum result, or – at the very least – negotiate withdrawal terms which left Britain closely tied to Continental Europe. For many the Brexit debate raised the long-established constitutional principle of the sovereignty of Parliament over the executive. Before 1689 that was a battle between the Crown and Parliament. In the twenty-first century powers are now vested entirely in the prime ministers, who have become increasingly presidential in their actions. Two prime ministers, Theresa May and Boris Johnson, claimed that the narrow referendum result represented 'the will of the people' and that it was their job to implement that will. Members of Parliament who opposed 'the will of the people' were denounced by Brexiteers as 'traitors to democracy'. Theresa May attempted to break the deadlock with an election in June 2017 but only succeeded in losing her parliamentary majority, although, as the Conservatives remained the largest party, she was able to form a minority government with the support of the right-wing Democratic Unionist Party in Northern Ireland. Mrs May was forced to resign after failing three times to persuade the House of Commons to pass an EU withdrawal bill that she had negotiated. She was succeeded by Boris Johnson, one of the leaders of the Leave.EU campaign, who purged the Conservative Party of opponents to British withdrawal before calling an election with the campaign slogan 'Get Brexit Done'. Johnson won the election with an overwhelming eighty-six-seat majority and Britain formally withdrew from the European Union on 31 January 2020. But the long and acrimonious debate raised disturbing underlying attitudes on immigration, race and national identity. It has also weakened Parliament's power to act as a check on the powers of an executive prime minister.

In January 2020, Cambridge University's Centre for the Future of Democracy reported that 60.3 per cent of the British electorate were unhappy with their political system. The researchers said that there was a global trend of falling trust in the ability of democratic politics to deliver good government, in the US and everywhere else in the world where the Anglo-Saxon political model has been adopted. Totalitarian countries, such as Russia and China, and countries which describe themselves as 'illiberal managed democracies', such as Hungary and Turkey, are actively using the dissatisfaction and polarisation in Britain and America to argue that parliamentary democracy is the politics of the past.

5

Liberty and Free Speech in the Modern World

A Mixed Blessing

Free speech is a mixed blessing. If you doubt this just ask anyone who has had their reputation trashed by the tabloid press on the basis of an out-of-context quote or exposed misdemeanour or sexual peccadillo of the sort which hypocritical journalists commit several times a day. How about political and business careers destroyed by deliberate lies and distortions that are protected by the constitutional armour of the first amendment? Or the military men and women whose lives have been lost by the leak of defence secrets? Then there is the use of the first amendment to undermine a fairer society by inciting hatred.

That is why over the years the first amendment has been qualified by legal statutes such as the law of libel and laws prohibiting treason and the incitement of hatred and violence. America and Britain have both long enjoyed a large degree of free speech, although in recent years they have slipped. Britain – the birthplace of modern-day free speech and a pioneer in espousing the merits of a free and vibrant press – lags behind most of the rest of its European neighbours at number 33 in the 2019 World Press Freedom index published by Reporters Without Borders and Index on Censorship. But at least the UK is not as far down the list as the home of the fabled first amendment. Twenty-first century America is 48th on the World Press Freedom index, just ahead of Senegal.

The compilers of the Press Freedom Index criticise the British government for its attacks on press freedom in the name of national security, and insufficient protection for whistleblowers and journalists and their sources. The ubiquitous police-operated closed-circuit television system has been branded a violation of the European Convention on

Human Rights and new anti-terrorism and crime legislation has been introduced that would restrict reporting and put journalists' sources at risk. Its proponents claim that restrictions are needed to combat the growing threat of terrorism. Its opponents counter that every new restriction to 'protect' democracy is a victory for those who oppose it. A similar argument is offered by the American Civil Liberties Union to promote unfettered freedom of speech and press: that any restrictions on free speech undermine the basic principle and play into the hands of the widespread censorship lobby.

Some of the World Press Freedom Index's harshest words have been reserved for the administration of President Donald Trump, bearing in mind that the president has sworn to protect the Constitution and the United States played a crucial role in enshrining freedom of speech in the UN Charter and encouraged it to be prominently incorporated in the constitutions of many post-colonial governments. Trump enabled and emboldened free press opponents by attacking the media as 'enemies of the people' and branded criticism of his administration as 'fake news'. Trump also attempted to block White House access to multiple media outlets. He even called for the revocation of some media outlets' broadcasting licences. The violent anti-press rhetoric from the highest level of the US government has been coupled with an increase in the number of press freedom violations at the local level, as journalists run the risk of arrest for covering protests or simply attempting to ask public officials questions. Reporters have even been subject to physical assault. Whistleblowers face prosecution under the Espionage Act if they leak information of public interest to the press, while there is still no federal 'shield law' guaranteeing reporters' right to protect their sources. Journalists and their devices continue to be searched at the US border, while some foreign journalists are still denied entry into the US after covering sensitive topics such as Colombia's FARC, or Kurdistan.

The Anglo-Saxons gave the modern world the concept of freedom of speech only to dilute it within their own borders in the face of the competing political pressures of national security, vested interests, political correctness, partisanship and inflated egos. Those in power have sought to curb freedom of speech because it exposes nefarious activities undertaken to retain power. Those seeking power recognise it as an essential tool for gaining power, only to jettison their support once it has served its purpose.

Hold the Front Page

Freedom of speech has become inextricably bound to a free press. The media – print, broadcasting and digital – are now the main conduits through which decisions are critically examined and political leaders are held to account. The importance of a free press emerged slowly in England during the seventeenth and eighteenth centuries before becoming entrenched in the first amendment of the US Constitution. It started with pamphlets and coffeehouses and gradually moved to the newspapers which dominated the communications scene before radio, television and, finally, the ubiquitous internet.

From the sixteenth century, Gutenberg's invention was churning out pamphlets. The first efforts focused almost exclusively on religious topics and clergymen used them to circulate their sermons. But they also conveyed news. We know about Elizabeth I's famous Tilbury speech on the eve of the arrival of the Spanish Armada because she ordered its publication in 1588 in a pamphlet entitled *To the Troops at Tilbury*. She also used the pamphlet format to justify the execution of Mary, Queen of Scots. During the English Civil Wars, individual pamphlets were used to give detailed reports of the battles. As the Age of Reason dawned, pamphlets became the weapons of choice for competing philosophers and politicians. The works were riddled with inaccuracies, half-truths, lies and fake news. They were, in short, the social media platforms of their day.

Pamphlets and the ideas they propagated needed a distribution system. This came in the form of the coffeehouse. The first known coffee shop was The Angel in the university town of Oxford. Opened in 1650, it quickly drew some of the world's top thinkers, but at the same time welcomed every class of society. Coffee had only just arrived on British shores and was a big hit with men such as Sir Francis Bacon, who extolled its virtues as a cure for smallpox, scurvy, headaches, gout and, of course, a hangover. Most important of all, the bitter black liquid was non-alcoholic, which increased the likelihood of sober and civil debates. The only entrance requirement was the purchase of an admission ticket which bought you coffee, access to the latest newspapers such as the *Oxford Gazette* and later *The Tatler* and *The Spectator* and a bewildering array of pamphlets. In addition, 'runners' were employed to sprint between shops to report the latest news. London was soon awash with coffee shops which were dubbed 'penny universities' because for the price of a single penny the denizens were provided access to the finest minds, the latest news and top-quality debates in which they were encouraged to participate. It is estimated that at the height of the coffee craze there more than 500 coffee shops in London alone.

The penny universities quickly spread to America, with the first opened in 1670. But there were differences between the British and American establishments. By the 1760s the coffeehouses (most of which doubled as drinks taverns) had evolved into incubators for rebellion. In 1765 the Royal Governor of Virginia, Francis Fauquier, was attacked by an anti-Stamp Act mob that gathered at the Williamsburg coffee shop R. Charlton's. When the British occupied Philadelphia during the American Revolution they closed the coffee shops. The most famous American coffee shop was Boston's Green Dragon Tavern, which was described by Daniel Webster as the 'headquarters of the Revolution'. It was in the Green Dragon that the Boston Tea Party was planned and regular meetings were held by the Sons of Liberty and the Boston Caucus.

As already discussed, the English establishment was all too aware of the power of the press from its earliest days. In fact, it was terrified of it. Throughout the sixteenth and seventeenth centuries attempts were made to control it through the infamous licensing laws, which finally succumbed to the tides of history and were allowed to lapse in 1695. But the powers that be continued to attempt to curb the media. It was not until 1774 that the British press was allowed to report parliamentary proceedings. Then there was the 1712 Stamp Act, which played a major role in laying the foundations for the American Revolution. The Act imposed a tax on all printed papers, advertisements and newspapers. Publishers were charged a penny for every printed sheet and a shilling for every advertisement – outrageously crippling sums in the eighteenth century. The newspaper proprietors found a way around the tax by varying the type faces and page sizes. The newspapers and pamphlets kept rolling off the presses.

The tax was introduced in the colonies after the Seven Years War. It was immediately attacked as an example of British tyranny and led to the 1765 Stamp Act Congress in New York. The meeting in what is now known as Federal Hall was the first time that the colonies had met as a group. It was also the platform for the stirring revolutionary demand from radical Boston lawyer James Otis: 'No taxation without representation.'

The non-renewal of the print licensing laws led to a flurry of political pamphlets and the establishment of Britain's first newspapers, *The Spectator* and *The Tatler*. The first newspaper published in America was the *Boston Newsletter*, which was founded in 1704 as a government mouthpiece. The second newspaper was *The New England Courant*, started by Ben Franklin's brother James in 1721. Both newspapers were comprised mainly of news from England. Readers wanted news about home and at the time that meant England. But by the 1740s American newspaper publishers were discovering that money could also be made from criticising the colonial governments. This led to the creation of America's first champion for freedom of the press. John Peter Zenger was a German immigrant who founded the *New York Weekly Journal*. In 1734 he was arrested for criminal libel after publishing a series of attacks on New York's royal governor, William Cosby. Zenger was acquitted and his victory established free press principles on both sides of the Atlantic and inspired the first amendment guarantees.

It was not all plain sailing for the newly founded press. The government had more censorious tricks up its sleeve. During the eighteenth century the British government tried repeatedly to introduce legislation to regulate the press. It failed every time, though not because Parliament regarded a free press as an essential bulwark for the protection of liberty. No, that thought required at least another fifty years to take shape. Its failure was down to the fact that legislators couldn't agree on the details of any regulation. As well as the Stamp Act, there was the 1704 sedition law. Lord Chief Justice Hope ruled that publications which maliciously undermined the affections of the people for the government of the day were criminal. Included in the sedition laws was any attempt to report the proceedings of Parliament. The iniquity of the sedition laws – along with the right to report parliamentary proceedings – became the special target of radical Whig MP and journalist John Wilkes. He paid a high price of periodic exile, prison, loss of his parliamentary seat and time in the stocks. But it paid off in the end. Wilkes won the support of the London mob and was hailed as a champion of liberty who laid down the principles of freedom of the press and won the right to report the proceedings of Parliament in Britain and Congress in America. He was also the ancestor of John Wilkes Booth, the man who assassinated President Lincoln.

It was left to the great codifier of English law, Sir William Blackstone, to set in legal concrete the importance of free speech and a free press on both sides of the Atlantic. Writing in his 1767 *Commentaries on the Laws of England*, Sir William argued:

> The liberty of the Press is indeed essential to the nature of a free state; but this consists in laying no previous restraint upon publications and not in freedom from censure for criminal matter when published. Every freeman has an undoubted right to lay what sentiments he pleases

before the public. To forbid this is to destroy the freedom of the press; but if he publishes what is improper, mischievous or illegal he must take the consequences.

But the issue of free speech still faced a rocky road through the passions that ruled during the War of Independence and its aftermath. During the war, loyalist newspaper publishers who dared to criticise the revolution found themselves run out of town, or country. In many cases their printing presses and offices were destroyed. The revolutionaries supported free speech as long as they agreed with what was said and printed. There was no mention of free speech or press in the Constitution as ratified in 1788. That document focused on the structure of the government rather than the rights that the government was designed to protect. Virginian James Madison viewed this as a major failing and immediately set out to correct it. He did so with the first ten amendments to the Constitution, which became known as the Bill of Rights.

The struggle continued in the infant United States. Despite efforts to construct a non-partisan federal structure, the country split into the Federalists led by John Adams and Alexander Hamilton, and the Republicans led by Thomas Jefferson. The split was complicated by the fact that the division assumed an international dimension. The Federalists sought closer relations with the former colonial masters in Britain while Jeffersonian Republicans favoured revolutionary France. The split was exacerbated by the 1795 Jay Treaty that returned Anglo-American relations to an even keel following the revolution. Not surprisingly, the treaty angered revolutionary France, which began seizing the cargoes of American vessels and demanding ransoms. There was a national outcry against not only the French but Jefferson's Republicans. The federalists led by Adams, who was elected president in 1798, forced through Congress the infamous Alien and Sedition Acts, which were a clear violation of the new Bill of Rights and a Federalist attempt to undermine the liberal leanings of Jefferson's supporters.

There were four pieces of legislation altogether. The law relating to free speech was the Sedition Act and it basically reinstated in America the 1704 draconian sedition laws of Lord Chief Justice Hope. The Alien Friends Act allowed the president to imprison or deport aliens considered 'dangerous to the peace and safety of the United States' at any time, while the Alien Enemies Act authorised the president to do the same to any male citizen of an enemy nation above the age of fourteen during times of war. The revised Alien Enemies Act remains in force to this day.

Twenty-five people were arrested under the terms of the Sedition Act. All were Republicans. Ten were convicted. Initial discussions involved the death penalty, but the final legislation limited sentences to hefty fines and imprisonment. Among the convicted was Jeffersonian congressman Matthew Lyon from Vermont. He made the mistake of telling a local newspaper that President Adams suffered from 'an unbounded thirst for ridiculous pomp, foolish adulation and selfish avarice'. He was found guilty of sedition, fined $1,000 and jailed for four months. In another case, Luther Baldwin was sentenced to prison because he drunkenly expressed the hope that a cannon salute to President Adams might find its way up the presidential backside.

The flagrant flouting of the first amendment split the country. Adams's stronghold in New England was 100 per cent behind it, while many of the Southern states opposed it. In Virginia and Kentucky there was even talk of secession. In New York Alexander Hamilton started to raise an army to fight the Southern rebels. The sedition laws rapidly grew in unpopularity and were the major factor behind the election of Thomas Jefferson as president in 1800. The laws were nullified in 1800 and 1801, but Jefferson found himself – like so many political figures before and after him – the victim of the freedom that he championed. One of those convicted under the Sedition Act was James Callender, a ne'er-do-well who had been secretly financed by Jefferson to challenge the sedition laws. After Jefferson's election victory, Callender used his secret dealings with the new president to blackmail him into giving him a government post. When Jefferson refused, Callender turned against him and was responsible for the revelation that the president had fathered a number of children by his slave mistress Sally Hemmings.

Callender also claimed that Jefferson had paid him to publicly call the revered George Washington a traitor. Harry Crosswell, publisher of the obscure upstate New York newspaper *The Wasp*, reprinted the allegation. Jefferson sued for libel. Ironically, Crosswell's valiant defence was handled by the arch Federalist Alexander Hamilton, who played a major role in drafting the sedition laws which Jefferson had nullified. The tables had completely turned, as so often happens in politics. Hamilton lost the case but re-established first amendment principles with his impassioned defence.

Free... Not so Free... Free, Not so...

As the nineteenth century progressed, Britain and America went down different paths in the free speech debate. The routes were largely determined by external political events. In Britain, the aristocracy was fighting a rearguard action against the fallout from revolutions in France and America. Free speech and a free press were viewed as being as big a threat as ever before by the hereditary Establishment. Continued imposition of stamp duties circumscribed the growth of the media, and with a few exceptions, such as Thomas Cobbett's *Political Register*, the newspapers were little more than money-making government mouthpieces with approved editorial copy filling the white spaces between advertisements. This continued until Britain started its era of parliamentary reform with the 1832 Great Reform Act. The gradual steps towards a universal franchise opened the eyes of an expanded British Establishment to the value of a free press and its role in preserving a representative government. Political philosopher John Stuart Mill spelled it out in his seminal work, *On Liberty*, when he argued that the highest value should be placed on truth and that truth can only be determined by opening it to constant debate in the form of a free press.

In America, westward expansion dominated national life and played its part in supporting free speech. Libertarian politics were an essential element in encouraging the development of newly acquired territories on the other side of the Appalachian Mountains. Part and parcel of this libertarianism was the right to say what one wanted. Protection of the first amendment became increasingly viewed as essentially an American principle. As for the Federalist Party, by 1820 it had virtually disappeared. Its oligarchical and monarchical tendencies reflected the values of the Old World and had no place in the new one.

The political climate aligned with fast-moving print technology and a revolutionary transportation and distribution system, the railways, to usher in the golden age of the newspaper. The centuries of debate that preceded this period meant that Britain and America led the way in establishing the importance and political power of the media. It was an age of rapidly expanding circulation, which in turn attracted advertisers who provided the financial security that ensured a free press. In America, the size of the country dictated that all the papers were essentially local in their editorial coverage. But that did not stop men such as Horace Greeley, Joseph Pulitzer and George Randolph Hearst from becoming major political figures not only in their respective localities but beyond.

It was in Britain where the press reached its apogee with *The Times* of London. By 1840 the newspaper's circulation was twice that of all its rivals combined and its editorial coverage mirrored the breadth of the British Empire. It was said that the second most important man in any world capital was the British ambassador; the first was the *Times'* correspondent. Editor John Thaddeus Delane laid the foundations for modern news coverage with his exposés. He was also the first to introduce the war correspondent, during the Crimean War. The reports of William Russell exposed the inadequacies of the British Army and helped Florence Nightingale establish the nursing profession. The foreign secretary, Lord Russell, complained: '*The Times* aspires not to be the organ, but the organiser of government.' When the paper was accused of leaking cabinet secrets, Delane replied: 'To accuse this, or any other journal, of publishing early and correct intelligence is to pay us one of the highest compliments that we can hope to deserve.'

The British government responded to the growing power of *The Times* by abolishing the last vestiges of the Stamp Act. This had the effect of creating competition for 'The Thunderer'. Within a few years *The Times* was being challenged by a host of competitors, each of them carving out their own profitable socio-economic niche. Fleet Street, the Street of Ink, the Street of Shame, became the centre of world journalism and the Mecca for every reporter who wanted to work at the top of his profession. It also became a political powerhouse and money-making machine that attracted the biggest egos and power brokers. Men such as Lord Rothermere, Lord Northcliffe, Lord Beaverbrook, Lord Thomson, Lord Cudlipp and Rupert Murdoch used their British national newspapers to accumulate vast wealth and power. They could literally make or break a British government. Freedom of the press was guaranteed less by formal laws than by the competition between these powerful press barons, who demanded what has become a traditional British liberty in return for their support and membership of the political Establishment. Their freedom of action was strengthened by financial independence created by the world's highest circulation and consequent large advertising revenues. The British national press was also able to pool its resources to create the first global news wire service – Reuters – which gave the British press, and by association Britain, a global reach. By the time the BBC was founded in 1922, the political and financial infrastructure existed to create an international, publicly funded broadcast news service which, arguably, remains the gold standard and template for every broadcaster.

In America, the press saw its role as standing slightly apart, providing hard news and criticising the governing classes rather than being part of the Establishment. It was an integral part of the system but from a semi-detached position. William Storey of the *Chicago Times* summed up the role of American newspapers when he said that his job was 'to print the news and raise Hell'. With the protection of the first amendment and an element of political clout, the regional newspapers did just that. At the national and state level, the free speech debate was handled mainly by the courts. But then for most of the nineteenth century the Supreme Court refused to hear the bulk of the first amendment cases because in 1833 Chief Justice John Marshal ruled that cases involving the first amendment were primarily the responsibility of the state governments.

Then came the First World War and the Espionage Acts of 1917 and 1918, which forbade support for the enemy in war time and 'any disloyal, profane, scurrilous or abusive language about the form of government of the United States or the flag of United States or the uniform of the Army or Navy'. President Woodrow Wilson wanted to extend the Act to include censorship of the press but was blocked by one vote in Congress. The Act, however, was widely used to imprison and fine individuals. The courts heard nearly 2,000 cases during the First World War, most of them ending with convictions, hefty fines and a term in prison. A slightly watered down version of the Act remained on the books after the war and was used in cases involving socialist politician Eugene Debs, Julius and Ethel Rosenberg, Pentagon papers whistleblower Daniel Ellsberg, Chelsea Manning, Edward Snowden, and WikiLeaks founder Julian Assange.

Despite some of the obvious political hypocrisy, the ideal of free speech was firmly implanted on both sides of the Atlantic by the outbreak of the Second World War – and then it withered again with the wartime paranoia about German, Italian and Japanese spies, followed by the McCarthy witch hunt. The establishment of Soviet-backed communist regimes in eastern Europe, the victory of the Chinese Communist Party in China's long-running civil war and Moscow's detonation of an atomic bomb in August 1949 raised the terrifying spectre of a red menace threatening to overthrow the American way of life. This was political grist to the mill of Joseph McCarthy, the newbie senator from Wisconsin who exploited the paranoia to rise to national prominence.

McCarthy was a master of the national mood and political theatrics who started his witch hunt in February 1950 with a speech in Wheeling, West Virginia, during which he waved a piece of paper which he claimed contained the names of 257 State Department employees who were known communists. Working hand in glove with McCarthy was FBI director J. Edgar Hoover who conducted illegal surveillance and compiled reports which he passed onto the Wisconsin senator and his staff. McCarthy orchestrated a witch hunt of 'fellow travellers' that ruined hundreds of thousands of lives. By 1952, the FBI had assembled nearly 450,000 files on alleged subversive groups and individuals. Prominent diplomats, army officers, teachers, actors, almost every section of American society was subjected to McCarthyism. Anyone with liberal leanings lived in constant fear of having their name dropped by Joe McCarthy. And if you had made the youthful mistake of at any time joining the Communist Party you could kiss goodbye to your job, career and possibly your citizenship. Actors such as Charlie Chaplin and Paul Robeson were forced out of the country. Distinguished diplomats Owen Lattimore and John Service were drummed out of the State Department and teaching positions. Those under investigation included Albert Einstein, Eleanor Roosevelt, Lucille Ball and Orson Welles. Anyone applying for a fishing licence in New York had to swear a loyalty oath because it was feared that communists would use the sport as cover to poison the city's water supply.

McCarthyism managed to cross the Atlantic where it was implemented by Britain's counter-intelligence agency, MI5. The organisation had been crusading against communism and the Soviet Union since before the Bolshevik Revolution. But now it had another reason to take a strong anti-communist position, and this had an impact on freedom of speech. Britain had emerged from the Second World War as the impoverished junior partner in the transatlantic relationship, but, at the same time, determined to retain its great power status for as long as possible. As part of this strategy it developed a close link with American intelligence that continues to be a cornerstone of the Anglo-American special relationship. To protect the special relationship (whether or not it still actually exists) British intelligence often toes the American line. A seat at the top table requires support for and acquiescence to American policies. In the 1950s it meant that MI5 placed an agent in the BBC with the specific job of uncovering any person suspected of communist sympathies. Later the security services created extensive files on a number of Labour Party MPs including deputy leader Harriet Harman, Labour Party leaders Michael Foot and Jeremy Corbyn, cabinet minister Peter Hain, and Labour guru Peter Mandelson. According to former MI5 agent Peter Wright, in his book *Spycatcher*, the agency even plotted to overthrow Labour Prime Minister Harold Wilson. The British government's failure to prevent publication of Wright's work was a major victory for free speech.

Possibly the longest-lasting damage to British freedom of speech was caused by the 1911 Official Secrets Act, which was last amended in 1989 and remains in force. This Act requires that anyone who is given access to secrets must sign a pledge to never reveal the secret involved, nor any other secret information to which they may become privy at any time in the future. Some journalists regard this arrangement as part of the cosy give-and-take nature of British journalism. Others see it as an effective gagging order, offering selected journalists secret titbits in return for which they can never speak about any other sensitive information.

The gradual move towards Western victory in the Cold War and relatively successful decolonisation gave a boost to Anglo-Saxon values, including the aspiration of free speech. It started with the 1948 Universal Declaration of Human Rights, which included a clause that stated: 'Everyone has the right to freedom of opinion and expression; this right includes freedom to hold opinions without interference and to seek, receive and import information and ideas through any media and regardless of frontiers.' Protection of free speech was written into Germany's Basic Law, and the European Convention on Human Rights. It also appeared in the constitutions of most newly independent states, although it was more honoured in the breach than the observance. The end of the Cold War even saw the introduction of a free press in Russia, although it ended with the rise of former KGB agent Vladimir Putin and his particular brand of nationalist-inspired totalitarianism. In America and Britain free speech suffered as a result of the attack on the World Trade Center on 11 September 2001. The subsequent War on Terror, with the invasion of Afghanistan and Iraq and attacks on Syria, created a climate of fear that sparked off anti-Islamic hysteria, which was dangerously and irresponsibly exploited by the populist right. Newspapers and broadcasters who railed against the populist right were attacked by political leaders as 'enemies of the people'. But the greatest impact on free speech came not from politics, but technology. The introduction of the Internet both opened and closed windows. It created opportunities for billions to access previously inaccessible information and news while at the same time providing a platform for hate and division.

Freedom of Speech Caught in the Web

The last Briton to have a major impact on freedom of speech on both sides of the Atlantic was Tim Berners-Lee. In fact, his impact was immediate and global and possibly greater than that of Johannes Gutenberg. Sir Tim Berners-Lee is the inventor of the World Wide Web, the Internet. The son of two computer engineers, Sir Tim was educated in London and Oxford and developed the concept and hypertext techniques for the World Wide Web while working as an independent contractor for the European Organisation for Nuclear Research (CERN). His invention earned him a knighthood, but not the billions piled up by other tech entrepreneurs. Sir Tim has gone the academic route and sits on various university committees responsible for monitoring the Internet. The IT money has been made in America, where entrepreneurs are able to access venture capital and a large and prosperous domestic market. It was left to men such as Facebook's Mark Zuckerberg to accumulate the cash and place the US in control of the twenty-first-century phenomenon of social media. In the first quarter of 2019, Facebook chalked up 2.38 billion monthly active users – roughly a third of the world population. In the same three-month period, its revenues were $15.08 billion, and that was after setting aside $3 billion to settle an ongoing Federal Trade Commission inquiry. Facebook also owns the popular social media site Instagram. The other big American social media giants are of course YouTube, Amazon, Instagram and Twitter; the latter the previous American president's preferred communications platform. The Chinese are also big in the social media world with WeChat, QQ and Weibo. They provide the Americans with some competition in developing countries, but their main strength is the nearly 1.4 billion Chinese. However, development of the Asian social media giants is hampered by government censorship known as the Great Firewall of China.

Then there are the bloggers, vloggers (video bloggers) and YouTube millionaires; anyone with access to a computer who has a story to tell, whether it is beauty secrets or military secrets. The traditional media had been a rich man's game. Owning a newspaper involved expensive finance for printing presses, paper, reporters, advertising sales people, marketing departments, offices, distribution networks, accounts, and a good PR team. The blogger only needed time to write and design a webpage. The cost was virtually nil. The result was an explosion in information and, in theory, freedom of speech.

The old print media were hamstrung by an economic model forged in the nineteenth and twentieth centuries. Their circulation figures were largely determined by their location, production schedule and physical distribution network. A complex web of machinery and working practices meant that it could take up to a day for news to make its way from the reporter's notebook to the consumer. Revenues were based on a combination of subscription plus advertising sales. The ideal model was a newspaper whose running costs were paid for by subscription with the profit derived from advertising. In theory, the global reach of the World Wide Web provided publishers with a global market. This did apply in a few cases, but most papers were limited by the local nature of their market. The old media were unable to compete with the new low-cost, web-based, real-time news sites. Circulation dropped. Advertising dried up and newspapers that had provided a vital service to their community closed.

In contrast, most of the social media sites were designed to exploit the immediate global reach of the World Wide Web. To achieve this they concentrated on niche, but globally available, editorial; sometimes very niche indeed. There is a website for those who believe that the earth is flat in part because there are enough people in the world who subscribe to that belief to support news in favour of it, and in part because there are people who find the idea funny. The extensive reach of the web also allows platforms to be built by extremists on the far left and right of the political spectrum: ultra-nationalists, Holocaust deniers, white supremacists, Jihadists and any other minority group driven by a sense of grievance and the will to pursue it. It gave a voice to those who had been hiding in the shadows, and by providing the platform increased their credibility and acceptability.

One of the best examples of political abuse of social media was the 2016 US presidential election. The Mueller Report said that there was no doubt that Russia used social media to influence voters in favour of Donald Trump. This view was shared by every US intelligence agency and for a long time dismissed by President Trump as it damaged the credibility of his election victory. The president's dismissal of intelligence reports only served to feed allegations of collusion between the Trump campaign and Moscow. It is almost impossible to determine if the Russian efforts had any impact on the outcome, and the Mueller Report found no evidence that the Trump campaign colluded or conspired with Russian internet trolls.

The economic model of social media has also changed the nature of news. Internet-based news, with a few exceptions, is entirely based on advertising revenue supported by large circulations. The viewer/reader is king along with as much data as can be accumulated related to their online habits. Companies such as Facebook use the data to sell highly targeted and effective advertising. This has raised serious concerns about privacy. So much so that the European Union has introduced General Data Protection Regulations (GDPR) to combat abuse of the sale of private data for commercial purposes.

Several governments have passed legislation to force the social media giants to remove hate speech from the platforms. The German Bundestag in January 2019 started to enforce a law that gives networks twenty-four hours to eject 'obviously illegal' postings. If they fail to do so, the platform providers face fines of up to $50 million. The British Parliament indicated that it would follow the German example. Other countries such as Russia and Vietnam, and even India, have introduced similar legislation, except that their definition of hate speech and fake news extends to criticism of the government, thus placing Facebook *et al.* in the unenviable position of becoming government censors or risk losing their commercially valuable position as global providers.

Mark Zuckerberg is reluctantly, and with great difficulty, complying with the regulations while at the same time maintaining that the laws regarding libel and hate speech that apply to the traditional media do not apply to social media. You cannot, argue social media lawyers, prosecute or in any way hold responsible the owner of a wall on which someone has posted an offensive message. Facebook and Twitter, they claim, is no more than a digital wall. Furthermore, any attempt to restrict users would be a violation of the first amendment, and the now almost universally accepted principle of free speech.

The issue is set to be high on political agendas around the world for many years to come as free speech advocates continue the age-old debate about the need, if any, for government regulation to protect national interest, ensure privacy and avoid abuse and incitement to violence. In the meantime, It remains to be seen which axiom will win: 'A lie travels halfway around the world before the truth puts its boots on' (alternatively attributed to Jonathan Swift, Mark Twain or Winston Churchill), or John Stuart Mill's assertion that 'truth always triumphs over falsehood'.

6

The Slave Trade

'Is Life so Dear ... as to be Purchased at the Price of Chains and Slavery?'

On 1 January 1863, President Abraham Lincoln issued the Emancipation Proclamation. America's African American slaves were freed. Actually, that is not true; they were only free in those states where Lincoln's authority was recognised, which meant the Union. The Confederacy ignored it. The slaves were not finally freed until the passage of the thirteenth amendment in December 1865. But that was only the start of a long rollercoaster ride that continues to this day.

It started off well enough. In 1866 the first Civil Rights Act was passed, which extended citizenship rights to the former slaves. In February 1870 the fifteenth amendment gave them the vote. This was too much for white Southerners who been reduced to penury by the folly of war and now faced the humiliation of parity with their former slaves. Through a process of violence, intimidation, segregation, economic racism and political chicanery they passed the Jim Crow laws which represented a de facto reversal of African American gains from the North's victory in the Civil War. African Americans in the former Confederate states were denied the vote and barred from whites-only schools, restaurants, hotels and toilets. They were made to sit at the back of the bus and denied access to all but the most menial of jobs.

Segregation and job discrimination continued for almost a century. It became widely accepted as a fact of American life in the North as well as the South. In 1912 Woodrow Wilson ordered segregation throughout the entire federal government. In 1921, President Calvin Coolidge appeared to pre-empt Hitler's *Mein Kampf* when he asserted, 'Biological laws tell us that certain divergent people will not mix or blend. The Nordics propagate themselves successfully. With other races the outcome shows deterioration on both sides.'

By the 1950s the smallest of cracks began to appear in the edifice of segregation. Then in 1955, fourteen-year-old African American Emmett Till travelled from Chicago to visit relatives in Money, Mississippi. While there, he allegedly wolf-whistled at a white woman. Emmett was lynched. He was shot in the head, and his eyes were gouged out. His mother brought the body back to Chicago and insisted on an open casket funeral, laying bare the violent horror of American racism for the entire world to see. Roy Bryant and J. W. Milam, the two men arrested for Emmett's murder, were acquitted by an all-white jury. Protected by the law of double jeopardy, the two men sold the story of their crime to *Look* magazine.

Emmett's murder and the subsequent acquittal of his murderers sparked off a series of boycotts, freedom rides, sit-ins, demonstrations and marches organised by the charismatic preacher Martin Luther King Jr, aimed at ending segregation and establishing equal rights for African Americans. In 1964 the Equal Rights Act was signed into law by former Jim Crow supporter President Lyndon B. Johnson. The following year the Jim Crow laws were overturned and in 1967 the Supreme Court declared illegal state laws banning interracial marriages.

But it became clear that the laws were no more than a legal veneer of respectability painted over centuries of prejudice stemming from the former slave status of African Americans. Despite representing only 12.7 per cent of the American population, African Americans in 2018 comprised a third of the country's prison population. In 2013 the median net worth of African American households was $11,000. The median net worth of white households was more than ten times that figure at $144,800. American police have been accused of being institutionally racist and the shooting of African American criminal suspects sparked off race riots in dozens of American cities between 1980 and 2015.

Then in 2008 it looked as if everything was about to change. An African American, Barack Obama, was elected President of the United States. Commentators talked of the start of a post-racial American society. In 2016 Obama was succeeded by Donald Trump, which many have interpreted as a white backlash. Trump has a history of racial prejudice. Many of his supporters and some of his key advisers were drawn from what is called the alt-right – a motley collection which includes white supremacists and ultra-right nationalists. President Trump exacerbated the situation when he refused to condemn Neo-Nazi marchers when they clashed with their opponents in Charlottesville, Virginia, during riots in which one person was murdered.

During the Trump presidency there were several incidents of African Americans being shot and killed by US police, culminating in the death of George Floyd, whose demise sparked off the protests and riots of the 'Black Lives Matter' movement. President Trump responded by heavily backing the police and the principle of law and order. This galvanised America's Black community to support Democratic Party presidential candidate Joe Biden and was a major contribution to Trump's defeat in the 2020 presidential election.

An NBC news survey in May 2018 – 155 years after Lincoln's Emancipation Decree and 54 years after the Equal Rights Act – revealed that 64 per cent of Americans believed that racism remained a problem. Forty-five per cent said it was worsening. Thirty per cent said it was the biggest source of division in America. Forty per cent of African Americans reported that they had been unfairly treated in a store or restaurant in the previous month. The legacy of slavery remains a major headache for the United States. It started with the British.

The Seduction of Queen Bess

Queen Elizabeth I was appalled when she was told that one of her favourites, Sir John Hawkins, had gone into the slaving business. The venture was 'detestable and would call down vengeance from heaven upon the undertakers', she said. Then Hawkins showed her the accounts. The queen immediately invested in his next slaving voyage in 1564. And that pretty much sums up the English attitude towards slavery. It was 'detestable', but they were prepared to hold their noses and turn a blind eye because the trade made shedloads of money. Over two centuries an estimated 15 million Africans were forcibly transported across the Atlantic. Some 3 million ended up in the United States. An estimated 30 million died before they even reached American shores.

English slave ships sailed from London, Bristol and Liverpool. The profits to their owners helped to finance Britain's industrial revolution and built many of its stately homes. New England followed suit. Boston, Salem, New London, New York, Newport, Providence, and Bristol, Rhode Island, were home ports for hundreds of slave-carrying ships. The mortar that binds the bricks of Beacon Hill is soaked in African blood. Then there are the industries that rose on the backs of the African diaspora. By no means did all of the slaves go to the colonies (later states) south of the Mason-Dixon Line. Many went to work in the sugar plantations of the Caribbean or the sugar and rice fields of Brazil. The money they earned for investors in England and America dwarfed the profits from the slave trade itself. The profits were used by colonials to buy the growing English manufactures. In 1770, 96 per cent of British exports of nails and 70 per cent of its wrought iron went to markets in the American and Caribbean colonies made rich by slave labour. About 15 per cent was absorbed by the domestic British market.

The British did not invent slavery. It has its roots in the dawn of time. Historians estimate, for instance, that 30 to 40 per cent of the population of the Roman Empire in the first century AD were slaves. The difference is that the African slave trade became based on a foundation of racial superiority, which subsequent generations are still trying to shed. If not banned, slavery was frowned upon in northern Europe from about the eleventh century. Instead, landlords relied on serfs and villeins whose ties to a manor were no more than the tiniest of tiny steps above slavery. There was, however, a booming trade in East African slaves run by Arab slave traders from the eighth century. This was centred on the island of Zanzibar which hosted an extensive slave market well into the late nineteenth century. Some of these slaves found their way into Renaissance drawing rooms in Genoa, Florence and Venice.

The Portuguese were the first in modern times to deal in the African slave trade. The first recorded slaves arrived in Portugal in 1441. There were twelve of them. They had been captured by captains Antao Goncalves and Muno Tristos in modern-day Mauritania. Eight years later the first proper slave ship – with 235 kidnapped Africans on board – arrived in Portugal, the result of a voyage by tax collector Lancarote de Freitas. By the beginning of the fifteenth century it was estimated that 10 per cent of the population of Lisbon were African slaves. The Portuguese dominated the African slave trade for the next two centuries, mainly as a consequence of a Papal Bull which gave them a monopoly on all trade with Africa. The Spanish, however, were keen to take a slice of the lucrative trade. Ignoring the Papal Bull, they jumped in and in 1476 Carlos de Valera of Castille arrived in Spain with the first load of 400 African slaves.

It could be argued that the transport of African slaves to America started with the best of motives. It was the brainchild of Dominican Friar Bartolome de las Casas who doubled as one of the early wealthy Spanish settlers in Hispaniola and Cuba. He quickly became appalled at the way the early conquistadores forced the indigenous people into slavery and in 1517 returned to Spain to urge King Charles V to save the indigenous people by importing slaves from Africa. The young king, who was also Emperor of the Holy Roman Empire, agreed and the great forced migration began. De las Casas ended up as the Bishop of Chiapas, and to give him his due, he turned against the African slave trade he initiated and is recognised as one of the first abolitionists.

The Spanish very quickly edged the Portuguese out of the slave trade. By the sixteenth century the Portuguese had built a string of heavily fortified castles along the West African coast which were nothing more than giant warehouses full of slaves waiting to be shipped to their European and American markets. But the Spanish controlled the vast American markets for the slave labour. Africans were needed to work and die in the gold and silver mines and the vast *encomiendas* that produced rice, indigo and the increasingly important sugar crop.

Charles V ensured Spanish dominance by selling the rights to a monopoly to provide African slaves to all the Spanish colonies in the New World. This monopoly was known as the *asiento*. The contractor (*asentista*) paid an agreed annual sum to the Spanish Crown to deliver a stipulated number of slaves. The first such contractor was a Genoese company that in 1517 agreed to supply 1,000 slaves over an eight-year period. In 1528 an agreement was reached with a German firm to supply 4,000 slaves. For its monopoly the firm paid 20,000 ducats annually to the Crown. Each slave was sold at a price not exceeding 45 ducats.

If anyone other than the *asentista* tried to sell slaves in a Spanish colony then the cargo would be confiscated and the captain and crew could be tried as pirates. This did not stop England's swashbuckling Elizabethan sailors, notably Sir John Hawkins and Sir Francis Drake. The two men are better known for capturing Spanish treasure ships, circumnavigating the globe and saving England from the Spanish Armada. But they were also England's first slave traders.

Captain John Hawkins, as he was then, made his first trip to the west coast of Africa in 1562. He was thirty years old. He bought 300 Africans and then sailed to Hispaniola (now the divided island of Haiti and the Dominican Republic) where he defied the *asiento* by exchanging them for a cargo of sugar, ginger and pearls. Some of the cargo he sold in Spain, where it was seized by the Spanish authorities because of his sale of slaves in a Spanish colony. Despite this, he made enough of a profit to seriously impress Queen Elizabeth.

Hawkins set off on his second slaving voyage in 1564 and his third in 1567. On the third voyage he took with him a young Francis Drake who was put in command of one of the slaving squadron's ships. The activities of Hawkins, Drake and other early English slavers were focused on skirting around the Portuguese and Spanish monopolies and selling their human cargoes in the Spanish colonies. There were, at the time, no English colonies and thus no English market for their 'goods'. The first slaves to be landed in what became the United States arrived in 1526 with the Spanish. The explorer, sugar planter and lawyer Lucas Vasquez de Allyon set off with a crew of 600 (including African slaves) from Hispaniola with orders to map and colonise the Eastern Seaboard. Where they went it is not quite certain but historians are convinced that they set up a colony on the Virginia coast. It lasted three months. De Allyon died and the 150 survivors sailed back to Hispaniola.

The first record of an African slave in one of the original thirteen colonies came in 1619. The Portuguese slave ship the *Sao Joao Bautista* sailed from Luanda in present-day Angola to Vera Cruz in present-day Mexico. On board were 350 slaves. But the captain only managed to sell 147 of his cargo in Mexico (then called New Spain) so he set sail for Jamaica where he disposed of another twenty-four. The *Sao Joao Bautista* then suffered a run-in with two privateers – the *White Lion* and *The Treasurer* – who relieved the Portuguese ship of the remnants of her slave cargo. They immediately set sail for the British colony at Jamestown. The *White Lion* arrived first and sold its twenty slaves to Governor George Yardley and a merchant named Abraham Peirsey. *The Treasurer*, captained by Captain Elfrith, however, encountered a seventeenth-century bureaucratic glitch when it arrived four days later. There were suggestions that Elfrith's letter of marque allowing him to attack Portuguese ships was invalid. This would make him a pirate and anyone who bought his goods could be tried as being complicit in piracy. He was refused permission to land the slaves so he sailed to Bermuda where he traded them for 50,000 ears of corn and entered the history books as the man who introduced African slaves to that British colony.

The slaves that arrived in 1619 may have been the first, but they were not the beginning of the African tsunami that later swept through the American South. That did not begin until the end of the seventeenth century and beginning of the eighteenth. Until then the Southern colonies relied primarily on indentured servants for their labour requirements. In fact, it is estimated that up to a half of all the white immigrants to the original thirteen colonies between 1606 and 1776 were indentured servants. And the practice did not stop with independence but carried on into the early years of the nineteenth century.

Indentures were bought and sold in five-year slots so a servant could be bought for five, ten, fifteen or twenty years. Some – such as convicted felons and prisoners of war – were sold for life. Their lives were little better than those of slaves. They could not leave their jobs or marry without the permission of their master and had no legal rights before the courts. Many were kidnapped as children and sold with false papers of indenture ship drawn up by unscrupulous ship captains. After the Monmouth Rebellion in 1685, hundreds of the rebels were sold as indentured servants in the West Indies and America. The same occurred during the earlier English Civil Wars when it was mainly the Scots and Irish who were transported.

The indentured servants were transported in the similar inhumane conditions as the African slaves. In some crossings, barely any of the immigrants survived. Between 1750 and 1755 it was estimated that the bodies of two thousand would-be indentured servants were tossed into New York harbor because they died on board before they could be offloaded. The indentured servants had one big advantage over the African slaves: they spoke English. They also had a major disadvantage: they died in greater numbers. The climate in the British-owned islands of the West Indies and in the Southern mainland was tropical. It was infested with malaria and yellow fever. The Europeans were physically ill-equipped for such hazards, whereas the African slaves had had generations of African weather and conditions to adapt.

Because the system of indentures was the accepted norm at the time, most of the early African slaves were not technically slaves but servants who were indentured for life. The indenture system, however, did not apply to the children of the Africans. They were born free – at first. By the mid-seventeenth century the plantation system was starting to take hold and English-speaking African children were a valuable commodity. So, the colonists turned to the Bible for a moral justification to bind the Africans with the chains of perpetual slavery. They found it in Leviticus chapter 25, verse 4, which told the pious colonials: 'Your male and female slaves are to come from the nations around you; from them you may buy slaves.'

The Bible was quickly backed up by the courts. In 1661 the Virginia Assembly ruled that Black slaves were to be 'perpetual servants'. Maryland followed suit in 1663 with the addition of a ban on interracial marriages. New York – whose slave population had grown when the colony was governed by the Dutch – was third in line in 1706 and the other colonies quickly followed suit. The exception was Georgia, which banned slavery until 1733. This was partly because the colony was populated mainly by convict labour and partly because the Spaniards in neighbouring Florida were offering freedom to any of the slaves in the English colonies who made their way to the Spanish colony. The Georgians were quick to make up for lost time on the slavery front.

England Rules the Waves – and the Slave Trade

African slaves finally started to arrive in large numbers after 1675 when the brother of Charles II, later James II, took the lead in forming the Royal African Company. Initially the British royal family was drawn to the west coast of Africa by tales of gold – tales that were completely true. The African Gold Coast roughly corresponds to modern-day Ghana. Gold from Ghana had been making its way to Europe since pre-colonial days and was the major draw for initial fifteenth-century Portuguese expansion into the area. Even today, the precious mineral makes up nearly 37 per cent of Ghanaian exports.

After the execution of Charles I, many royalist officers turned swashbuckling privateers. Two of the most famous were the king's cousin Prince Rupert of the Rhine and Sir Robert Holmes. They travelled to what was then known as the Gold Coast and returned to the exiled court with stories of riches. Almost as soon as the Stuart family was restored to the British throne in 1660, Prince Rupert and Sir Robert persuaded the king and his brother to establish a company to drive out the Dutch who then controlled the Gold Coast and Guinea.

The company was set up and Sir Robert was despatched with a fleet of Royal Navy ships to kick out the Dutch. Initially the company was called the Company of Royal Adventurers of England Trading into Africa. In 1663 the company was given a royal charter and rechristened the Royal African Company. At first the company focused entirely on the gold trade and in 1665 hauled back to England the not inconsiderable sum of £200,000 in gold. It made another £100,000 dealing in ivory, hides, pepper and dyewoods.

Then British influence crept eastwards around the Bight of Benin and the Gulf of Guinea onto the Slave Coast. The British expansion coincided with the growth of British sugar plantations in the Caribbean and the virtually insatiable demand for sugar in Europe. Growing and harvesting the sugar required a large labour force working in a harsh climate very similar to that of the west coast of Africa. The Royal African Company quickly spotted the demand, and within a very short time the slave trade had overtaken gold mining. By 1690 the company was the main supplier of slaves to the English sugar plantations in the West Indies. Because the company was closely associated with the Stuarts, its fortunes waxed and waned in tandem with those of the restored royal dynasty. They were also tied to the success of the Dutch, who were proving difficult to dislodge from the Gold Coast. The seventeenth century was the Dutch golden age and the Stuarts fought and lost two naval wars against the Netherlands in 1664–67 and again in 1672–74. The first war, however, did lead to New Amsterdam becoming New York.

As far as slavery in America was concerned, the formation of the RAC was the real start. Because of the company's royal connections, it became official government policy to encourage the colonials to buy slaves. In 1650 there were only 300 slaves in all of Virginia. By 1700 they were being imported into the Southern colonies at the rate of a thousand a year. The end of the Stuart dynasty and the accession of William and Mary in 1688 spelled the beginning of the end for the monopoly status of the Royal African Company. In 1698 its royal charter was removed and the trade was opened to all English merchants. By 1710 the free-for-all had quadrupled the number of Africans transported across the Atlantic.

However, the biggest boost came with the end of the War of the Spanish Succession. The Europe-wide tussle over who succeeded to the Spanish throne ended with Britain as top dog. More importantly, from the point of view of the slave trade, the British were granted the much sought-after *asiento*, which gave them the monopoly on the slave trade in the British, Spanish and Portuguese colonies. The *asiento*, harnessed to British's nascent industrial revolution and the development of the plantation system in the West Indies and the Southern colonies on the American mainland, meant that the slave trade rocketed. It has been estimated that between 1713 and 1776 an average of 70,000 slaves a year crossed the Atlantic. The census of 1790 showed a slave population in the newly born United States of 697,897 out of a total population of 3,929,214. The economies of the states below the Mason-Dixon Line had become totally dependent on slave labour.

The *asiento* also spelled the beginning of the end for the Royal African Company as it enabled more and more English merchants to enter the slave trade. The company was finally wound up in 1750 but by that time the English merchant navy was so powerful that two-thirds of the Africans who crossed the Atlantic did so in English ships and continued to do so until the British banned the trade in 1807. The first English city to benefit from the slave trade was London, possibly because it was the seat of government and the Royal African Company was a government monopoly. At the start of the eighteenth century Bristol had overtaken the capital but in turn was surpassed by the north-western port of Liverpool. In 1764, Liverpool had seventy-four ships carrying slaves from Africa to America. By 1771 the number had grown to 107 and they were bigger, faster and carried more slaves than the previous generation.

Liverpool's big advantage over Bristol and London was its proximity to the industrial heartland of Manchester. Textiles, guns and cooking utensils were being churned out by the British industrial revolution, loaded onto ships in the nearby Liverpool docks, carried to West Africa, traded for slaves which were transported to the West Indies and the Southern American colonies where they were traded for sugar, rum, rice, indigo, cotton and tobacco before heading back to Britain. Each voyage was estimated to make a minimum profit of 30 per cent from slaves alone. The second leg of the voyage, which carried the slaves, became known as the Middle Passage. The money from the slave trade turned Liverpool into the greatest port in the world and what was not spent on improving the docks was invested in textile mills, coal mines, quarries, railways, foundries, steel mills, armaments factories, roads, potteries and thousands of stately homes.

Of course, the slave traders did not act alone. They rarely landed armed gangs on the African coast and physically forced Africans into the holds of their ships. Complicit in the trade were the chiefs and kings of the African continent. They would regularly raid neighbouring provinces and villages for men, women and children who would be imprisoned in European-built forts that dotted the African coast or in the smaller barracoons, usually run by the dregs of European society. In the local dialects the word for war became synonymous with slave raids. By the start of the eighteenth century most of the populations of the West African coastal communities had been decimated and the slave raiders were forced to travel several hundred miles inland to capture their prey. They were chained at the neck and ankles and marched to the coast in long lines called coffles. The same word is used to describe a long line of pack animals tied together.

Many of the captured Africans died on the march from the interior to the sea. They were the lucky ones. They avoided the horrors of the Middle Passage. The ships were small, between 300 and 400 tons. Probably the most infamous of the ships was the *Brookes* because of a diagram the captain drew showing how the slaves were packed into the hold to allow him the maximum cargo. The diagram became a major weapon in the campaign for the abolition of the slave trade. The *Brookes* weighed 350 tons and was 100 feet long and 25 feet wide at amidships. It had a total of 3,000 square feet of deck space. The diagram showed 454 slaves, which allowed six foot by one foot and four inches for each man, five foot ten inches by one foot four inches for each woman, and five foot by one foot and two inches for each boy. On one voyage the *Brookes* managed to 'tight pack' the slaves by packing them in lines between each other's knees. Another method of 'tight packing' was to force the slaves to lie on their sides rather than their backs.

There was an ongoing debate between slave captains between those who argued in favour of 'loose packing' and those who preferred 'tight packing'. Loose packers, as the phrase suggests, preferred to give the slaves more room and better food. The tight packers squeezed them into every nook and cranny. The two opposing views had one thing in common: they approached the issue in cold and calculated business terms. The loose packers maintained that their system reduced the mortality rate and enabled the captains to obtain a better price for each slave when they reached the West Indies or American mainland. The tight packers worked on a percentage basis. Yes, more Africans died, but because there were more of them aboard that meant that a greater number reached the slave markets on the other side of the Atlantic. The tight packers were in the ascendant throughout the eighteenth century. The outcome was, according to a 1788 report by the British Privy Council, that nearly half of the slave cargoes died in port, in transit or were so weakened by the rigours of the voyage that they died shortly after landing in the New World.

The minimum length of the Middle Passage voyage was three weeks. Often it was longer as the ships had to pass through the Doldrums at five degrees north and south of the equator. During the passage the slaves were brought on deck for most of the morning and early afternoon where they were fed two meals, which usually consisted of yams, rice, millet, cornmeal, salted beef and water. The men were constantly chained. The women and children were usually allowed to roam freely. The slaves were exercised by forcing them to sing and dance. If they didn't do so, they were whipped. While the slaves were on deck, the crew went below to scrub the slave quarters, which were covered with faeces, urine and bloody mucus. There were bucket latrines below deck, but it was almost impossible to reach them because the slaves were so tightly packed, manacled together in pairs and with little more than a couple of feet of headroom. The slaves had little choice other than to relieve themselves where they lay and to lie in their own filth. The result was widespread dysentery as well as smallpox, yellow fever and a host of other diseases. If a slave died, he or she was pitched overboard. If they fell ill with dysentery or smallpox they were also pitched overboard to prevent the disease spreading throughout the ship.

Most of the ships had air holes that allowed fresh air to circulate through the slave decks. Often, sails were arranged to direct the air through the holes for maximum effect. But if the ship encountered rough seas the slaves could be confined below deck for days on end. The sails were taken down and the air holes closed. The results were predictable.

It was said that a slave ship could be smelled from 5 miles away. The ships usually headed for the British West Indies. The two favourite destinations were Barbados and Jamaica. The former was a British colony from 1627 and the latter from 1650. As soon as the British sorted out the pirate problem, the two West Indian colonies became the centre of the British sugar cane industry which sprang up to satisfy the Europeans' newly discovered sweet tooth. Sugar also provided the distilled ingredient for that other favourite – rum.

Growing sugar cane was a labour-intensive industry best done on large plantations that could offer economies of scale. The conditions on those hot, humid plantations were horrific and a large proportion of the slaves quickly died from disease or exhaustion. The slave trade was required to maintain a steady flow of workers to replace the dead. Only about ten per cent of the slaves that reached American shores travelled directly from Africa to one of the thirteen colonies. The slave trading link between the West Indies and the mainland started with the founding of the colonies of North and South Carolina in 1663. The Carolinas were created by the newly restored King James II, who sold the land to eight British peers who in turn recruited plantation owners from Barbados and Jamaica to settle the territory. They came with their slaves, the plantation system and a slave trade link between the West Indies and the Southern American colonies.

The big cash crop in the Carolinas became rice, which, ironically, appears to have been introduced to the English colonies by the African slaves themselves. The success of rice and the links with Barbadian planters meant that slavery took hold in the Carolinas sooner and faster than the earlier settlement of Virginia. By 1720, two-thirds of the population were Black African slaves. The plantation owners slept uneasily in their beds at night for fear of slave revolts. Their fears were justified. In 1739 about eighty South Carolina slaves revolted under the leader of an African called Cato. The slaves decided to march to Spanish Florida where the authorities promised freedom to runaway slaves from the English colonies. On the way they set fire to several plantations and murdered white settlers. A militia was quickly formed, intercepted the escaping slaves and in a pitched battle killed most of them. Those that survived were sold to plantations in Barbados. The following year the South Carolina Legislature passed the Negro Act, which forbade the assembly of slaves and their education. It also banned the importation of African slaves for ten years because most of the revolting slaves had come directly from Africa. The Act also restricted the right of slaveholders to free their slaves and introduced penalties for harsh treatment of slaves.

Slavery, however, was not confined to below what became the Mason-Dixon line. Quaker William Penn had slaves, as did founding father Benjamin Franklin and the Massachusetts witch-hunting evangelist and medical scientist Cotton Mather. Among the Northern colonies, New York had the largest number of Northern slaves because the Dutch settled it at a time when they were major players in the slave trade. In 1700 there were 2,170 slaves in New York out of a total estimated population of 19,000. By 1770, both the slave and total populations had increased tenfold.

New York, however, was a Northern exception. The next largest slave population in 1770 among the eight Northern colonies was Pennsylvania with 5,561 slaves out of a total population of 240,057. Between all the Northern colonies in 1770 there were 49,546 slaves out of a total population of 1,103,185. Whereas in the five southern colonies there were 411,196 slaves out of a total population of 994,434. The fact is that the climate and conditions of the Northern colonies did not lend themselves to the plantation system and without the plantations there was not the same need for slaves. The relatively few slaves in the North were usually household slaves for the very wealthy or they worked as artisans in the North's growing industries. Benjamin Franklin's two household slaves were known as George and King. Franklin himself eventually became a fierce abolitionist, freed his slaves and fought for the education of all freed slaves.

That does not mean that the Northern Yankees had anything approaching clean hands. They may not have been big slave owners, but they were big in the slave trade, especially the puritanical New Englanders. The first known American ship built especially for the slave trade was the *Desire*, which rolled off the Salem, Massachusetts, shipyard in 1638. She was only 120 tons and 79 feet long and on her maiden voyage carried a cargo of Native Americans to the West Indies. They soon died and the *Desire* returned with a cargo of African slaves who survived. Thereafter, the ship confined her operations to carrying rum to Barbados and slaves to New England. The last ship to land a cargo of slaves was an American slaver in 1860.

The New England slave traders found it difficult to break into the main source of African slaves – the west coast of Africa – so they travelled around the Cape of Good Hope and broke in a new market in Madagascar. Tiny Rhode Island became the leading slave trading colony. Their ships started operating in 1652 and by the middle of the eighteenth century Newport overtook Boston as the number one source of American-built and managed slave ships. It is estimated that the Rhode

Island merchants carried 100,000 slaves from Africa to the American colonies. Several of the colony's leading citizens were heavily involved in the slave trade. They included Aaron Lopez, who founded Brown University and several libraries with money from the trade. The Wanton family provided four governors of Rhode Island and Esek Hopkins rose to become commander-in-chief of the Continental Navy. The success of the Rhode Islanders was built on their own triangular trade, which neatly avoided the mother country. The colony built rum distilleries and they would transport the rum to Africa where they would trade the liquor for slaves, whom they would carry to the West Indies where they would pick up sugar and molasses to bring back to Rhode Island to be distilled into rum. At the same time a number of industries sprang up to service the slave trade. There were the shipbuilding yards, sailmakers, rope makers and iron foundries to forge the chains and manacles, and finally the distilleries. In 1770, Samuel Hopkins, pastor of the First Congregation Church in Newport, wrote that Newport 'has been, in a great measure, built up by the blood of Africans'.

Stopping the Slave Trade

As the Americans were struggling to reconcile the high-flown ideals of the Declaration of Independence and the US Constitution with the institution of slavery, British abolitionists were taking practical steps towards the end of the practice by pushing Parliament to ban the slave trade. The primary force behind this campaign was the independent evangelical MP William Wilberforce. In 1787 he formed he formed the Society for Effecting the Abolition of the Slave Trade. The group became known as the 'Clapham Sect' because it was based in the south-west London suburb where Wilberforce and most of his wealthy friends lived. The focus was on stopping the trade between Africa and the British sugar plantations in the West Indies, but it impacted on the US as many of the West Indian planters sold their slave surplus to the American southern states. The breakthrough came in 1807 with Parliament voting to abolish the slave trade in the British Empire. You could still own slaves, you just couldn't transport them from Africa to the West Indies. The following year the Royal Navy set up the West Africa Squadron to enforce the ban on the slave trade. At its height, the West Africa Squadron employed a sixth of the Royal Navy's fleet. Between 1808 and 1860 it captured 1,600 slave ships and freed 150,000 Africans. The Americans paid reluctant lip service to suppressing the slave trade at the Treaty of Ghent that ended the War of 1812. Article 10 of the treaty committed the US to using 'their best endeavours' to fight the slave trade. In 1820 Congress passed a law declaring that any American who worked on a slave ship would be condemned as a pirate and hanged, a law recognised more in the breach than its observance. By 1840 several European and Latin American navies had joined the West Africa Squadron. The American navy was conspicuous by its absence. Slave ships continued to operate out of the States, especially New England, but no American sailors were arrested for piracy until the Civil War. The political differences between slave and non-slave states were too finely balanced to risk by cooperation with previous colonial masters.

The hope on both sides of the Atlantic was that slavery would die out as the plantations in the West Indies and America would be unable to maintain slave numbers without a steady influx from Africa. But by 1807 there were enough slaves in the West Indies and American South to enable the slave owners to replace through breeding programmes those who became ill or died. In 1823, William Wilberforce formed the Anti-Slavery Society to fight for the total abolition of slavery throughout the British Empire. In the first year of operation, 250,000 anti-slavery pamphlets were distributed. The society started its operations in London, but branches had quickly sprung up in Manchester and Edinburgh. A centrally controlled committee was established which sent out speakers around the country leading to the establishment of hundreds of abolition societies. The campaign bore fruit in 1833 when Parliament voted for emancipation throughout the empire. Wilberforce died five days later.

One of those who attended the funeral service was William Lloyd Garrison, who walked behind Wilberforce's bier. The year before the Bostonian had helped to form America's first effective abolitionist organisation, the New England Anti-Slavery Society. By 1840 the American Anti-Slavery Society had 100,000 members. They had strong support from the British who, now that the empire had been dealt with, shifted their full attention to America. British abolitionists supplied money, literature, campaign tactics and speakers. One of the most famous speakers was George Thompson, who crossed the Atlantic. His fiery rhetoric is credited with encouraging the formation of an estimated 150 local abolitionist societies. It also resulted in a backlash against the abolitionist movement. President Andrew Jackson, himself a major slave owner, attacked Thompson as a foreign troublemaker and his meetings were often marked by violent pro-slavery demonstrations. In the end Thompson was forced to flee for his life back to Britain to 'escape the assassin's knife'. Thompson returned in 1850 when he was better received as the abolitionist cause had by that time become entrenched in the North. Garrison was also attacked. The state government of Georgia placed a $500 bounty on his head to be given to anyone who captured him and brought him before a Georgia court. Various individual planters went a step further and issued dead or alive posters. On one occasion, pro-slavery demonstrators burned his effigy outside his home and nearly managed to tar and feather him. He followed Thompson's example and fled to England where he stayed for a year building more contacts with and collecting more money from British abolitionists.

The battle over slavery also had the effect of creating two African colonies for freed slaves established by Britain and America. The first was Sierra Leone, created by the British in 1787 as a home for freed American slaves that had fought with the British Army in the War of Independence. The US considered sending some of its freed slaves to Sierra Leone. Instead, in 1820, Liberia was founded by the American Colonisation Society with government aid. The move had the support of key founding fathers: Thomas Jefferson, James Monroe and James Madison. Monroe was president at the time and the capital, Monrovia, was named after him. The creation of Liberia had widespread popular support. The South wanted the removal of any freed African Americans as they feared they would spread discontent among the slaves. The North didn't want them either. They were opposed to the institution of slavery but heavily prejudiced against any Blacks in their midst. Liberia was a failure from the start. Between 1820 and 1843, 4,571 freed American slaves were transported to West Africa. By 1847, when the colony declared independence, three-quarters had died. Those who survived grabbed political control from the indigenous African population and shortly after independence passed legislation blocking them from voting or holding public office. The clash between the descendants of American slaves and indigenous Africans continues to this day and is one of the main reasons that Liberia is one of the poorest, most corrupt and worst governed states in the world. Sierra Leone is not much better, possibly worse.

The greatest fear of the Southern states was a slave revolt. This fear appeared to be justified by a four-day rebellion led by the Black preacher Nat Turner in August 1831. One hundred and twenty men, women and children were killed before the revolt was brutally suppressed. As a result of Nat Turner's rebellion, the Southern states restricted the rights of assembly among all Blacks (freedmen and slaves), banned the possession of firearms by all African Americans, criminalised the possession of abolitionist literature and required white clergymen to be present at all African American church services. The draconian measures helped to drum up support for the abolitionist cause on both sides of the

Atlantic. This reached its climax in June 1840 at the World Anti-Slavery Convention in London, which was attended by fifty-three American delegates. The US contingent was unpopular with the dominant British. For a start, there was a disagreement over whether the American female delegates would be allowed to attend. They were eventually allowed in after an intervention by Garrison, but they were segregated behind a screen and refused the right to speak. The British were also disappointed by the Americans' refusal to take stronger action in the cause of abolition. The Americans, on the other hand, were of the opinion that the difficult political problems at home required careful handling, especially as the abolitionists were at that time in a minority in the Northern states.

By 1840, both America and Britain were in the depths of a recession. It started with the Panic of 1837. The earlier part of the decade had left the British banks awash with investment capital. They put their money into the fast-expanding American South and West, especially transport links. Improved transport, however, resulted in a precipitous drop in the price of the cotton crop that was the main collateral for the planters' loans. When the Southern plantation owners defaulted, both the American and British economies suffered. The unfortunate financial effect was that there was very little money available in either Britain or America to finance the abolitionist cause and interest languished until Congress passed the 1850 Fugitive Slave Act, which required that runaway slaves be returned to their owners even if they had escaped to a free state.

The passage of the Fugitive Slave Act had two major effects. It dragged British Canada into the debate because slaves were no longer safe after crossing the Mason-Dixon line that separated North and South. The British government took a stand and provided safe refuge in Canada to any runaways who made it across the border. The Fugitive Slave Act also energised Harriet Beecher Stowe to write the abolitionist novel *Uncle Tom's Cabin*. The 1852 book has been criticised by modern commentators as an insipid melodrama that reinforced nineteenth-century African American stereotypes, but it also inspired millions to line up behind the abolitionist cause and is regarded as one of the most influential books in history, as well as the world's first blockbuster novel. In 1853, Ms Stowe made a speaking tour of Britain which raised millions for the abolitionist cause, as well as selling an astonishing 1.5 million copies of her work, far outstripping the estimated half a million copies sold in the US. The book spawned a Broadway play and a score of pro-slavery counter-novels written by Southern writers trying to portray slavery as a paternalistic, Christian institution aimed at improving the lot of African Americans. The American public was forced to choose whether it was for or against slavery, and in making the choice the country moved inexorably closer to civil war. At the height of the war, in 1862, Ms Stowe visited the White House and Abraham Lincoln is reported to have greeted her with the words: 'So you are the little lady who started this great war.'

With the end of the Civil War and the Emancipation Decree the British public lost interest in the plight of African Americans. They were free. The issue was over, done and dusted. The South's Jim Crow laws that followed the Reconstruction period and the clear American discrimination and prejudice against its Black population were of little concern to the British public until well into the twentieth century. This is mainly due to the fact that the British did not have particularly clean hands when it came to the treatment of their colonial subjects, which ranged from paternalistic to downright exploitative. Blacks, whether in Africa or the Caribbean, were particularly hard done by. For centuries they had been regarded as an inferior race and it was difficult to reverse that mindset. Until the 1950s most public places in the British colonies were segregated along the same lines as in the American South. In the Caribbean and Bahamas, the countries were ruled by London-appointed governors advised by an almost exclusively white executive committee. In South Africa, the Afrikaner descendants of the first Dutch and Huguenot settlers are blamed for apartheid. They did indeed create a legalised and systemic race-based system from 1948, but the foundations were laid by the British. The Glen Grey Act of 1894 put limits on the amount of land Africans could own. Blacks were denied the vote in 1905 and restricted to living in certain areas. The infamous pass laws were a British creation. When South Africa was given self-governing dominion status the Africans were banned from holding political office and total political control was handed to the white population. The 1923 Urban Areas Act introduced residential segregation and in 1926 Africans were banned from skilled trades.

The first cracks in the segregation policies of the American South appeared in 1954 when the US Supreme Court ruled that racial segregation in public schools was unconstitutional. The move started the civil rights movement, which eventually culminated in the 1964 Civil Rights Act that banned discrimination on the basis of race, sex, colour, religion or national origin. But for many African Americans the civil rights legislation was too little too late. They demanded positive discrimination to redress the balance of centuries of slavery and bigotry.

Despite the colonial experience and their role in the slave trade, the British regarded themselves as having a more enlightened view of race issues than their American cousins. This is partly because for centuries the British Isles had a homogenous white population. This changed after the Second World War with the end of empire and a labour shortage in the UK. The British Nationality Act of 1948 allowed the 800,000,000 subjects in the British Empire to live and work in the United Kingdom without a visa. The result was a gradually increasing influx of economic migrants: 3,000 in in 1953, 46,800 in 1956 and 136,400 in 1961. As the numbers grew, so did the opposition from the indigenous population who blamed African and Asian immigrants for strains on the welfare state and the National Health Service, plus a lack of jobs, and crime. The first attempt to restrict immigration was the 1968 Commonwealth Immigrants Act, which required immigrants to be connected by birth or ancestry to a UK national. Immigration numbers, however, continued to rise and were boosted by the freedom of movement rules after Britain joined the European Union. The perceived problems and prejudices caused by immigration were recognised as one of the main reasons for the 2016 referendum vote to leave the European Union.

The US, meanwhile, faced a problem with illegal economic migrants from Central America. In 2017 there were an estimated 10.7 million illegal immigrants in the US. Public fear of a Mexican 'invasion' was one of the main reasons for the election of Donald Trump in 2016, who promised a major crackdown on undocumented immigrants and a wall along America's southern border. The African American population, which is almost entirely descended from the slave trade, makes up 12.7 per cent of the US population in 2020. The Hispanic and Latino immigrants have overtaken them and make up 17.8 per cent. The white population is now 60.7 per cent and is predicted to be in a minority by 2050. This has helped to create a rise in the number of white supremacist groups who fear that their long-established hold on the reins of political and economic power are threatened.

The race issue that began with the British control of the slave trade and continued with the mistreatment of African Americans remains a problem and stain on the national character of both countries and another tangle of dark Anglo-American roots which helps to bind the two countries together.

7

I Believe

Nasty, Brutish and Short

It is difficult to overstate the importance of Christianity in Anglo-American history. Life was hard for 99 per cent of medieval Britons. They worked in the field for roughly fifty years and then died. There were a few joyful breaks on the way: first love, marriage, surviving children. But these were blips in a life of unremitting drudgery punctuated by disease and the death of loved ones. Their time on Earth was made bearable by the belief that there was a better life waiting for them at the end.

The vast majority of medieval Britons were illiterate and ignorant. In the twenty-first-century secular world we demand logically determined scientific proof to justify almost every decision and action. Not so then. There were no microscopes, telescopes, computers or DNA tests. The sun set. The sun rose. And there were four seasons in the year. How they occurred was a mystery which could only be explained by the existence of a higher being. Only a handful of the aristocracy could read and write. Book learning was left to the priests and for them there was only one book of any significance: the Bible. It is unsurprising, therefore, that right up to relatively modern times your average Briton spent most of his or her time thinking about and talking about Christianity and preparing for the glorious afterlife it promised. What they believed and how they believed it became a determining factor not only in British life but also in American history.

As far as Britain and America are concerned, for religion, simply read Christianity. But that in itself is a wide and all-embracing catch-all. Some claim there are more than 30,000 different Protestant denominations. Most of them consist of one or two churches and a fiery preacher, but there are at least 180 major Protestant churches in addition to the Roman Catholic Church. Christianity first reached British shores courtesy of the Romans. And then they took it away. The Romans – in common with every empire in history – eventually overreached themselves. Emperor Diocletian tried to remedy the problem in AD 185 by splitting the empire into a western half ruled from Rome and an eastern half ruled from what became Constantinople, now Istanbul. But that did not solve the problem of the Goths, Visigoths and Huns who swept out of central Asia in pursuit of the riches of imperial Rome. By the end of the fourth century they were knocking on Rome's gates, and in AD 410 the Emperor Honorius withdrew the Roman garrison from Britain to protect the heartland. He told Romano-Britons: 'Look to your own defence.'

By then the Romano-Britons (who were basically Romanised Celts) faced problems of their own in the Angles, Saxons and Jutes. The Anglo-Saxons came from modern-day Denmark, the Netherlands and north-west Germany. They were probably pushed out of their homes by the westward-marching Goths and Huns. However, no one knows for certain because Roman civilisation was little more than a veneer over traditional Celtic tribes. When the Roman troops left so did the lawyers, administrators, scribes, clergy, merchants and all the trappings of civilisation. There was no one left to protect, administer, trade, or record events. The last Roman to leave switched off the lights and England was plunged into the Dark Ages. The next 200 years is pretty much guesswork. But based on what emerged from the seventh century onwards, the tribal Anglo-Saxons successfully dislodged the Celts from England and pushed them into the western corners of the British Isles – Ireland, Wales and Cornwall. Then they started fighting among themselves and gradually carved out a series of what could loosely be called kingdoms – Northumbria, Mercia, Anglia, Kent, Wessex and others. The invaders' religion was polytheistic paganism, which means they believed in lots of different gods, none of whom were in any way connected to Christianity. Exactly which gods seems to vary from region to region but the Norse gods such as Thor and Odin were among the most familiar. There were regular animal sacrifices and the Angles and Saxons were fond of sacred places such as streams or particular trees.

This does not mean there were absolutely no Christians. Christianity never actually left the British Isles. It just wasn't practised by the Anglo-Saxons. The religion moved westward with the Celts and during the Dark Ages was centred on Ireland, which regularly sent missionaries to Wales, Cornwall and north-west England. This church had no contact whatsoever with Rome for 200 years and developed its own religious customs. There were differences over the date of Easter, the haircut of priests and monks, the baptismal service and the procedure for consecrating bishops. The biggest difference, however, was not over religious rites but power. The Roman Catholic Church was highly centralised and saw itself as the successor to the Western Roman Empire. The Celtic Church was organisationally looser as it emerged from the tribal structure of the Celts. The effect of these basic differences was a power struggle as both churches demanded the right to control the road to heaven.

Osiwu, the King of Northumbria, broke the deadlock. He called a council of the leaders from both Christian churches at the Abbey of Whitby in 664 to decide which would be the official religion in his kingdom. As Northumbria was then the dominant Anglo-Saxon kingdom, the one that won the debate would win control of souls for the rest of the British Isles. Rome won and its victory was a landmark in British and American history. If Celtic Christianity had triumphed there probably would not have been a Reformation because there would have been no oppressive Roman Catholic Church to rebel against. This would have meant no – or extremely different – Puritans, Methodists, Baptists, Quakers and Presbyterians whose oppression by the Anglican Church pushed them towards American shores.

Instead, for many more centuries Britain had a religion which was governed from a city a thousand miles away. It was a religion with its own armies, political directorate and powerful weapons such as the threat of excommunication, interdiction and the flames of Hell. Its legions of priests, nuns and monks were subject only to Church law. The Church paid no tax to the king but everyone paid ten per cent of their income to the Church. The medieval British also had to pay for baptisms, confirmations, marriages, burials and indulgences to escape purgatory, and people were encouraged to give men and land simply because it helped God's representatives on Earth. Most of all, the Roman Catholic Church was the most powerful institution in medieval Britain because it retained a hold on its claim to be the sole conduit between men, women, children, kings and God. By the fourteenth century, the Church owned roughly a third of England, making it the wealthiest landowner by far. It was powerful, and, as the saying goes, power corrupts.

Enter John Wycliffe, England's – and, by association, America's – first Protestant. He arrived on the scene only a few years after the Black Death struck Britain in 1348. Most theologians believed that the plague was sent by God to punish the wicked for their sins. Wrong, said Wycliffe. It was sent by God as a punishment for the sins of the Roman Catholic

Church. With up to half of the population dead from the plague, Britons were open to new ideas and Wycliffe's found particularly fertile ground. He not only believed that the Church hierarchy was riddled with sinners; he was opposed to the pomp and ceremony of the Romanism. Praying to saints, he argued, was a form of idolatry. Prayers for the dead, papal pardons, pilgrimages, confession, baptism, indulgences, intercessions and even the priesthood had no scriptural basis, and the Bible should be written in English so that everyone could read it instead of learning the Word of God second-hand through the only person in a parish who could understand Latin, the priest.

The people who followed Wycliffe were called Lollards, based on the Old Dutch for 'mutter', which described the sound of much of their services. For a while the Lollards captured political as well as religious influence. One of their supporters was John of Gaunt, third son of Edward III and one of the most powerful men in fourteenth-century England. Gaunt saw the Lollards as a route to securing the riches of the Roman Catholic Church for the English throne and the aristocracy. Two things changed his mind and that of the young Richard II. The first was the Peasants' Revolt of 1381. Most of the peasants were Lollards inspired by the preaching of Wycliffe and an itinerant priest called John Ball who took Lollardy to the next – and unacceptable – level of attacking the political authority of the king as well as the Roman Catholic Church.

The final straw was Wycliffe's view on transsubstantiation, which to this day is the major doctrinal difference between the Protestant and Roman Catholic churches. Rome insisted that during a church service the bread and wine is actually transformed into the body and blood of Jesus. Wycliffe said that was wrong. He instead pushed the idea that there was a 'real spiritual presence' in the sacraments but that that the body and blood of Christ did not physically change into bread and wine. The bread remained bread but was also the body of Christ and the wine remained wine but was also the blood of Christ. Later Protestants would take this a step further and argue that the wine and bread merely represented the blood and body of Christ. Anyway, Wycliffe fell out of favour and by the time of his death in 1384 had been thoroughly suppressed. But the seed had been planted. It just took nearly 200 years to start to bear fruit.

Protesting Protestants

On 31 October 1517, the German priest Martin Luther sent the Archbishop of Mainz a list of complaints about the Roman Catholic Church. Many of his points were a rehash of Wycliffe's assertions.

For good measure, Luther also nailed his ninety-five theses to the door of All Saints' Church in Wittenberg. Between the time of Luther and Wycliffe there had been a major technological development in Europe – the invention of the printing press. Almost immediately, Luther's theses were being printed and circulated out of the European print capital of Nuremberg and a pamphlet war started between the German rebel priest and opponents in the Church. One of his opponents was England's Henry VIII, who wrote a pamphlet entitled *Defence of the Seven Sacraments*. This attacked Luther and supported the Church. In return for his support, Pope Leo X gave the king and his heirs the title of 'Defender of the Faith'.

During those intervening years the Wars of the Roses had left the English body politic badly scarred and the conflict was still fresh in the public mind. In fact, there were many who disputed Henry VIII's right to the throne. For that reason, Henry believed that a male heir was essential to prevent England from slipping back into another disastrous civil war. Unfortunately, Henry's wife, Catherine of Aragon, went through seven pregnancies but only one survived to adulthood – a girl, Mary. By 1525, Catherine had reached menopause. The king was convinced that his marriage was cursed because Catherine had been married to Henry's older brother Arthur before she wed Henry. The Bible specifically forbade marrying your brother's wife. Leviticus chapter 20 verse 16 is crystal clear on the subject: 'If a man shall take his brother's wife, it is an impurity; he hath uncovered his brother's nakedness; they shall be childless.' Because of Catherine's previous marriage, Henry had sought and received a papal dispensation. But he now believed papal intervention had failed, and he was damned to be denied a male heir. Catherine claimed to her dying day that the Biblical block was inconsequential because her first marriage was never consummated. This is quite likely, because when Arthur died in 1501 they were both teenagers who had been wed for only six months. The king did not believe his queen, or chose not to, and besides, by this time (1525) he had fallen for raven-haired beauty Anne Boleyn. He wanted an annulment for political and personal reasons, with a bit of royal lust thrown in for good measure.

Annulment and/or divorce, however, were difficult in the sixteenth century. It was especially difficult for monarchs who had to consider the political ramifications alongside all the other human and legal problems that accompany a marital split. In this case the political problems proved insurmountable. Catherine was a Hapsburg who at that time ruled Spain and – through the Holy Roman Empire – most of Eastern and Central Europe. On top of that the Pope, who needed to approve the annulment, was being held captive by Catherine's nephew, the Emperor Charles V. Catherine refused to leave her throne, her nephew backed her up and the Pope had no choice but to obey the commands of his captor the emperor.

Henry was stuck. He needed the services of a first-class medieval legal eagle. He found one in the form of Thomas Cromwell, who became chief minister to Henry VIII and later Earl of Essex. Cromwell was a graduate of Cambridge, which was a hotbed of anti-Catholic sentiment (Oxford took the opposing position). Cromwell's solution therefore was simple: Henry VIII should break away from Rome and become the head of his own Church of England. This took some persuasion. Henry was not by religious inclination a Protestant. Cromwell was. But Cromwell had several aces up his sleeve. Two of them were the lack of a male heir and the king's lust for Anne Boleyn. The other was the vast wealth of the Church, which the financially hard-pressed Henry would control if he was its head.

Over a ten-year period, Cromwell – with the king's grudging approval – pushed through Parliament a series of laws that annulled the marriage of Henry and Catherine, validated the marriage with Anne Boleyn, bastardised Catherine and Henry's daughter Mary, stopped the English Church from sending money to Rome, forbade all appeals or contact with Rome, dissolved more than 800 monasteries and confiscated their wealth, and declared Henry VIII head of the Church in England. Religious differences did not end with Henry's Act of Supremacy. Religion had always been part of, but one step removed from, politics. Now it was firmly in the political arena and was to be the number one political football for at least the next 150 years, a period which included the birth of colonial America.

The English monarch now had control over his subjects' religious lives and beliefs as well as their secular world. In theory this made him all-powerful, but in practice the monarchy had over-reached itself. Henry's assumption of religious powers came at a time when the previously assumed infallibility of the Church was being increasingly questioned. By cloaking itself in a religious aura, the monarchy laid itself open to the same questioning – in the political as well as the religious sphere. While other European monarchs were growing in autocratic power, the English throne started on the long road to constitutional monarchy. There would be plenty of potholes on the road including the English Civil Wars, Oliver Cromwell, more religious dissent and a revolution in America.

One immediate positive impact of the break with Rome was that Henry VIII managed to sire a son. Edward VI was the fruit of his third marriage, to Jane Seymour (Anne Boleyn was beheaded). Edward was the first English monarch who could truly be called Protestant. His father was certainly not a Protestant; he was a Catholic who was the head of his own Catholic church. By the time Edward ascended the throne as a boy king in 1547, the teachings of Wycliffe and Luther had been added to by the likes of the French theologian John Calvin and the fiery Scots preacher John Knox. Lollardy had taken a firm hold in parts of Germany and major segments of the British court. The Archbishop of Canterbury, Thomas Cranmer, was a devout Protestant and took responsibility for ensuring that Edward travelled the dissenting path.

Unfortunately for the nascent Protestant Church in England, Edward died in 1553, just six years into his reign. If Edward had lived longer it is quite possible that a more pronounced form of Protestant Christianity would have become the official religion of England and groups such as the New England Puritans would have felt more comfortable staying at home. Edward was succeeded by his sister Mary, who had been rigidly educated as a Roman Catholic by her mother, Catherine. Henry VIII had divorced her, but Catherine was allowed to stay in England and raise her daughter. And she did, as a devout Protestant-hating Roman Catholic. During Mary's five-year reign, England returned to the Roman fold and 283 leading Protestants were burned as heretics and more than 800 fled into exile. When Elizabeth came to the throne in 1558, Rome was again renounced and the religion was switched back to the Protestant cause. This time, however, the Church of England, or Anglican Church, settled into a compromise forged by the new queen.

This did not satisfy Pope Pius V. The new English Church recognised the monarch as its head rather than the Pope. This was unacceptable. Control of the Church meant control of souls and in the sixteenth century that easily translated into political power. In 1570 the Pope issued his bull Regnans in Excelsis, which excommunicated the queen and called on her subjects to rise up against Elizabeth and assassinate her. The papal bull inspired a number of assassination attempts. In 1571 the Ridolfi Plot – named after the Florentine banker who financed it – intended to assassinate Elizabeth and replace her with her cousin Mary, Queen of Scots. The 1586 Babington Plot was pretty much the same scenario. In October 1583 John Somerville was arrested for trying to shoot the queen and in 1584 Welsh MP William Parry was arrested in her garden and later hanged. There was the Barge Plot, when an unknown marksman tried to shoot the queen while she was travelling down the Thames and hit one of her bargemen instead. Finally, there was the attack of the Spanish Armada in 1588.

Despite the numerous attempts on her life, Elizabeth I was remarkably devout, practical, tolerant and traditionally minded. She was opposed to Catholicism because she was against the control of Rome, but she was not against Catholics practising their faith as long as they did so quietly. She was raised in a church of priests, vestments and genuflections. The ritual of the Catholic Church represented a secure continuity for her, as it did for many of her subjects. So she fought to keep them against strict Calvinists such as the Puritan MP and explorer William Strickland and Archbishop John Whitgift.

Purer Puritans

William Strickland (who is credited with introducing turkey to the English diet) was the leader of the Puritans in the House of Commons, and largely due to his leadership Parliament – especially the Commons – became the focal point for anti-Catholic, anti-Pope and pro-Puritan sentiments in England. The queen managed to keep the Protestant zealots in check and followed the middle course by careful housekeeping. The Tudor government was structured so that the monarch could dispense with the services of Parliament as long as he or she didn't need money. If the monarchy needed extra cash it needed the approval of the legislature. Queen Elizabeth summoned Parliament only thirteen times in her fifty-five-year reign and each time it only met for a few months.

By the time James I succeeded to the throne in 1603, the Puritans had become strong enough that a petition signed by a thousand Puritan clergymen could be presented to James as he made his way from Scotland to London to assume his duties. Known as the Millenary Petition, it called for the end of wedding rings, a ban on surplices and the term 'priest', strict observance of the Sabbath and a ban on making the sign of the cross. James managed to fend off the petition with a promise to convene a Protestant committee to rewrite the Bible, which became known as the famous King James Version.

James I's inclination was to follow the path of tolerant moderation laid down by Elizabeth. He would have been more successful in this course if it had not been for the Gunpowder Plot, the conspiracy of Catholic rebels to blow up Parliament and James with it on 5 November 1605. It was thwarted at the last minute when one of the conspirators, Guy Fawkes, was discovered in the parliamentary cellars guarding thirty-five barrels of gunpowder. Ever since, 5 November has been celebrated with fireworks and a bonfire at which Guy Fawkes is burned in effigy while some crowds shout: 'Down with the Pope.'

The Gunpowder Plot pushed Protestant England over the edge into Catholic witch hunts. Papists were branded as murdering traitors and legal action had to be taken to protect the liberties of Englishmen, a cause which had now become inextricably linked to Protestantism. The legal action took the form of the Popish Recusants Act which barred Catholics from the law and medicine, prevented them from acting as a trustee or guardian, forced them to take a new oath of allegiance, made it high treason to obey Rome, and forced all English people to attend a service in an Anglican church at least once a year.

The Puritan-dominated Parliament was also strengthened by the king's free-spending habits. Unlike Elizabeth, James was bad at balancing the royal books. He quickly ran up debts of £600,000 that strained relations with the parliamentary holders of the purse strings. The dispute infuriated James who was a firm believer in the divine right of kings and thought that Parliament should simply rubber-stamp his God-inspired demands. Parliament, however, believed that the king's contract to rule was through them rather than a divine being. Years of the Protestant Reformation had endowed Parliament with a growing streak of political independence. James I, however, was successful at holding back the clerical demands of the Puritans and gradually the structure and doctrines of the Church of England emerged. The clergy were allowed to marry, but services were conducted by priests in vestments. The congregations kneeled to pray. There were confirmations and baptisms as in the Roman Catholic Church. Wedding rings were exchanged. In fact, the only real difference was that the head of the Church was the king instead of the Pope in Rome.

The Puritans, however, remained a potent force. By 1610 they had become a mainstream dissenting voice and as such they spawned even more radical Protestant dissenting groups. One of these groups was called the Separatists. The Puritans wanted to purify the Church of England. The Separatists, as the name suggests, thought that the Church of England was every bit as corrupt as the Roman Catholic Church and wanted to break away entirely. The Separatists were persecuted for their beliefs. Because of the close connection between religion and politics, they were seen as a threat to the state. The east of England was a hotbed of Separatist theology. And one particularly hot coal in that bed was based in the tiny village of Scrooby on the Lincolnshire, Nottinghamshire and South Yorkshire borders. Today the village is more of a hamlet with a population of little more than 300 souls. At the start of the seventeenth century Scrooby souls were holding secret church services in the home of William Brewster who occupied the local manor house. Their meetings were conducted in secrecy because, under the 1559 Act of Uniformity, it was illegal to attend church services unless the church had signed an allegiance to the Church of England. The Scrooby Separatists refused to sign any such agreement and thus faced imprisonment, fines and possibly even death.

As well as being the local postmaster, Brewster had spent some time in the Netherlands with the British Embassy there. The Dutch were at the time much more amenable to the myriad of Protestant groups, and so Brewster used his Dutch connections to move the Scrooby congregation to Leyden before the English legal net closed in on the dissenters' activities. However, they were unhappy in Leyden. It was foreign. They were unable to find suitable jobs. Their children were being corrupted. Their English identity was being subsumed into Dutch life and the long and bloody Thirty Years War was looming large on the political horizon. Back in London all the talk was of finding settlers for North America. Religious beliefs were secondary, if considered at all. What was required was a flock of people prepared to risk their lives in a new, unknown land for the benefit of rich investors. The settlement at Jamestown, Virginia, had established a beach head, and the investors – the London Company – were looking for settlers to establish themselves in the northern part of the American east coast in a place they called New England. The Separatists were unconcerned about the dangers. God would protect them. A delegation was despatched to London and they managed to negotiate a sweet deal with one of the investors, Sir Ferdinando Gorges. Each colonist was given a share equal to the share held by a British-based merchant. They had equal standing with the British merchants and could ignore their advice.

On 16 September 1620, colonists left the British port of Plymouth on two ships: The *Mayflower* and the *Speedwell*. As well as the Scrooby congregation, there were Separatists from London and Southampton, indentured servants, crew and artisans as well as 311 servants. The latter ship failed to live up to its name; it was neither speedy nor well. It sprung a leak and made it only 2.4 nautical miles to Dartmouth. The ship, laden with most of the colony's supplies, put in for repairs and the *Mayflower* continued the voyage on its own. Somewhere in mid-Atlantic, the Scrooby Separatists drew up the Mayflower Compact, which is dealt with more thoroughly in the chapter on law. Suffice to say that the compact is regarded by many as one of the foundation stones of American democracy, not so much because of what it said as because it said anything at all, at a time when most people kept their mouths shut, their quill pens in their inkwells, and did what they were told.

The decision to continue without the supply ship *Speedwell* proved to be nearly catastrophic. The colonists landed on the coast of New England at the start of winter on 9 November 1620, after a miserable sea voyage. They didn't start building their settlement at New Plymouth until Christmas Eve. Within three months half of the colony was dead and buried in the frozen ground. Initial relations with the local Poakhonet and Massachuset peoples were bad. Their first encounter involved shots being fired by both sides, arrows by the Native Americans and guns by the Pilgrims. It was not the Native Americans' first meeting with Europeans. Several years earlier a group of Englishmen had raided their village and carried off a number of the inhabitants as slaves. One of them was a Native American named Squanto who was rescued from enforced servitude by the aforementioned Sir Ferdinando Gorges. Squanto was taught English and sent back to America. On his return he discovered that his entire village had been wiped out by bubonic plague carried by Europeans.

Squanto was taken in by the Poakhonet and in the spring of 1621 he and another Native American – Samoset – established themselves as a go-between for the indigenous people and the interlopers. He persuaded the local chieftain Massasasoit that the English were a powerful force to be accommodated rather than defeated. As far as the Pilgrims were concerned, he taught them how to fertilise the soil and which crops would thrive in the New World. Squanto took on the role of diplomat. The result was the first Thanksgiving feast and a peace treaty which allowed the Pilgrims to establish roots.

The Pilgrims were sent to New England to catch fish, chop timber and gather furs that would make money for the British investors. The truth is that in the early years of the settlement they were too busy fighting for survival to focus on money-making ventures. By 1626 the merchants had more or less thrown in the towel and written off the colony as a bad investment. The colonists, however, stayed. For them religious freedom was more important than cash. They were soon joined by other dissenters who were coming under increasing pressure in England. The problem was the growing dispute between the monarchy and the Puritan-dominated Parliament. The growing divide between Parliament and Crown had as much to do with religion as the differing views on the divine right of kings. It started even before the coronation of Charles I when he married the French – and Catholic – Princess Henrietta Maria in 1625. The Puritans were strongly opposed to the match. Charles knew they would be and headed off an early clash by consummating the union before Parliament had a chance to meet. This was just the start. Henrietta Maria refused to participate in the coronation because it was a Protestant ceremony; Charles sent English ships to France to help suppress the Protestant Huguenots and entered into a secret agreement with his new brother-in-law, France's Louis XIII, to ease restrictions against Catholics.

The first year of Charles I's rule set in motion a disastrous snowball of events that eventually ended with the king being swept from the throne, his execution and eleven years of joyless and dictatorial government. It also resulted in the emigration of thousands of Puritans to America, either were fed up with arguing with the king's men, oppressed, or in search of a place where they could practise their all-consuming religion unfettered by what they regarded as the shackles of Popishness.

Practical Puritans

There was a distinct difference between these colonials and the 1620 Pilgrims. For a start, they were members of the Church of England. The original Pilgrims had separated themselves from the Church and formed their own religion. The Puritans wanted to purify their mother church by purging it of the ceremonies and traditions that it inherited from Rome. They were also Calvinists. They believed that because of Adam's original sin man was totally corrupt. Evil was behind every rock and tree and the world was a stage for a struggle between good and evil. Furthermore, they felt there was a covenant between God and man based on God's agreement with Abraham. Abraham was given salvation, but took on obligations. The idea of this covenant dominated relationships at all levels. Thirdly, the covenant was only available to the elect (i.e. themselves). not all of humanity.

Of course, the Puritans developed divisions like any group of humans. There were the Episcopalians, who were closest to the Church of England and favoured the retention of bishops; the Presbyterians, who were linked to the Church of Scotland and wanted to replace bishops with elected clergy; and the Congregationalists, who believed in the autonomy of the local church. All of them accepted the Bible as the literal word of God and almost the only written guiding influence in their lives.

Puritan families were patriarchies based on their interpretation of the Bible. The husband reigned supreme and was God's chief representative in the family unit, with women expected to be pious and obedient. The relationship between employee (or master) and servant was linked to that between a parent and child. The master of the house was expected to ensure that all servants followed the Bible's teachings and in turn the servants were educated, housed, fed and cared for on the same terms as a parent and child. Just as parents were expected to uphold Puritan religious values in the home, masters assumed the parental responsibility of housing and educating young servants. Older servants also dwelt with masters and were cared for in the event of illness or injury.

Like most people on both sides of the Atlantic, the Puritans believed in the active existence of the Devil and his ability to control souls and minds for evil purposes. Witches, they argued, were an everyday fact of life, hence the infamous Salem witch trials. But the Puritans of Salem were only following the example of their English brethren. In the 1640s Puritan preacher Matthew Hopkins took advantage of the upheaval of the English Civil Wars to declare himself 'Witch finder General'. Working with his assistant John Stearne, he travelled through the eastern English counties of Suffolk, Essex, Norfolk, Cambridgeshire and Huntingdonshire in search of the devil's disciples. Between 1644 and 1646 he is believed to have been responsible for the deaths of about 300 women. To put this figure in perspective, it is believed that just fewer than 500 English women died as a result of accusations of witchcraft between the fifteenth and eighteenth centuries.

Hopkins died in 1648, but the year before his death he published *Discovery of Witches*, which found its way across the Atlantic to the Massachusetts Bay Colony. Governor John Winthrop credited the book with being the inspiration and guiding light for the first bout of the Salem witch trials from 1648 to 1663, which led to the deaths of fifteen women and two men. The book was dusted off again for the second round of trials in 1692–93 when nineteen were executed. There were accusations of witchcraft elsewhere in colonial America but nothing on the same scale or with the same consequences. In Virginia an estimated nineteen people were accused of witchcraft. All but one was acquitted. The unlucky guilty 'witch' was imprisoned for ten years. In Pennsylvania two women were accused and quickly acquitted. The liberal-minded William Penn is alleged to have said: 'I know of no law against riding on a broomstick.' The Salem witch trials remain a permanent reminder of the dangers of religiously inspired mass hysteria and a blot on the history of Puritanism and Massachusetts. But the Puritans' and the Mayflower Separatists' strong belief in their role as agents of God led them to make major political contributions as well.

The first – the Mayflower Compact – was signed and sealed while the Separatists were still being tossed about in the North Atlantic. To truly understand the importance of the document you have to place it in context. The colonists were travelling thousands of miles from their homes and seat of government in an era when crossing the ocean was costly, dangerous and took a long time. They needed a structure to avert the danger of slipping into anarchy in the New World. But the colonists were coming from a highly structured society where almost everyone was born and died in their social class. Governance was by a handful of men largely on the basis of their birth. None of those men were available. The Compact which committed the forty-one signatories to 'agree to enact, constitute and frame just and equal laws' was a recognition that they were on their own. The thought must have been both liberating and terrifying, but the way these Englishmen dealt with it established a written foundation for independence of thought and action which eventually led to political independence.

Another important document was a sermon by the newly appointed Governor John Winthrop. Once again the words were written while the colonists were still at sea. This time the ship was the *Arabella* and the year was 1630. In his sermon, Governor Winthrop laid out his vision of what America would become. 'We shall be,' he said, 'as a city upon a hill. The eyes of all people are upon us.' This concept of America as an example for the rest of the world to follow is another key element in the American political bedrock.

John Winthrop served as governor of the Massachusetts Bay Colony continuously until his death in 1649. He ensured that the Puritan religion was at the core of the colony's initial political structures – for a time. In 1631 Winthrop required all voters to be members of a local Puritan congregation. The idea was that the government would be good because it was elected by good and righteous citizens who had in turn been elected by God. However, it soon became apparent that Winthrop's religiously motivated diktat was impractical. Within a few years non-Puritan settlers started arriving in New England and the second- and third-generation Puritans just didn't have the same enthusiasm and commitment as their forebears, or they simply moved to new lands in the untapped American wilderness. By the 1690s membership in the Puritan Congregationalist churches had plummeted to 30 per cent of the colony's population. At the same time adherents of other faiths began to appear. By 1675 Baptists, Presbyterians and Quakers were all starting to make their mark in Massachusetts. There was a general recognition, however, that the key to success in the New World meant cooperation as laid down in the Mayflower Compact. Their support, therefore, was required, so gradually the franchise was extended borough by borough to the unchurched and the landless.

Billy Penn

Massachusetts was not the only colony founded on religion. Maryland was created as a haven for Catholics and Pennsylvania was a refuge for the new religion of Quakerism. The Quakers were the religious brainchild of George Fox. Born in 1624, he was raised as a devout Leicestershire Puritan. Fox came of age at the height of the English Civil Wars when religious and philosophical ferment went hand-in-hand with political upheaval. In the case of Fox this meant going several steps further away from the Church in his ideas and practices.

The Puritans opposed many of the trappings of the Church of England which they reviled as a continuation of Roman practices. These included vestments, icons, incense and ornate music. The only practices they allowed in their services were those that were specifically mentioned in the Bible. They even banned the celebration of Christmas. They did not, however, do without ministers, religious services or, most important of all, churches. George Fox and his Quakers did. Fox preached that religious rituals should be ignored and that every person had a direct relationship with God and that God's omnipresence meant that He 'did not dwell in temples made by man'. These core beliefs led to radical political thoughts. If everyone had a direct relationship with God, then women should have equal rights; indeed, many of the early Quaker preachers were women. By the eighteenth century, the belief in this equal relationship meant that the Quakers were among the first – and leading – advocates for the abolition of slavery.

The presence of God in everyone also underpinned Quaker pacifism. There is, argued Quakers, 'that of God' in everyone. You would not kill God, so you don't kill people because of the presence of God in people. Quakers also refused to remove their hats before the king or the British nobility. The reason? All men, Quakers maintained, were created equal. Swearing an oath of loyalty to the king was also a no-no. They maintained that doing so was a breach of Jesus's commandment to avoid swearing. These religious and social beliefs migrated into the political sphere when they reached American shores. All of this was complete and total heresy in mid-seventeenth-century England, especially during the eleven years of the Puritan dictatorship from 1649–60. Consequently, the Quakers were persecuted and George Fox spent his life in and out of prison. When Charles II was restored to the throne, the persecution and imprisonment of Fox and other Quakers initially continued, but gradually conditions improved and in 1687 and 1688 Charles II's brother, James II, signed the Declaration of Indulgence, which established religious freedom in England by abolishing penal laws enforcing conformity to the Church of England. This meant that Roman Catholics and the growing number of Protestant dissident churches were free to worship – including the Quakers.

The Declaration of Indulgence was largely the result of the efforts of George Fox's disciple William Penn, the founder of Pennsylvania and probably history's most famous and influential Quaker. Penn owed his success to his father Admiral Sir William Penn, who established strong royal links when he was tasked with bringing Charles II back to England in 1660, and later, when he served directly under his brother the Duke of York, the future King James II. As expected of a keen royalist, Sir William was a devout Anglican. From his teen years, his son William was not. He initially toyed with Puritanism but eventually embraced the Quaker faith. The result was an extremely unhappy Penn household with young William being periodically disinherited and then reinstated or thrown into prison and then released after his father's intervention. In the end, the elder Penn came to respect William's iron-clad determination and strong beliefs, and shortly before he died in 1670 he wrung a promise from the king's brother, the Duke of York, that he would assume the role of royal protector for his prodigal son.

The future James II also had a financial incentive to help William Penn. The estate which the younger Penn inherited from his father included a loan to James of the then huge sum of £16,000. The two men decided to solve the problem of the Quaker heresy and the king's debt by the king's grant of 45,000 square miles west of New Jersey and north of Maryland. At the time it was the largest personal land grant in history. William Penn named the new colony 'Sylvania'. James II added the prefix 'Penn' in memory of the elder Penn. The land grant was signed in 1681. Almost immediately, William Penn was on a boat across the Atlantic. Drawing on his religious, political and legal travails back in England, and centuries of English legal tradition, he drafted a charter for his new colony which would find clear echoes in the later US Constitution. All men were guaranteed free elections, freedom of religion, freedom of thought, freedom from unjust imprisonment and a free and fair trial by jury.

Within a few years, the Quaker authorities in England and Wales were complaining that their congregations were being stripped of membership because of the flood of immigrants flowing into Pennsylvania. And because of William Penn's strong stand on religious freedom, other Protestant religions also poured into the colony from across Europe. The Quakers, however, dominated the political, social and economic life of the colony right up until the middle of the eighteenth century. Their values remained much longer.

Maryland: Religious Battleground

Maryland is generally regarded as being founded as a refuge for England's persecuted Roman Catholics. That was one of the main reasons for its creation. But the fear and hatred of Rome crossed the Atlantic and meant that the colony never became the true refuge that its founders intended. Instead it became a target for the Puritans in New England and the Anglicans in Virginia. Maryland was the brainchild of George Calvert, the first Lord Baltimore, who was Secretary of State to James I and a keen advocate of colonisation. He was an early investor in Virginia and the instigator of a failed attempt to settle Newfoundland. In 1625 he made the controversial decision to convert to Catholicism and almost simultaneously resigned his public offices. Being a Catholic was political death in early seventeenth-century England. The memories of the Reformation, the Spanish Armada and the 1605 plot to blow up Parliament were still fresh in the public consciousness and would remain so for many more years.

Calvert, however, remained close to the king, who rewarded him on his withdrawal from service with the hereditary title of Lord Baltimore. The newly created peer quickly became one of the leading Catholic figures in England and a protector of his religious brethren. In that capacity he asked the king for a land grant in America to which the unwanted English Catholics could flee. It was granted five weeks after George Calvert died in 1632. It was left to his son, Cecil – the second Lord Baltimore – to complete the task. Cecil, however, was not particularly interested in trying his hand in the American wilderness. He stayed behind at Kiplin Hall in Yorkshire to look after family affairs on the home front and defend the colony's political interests at court and in Parliament. The job of running the colony was delegated to his younger brother Leonard who was dispatched as the first governor of Maryland, named after James I's Catholic wife, Henrietta Maria.

Shortly after arriving in Maryland, Leonard Calvert clashed with the Virginian planter cum politician cum trader William Claiborne who had secured the rights to a trading post on Kent Island in the Chesapeake Bay, and, inconveniently, in the middle of the Maryland. The deal was signed the year before the king granted Maryland to Lord Baltimore. The king either knew nothing about Claiborne, or conveniently ignored him. This led to a series of battles between Virginia and the new colony of Maryland with control of the Chesapeake Bay see-sawing between the two. Land claims were ostensibly at the root of the problem, but the underlying rivalry between Catholics and Anglicans soon overtook the pursuit of mammon. Claiborne and his Virginia-based political successors could 'not be trusted' and the same sentiments were expressed by Calvert about Anglican Virginians. By the end of the seventeenth century, Kent Island was firmly under the jurisdiction of Maryland, but Virginia continued to lay claim to it right up until 1776.

Maryland had an even more difficult relationship with the Puritans to the north. They had a deeper hatred of Catholics, especially during the English Civil Wars from 1642 to 1651. It was during the war that the Maryland government passed what is generally regarded as the first American law in favour of freedom of religion. The 1649 Maryland Toleration Act promised religious toleration for all those who accepted the Holy Trinity. The Catholic-dominated Maryland Assembly did not pass the law because of a philanthropic civil rights movement or a wave of ecumenicalism. It passed the Act to protect Maryland's Roman Catholics from persecution by the growing number of Anglican and Puritan settlers.

The Calvert family had a difficult time holding on to their tenure of Maryland during the English Civil Wars and the Cromwellian Protectorate that followed it. English Catholics sided with the Royalist cause during the conflict while Parliament was dominated by Puritans. Belief in the divine right of kings found a more willing audience among the traditionally minded Catholics. The Maryland government remained devoutly loyal to the Royalist cause and all the settlers were made to swear an oath of loyalty to the king. In 1650 Maryland's Puritan settlers revolted against the Catholic Calverts, abolished the Toleration Acts and established a government prohibiting both Catholicism and Anglicanism. Catholics were also banned from holding public office.

Back in England, Cecil Calvert, the second Lord Baltimore, raised a small navy and sent it off to Chesapeake Bay. At this stage William Claiborne re-entered the fray with the help of the piratical Captain Richard Ingle, a Puritan supporting the Parliamentarian cause against Catholics. The result was the Battle of the Severn on 25 March 1655, near present-day Annapolis. The battle was the only clash of the English Civil Wars on American soil, and it occurred five years after King Charles was beheaded, though it is regarded by some as the last battle of the war. The anti-Catholic forces won and a Puritan government remained in power until 1658, when Lord Baltimore was reinstated as the proprietor of Maryland and the Toleration Acts were back on the law books. Cromwell had died that same year and Maryland had become a pawn between Puritans and those clamouring for an end to Cromwellian excesses and a restoration of the monarchy. Two years later, a monarch was back on the English throne.

But the religious differences and turmoil were far from over. Charles II was succeeded by his brother James II, whom Parliament, probably correctly, suspected of planning to return England to the papal fold. They organised his overthrow by the Dutch Protestants William and Mary. This was what the Maryland Protestants were waiting for. In 1689 they overthrew the government of Lord Baltimore and Maryland became a royal colony. The Calvert family, however, refused to give up. The fourth Lord Baltimore figured out that the root of his family's see-sawing fortunes was the conversion of his ancestor to the Catholic faith. So, in 1715 he converted back to Anglicanism and George I rewarded him by restoring the hereditary proprietorship to the Calvert family, who remained in charge of the colony's affairs right up to 1776.

Virginia Cavaliers and the Great Hodgepodge

From its very inception Virginia was religiously and politically Anglican, which is another way of saying steadfastly tied to the Church of England and the Crown. It was and remained a preserve of the younger sons of the British nobility and landed gentry who used their connections to carve out huge tracts of land from which they could create fresh fortunes. When the Massachusetts settlers crossed the Atlantic they took with them Puritan preachers. When the Calverts sent their people to Maryland they were accompanied by Catholic priests. The Virginians, the first English people to settle in North America, brought Anglican priests and made certain that everyone who accompanied them was a member of the Church of England.

Between the initial Jamestown settlement in 1609 and 1624 when the founding Virginia Company went bust, the London backers paid for twenty-two ministers to be sent to the colony. In 1616, when there were only 350 settlers, there were four Anglican priests to minister to their souls. The company's original charter of 1607 declared that one of the company's main aims was to propagate the 'Christian religion to such people as yet live in darkness and miserable ignorance of the true knowledge and worship of God' – that is, the Native Americans.

After Virginia became a royal colony in 1624 Anglicanism was named as the colony's official religion and taxes were levied to support it. Both North Carolina and South Carolina – whose dominant settlers were drawn from the same genteel English stock as Virginia – followed suit in 1680 and 1710 respectively. In 1640 there was an attempt to establish a Puritan settlement in Virginia south of Jamestown. A group of about seventy Puritans wrote to a New England preacher asking him to join them. He did, but was gone by 1650. Virginia's Governor William Berkeley threw out not only the Puritan ministers but the entire congregation. They fled to Maryland where they became a headache for the Calvert family.

Although Anglicanism got off to a flying start in the South, it quickly faltered. In 1661 only ten of Virginia's fifty parishes actually had a resident clergyman. The reason was simple: the initial crop of priests had been drawn to the New World by the lure of riches just like every other settler, but as reports of disease, hostile Native Americans and early graves filtered back to England, the clergy became increasingly reluctant to leave their comfortable British parishes. By the 1680s the priest shortage meant that entire parishes of children were being denied the basic sacrament of baptism. This vacuum was filled by other up-and-coming denominations such as the Baptists, who were founded by John Smyth in 1609, and the Methodists, who emerged in the first half of the eighteenth century out of the teachings of John and Charles Wesley. The latter were given their start in the colonies by General James Oglethorpe, the first Governor of Georgia, who invited the Wesleys to his colony in 1735. By the time Charles Wesley died in 1788 there were an estimated 500 Methodist preachers in the nascent United States.

The Methodists, Baptists and other Protestant sects were successful partly because they had no political connections and partly because they were prepared to go anywhere and preach in the open air. The Anglican priests, in contrast, insisted on all the proper religious trappings including vestments, silver plate and a sturdy church building. They were also seen as politically linked to the British Establishment. The head of the Church of England was the monarch who, on the advice of Parliament, appointed all the bishops. They in turn wielded direct political influence by sitting in the House of Lords.

Another part of the appeal of the non-conformist sects was that their clergy were less corrupt than those of the Church of England. When it came to power, money and influence, there was little difference between the medieval Roman Catholic Church and the Church of England. In fact, if anything the Anglican institution of the late seventeenth and early eighteenth century was more dissolute than its earlier Roman counterpart. Some of the English parishes had large estates attached to them which provided the incumbents with handsome incomes. The livings for those parishes were bought and sold like any other commodity. Often the priest (or vicar) never lived in the parish to which he was assigned, instead employing a curate to look after parish affairs while he spent his time enjoying London fleshpots or touring the Continent.

The colonial settlers outside of the South had fled England to escape from what they perceived to be an amoral and scandalous Church. It is because of this that they so vehemently opposed one of the religious demands of the Anglican-dominated South – the appointment of a Church of England bishop for North America. Such an appointment, argued the Puritans in New England, the Quakers in Pennsylvania, the Dutch in New York and the Catholics in Maryland, would curtail their hard-won religious and political freedoms and undermine their reasons for leaving the comforts of England for the dangers and uncertainties of America. Throughout the colonial period, North America (including Canada) came under the auspices of the Bishop of London, who also argued continuously for the appointment of a North American bishop. This was continuously blocked by opposition from the northern half of the eastern seaboard. As John Adams, the second US president, wrote, 'the apprehension of episcopacy' contributed as much as any other cause to the American revolution: 'The objection was not merely to the office of a bishop, though even that was dreaded, but to the authority on which it must be founded.'

The Anglican Church became a top target for patriots during the War of Independence. An estimated 75 per cent of the clergy were forced to flee back to England or Canada. The royal coat of arms which decorated many churches was torn down and a number of churches were burned. The Anglican Church in America, which became the Episcopal Church, took decades to recover and has ever since been associated with America's Establishment forces in the same way the Church of England is linked to political conservatism in Britain.

One of the biggest blows to the Anglican Church, and by association British political authority, was an evangelical movement which swept both colonial America and Britain in the 1730s and 1740s. It was known as the 'Great Awakening' in America and the 'Evangelical Revival' in Britain. It started almost simultaneously in New England and Britain and both sides of the Atlantic fed each other's fresh brand of emotional religious revival.

The main figures were British-based Methodist preacher George Whitefield, a follower and contemporary of the Wesley brothers, and Jonathan Edwards and Gilbert Tennent in Massachusetts. Whitefield pioneered open-air preaching with gatherings in Wales and within a few months was preaching to London crowds numbering in the tens of thousands. In 1738 he followed in the footsteps of the Wesleys and repeated his successes in Georgia. The following year he returned to America and preached primarily in the middle colonies and New England. Tennent and Edwards meanwhile had started in 1734 by laying a heavy emphasis on a return to the basic Calvinist theology of the early Puritans. They gave particular prominence to followers forming an emotional and personal religious experience. This emphasis on the individual had both a religious and political consequence. Followers turned their back on formal religious structures in both the Anglican churches of the South and the Congregational churches of New England. In the latter region, there were ninety-eight church schisms as a result of the Great Awakening.

Politically, the Great Awakening is credited by some historians with contributing to the general social and philosophical atmosphere that led to the American Revolution. Breaking with the Church made it easier to break with the homeland. On top of that, the evangelists' emphasis on personal relationships with God led the colonials to place greater importance on individual liberties. Revivalism in England eventually failed to penetrate the brick wall of the Established Church. But in America – where the concept of religious freedom was already a fact of life – it helped to create the country's rich and intricate religious tapestry.

The founding of America coincided with the Reformation and the English Civil Wars. The Cromwellian rule which followed was the result of a religiously fuelled political revolt. In the heady mix of the times it spawned dozens of different Christian sects in England, all of whom claimed a special relationship with God. When the monarchy was restored there was a limited tolerance of the new religions but dominance was allotted to the Church of England and Anglicanism. Complete freedom of religion could only be found across the sea in America. Seekers, Ranters, Antinomians, Baptists, Lutherans, Methodists, Seventh Day Baptists, Quakers, Puritans, Separatists, Catholics, Soul Sleepers, Adamites, Diggers, Levellers, Anabaptists, Mennonites, Behmenists, Muggletonians, and many others made the journey across the Atlantic. When they arrived in colonial America the impetus that drove them to split from their religious roots also drove them to continue to multiply through division, with each new branch renewing the original fundamentalism that motivated the first pilgrims.

Never the Twain

The strength of religious observance and conviction is one of the biggest differentiators between America and Britain. According to a survey by the British Humanist Association in 2014, only 41.7 per cent of the

British population identified as Christians; only 16.3 percent belonged to the Church of England; 10 per cent are regular churchgoers; 3 per cent regard themselves as 'seriously religious'; and 60 per cent said they were not religious at all. In the US, a similar survey by the Pew Research Centre in 2013 reported that 80 per cent of the American population regard religion is an important part of their lives, 37 per cent go to church every week and a quarter of Americans believe in the literal word of The Bible (the world was created in seven days, it is about 6,000 years old, Adam was moulded by God from clay, etc.). The differing attitudes towards religion have a huge impact on the politics and cultures of both countries. For instance, Britain and America are often opposed on issues such as capital punishment, abortion, gay rights, medical cloning and policies towards Israel. Probably the main reason for the continuing strength of religion in America is that it is quite simply a major part of the country's historical DNA. Religious dissenters fled England in search of religious freedom and the quest for freedom is at the core of the American psyche. The wide range of Christian religions also created a highly competitive free market in religion, which drove Americans to make a choice and then to justify it with religious zeal. In contrast, the British state-run Church of England acted as a dead hand on piety. The British clergy became corrupt and inextricably linked to the conservative political establishment. Bishops sat in the House of Lords and were appointed by the government on the basis of their political leanings. Nepotism was rife. More than half of the priests were appointed by the local aristocracy who chose their relatives who, in many cases, used substantial incomes from their parishes to employ curates to run the churches so that they could indulge in the London social scene or fox hunting.

While British religion started a long period of ossification after the War of Independence, the Americans started what has been called the 'Second Great Awakening'. This wave of post-independence evangelism was noted for revivalist or 'camp meetings' which became a regular feature of American evangelical services. The meetings had their roots in the eighteenth-century Scottish Presbyterian 'communion season' or 'Holy Fair', when Presbyterian ministers would travel to the remote Scottish Highlands where they would conduct a week of sermons that concluded with a communion service. The format was ideal for reaching the American frontiers and the first recorded instance in the US was in June 1800 at the Red River Meeting House in Logan County, Kentucky. Only a few hundred attended this meeting, but up to 10,000 are believed to have travelled to the second revivalist meeting at Cane Ridge, Kentucky – roughly 10 per cent of the state's population at the time.

Cane Ridge became the religious pattern for American revivalist meetings for decades. It was organised by the Presbyterians but there were also clergy from Baptist, Methodist and other churches. There was usually one large physical structure but simultaneous meetings would be held outside. The services were punctuated with hymns, public conversions and confessions, eye-rolling, fits, healing sessions and loud sermons focused on the sins of the congregation. The denominations that encouraged the revivals believed in man's spiritual equality before God, which led them to recruit members and preachers from a much wider social class than was the case in England. The preachers were called 'circuit riders'. They would travel a frontier circuit armed with little more than a Bible, stopping in remote communities to organise a week-long revivalist service. For many of the frontier communities this was the only church service they might attend all year and they might come from a hundred miles or more to practise their religion. The camp meetings also became a major event in the social and business calendar of the American frontier as it might be the only time that the far-flung communities met and mingled. The preachers relied entirely on the collection plate for their income. The result was that the travelling clergy became increasingly entrepreneurial, and they quickly realised that fiery sermons and saved souls converted into hard cash.

Although the Church of England was much more staid in its religious observances, the same could not be said of the British branch of dissenting religions such as the Methodists, Quakers, Baptists and Presbyterians. They provided almost all of the Bibles, hymnals and religious tracts as well as a significant number of the early circuit riders to the American frontier. The slavery issue, however, divided British and American churches in the period between independence and the American Civil War. The British found Americans' support for slavery unforgivable. They were particularly upset by the Southern and Western states' use of Biblical verses to justify their treatment of African Americans. Their opinion of the Northern states – whom they regarded as turning a blind eye to the evil of slavery – was only slightly higher. Religious relations across the Atlantic improved after the Civil War, but by then the evangelical revivalist approach to Christianity was firmly entrenched in American society it would remain so – with its highs and lows – to the present day.

As already stated, one of the main reasons the Puritans fled to America was to escape the restrictions of the state-supported Anglican Church. They were Calvinists who believed in a personal relationship with God without the interference of bishops and politicians. Ironically, they ended up with a state-supported Congregational Church in New England. Right from the start, in colonial Massachusetts only its members were allowed to vote and it was supported by the taxpayers whether they were members or not. It was until 1689, when the colony's charter was changed, that non-Congregationalists were allowed to vote, although they were still subject to property qualifications, and the taxpayers continued to pay the running costs of the Congregational Church. This system was extended to include Connecticut and New Hampshire and continued after the revolution. Not surprisingly, non-Congregationalists felt that they were discriminated against under Article Six of the Constitution, which says that 'no religious test shall ever be required as a qualification to any office or public trust under the Constitution' and under the first amendment guaranteeing freedom of religion. In 1801 Baptists in Danbury, Connecticut, wrote to newly elected President Thomas Jefferson complaining that their state's support for Congregationalism involved an inherent bias against other churches and that 'no man ought to suffer in name, person or effects on account of his religious opinions (and) that the legitimate power of civil government extends no further than to punish the man who works ill to his neighbour'. Jefferson wrote back supporting the Danbury Baptist Association and confirmed that the US Constitution established a firm 'wall of separation between church and state'. The Congregational Church was eventually disestablished in Connecticut in 1818 and in New Hampshire a year later. Massachusetts did not follow suit until 1833.

Jefferson's letter was not the first – or last – word on the issue of separation of Church and State. James Madison, the man regarded as the 'father of the Constitution', and a close friend of Jefferson, tried and failed to insert a clause in the Constitution clearly stating the separation of Church and State. In the absence of a clear constitutional directive, Jefferson's interpretative letter has been used as the legal benchmark in successive Supreme Court and congressional decisions. The first battle came just as the Civil War came to an end. In 1864 a group of eleven Protestant churches formed the National Reform Association to campaign for a constitutional amendment which unequivocally declared the US 'a Christian nation'. The proposal was really aimed at stemming the late nineteenth-century immigration flood, but it won broad public support on religious grounds as well. It did not, however, win support in Congress. The House of Representatives threw it out at the committee stage.

The failure of the National Reform Association to win Congressional backing was a setback for the 'Christian nation' fundamentalists. But the 1925 Scopes Monkey Trial was a disaster. At issue was the teaching of evolution in Tennessee's public high schools, which was banned by the state's Butler Act. The newly formed American Civil Liberties Union had been searching for a science teacher to challenge the state. They found him in the form of Jonathan Thomas Scopes. To lead the prosecution of Scopes, the state signed up William Jennings Bryan, three times a presidential candidate and, since 1920, the leader of the anti-evolution fundamentalist Christian movement. Opposing him was Clarence Darrow, the most prominent trial lawyer of his day and an avowed agnostic. Scopes and Darrow lost, but it was a pyrrhic victory for the fundamentalists. The trial was reported by newspapers across the country. Bryan's religious arguments were shattered and the judge was exposed as biased. The guilty verdict was appealed to the state Supreme Court, which upheld all the main points of the conviction but managed to throw out the case on a legal technicality because they found it an embarrassment to Tennessee's reputation. William Jennings Bryan died suddenly five days after the trial. His death left a void in the leadership of the fundamentalist movement. This, combined with the publicity of the trial and an increasing interest in the benefits of science, put the American fundamentalist movement on the back foot for nearly half a century. The Butler Act, however, remained on the Tennessee statute books until 1967 and creationism is still taught in fourteen American states.

America's evangelicals came storming back in the 1970s. There were several reasons for this revival: the 1973 Supreme Court decision *Roe v. Wade*, which legalised abortion; a backlash against the liberal counter-culture of the 1960s; and a patriotic kick back against the anti-war demonstrations of the Vietnam era. Abortion became a touchstone for what was quickly termed the 'Christian Right', but the other two issues were vital in allying the evangelical cause with conservative political values. In 1979 Baptist Pastor Jerry Falwell explicitly linked evangelicals to political activism with the formation of the 'Moral Majority'. At the same time, Paul Weyrich of the Free Congress Foundation went about embedding the Moral Majority in the Republican Party. The turning point was Falwell's endorsement of Ronald Reagan in the 1980 presidential elections. With Falwell's backing, Reagan secured two-thirds of the evangelical vote and the alliance between Republicans and the Christian Right was sealed. The leaders of the evangelical movement had proven that they could deliver votes to politicians who backed their policies. Their large base of activists was driven not by support for a set of political values but a powerful, deep-seated and infallible belief backed by the word of God. Evangelicals did more than provide a large bloc vote. They were a coalition of activists who were prepared to print and distribute leaflets, make phone calls, contribute cash and knock on doors because they believed that supporting the Republican Party was God's work.

By the 2016 election, the link between the Republican Party and the Christian Right had become so strong that it was inconceivable that the party could win a presidential election without the endorsement of the Christian Right. It was thus surprising to many that Donald Trump – the thrice-married, self-confessed playboy who rarely attends church – won the overwhelming support of America's evangelical movement. He did not start off that way. During the primaries he was garnering only about a third of the Christian vote. But at a September 2016 meeting in Trump Towers, the Republican nominee persuaded a key group of evangelical leaders that he would be their man in the White House. In 2016 Donald Trump received 81 per cent of the white evangelical vote, which represented a bloc vote of approximately 23 per cent of the electorate. At the end of 2019, 90 per cent of avowed evangelicals opposed the impeachment of President Trump and half of them believed that he had been sent by God.

The Christian Right's policies extend beyond domestic issues to a strong pro-Israeli position fully supported by President Trump. The evangelical support for Israel has a Biblical foundation. The Old Testament is clear that the Jews have been chosen by God to rule over Israel. Furthermore, many evangelicals claim that the re-establishment of the state of Israel will be followed by a major battle at the ancient Israeli site of Armageddon that will end with the Second Coming of Christ. Trump's pro-Israeli policies such as recognition of Jerusalem as the Israeli capital and support for West Bank settlements was judged by many on the Christian Right as hastening the Second Coming. According to a May 2018 *Washington Post* survey, 36 per cent of Americans believe the Bible is the literal word of God and therefore should be accepted without question. Some 59 per cent of Americans accept support for Israel because of the Armageddon prophecy.

8

British Disasters that Made America

Why Immigrate?

Immigration, in the form of mass migration or flights from war, persecution or poverty, has always been a determining factor in history. Prehistoric humans moved when they had depleted the local stock of game and berries or depleted the soil through agriculture. The Jews can boast of the earliest recorded forced migration when famine forced them out of Palestine and into Egypt. Four centuries later they fled persecution and slavery back to Israel. In fact, the Jews are history's longest refugee story. Their expulsion from Jerusalem in AD 70 started centuries of wandering. Through the medieval period and beyond the Jews have been expelled from England, Spain, Lithuania, Poland, Portugal, Bohemia, Italy, Bavaria and Ukraine, as well as suffering legal discrimination and massacres elsewhere. At the turn of the twentieth century they were subjected to pogroms in Russia and after that came the Holocaust.

Natural disasters have also played a major role in the world's immigration story. Famine on the Russian steppe is a likely factor in pushing the Huns and Goths to the gates of Rome. The Angles and Saxons are believed to been prodded across the English Channel by continuing pressure from the east. And, of course, the Celtic tribes that remained in England after Roman abandonment were forced into Ireland and Wales by the Angles and Saxons.

The modern world remains vulnerable to the same pressures. The Palestinians have been pushed out of their homes by Jews returning to what they believe is their God-given homeland. War in Syria forced millions to seek refuge in Europe. Creeping desertification and the bright lights of Paris, London and Rome have driven millions of Africans to risk their lives crossing the Mediterranean in flimsy, overcrowded and unseaworthy craft. Persecution of Myanmar's Rohingya Muslims has led to hundreds of thousands fleeing across the border to sanctuary in Bangladesh. Gang warfare, civil wars and poverty have played their part in dislodging Latin Americans from their Mexican and Central American homes and set them on the road to a free and stable United States. At some time in the next few decades, the 53,000 residents of the American-owned Marshall Islands are expected to arrive in the US as the rising waters of climate change claim their Pacific homes.

For the most part, immigrants don't want to move. They don't want to abandon familiar certainties, family, friends, and the safety net of their culture for the uncertainties of an unknown world. Some may have been seduced by Hollywood-inspired promises of a better life or the glossy travel brochures of Europe. But by and large they would rather stay at home. When they do move they often try to compensate for their cultural loss by recreating the culture of their homelands in the new land. They mix with people from their own country. They speak their mother tongue among themselves, cook meals that their mothers and grandmothers made, practise the religion of their ancestors and, if possible, import the laws and customs of their homelands. It is, for example, almost impossible to find an American abroad who fails to celebrate Thanksgiving.

The British in America were no exception. In fact, in many ways, they wrote the ultimate immigration rule book. After no more than a desultory attempt at peaceful coexistence with the Native Americans, they set about supplanting the existing residents and importing en masse British laws, customs, beliefs, society, language, religion and culture to the New World. New England was called New England for a reason. The men and women who made the journey would have preferred, just like their ancient and modern counterparts, to have stayed home. They risked their lives to cross the Atlantic and set up home on the other side of the ocean. To start there was the sea voyage, which could quite easily end with the ship sinking or disease striking you dead before you reached American shores. Once in America, the natives could be distinctly unfriendly. In the Second Powhatan War in 1622, a third of the struggling Virginia colony was wiped out by Native Americans on a single day in March. If the natives didn't get you, then disease would. Yellow fever, cholera, malaria, and dysentery were all rampant in the colonies. There was also the problem of starvation. In 2013 archaeologists discovered signs of cannibalism among the Jamestown colonists. In the winter 1609/10 all but sixty of the original 500 Virginia colonists died of starvation or disease. In fact, it was not until the turn of the eighteenth century that the number of colonists being born and surviving to a reasonable age was greater than the new arrivals from abroad.

So what was happening in Britain that made the American colonials risk their very lives in a disease-ridden land far from home and inhabited by hostile natives? What drove them from the sanctuary of familiar hearth and home?

'Bad World for Poor People'

Big problems and opportunities started with the bubonic plague. The disease reached British shores in June 1348. Within eighteen months about 40 per cent of the population of England and Wales were dead. That was the first and worst of the outbreaks of plague. There were more to come. Between 1348 and 1665 there were nearly forty plague outbreaks, reducing the population between 10 and 20 per cent each time they struck. They did not stop until the Great Fire of London reduced the capital to ash and presented the unique opportunity of rebuilding the city with an underground sewage system, which banished the disease-carrying rats to a life as troglodytes.

Dead bodies, abandoned villages and overcrowded cemeteries were not the only consequence of the Black Death. The plague also heralded the beginning of the end of the feudal structure, weakened the political stranglehold of the Roman Catholic Church, and set in motion social and market forces which had a later effect on the settlement of America. For a start, the Church took a big hit. Worshippers crammed into pews to pray for their lives only to continue dying. It became starkly apparent that the Church could do nothing to save their earthly lives and this raised doubts about Catholicism's soul-saving abilities, which in turn led to the rise of alternative Christian beliefs such as those of the fourteenth-century Lollards. The power of the Church was further damaged by the fact that many of the plague's victims were treated in monasteries, which performed the medieval role of primitive hospitals. Thus the numbers of tending clergy were depleted more than any other sector of society and never again reached their earlier level.

The economic consequences were even greater as inevitable market forces mobilised to the fill the vacuum left by the collapse of a social and economic structure. The feudal economy relied on large numbers of low-paid peasants and serfs legally tied to a manor and working at labour-intensive agricultural jobs. The loss of half the workforce meant that the nobility had to pay more to those who remained. For the first time in history, English workers had bargaining power. However, it took a while for those at the top to realise it. The king kept on fighting the Hundred Years War with France despite the effects of the plague. With a much-reduced population he had to increase taxes to pay for the war, which led to the 1381 Peasants' Revolt. The labour shortage also spelled the end of serfdom, although it was not officially gone until Elizabeth I decreed its end in 1574. The aftermath of the plague started the English poor on the road to thinking that there must be something better than working for the lord of the manor until you dropped.

The consequences of the plague also forced landowners to adapt to changed economic circumstances. With fewer workers they needed to devise ways of exploiting the land with fewer people. Early medieval English agriculture – which represented 90 per cent of the economy and employed 90 per cent of the people – was mainly arable and based on the open field system. Individual serfs and/or peasants each farmed a strip or strips of land which were tied to a manor and which were situated in an open field. Although individuals were responsible for their own separate strips, there was a communal cooperation involving crop rotations and fallow fields. Whether the crops were vegetables or grains, production was labour intensive.

The answer that the landowners came up with was to switch from producing crops to raising animals, in particular sheep, whose wool was sold to Dutch merchants. The damp, cold English climate produced superior wool, which was soon in demand throughout Europe and led to an economic boom in the sheep-producing areas. Sheep needed to be kept in fields that were enclosed, either with stone walls or hedges, completely altering the agricultural landscape. The wool boom actually started more than a century before the Black Death, but the plague significantly speeded up the trend from arable to pastoral farming.

By 1400 things started to pick up again. Although rats kept spreading disease in unsanitary living conditions every twenty years or so, the population reductions were never again as big as they were in the mid-fourteenth century. The increased wool production brought in cash, which meant that there was more money to go around in a reduced population that required less food. The 1400s were generally considered a golden era for the common folk of England. But things started to change again in the 1500s. Basically, the good times had become too good. During the Tudor years the population grew by 25 per cent and there was a growing number of vagrants who were forced off the land by to make room for the more profitable sheep. Henry VIII's dissolution of the monasteries did nothing to help. The religious houses had played a major role in providing housing and work for the poor. On top of that, the monks themselves were made homeless. The number of vagabonds wandering the highways and byways of England rose exponentially. It has been estimated that in the city of Norwich alone, 25 per cent of the population required poor relief. As historian R. H. Tawney observed, 'The sixteenth century lives in terror of the tramp.'

The government response to the poverty problem involved both carrot and stick. The reigns of Henry VIII and his young son Edward VI leaned more towards the stick approach. Vagrancy was dealt with particularly harshly as the vagrants (or vagabonds) often turned to crime to survive. In a throwback to earlier times, vagrants when first apprehended were sent back to the parish of their birth where they were either whipped or put into stocks. For a second offence an ear was cut off, or, as was the case during the reign of Edward VI, they were branded on the chest with a letter 'V'. A third offence landed them in prison or, in some cases, on the gallows. During Elizabeth I's reign the carrot approach was employed more often. There was a greater acceptance that poverty was a social condition rather than a result of lapsed morals or divinely ordained. Gradually, a series of poor laws were passed helping the sick, disabled and those who had fallen on hard times. These culminated in the 1601 Poor Law, which decreed that every parish had to collect money from its citizens to help the poor. The poor were herded into workhouses, where, in return for food and shelter, they provided free labour. It was an improvement, moving the poor off the streets, but it did not end the poverty brought about by a surplus of workers.

This excess of labour fed the colonisation of America in the seventeenth century. The London-based merchants with stakes in America raided the workhouses and even the prisons for men prepared to risk their lives in the new colonies. They were mainly agricultural labourers who would be assigned to a master as an indentured servant for anywhere between four and twenty years. As indentured servants they were practically treated as slaves. In seventeenth-century Virginia half of the immigrant population was indentured servants. They had to be desperate men and women. The chances of survival in the New World were slim. For example, between 1607 and 1624 about 30 per cent of the workforce died every year from dysentery, typhoid, malaria or yellow fever. It was not until the end of the seventeenth century that indentured servants from England were replaced by slaves from Africa. In the eighteenth century, Georgia's founder James Oglethorpe turned to Britain's overcrowded debtors' prisons to populate his new colony with the 'worthy poor'.

The English Civil Wars

There is nothing quite like a war for displacing people and forcing them to search out new places to resurrect shattered lives. Civil wars are particularly useful in that respect because people are forced into supporting one side or the other. When one side wins it invariably takes revenge on the other, providing another good reason for the defeated faction to look elsewhere. Seventeenth- and eighteenth-century England, Scotland, Wales and Ireland were spattered with these home-grown conflicts. The biggest and most dramatic were the English Civil Wars that were conducted in two parts between 1642 and 1649. It cost the life of one king and about 100,000 other lives. It also resulted in an estimated 50,000 making the dangerous 3,000-mile journey across the Atlantic – either voluntarily or as transported prisoners.

Remarkably, it is estimated that between 10 and 25 per cent of the population of the north-east returned to England during the civil wars to fight for the Puritan and Parliamentary cause against the Royalists whom they felt had persecuted them and forced them to seek refuge in America. In 1639 the Puritan minister Richard Mather christened his son Increase to mark the rising population of Massachusetts. Two years later, a second son was named Return to denote the growing number of colonists returning to the mother country. Among those who returned was David Yale, whose son Elihu endowed a college in New Haven without ever returning to America. And in 1645, the nephew of Massachusetts governor John Winthrop, George Downing, returned to fight for Cromwell's army. He eventually ended up a successful London property speculator whose building projects included one of the world's most famous roads – Downing Street. Edward Winslow, who is credited with writing the story of the first American Thanksgiving, left in 1640, never to return to New England.

As discussed, Charles I was a strong believer in the divine right of kings as set out by his father James I in a speech to Parliament in 1610:

[The state of monarchy] is the supremest thing upon earth, for kings are not only God's lieutenants upon earth and sit upon God's throne, but even by God himself they are called gods. There be three principal [comparisons] that illustrate the state of monarchy: one taken out of the word of God, and the two other out of the grounds of policy and philosophy. In the Scriptures kings are called gods, and so their power after a certain relation compared to the Divine power. Kings are also compared to fathers of families; for a king is truly *parens patriae* [parent of the country], the politic father of his people. And lastly, kings are compared to the head of this microcosm of the body of man.

This statement of belief was not new. It predated the Romans and there are a number of Biblical references to support its religious roots. The belief was still widely held through England, but the middle-class gentry were beginning to doubt it in tandem with their break from the Catholic Church.

Despite his outdated views, Parliament had a reasonable relationship with the first member of the Stuart dynasty to sit on the English throne. His son was a different matter. For a start, Charles I was a High Church Anglican (or Arminian) who married a French Catholic princess and sent troops to support the French king against Protestant Huguenots. All of this rankled with the strict Puritan-dominated Parliament. Charles I decided it would be easier to rule without the legislators so he dissolved Parliament in 1629. It remained dissolved until 1640, when lack of funds and a war with Scotland forced the king to summon it anew to ask for funds.

The king did have other sources of revenue. There was the income from his own land plus royal fines and special taxes involving merchant and naval ships. But these funds were limited. If large sums were required then the consent of Parliament was needed and problems with Scotland – the Bishops' Wars – required large sums. When Parliament was recalled it refused to release the necessary funds unless the king agreed to certain demands such as the right for Parliament to be convened at least every three years, parliamentary control of ministers and the end of the king's right to dissolve it. Parliament also demanded that its approval was required for all taxes and that taxes imposed directly by the monarch were illegal. All this was too much for Charles, who in January 1642 sent 400 men to Westminster Hall to arrest his five leading opponents in the House of Commons. They successfully fled, protected by the Speaker of the House. The stage was set for war.

Charles I officially mustered his army in August 1642 after the garrison at Hull refused to let the monarch enter the city to equip his forces. Simultaneously, Parliament was raising an army of 10,000 volunteers under the Earl of Essex, Robert Devereux. The first pitched battle was fought at Edgehill on 23 October 1642. It was quickly followed by a clash at Turnham Green outside London and the king was forced to retreat to Oxford, which became his headquarters for the duration of the war. Geographically, the war started with the Parliament forces in London, the south and the east. The king initially held the north, Wales and the west of England. Gradually he was pushed out of the north and south Wales and most of the West Country except for the Royalist strongholds of Devon and Cornwall.

The Scots played a vital role in the war, switching sides at key moments. The Scots were divided by royalists led by the Marquis of Montrose and Presbyterian Covenanters who had enjoyed a loose political control of Scotland since 1639 and were generally sympathetic to the parliamentary cause. The Bishops' Wars started because the king wanted to impose his High Church Anglicanism on Scotland as part of a plan to unite the two countries. Scottish opposition taught him the folly of his ways. So, as soon as fighting broke out, he promised the Covenanters that he would impose Presbyterianism on the English. This, of course, only strengthened popular support for the Parliamentarian forces. When the English Royalist forces were defeated, the king surrendered to the Covenanters who then turned on Charles by handing him over to the Parliamentarian forces in 1645. This ended the first phase of the English Civil Wars, but more was to follow.

Almost as soon the Scots had handed over the king they started falling out with the Parliamentarian forces over Parliament's refusal to introduce Presbyterianism in England and fears that the victors would force political union on Scotland. The consequence was an invasion by the Scottish Covenanters to rescue the king they had just handed over to his enemies. They were defeated by Oliver Cromwell's New Model Army at the Battle of Preston. Cromwell went on to conquer Scotland and sent thousands of Scots to the Caribbean, Virginia and the Carolinas to work in the fields as indentured servants – the start of the Scottish migration to America.

The Irish also joined the fray before the formal start of the English Civil Wars and suffered even more than the Scots. English domination of Ireland dates back to early Norman times with the English control waxing and waning, usually in relation to events in England. Whenever England became obsessed with its own problems, such as during the Black Death and the War of the Roses, the Irish took the opportunity to assert their independence. The Tudors crushed them in the sixteenth century with the last big stand at the Battle of Kinsale in 1601. The first part of the seventeenth century saw the foundations laid for the Ulster plantation with settlers imported from England and Scotland to colonise the northern part of Ireland, creating a problem which continues to bedevil Anglo-Irish relations, Anglo-American relations and Anglo-EU relations. The Irish Catholic reaction to the Ulster plantation led to a civil war in which, by 1640, the Catholics had gained the upper hand. When fighting broke out in England between Royalists and Parliamentarians, the Irish Catholics formed their own de facto government called the Irish Catholic Confederation, which declared itself for Charles I. They felt no great loyalty to the king; they just regarded him as a better option than the Puritan-dominated, anti-Catholic Parliament. Only a handful of Irish actually fought with the Royalist forces in England, but about 2,000 are believed to have fought with the Royalists in Scotland.

The Irish were right to be worried about the Parliamentarian forces. After Charles I was beheaded in 1649, Oliver Cromwell's New Model Army turned its attention towards Catholic Ireland to end the Irish Catholic Confederation which had recognised Charles II as ruler of England. The outcome was a religiously inspired Cromwellian genocide. No accurate records were kept of those killed but the estimates begin at 200,000 out of a population of approximately 1.5 million. The Catholics were also forced off their land, which was given to Cromwellian soldiers and more Protestant settlers from England and Scotland. An estimated 50,000 were sold as indentured servants. Some went directly to Virginia and the Carolinas but most of them were sent to work in the sugar cane fields in newly acquired Caribbean island colonies. Eventually, the bulk of these Irish found their way to America. This was the first forced Irish migration to America, which was surpassed only by the Irish potato famine of 1845–52 when 1.5 million Irish crossed the sea to America.

Fleeing Cromwell for Virginia

It wasn't just the Scots and Irish who fled England as a result of the English Civil Wars. Those who supported Charles I and, after he was beheaded, Charles II found England an inhospitable place. Oddly enough, the number of reprisals was limited. Oliver Cromwell realised that he needed to work with the English gentry who supplied the backbone of the government machinery. There were exceptions. First of all were Catholics. He hated them with a passion and persecuted them. His war in Ireland was as much a religious crusade as a reassertion of English authority. Next was anyone who was found to have actively plotted for his overthrow and the restoration of the monarchy in the form of Charles II, who found refuge in France. There were attempts to overthrow the Protectorate organised by what was known as the Sealed Knot Society. All were uncovered by Cromwell's spy chief, John Thurloe, and squashed.

But even if Cromwell wanted the gentry to stay, many of them decided that England under the rule of first a Puritan Parliament followed by a religious zealot was not for them. The Cavaliers, as they were known, were a fun-loving group who enjoyed parties, theatre and fine clothes. During the Protectorate England resembled the ISIS Caliphate of the twenty-first century. Theatres and dancing were banned. Women were forced to dress in black from head to toe. Working on the Sabbath could land you in prison. This encouraged many of the Cavaliers to flee their homeland. Some joined Charles II at his French court in exile. But a good number went to Virginia.

The Governor of Virginia, Sir William Berkeley, was a close friend of Charles I, who in 1641 appointed him Governor of Virginia. He developed the plantation system and his Green Spring plantation became an agricultural model for the rest of the colony as he developed new and better strains of tobacco, diversified crops, and introduced rice and silk production. He was also instrumental in the introduction of African slaves to the plantation system. Sir William was a keen supporter of the monarchy, High Anglican Church worship with as many popish trappings as possible, the divine right of kings and the notion that the aristocracy formed the bedrock of society. To this end he set out to recreate a hierarchical England in the South. In this way Virginia became markedly different than the more egalitarian north. The colonies around Massachusetts may have been called New England, but colonial Virginia was olde feudal England transplanted in the New World.

The English Civil Wars and the lopping off of the head of Charles I was a major boost for Sir William's settlement strategy. As soon as he heard of the death of the king, Berkeley declared Virginia a supporter of his son Charles II and offered the colony as a political asylum for disaffected Royalist 'gentlemen' seeking to flee Cromwell's joyless rule. He even suggested that Charles II sail to Virginia where he would be crowned King of America. And they came. Not as many as many as later Virginians claim, but a significant number so that by the time Berkeley died in 1677 the population of the colony had grown from 8,000 to 40,000. Those members of the aristocracy that did sail across were usually the second and third sons of aristocratic families. The first sons inherited the title and English property, even under Cromwell, and remained in England. Among those who crossed the Atlantic was George Washington's great-grandfather John, who left Sulgrave Manor in Northamptonshire for Virginia. By 1670 the upper house of the Virginia legislature mirrored the English House of Lords in that every member was related by blood or marriage to every other member. Almost the same could be said of the lower house as well.

Sir William Berkeley's defiance of the Parliamentarian forces had other economic and political effects. Parliament banned all trade with Virginia and allowed privateers to seize ships carrying goods from Virginia as well as other British colonies that backed the monarchy including Antigua, Barbados and Bermuda. Parliament also passed the first of many Navigation Acts, which decreed that the colonies could only trade with England and their goods could only be transported in English ships. The Navigation Acts – which continued in the British Empire in several different forms until 1849 – were one of the first instances of English laws suppressing colonial economies. They encouraged the colonies to circumvent English trade restrictions. Sir William Berkeley, for instance, bypassed England by trading with the Netherlands through the Dutch colony at New Amsterdam (later New York). Such links later helped to forge closer ties between the colonies.

Sir William reluctantly surrendered to the Parliamentarian forces in 1652 when an English fleet anchored off the capital at Jamestown with its guns pointed to the shore. Sir William was forced to step down, although he was allowed to stay at his Green Spring plantation. Parliament imposed first Richard Bennett and then Samuel Matthews as governors. Two months before the restoration of the monarchy, Virginians were allowed to elect a governor and Sir William was swept back into office. Unfortunately, his final seventeen-year administration was not as propitious as his first eleven years in charge. The colony suffered hurricanes, wars, disease and economic disasters. In 1677 the king was forced to recall Sir William, who died shortly afterwards in London. However, the social system he established, of an almost feudal political and economic structure, was firmly established. It bred a political cadre which was firmly committed to the liberties established by English law and precedent but opposed social equality. John Randolph, the great-uncle of Thomas Jefferson, summed up the attitude of many of his colonial compatriots when he said: 'I love liberty and hate equality.' It was his attitude that justified a system of enslavement for millions of Africans for the benefit of a few thousand wealthy plantation owners and eventually led to the American Civil War in which 620,000 lives were lost.

The Cavaliers of Virginia have produced more American presidents than any other state (eight), including four of the first five. Its sons include US Chief Supreme Court Justice John Marshal, Confederate general Robert E. Lee, explorers Lewis and Clark, and polar explorer Robert Byrd. The First Families of Virginia (usually referred to as the FFVs) are still firmly ensconced in the hunting country of Middleburg where they ride to the hounds in English hunting jackets. At their best they are a happy mix of confidence, noblesse oblige and a strong sense of duty and service. At their worst they are self-entitled, arrogant snobs; very similar to the upper-class relatives they left behind in England.

Welshmen and Northerners

England has been politically and socially divided since Henry VIII's Reformation and dissolution of the monasteries. London and the prosperous south-east have been the centre of the Establishment. The West Country, Wales and the north of England have hosted anything that is construed as anti-establishment. In the twentieth and twenty-first centuries (until very recently), the north and Wales have been the political base of the Labour Party. From the sixteenth to the eighteenth centuries your politics were reflected in your choice of church. The Establishment was Church of England, also known as Anglican and later, in America, Episcopalian. Church membership was solid in London and south-east England. In Wales and the north they either remained faithful to the Roman Catholic Church or joined up with one of the dissenting churches such as the Anabaptists, Quakers and the Methodists.

The 'Dissenters', as they were known, faced persecution from the authorities because the Church of England was the religious arm of the government, and gave the government power over the destination of men's souls. The Quakers were singled out for an especially hard time because their beliefs led them to espouse dangerous ideas about equality. This found its practical expression in the refusal of Quakers to doff their hats to their 'superiors', pay the required tithe to the Anglican Church, or serve in the militia, and led them to oppose the lucrative slave trade. The Quakers were founded during the English Civil Wars by the aforementioned George Fox, who found a ready audience for his preachings in the north-western county of Lancashire and established a base at Swarthmoor Hall. In 1657, he was visited by a young Welshman named John ap John and the seed was planted for mass Welsh emigration to America.

The Welsh had even more of a reason to be dissatisfied with English dominance and the Anglican Church. The history of Wales has been one long struggle to retain a national identity in the face of their overbearing English neighbours. Two of the traditional repositories of nationalism are language and religion. Wales was not a popular destination for seventeenth-century Anglican priests. As a result, the priests they did get were generally poorly educated, corrupt and, worst of all, could not speak Welsh. In 1657, John ap John returned to Wales with George Fox and toured the country. Fox did not speak Welsh, but John ap John acted as his interpreter and the simplicity of the Quakers' silent meetings appealed to the Welsh. Tens of thousands of them were converted to the Quaker faith – and were almost immediately persecuted.

The Quakers were of course saved from a life of fines and imprisonment by William Penn, whose father was one of the creditors of Charles II, which led him to receive a massive land grant which included Pennsylvania and a big chunk of present-day Delaware. The land, it was agreed, would be used as a refuge for Quakers and other dissenting religions. Welsh Quakers in particular flocked to what became Pennsylvania, and in Delaware they established a Welsh-speaking 100-square-mile colony called the Welsh Tract. By 1700 an estimated 30,000 Welsh Quakers had emigrated to Pennsylvania and the Quaker congregations back home were complaining that they had been stripped of their membership. It was not just Quakers who left for Pennsylvania. George Fox and William Penn also had close links with Anabaptists, Mennonites and Amish in the Dutch and German-speaking parts of Europe. These became the ancestors of the Pennsylvania Dutch or Amish communities of Pennsylvania whose strict interpretation of the Bible means they refuse the conveniences of modern life such as cars, television and computers.

Welsh Quakers were a major political power in Pennsylvania's early political life. By the early eighteenth century, about 20 per cent of the colony's population were of Welsh descent. In 2019 there are about 2 million Americans claiming Welsh ancestry. The Welsh did not remain in Pennsylvania. At the end of the eighteenth and early nineteenth century they spilled over into Ohio where they dominated the local coal mining areas. Jackson County, for instance, was referred to as 'Little Wales', and Welsh was commonly spoken there up until the 1950s. Several signatories to the Declaration of Independence were Welsh and in the nineteenth century several important American universities were founded by the descendants of Welsh Quakers, such as Bryn Mawr, Swarthmore, Cornell, Duke, Johns Hopkins and Haverford.

Rebels and Crooks

One of the enduring American myths is that colonial Americans were drawn across the ocean by the lure of new and exciting lands. This is true for some, but not for many. Most of them were reluctant travellers. They fled the comfort and security of home because of persecution, war, famine and extreme economic hardship. And some of the immigrants were forced onto transport ships as prisoners of war or – in many cases – as criminals.

The fate of Irish and Scottish soldiers defeated in the English Civil Wars and the flight of Royalist sympathisers has already been discussed. But the unrest that plagued Britain in the first half of the seventeenth century continued into the second and well into the eighteenth as various claimants to the throne rose and fell. The first such unsuccessful effort was led by the man with the weakest claim to the throne. The Duke of Monmouth was the eldest of the many illegitimate children of King Charles II. Bastards were blocked from succeeding to the throne, but he was Protestant in opposition to the legitimate James II, who was Catholic. The fact that he was even able to raise an army was testament to the unpopularity of James II.

It was Monmouth's popularity with the dominant Protestants that led to his exile in 1679 to the Dutch United Provinces. The same popularity persuaded Monmouth to sail back to England after James II succeeded his brother in 1685. He landed at Lyme Regis with three ships and declared himself king. But his 'reign' was short-lived. After marching around the West Country, Monmouth's forces were soundly defeated at the Battle of Sedgemoor in July 1685.

The Monmouth Rebellion was another boon for the advocates of forced immigration. James II instructed Lord Chief Justice George Jeffreys to head westward to dispense British justice to the captured rebels. In less than a month, Judge Jeffreys managed to try more than 1,300 rebels. 320 of them were hanged. More than 800 were transported to work in the sugar cane fields of Barbados and Jamaica, and the remainder were imprisoned and flogged. The king rewarded Judge Jeffrey's swift and sure dispensation of justice with a promotion to Lord Chancellor. History has rewarded him with the epithet of 'the Hanging Judge'. Most of those who were transported to the West Indies quickly fell victim to disease. Those who survived included pirate crews, who became an integral part of the seventeenth- and eighteenth-century folklore of the Caribbean and the eastern seaboard. The rest eventually found their way to Georgia, North Carolina, South Carolina, Virginia or Maryland – or went back to England.

Only three years after Monmouth's abortive coup, James II was overthrown by the combined efforts of Parliament and William of Orange in the Glorious Revolution. James's strident Catholicism and regular clashes with Parliament were too much for the MPs, so they invited William and his wife Mary, niece of James II, to take the throne. William landed with a large army at Brixham in Devon and marched to London. So unpopular was James II that William was totally unopposed. James fled to France, dropping the Great Seal into the Thames as he went. Parliament decreed that the king's flight and treatment of the seal

1. The iconic White Cliffs of Dover stand guard over the English Channel as one of the country's most iconic geographic features. The cliffs and the channel were created 425,000 years ago when the North Sea broke through a massive ice dam. (Jeff Pardoen under Creative Commons)

2. Britain's coal mines provided the fuel which powered the Industrial Revolution. (Wellcome Collection)

3. The enormous Mississippi River. Its basin is the fourth largest in the world and one of the reasons for America's economic success. (Ken Lund under Creative Commons)

4. It took sixty days for the Puritans to cross a storm-tossed Atlantic in 1620 on the *Mayflower*. Today passengers fly over it in a few hours.

5. Britain provided the technology and the Mesabi Range provided America with the raw material of iron that enabled it to become the world's number one steel producer. (McGhiever under Creative Commons)

6. Abraham Lincoln signed the Emancipation Proclamation on 1 January 1863, but in 2018 two-thirds of the country's prison population were African Americans. (Mead Art Museum)

Anglorum diadema tenens sceptrunque paternu Hác forma insigni sortis Elisa nitet

POSVI DEVM
ADIVTOREM MEVM

HONI SOIT QVI MALY PENSE

NATA GRONEWICIAE
ANN. ☧ M D XXXIII.
VI. EID. SEPT.

ELISABET D. G. ANG. FRAN. HIB. ET VERG. REGINA
FIDEI CHRISTIANAE PROPVGNATRIX ACERRIMA

Tristia dum gentes circum omnes bella fatigant
Cæcíque errores toto grassantur in Orbe,
Pace beas longa, vera et pietate Britannos
Justitiæ et Regni moderans sapienter habenas.

Ô Flos labe carens, fidei sanctissima cultrix,
Chara domi, celebrisque foris Dei et vnica cura,
Lux pietate nitens, Virtus tua et inclyta facta
Sic faciant tandem te Coelica Regna videre.

Honoris ipsius causâ æri incidebat Crispianus Passæus Belga . 1592 .

7. Queen Elizabeth I was appalled that one of her favourite sea captains, Sir John Hawkins, had become a slave trader – until she discovered how much money he made. (Metropolitan Museum of Art)

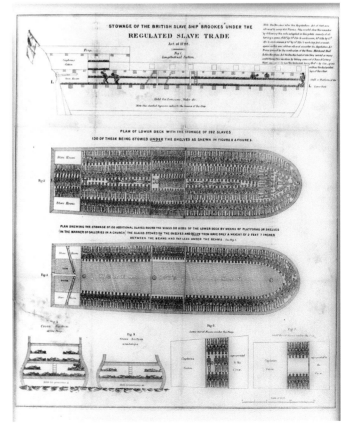

Above: 8. Slaves in the American south. After the founding of Charleston in 1670 the South Carolina port became the main entry point for African slaves. (Library of Congress)

Right: 9. This diagram of the slave ship *Brookes* caused a major stir when it was published in 1788. It showed 454 slaves packed into a 350-ton ship 100 feet long and 25 feet wide. (Library of Congress)

10. William Lloyd Garrison in 1840 helped to form America's first serious abolitionist organisation, the New England Anti-slavery Society. (Liljenquist Collection)

11. Harriet Beecher Stowe was the author of the anti-slavery bestseller *Uncle Tom's Cabin*. When she visited the White House she was greeted by Abraham Lincoln with the words: 'So you are the little lady who started this great war.'

12. The US Supreme Court has repeatedly acknowledged America's debt to John Lilburne whose legal battles led to the abolition of the Star Chamber, the reaffirmation of the jury system and established the defendant's right against self-incrimination.

THE BILL OF RIGHTS,

PASSED IN 1689,

THE FIRST YEAR OF WILLIAM AND MARY.

An Act declaring the Rights and Liberties of the Subject, and settling the Succession of the Crown.

WHEREAS the Lords Spiritual and Temporal, and Commons, assembled at Westminster, lawfully, fully, and freely representing all the estates of the people of this realm, did upon the thirteenth day of February, in the year of our Lord one thousand six hundred eighty-eight, present unto their Majesties, then called and known by the names and style of William and Mary, Prince and Princess of Orange, being present in their proper persons, a certain declaration in writing, made by the said Lords and Commons, in the words following, *viz.*

" WHEREAS the late King James the Second, by the assistance of divers evil counsellors, judges, and ministers employed by him, did endeavour to subvert and extirpate the Protestant religion, and the laws and liberties of this kingdom ;

" 1. By assuming and exercising a power of dispensing with and suspending of laws, and the execution of laws, without consent of Parliament.

" 2. By committing and prosecuting divers worthy Prelates, for humbly petitioning to be excused from concurring to the said assumed power.

" 3. By issuing and causing to be executed a commission under the Great Seal for erecting a Court called, *The Court of Commissioners for Ecclesiastical Causes.*

" 4. By levying money for and to the use of the Crown, by pretence of prerogative, for other time, and in other manner, than the same was granted by Parliament.

" 5. By raising and keeping a standing army within this kingdom in time of peace, without consent of Parliament, and quartering soldiers contrary to law.

" 6. By causing several good subjects, being Protestants, to be disarmed, at the same time when Papists were both armed and employed contrary to law.

" 7. By violating the freedom of election of Members to serve in Parliament.

E

13. The first Bill of Rights was not American. It was British. It established the constitutional supremacy of Parliament after the overthrow of Britain's Stuart dynasty.

14. Henry VIII was certain that his marriage to Catherine of Aragon was cursed because he married his brother's wife. The subsequent divorce led a split with Rome, the establishment of the Church of England and the Reformation. (Metropolitan Museum of Art)

15. The 1605 Gunpowder Plot pushed Protestant England over the edge into Catholic witch hunts and strengthened the hand of the Puritans. Depicted here is the execution of some of the plotters. (Wellcome Collection)

16. Matthew Hopkins was England's self-appointed 'Witchfinder General'. He was responsible for the deaths of 300 women and set the template for the Salem witch trials.

17. The clash between King Charles I and Parliament, and the king's execution in 1649, marked the beginning of the end of the principle of the Divine Right of Kings. (Metropolitan Museum of Art)

18. Catholic Lord Baltimore established Maryland as a refuge for persecuted Catholics, but the colony became a target for the New England Puritans and the Anglicans of Virginia. (New York Public Library)

19. The log cabin church at Cane Ridge, Kentucky, attracted thousands for America's first evangelical revivalist or 'camp meeting'. The religious events that became a regular feature of frontier life had their origin in the travelling Scottish Holy Fairs. (Library of Congress)

20. Thomas Jefferson – the author of the Declaration of Independence and the third US president – established the principle of separation of Church and State which has been repeatedly cited by the US Supreme Court. (Metropolitan Museum of Art)

21. Edmund Burke was colonial America's champion in the British Parliament. He said that from a legal point of view the British government had every right to tax the colonists, but from a political point of view they were sowing the seeds of rebellion. (Metropolitan Museum of Art)

22. John Wilkes was the ancestor of John Wilkes Booth and a champion of a free press who secured the right of newspapers to report parliamentary proceedings.

23. Oliver Cromwell established the rights of Parliament at the point of a sword and his military dictatorship drove thousands to America. (Metropolitan Museum of Art)

24. Virginia's House of Burgesses was America's first legislature and was modelled on the British Parliament with an appointed upper house and a lower house elected by property owners. (Library of Congress)

25. Adam Smith's book *Wealth of Nations* put paid to the age of mercantilism and ushered in the principles of *laissez-faire* economics, capitalism, free enterprise, division of labour, free markets, wage competition and the 'invisible hand' of the marketplace.

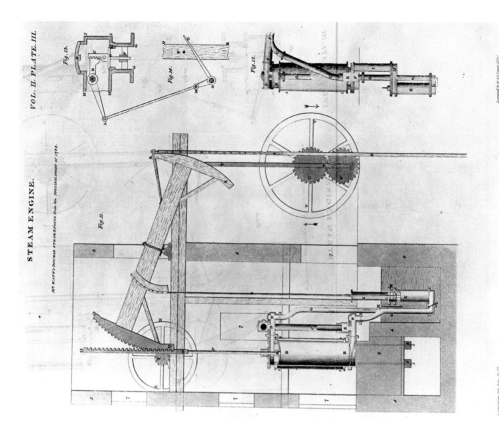

Above: 26. The steam engine invented by James Watt powered the industrial revolution on both sides of the Atlantic. (Library of Congress)

Left: 27. British Prime Minister Margaret Thatcher privatised large sections of Britain's welfare state and was a major influence on President Ronald Reagan's foreign and domestic policies. (Thatcher Estate)

28. President Woodrow Wilson brought America out of its self-imposed isolationism to fight alongside Britain in the First World War. When the war ended the country retreated into its shell. (Library of Congress)

29. The European Economic Recovery Programme (Marshall Plan) was announced by US Secretary of State George C. Marshall. It laid the foundations for Britain and Europe's post-Second World War economic recovery. (US Department of State)

Above: 30. Britain was one of the few Western countries to provide unquestioning support to the US in the 2003 Iraq War; support for which Prime Minister Tony Blair paid a heavy price. (Sgt Jose E. Guillen/US Marines)

Left: 31. President Donald Trump has golf courses in Scotland and Ireland and promised Britain a 'great' trade deal in the wake of the UK's vote to leave the European Union. (Office of the President of the United States)

constituted an abdication and declared William and Mary co-monarchs. James never accepted the abdication ruling and plotted from exile in France to return to the English throne.

In France, the Stuarts in exile managed to gain the recognition of the French court and the Vatican. And because the dynasty had started in Scotland, they had a strong support base there. This was strengthened by the 1707 Act of Union between England and Scotland, which combined the two parliaments and ended Scottish independence. All of this persuaded James Edward Stuart, son of James II, to make an attempt in 1715 to seize the throne. He landed in northern Scotland and gathered an army of supporters who became known as Jacobites. The Jacobites had some initial successes but after five months James was forced to flee back to exile in France. His son – who became known as Bonnie Prince Charlie – had more success, but not enough. He also landed in Scotland, won control of it and was proclaimed King of Scotland. He then marched on England and reached Derby in the Midlands before he realised that promised French support was not forthcoming and marched back to Scotland to regroup. There he was decisively defeated in 1746 at the Battle of Culloden outside Inverness and was forced, like his father before him, to flee back to France.

The English authorities more or less overlooked the Scottish support for the Stuarts the first time around, but after the 1745 Jacobite rebellion, they decided to crush the geographic base of the Jacobite rebellion, Scotland. Symbols of Scottish identity, such as the kilt and bagpipe, were banned. It was forbidden to speak Gaelic. Scotsmen were prevented from carrying weapons and the clan chiefs were stripped of their political power. Anyone caught breaking the law faced transportation to the colonies. And thousands were sent as indentured servants who, when their ships landed in the New World, were sold as unskilled labourers to masters in America.

Ironically, these Scots emerged as some of the most loyal subjects of George III during the American Revolution. One group of Highland Scots settled in the Mohawk Valley in New York and during the revolution formed the King's First American Regiment, who fought in kilts to the skirl of the bagpipes. The regiment famously defeated Washington's troops at the Battle of Brandywine. After 1783, the regiment was disbanded, and the Scots settled in Canada with their wives and children. Over the years the Scots became known as the backbone of the British Empire. In the United States, it is estimated that up to 25 million Americans – 8.3 per cent of the population – can claim Scottish or Scotch-Irish ancestry.

The first Scots to reach America even preceded the Pilgrim Fathers. Viking explorer Leif Erikson spent a year on the west coast of Scotland before sailing for Greenland and ending up in what he called Vinland and what we call America. A large number of his crew were Scottish. The Icelandic sagas record that two of them were Scottish slaves named Hati and Hekja who were used by Erikson as scouts in the New World.

The eponymous figure of Uncle Sam has Scottish links. He is based on one Samuel Wilson whose parents hailed from Greenock on the west coast of Scotland outside Glasgow. Scots have made major contributions to America's development and history across a wide range of disciplines. Some of the notable Scots Americans are Andrew Carnegie, Alexander Graham Bell, Alexander Hamilton, Washington Irving and Edgar Alan Poe. It is said that three-quarters of American presidents can claim Scottish roots.

A number of the Scots Americans claim their Scottish roots via Ireland. The link between the countries is both strong and old and coincided with the settlement of America. The English have been in and out of Ireland since Norman times, but in the seventeenth century the battle for dominance in Ireland was injected with an incurable religious virus. England broke with Rome and Ireland remained steadfastly loyal to the Vatican. Protestant England now had a God-given right to conquer Ireland and the Catholic Irish didn't help by supporting anyone who opposed the Protestant cause in England and Scotland. After a series of successive military victories, the English concluded that the best way to maintain political power of their troublesome Catholic neighbour was to kick Catholics off their land and give it to Protestant settlers.

The earliest Irish settlers were prisoners sold as indentured servants after the wars with Oliver Cromwell and William of Orange. The biggest migration, however, came after the 1845 arrival of *Phytophthora Infestas*, better known as potato blight. The blight infected potato crops throughout Europe but its impact was felt most strongly in Ireland because of the social and economic conditions and the British government's response. Developments in the century before ensured that Irish peasant farmers would suffer the brunt. In 1801 Ireland formally joined in a political union with England, Scotland and Wales and was ruled by Parliament in London. The English landlords turned over the bulk of the land to grazing cattle and growing grain. This forced the large number of subsistence peasant farmers to maximise the output of their small plots with the plant that produced the greatest calorific return – the humble potato. Finally, the economic philosophy of the day – laissez-faire – dictated against government interference. The 'invisible hand' of the market would set matters right.

The tragic outcome was that between 1845 and 1849 an estimated 1 million Irish people died of starvation or disease brought on by malnutrition. Another million were forced to emigrate, the vast majority of them to the United States. By 1851, Irish immigrants comprised an estimated 25 per cent of the populations of New York, Boston, Philadelphia and Baltimore and the population of Ireland had been reduced from 8.2 million to 6.5 million.

The Irish were the first big national/ethnic/religious group of immigrants to face a wall of prejudice when reaching the United States; partly because they were poor, but mainly because they were entering a society dominated by white Anglo-Saxon Protestants whose English ancestors had for centuries treated the Irish Catholics as an inferior species. The words 'No Irish Need Apply' became a common sight outside boarding houses and on job advertisements throughout America, but especially in the east coast cities where the immigrants gathered. Prejudice reached a peak in the mid-1850s with the creation of an anti-Irish immigration political party known first as the Native American Party, then the American Party and finally as the Know Nothing Movement. Dominated by white Anglo-Saxon Protestants, they were a near clone of seventeenth-century Cromwellians. They claimed that the Irish Catholics were being directed by the Vatican and were plotting through their priests to seize political control of the United States. The anti-Irish nativist movement, as it was also called, reached its peak in the 1856 elections and then gradually died down; but anti-Catholic prejudice continued in organisations such as the Ku Klux Klan.

The Irish, in common with almost every American immigrant group, gradually won acceptance from the rest of American society and made its mark. As of 2019, more than 33 million Americans claimed Irish roots. The population of the Irish landmass (Northern Ireland and the Republic of Ireland) was only 6.65 million in 2019. Everyone knows of the Irish roots of John F. Kennedy, the first non-Protestant to be elected president. But not as well documented is that Barack Obama, who broke the presidential colour bar, also had Irish ancestry. Other famous Irish Americans include golfer Ben Hogan, crooner/actor Bing Crosby and impresario Ed Sullivan.

The Disaster of Success

The US emerged from its civil war a major world economic power. The battle to preserve the Union forced at least the Northern states to rush to build troop-carrying railways, roads, ports and ships; develop munitions and textile industries and steel plants; and dig for coal to provide the energy to run them. The result was a massive spare capacity, which allowed freebooting capitalists to quickly and effectively beat American swords into American ploughshares. In 1830 America's share of world manufacturing output was 2.4 per cent. It grew to 7.2 per cent at the outbreak of war in 1860 and stood at 14.7 per cent in 1880. 1n 1900 the US overtook Britain and emerged as the world's major industrial nation with 23.6 per cent of the world's manufacturing capacity. To create this wealth in so short a time required the importation of a huge workforce – far more than could be recruited from Britain, which, after all, needed workers to run its own satanic mills and protect the empire. So America looked elsewhere: Italians, Swedes, Germans, Poles, Jews, Poles, Russians, Chinese, Japanese, any people who were susceptible to the lure of the American dream because of war, famine, poverty or religious or political persecution in their homelands. The bosses didn't care. They just needed bodies. And they came: 12 million of them between 1870 and 1900.

The industrialisation of America created vast wealth, the distribution of which mirrored that of Dickensian Britain. Economic historians estimate that 4,000 families representing less than 1 per cent of the US population controlled more half of the country's wealth. A social structure was emerging that aped the class-ridden British societies that the colonials had fought to free themselves from a hundred years before. The late medieval College of Arms (1484), *Debrett's* (1769) and *Burke's Peerage* (1826) painstakingly recorded British family histories, titles and bloodlines so that the aristocracy was equipped with the information required to protect its wealth and political power. In the latter half of the nineteenth century, 99 per cent of the country's land was owned by just 1,000 families. The US equivalent of the British aristocracy were the robber barons who accumulated massive fortunes partly through stock market manipulations and financial chicanery that put them in control of America's industrial complex. Their social bible was first produced in 1887 by newspaper society columnist Louis Keller. It was called *The Social Register* and contained the names of 5,000 socially acceptable and wealthy individuals, most of whom were descended from the early British colonial settlers. *The Social Register* continues and in 2014 listed 25,000 upper-class Americans who are encouraged to socialise, conduct business and mate with the denizens of the pages of the register in order to protect their collective position in society.

The wealth, power and position of the British aristocracy was based on land ownership and a complex web of marital alliances and affirming titles that could in most cases be traced back to the Norman Conquest. But the problem was that by the mid-nineteenth century ownership of land had been replaced by factories and coal mines as the source of the nation's wealth. And the owners of this wealth were not the titled aristocracy but nouveau riche entrepreneurs, factory owners, merchants and bankers who had been socially excluded with the epithet 'trade'. The tradespeople responded with increasingly ostentatious and opulent displays of their wealth, which challenged the social and political position of the hereditary aristocracy who in turn were pushed into increasingly obscene displays of their own wealth, which they could ill afford and which gradually ate into their asset base. It quickly became apparent that the *nouveaux riches* needed to be given a stake in the Establishment in order for the Establishment to remain on top. Consequently, some of the industrialists were given titles, but most important of all their daughters were reluctantly allowed to marry into the aristocracy in return for large dowries that were spent on maintaining crumbling stately homes and lavish entertainments. This worked quite successfully for a while, but the stock of wealthy British industrialists' daughters started to run out. So the British aristocracy turned to the more *nouveau* and more *riche* Americans.

To facilitate these links a matchmaking agency was established in New York headed by the American wife of the British baronet general Sir Arthur Paget. Heavily chaperoned trips were arranged for prospective wealthy American brides to display their charms during the London social season from February to August in a whirlwind of teas and balls. Between 1870 and 1930, an estimated 350 American heiresses brought $2 billion into the British aristocracy. The best known example was Consuelo Vanderbilt, the daughter of railway magnate William Kissam Vanderbilt, the richest man in America, who coughed up $75 million and $200,000 a year for life to secure for his beautiful daughter a loveless marriage to the 9th Duke of Marlborough, who desperately needed the cash for save his crumbling Blenheim Palace. Consuelo's marriage, however, paled into historical and political insignificance when compared to the 1874 marriage of Jennie Jerome to the 9th Duke of Marlborough's younger brother Lord Randolph Churchill. Theirs was – unusually for the time – a love match although the financially strapped Lord Randolph did secure a reasonable dowry to help finance his political career. But the most significant outcome of their union was Sir Winston Churchill, who went on to organise the Anglo-American alliance and special relationship which saved the world for democracy.

The spokesperson for Americans in late nineteenth-century Britain was the novelist Henry James. He maintained that Britain was the best of all possible worlds for well-connected Yanks. The liberal-minded and educated American was free of the class baggage that infected British society, which meant that they were free to enjoy a wide range of social activities in the most powerful and cultured country in the world. The ere of the free-spending transatlantic elite became known as the 'Gilded Age'. Not because of the money spent, but because the ostentatious wealth displayed by a few was no more than a thin gilt veneer over an increasingly rotten and unequal society. As wealth started to accumulate in the hands of a few, the bulk of the population continued to suffer unsanitary and overcrowded housing, poor working conditions and pay, bad diet, insecure employment and illness. To a slight degree the resentment that arose was offset by the bread-and-circuses element provided by the aristocracy as reported in the increasingly popular penny press. But it was not enough. The working classes demanded their share of the wealth. British law had for centuries prohibited the formation of trade unions to demand higher wages and better conditions. In 1834 the Tolpuddle Martyrs were transported to Australia for forming an agricultural workers' union in Dorset. Their pardon two years later opened the door to the legalisation of trade unions. From then on, Britain took the lead in the establishment of trade unions at home and abroad. In 1864, London hosted the International Workingmen's Association, which asserted that workers around the globe had the right to organise themselves and demanded an eight-hour day and a reasonable wage. In 1868 a group of trade unionists from across the British Isles met in the Mechanics Institute in Manchester and formed the Trades Union Congress to campaign for better conditions for its members. It soon became apparent that the best way to achieve its ends was through political power in Parliament. In 1898 the Labour Party was formed to that end and through its alliance with the TUC managed within just twenty years to supplant the Liberal Party as the main rival to the Conservative Party.

The American courts – using the precedent of English law – were initially just as tough on any attempts by American workers attempts to organise themselves. In the first half of the nineteenth century there were twenty-three prosecutions involving workers who tried to use their collective bargaining power to negotiate better conditions. The charge was criminal conspiracy. But changes in English law and changes in public perception gradually led to the acceptance of trade unionism in America. Among the first industries to be organised was the railways. The Brotherhood of Locomotives and Trainmen, founded in 1863, later became known as the International Brotherhood of Teamsters. In

1881 the umbrella trade union organisation the American Federation of Labour was formed to follow the British example of the TUC to fight for working men's rights across a wide range of industries. The AFL, however, did not follow the British example of establishing a political arm. Problems related to racial discrimination, an innate libertarianism and a can-do optimism that encourages workers to believe that the children of an American docker can grow up to become doctors kept the AFL (later the AFL-CIO) out of the directly participatory political arena. Today they are more associated with the Democratic Party, but pride themselves on working with politicians from both main parties.

The Gilded Age came to an abrupt end on 28 July 1914. And the First World War signalled the end of the supremacy of the British aristocracy as well. The British upper class were drawn from the centuries-old tradition of a warrior class. They were the mounted knights who were taught to lead by example in charges against the enemy. It was only right and proper for them to do so; they had the biggest stake in the system. It was therefore natural that the war's officer class was drawn almost exclusively from the upper crust. And when the balloon went up and the whistles blew they were the first ones to climb out of the trenches and be drilled between the eyes by a German bullet. The upper reaches of British society had also been the traditional reservoir for political leadership in peacetime Britain and an almost bottomless talent pool for the empire. Both of those sources had run dry on the fields of Flanders along with the money to maintain Britain's pre-eminent position in the world. America had managed to stay neutral for the first three years of the war and emerged as the richest nation in the world. The end of the war signalled the start of the American century and a new type of British immigrant to America.

The US was now an economic giant but not ready, willing or able to shoulder corresponding international political and military responsibilities. President Woodrow Wilson's dreams of a world governed by the values of 1776 and led by a rich, dynamic, young America were dashed by an isolationist Congress. America took its money, invested in its industries and spent the profits on flappers, Prohibition gin, flagpole sitting, Model Ts, gangsters, Hollywood, baseball, barnstorming aviators and boundless hedonism. It was the Jazz Age. The wartime survivors in Britain made a stab at emulating their American cousins, but the antics of London's 'Bright Young Things' were a pale imitation of New York's non-stop party. So a large number of the British aristocracy simply upped stakes, turned their backs on grey British skies and headed west to make money and enjoy life.

Then on 24 October 1929 the music stopped. The freewheeling and unregulated New York Stock Exchange that had fuelled the Jazz Age crashed and dragged America, Britain and the rest of the world into the Great Depression. The depression was an American-made disaster that dictated that few people emigrated because there was nowhere better to go. Both sides of the Atlantic entered an economic hibernation in an attempt to last out the financial storm, only to have their financial troubles explode into the Second World War in September 1939. The Second World War completed the task of establishing American supremacy and destroying the British Empire that had started with the last war. Rationed, cash-strapped, bombed-out Britain was again contrasted with increasingly wealthy and unscathed America, which emerged from the war prepared to take the burden of world leadership from British shoulders. America was again the fun place to be, but now it was the place to be for power and influence as well.

But in September 1940, Britain was five long years away from worrying about the post-war period. It was the height of the Blitz and the Battle of Britain. Hitler was massing troops on the Atlantic coastline in preparation for a seaborne invasion. There were real fears that Britain would fall. Churchill promised to 'fight them on the beaches' and 'never surrender'. But privately he had a plan B. Key to this plan was passing the military baton to the United States so that they could continue the fight against Nazism should Britain succumb to overwhelming odds and fail. To that end Churchill despatched one of his top scientists, Sir Henry Tizard, to the US with a black metal suitcase drilled with holes and stuffed with documents. The holes were needed to ensure that the case sank in case of a German U-boat attack. The documents were details of Britain's top military secrets including a prototype atomic bomb, airborne radar systems, jet engine technology, rocket technology, gun sights, chemical weapons technology and the cavity magnetron which produced microwaves. The mission was a success. America agreed to become the arsenal of democracy, but the price Britain paid in trading its secrets for security was high. The atomic secrets meant that America – not Britain – became the first nuclear power. Jet engine patents enabled Boeing and Lockheed to dominate the military and civil aviation industries and the cavity magnetron produced the microwaves that were vital for modern-day telecommunications as well as the ubiquitous microwave oven. The Second World War was a British disaster that drove priceless ideas across the Atlantic and played almost as big a role in building prosperous post-war America as did its people.

Britain has over the centuries enjoyed an enviable academic record. Universities such as Oxford, Cambridge, St Andrews, Manchester and Edinburgh have throughout their long histories been regarded as the world's top centres of learning. The scientific achievements, research and intellectual skills that they fostered played a vital role in building a stable and prosperous Britain. But in the 1950s and 1960s British academia suffered from post-war privations caused by the transfer of technology and lack of money to invest in facilities and salaries. America suffered no such problem and set about luring the cream of the British intelligentsia with first-class research facilities and attractive salaries. In 1963, Britain's Royal Society warned that the UK was suffering a 'brain drain'. This eventually resulted in increased government investment in research, and the opportunity for cooperation with, and investment from, Europe was one of the factors behind Britain joining the European Economic Community in 1973.

In the globalised twenty-first century the issue of which country owns which patent has become less significant as products are composed of hundreds of different components produced in far-flung parts of the world before being assembled by the most cost-effective assembly line. London has become a commercial outpost of New York, Los Angeles, San Francisco and Chicago and vice versa. Executives regard the 'red eye' business flights across the Atlantic as part and parcel of their jobs. Academics are as comfortable in the ivy-covered walls of Harvard as the dreaming spires of Oxford. This new Anglo-American order of international high-fliers has replaced the Transatlantic aristocracy of the 'Gilded Age'. Wealth – conspicuous wealth – remains one of the qualifications for membership, but bloodlines have been replaced by knowledge and ability. However, this new upper echelon is no less despised and envied than its nineteenth-century forerunner, as a growing tide of nationalism reacts to the globalised economy by accusing the new leaders of living in an out-of-touch bubble and dismissively brands them as the 'metropolitan elite'.

9

Money, Money, Money

The Hip Thigh Bone Theory

And so to the hip thigh bone theory of world economics. The theory is based on the 1920s African American spiritual 'Dem Dry Bones'. The ditty was based on a Biblical passage in which a collection of dry bones reassembled themselves before the astonished eyes of the prophet Ezekiel. The foot-tapping, hand-clapping spiritual is a roof raiser in evangelical churches around the world. It is also a popular song in young children's anatomy classes. It is a perfect metaphor of how the rapidly shrinking and increasingly connected world has become ever more dependent on its constituent parts (or bones) working together.

The twenty-first-century world has become totally interconnected. In fact, the bones that comprise the skeleton of our globe are not so much connected as fused and then overlaid with a complex web of nerves, muscles, sinews, international political and trade organs, and a protective skin of military alliances. At times it seems that the only thing missing from this metaphor is a functioning brain.

The fact is that if Americans want iron ore for their steel mills it is best to have a quiet word with the Swedes or Canadians. If the farmers in Kansas need phosphates to fertilise the amber waves of grain or the fruited plain, it is best to be nice to the Moroccans. For tin cans think Africa and Australia. If a suburban family in Westchester wants to build a brick house they need sand – that probably means China or New Zealand. As for oil, well, just think of an unstable part of the world, smile nicely and thrust out a fistful of dollars.

America is not alone in its needs. Central and Western Europe are heavily dependent on Russian natural gas. Landlocked Bolivia depends on good relations with Peru and Chile to export and import its goods by sea. Oman and Iran together control the Straits of Hormuz and the entrance to the Persian Gulf, and the Vietnamese rice paddies are at the mercy of the Chinese who control the water flowing from the Himalayas. China also has under its soil an estimated 70 per cent of the world's rare earth deposits, a vital component in the computer industry.

The world is not just connected by trade and natural resources. The complex and interwoven financial structures that grease the wheels of commerce are increasingly important. There may be so-called national exchanges in London, New York, Hong Kong, Frankfurt, Tokyo and Dubai, but in our twenty-four-hour world, all these exchanges now operate as one global trading floor fed with information from 24/7 global news operations.

Manufacturing has also become international. Toyota is the world's largest car manufacturer with annual revenues in excess of $200 billion in 2017. It has 200 suppliers from twenty-eight countries. General Motors is America's largest motor manufacturer and the fourth largest in the world after Toyota, Hyundai and Volkswagen. The constituent parts of its vehicles come from thirty-seven different countries. It is common for the brakes to be made in one country, the axles in another and the crankshaft in a third. Then they are all shipped to assembly plants which, in the case of Toyota, are based in twenty-six different countries. This global to and fro enables the manufacturers to buy from suppliers close to essential resources and a skilled workforce, as well as delivering economies of scale. Placing assembly plants around the world means that the finished products can reach their world markets without crippling transport costs and this in turn means lower prices for the consumer as well as higher profits for the shareholders.

Service industries have also become internationalised. It is not unusual for a high-priced international New York or London-based law firm to outsource its backroom work to South Asia. These could include its accountancy operation, answering service, secretaries, or even the staff required for drafting legal documents. The London-based media giant Thomson-Reuters has moved its editing operations to India to exploit a willing, highly skilled and relatively inexpensive labour force that can now be reached in nanoseconds via the Worldwide Web.

The improvements in communications and transport have spawned a host of international bodies to regulate and provide a framework for loans, trade negotiations, investments, communications enhancements and political and security cooperation. The World Bank in the financial year 2018/19 approved loans totalling $4.3 billion for capital projects in the developing world. Its sister organisation the International Monetary Fund (IMF) is charged with encouraging and maintaining sustainable global growth by channelling money from wealthy countries to those that require cash for political and economic stability. In 2018/19 IMF loans included $6 billion to Pakistan. Other big recipients were Colombia, Argentina, Barbados, Angola, Morocco, Ukraine and Ecuador. On the principle that a rising tide floats all ships, free trade is generally regarded as a good thing for almost everyone. The World Trade Organisation (WTO) provides a negotiating platform to handle disputes and ensure that trade is as free as possible. The World Health Organisation (WHO) coordinates the work of health agencies and ministries worldwide. It has been one of the reasons for the successful fight against smallpox, malaria, tuberculosis, polio and other diseases. The United Nations Educational, Scientific and Cultural Organization (UNESCO) protects valuable world heritage sites for future generations. The International Labour Organisation (ILO) protects workers' rights, and the 2015 Paris Climate Change Agreement was intended to coordinate activities to protect the environment from the effects of global warming. All the above, and other agencies, come under the aegis of the United Nations, which also has a political and security arm under the umbrella of the UN General Assembly (UNGA) and the UN Security Council. They control 110,000 peacekeeping forces in fourteen countries across four continents – second only to the number of US troops deployed overseas.

As well as global bodies, there are myriad regional organisations designed to promote local cooperation in the political, economic, trade, security and military spheres. The two most successful are the European Union (EU) and North Atlantic Treaty Organisation (NATO) which together have provided a security and economic framework which kept Russia at bay, won the Cold War and created prosperity and political stability in Europe through the creation of an interdependent trading bloc that has become the largest of its kind in the world. Other organisations include the G7 group of the biggest industrialised economies; the G20, which represents the top twenty countries; the African Union (AU), comprised of the fifty-five African countries; BRICS (Brazil, Russia, India, China and South Africa); the Shanghai Cooperation Organisation, which is made up of China, Russia and the Central Asian countries of Kazakhstan, Kyrgyzstan, Tajikistan, and Uzbekistan; the Asia-Pacific Economic Cooperation (APEC) has twenty-one members who border the Pacific Rim; and South America's Mercosur, which manages a free trade zone and customs union between its four full members, Argentina, Brazil, Paraguay and Uruguay. Generally speaking, increased international trade and communications has pushed countries into seeking economic, political and military alliances to protect their trade, create economies of scale, guarantee markets for their goods and services, and protect their territories.

The upside of the hip thigh bone theory of the world is that hundreds of millions have been lifted out of poverty since the end of the Second World War. There have been wars, but in most cases they have been limited in scope compared to the past. Planet Earth has enjoyed an unparalleled period of peace and prosperity. But there is a downside. The coronavirus pandemic exposed the health risks as an estimated 107,000 flights a day spread the disease to every corner of the globe within a matter of weeks. It strengthened the positions of anti-globalists who argued that the pandemic demonstrated the world's over-dependence on China for key manufacturing industries.

The emphasis on regional and global cooperation has also led to the rise of multinational companies and a de-emphasis on corporate national identities. Japanese car manufacturers are no longer competing against their American counterparts. Toyota's assembly plants in twenty-six countries are competing against GM's operations in thirty-seven countries. Globalisation improves products, lifts millions out of poverty and improves quality as well as lowering consumer prices. But it is also accused of exporting jobs and encouraging unbridled immigration, and the employment of cheap illegal workers who exacerbate racial divisions by apparently undermining national homogeneity. President Donald Trump led the counter-attack against globalisation with his America First campaign. He was successful in turning it into an international effort by securing the support of parties such as the Alternative for Deutschland (AfD) in Germany, Marine Le Pen's National Rally in France, Matteo Salvini's League in Italy and the pro-Brexit parties in Britain. Conservative populist personalities such as Hungary's Viktor Orban, India's Narendra Modi, Brazil's Jair Bolsonaro, Israel's Benjamin Netanyahu and even Russia's Vladimir Putin have ridden the wave. These political figures have exploited variations of the democratic system to tap into a politically charged reservoir of emotion and fear to secure political office. Of course, the democratic pendulum has a habit of swinging both ways, which is both its strength and its weakness. With the communications and transport genii out of their bottles it is difficult to imagine that even the most populist politician can stuff globalism back into a nationalist-oriented trading system without causing irreparable damage to the democratic institutions that put them into office.

Britain has played a major role in the development of the economic philosophies and structures which created the current world trading patterns currently dominated by the US. Britain established the triangular trade that laid the foundations for America's successful colonial trade. Its joint-stock companies were the forerunners of modern-day shareholder-owned large American corporations. British economists provided the philosophical foundations for the American economy. The first truly multinational companies were British and the pursuit of free trade has been the policy of successive British governments since the first half of the nineteenth century. In the twentieth century socialist economics forged the British welfare state, which inspired America's social services, while the Thatcherism of the 1980s reintroduced a large dose of free market economics.

Pottery and Silk

Global trade has been around since prehistoric times. The volcanic glass obsidian was valued by early man as a ceremonial cutting tool and has cropped up in archaeological digs in different parts of the world thousands of miles from its source. It is known that the Danube River was a major cross-European trading route stretching from its headwaters in the Swiss Alps to the Black Sea. Prehistoric Celts discovered that the best giant stones for the 5,000-year-old Stonehenge came not from an English quarry but from the west coast of Wales 150 miles away. Some of the earliest examples of writing record shipments of grain between the civilisations of the Fertile Crescent and modern-day India. In those days there was no such thing as free trade or regulated trade. To move goods was an expensive and laborious process. If it was going overland it travelled slowly by camel or cart over near non-existent roads. If it went by sea the sailors had to wait for the tides, winds and monsoons. They stayed close to land in case a squall suddenly sprang up. There were pirates and bandits. Every time a trade caravan crossed a border or rested in a town or at an oasis there were taxes to be paid. If a ship pulled into a port there were port duties. Trade was a risky business. But high risk meant high profits. The risks also meant high prices, so that most of the long-distance trade was in luxury goods for the gratification of a wealthy elite.

The most famous of the ancient trade routes was the Silk Road from China to Europe. Actually, the term Silk Road is a misnomer. There was not one road but a series of different routes. At either end were the two great civilisations of the ancient world, China and Rome, but the routes between were varied and often the traders travelled only part of the long journey before returning home. Perhaps the most famous and glamorous was the overland route across the Gobi Desert, over the Hindu Kush, through Afghanistan, Persia, modern-day Iraq, Syria, Lebanon and Turkey to Constantinople, where goods were loaded onto ships bound for Rome. Other routes were more sea-based and took in the spice islands of Indonesia and Ceylon as well as both coasts of India before heading across the Arabian Sea to the markets of Zanzibar where they loaded up with African goods before sailing into the Red Sea and across Egypt to the Mediterranean. Modern China is recreating the old Silk Road with its one-belt-one-road initiative. It uses many of the same routes, but instead of camels and sailing ships employs dedicated railways, pipelines, tankers, cargo planes and giant container ships. The cargoes still include silks and spices, but these have been dwarfed by hundreds of billions of dollars of modern manufactured goods.

The ancient route was severely truncated in the fifth century after the eternal city was repeatedly sacked by Goths, Vandals and Huns and western Europe plunged into the Dark Ages. The new political and cultural heart of the Roman Empire was Constantinople, which became the western terminus for the Silk Road. The spread of Islam in the seventh, eighth and ninth centuries threw up another obstacle to east–west trade as the clash between Islam and Christianity blocked Europe's access eastwards to the benefit of the Islamic world. The Western Europeans partially revived their interest in things Asian during the Crusades, which stretched from 1096 to 1291. It was a tantalising taste fed by the tales of traders such as Marco Polo. Then, in 1453, Constantinople fell to the forces of Islam and the Ottoman Empire, which effectively turned the Mediterranean into an Islamic lake. The decision of the Portuguese to sail around Africa and Christopher Columbus's trek westwards was based on the need to outflank a hostile Islamic world to reach the riches of the East and defeat the forces of Islam. Up until 1492, England was a geopolitical backwater on the edge of the known world. The discovery of America moved it to the centre.

An Economy of Plunder and Mercantilism

Medieval England was the ultimate in the survival of the fittest. Monarchs and their aristocratic retinues were not chosen for their book learning. Many of them were illiterate. The most sought-after quality for a political leader was the ability to succeed in battle. There was trade across borders. The cold and wet British climate produced a particularly profitable strain of wool. But the main source of income for governments came through pillage and plunder and the acquisition of territory that produced tributes and taxes. In 1400, roughly 60 per cent of the English population worked in agriculture, and most of them struggled to put enough on the table to keep their families alive. Successive English monarchs and aristocrats managed to finance their activities through a succession of wars in Scotland, Ireland, Wales and France, as well as by fighting each other. The pillage-and-plunder approach to economics crossed the Atlantic to the New World. It is estimated that the Spanish killed 8 million South American natives in the first genocide of the modern era. They enslaved millions more who were used to mine 181 tons of gold and 16,000 tons of silver at the height of the Spanish Empire from 1500 to 1650. Colonies had one purpose and one purpose only: to create wealth for the colonial power. This was the age of mercantilism.

Mercantilist economies worked on the basis of a country acquiring a one-way favourable balance of trade, a simple win/lose world economic system based on the acquisition of precious metals, mainly through conquest and followed by trade. The Spanish and the Portuguese started it, but the English were quick to follow suit. Mercantilism dominated European economies from the sixteenth to the late eighteenth centuries. In England, the high priest of mercantilism was Sir Thomas Mun, a director of the East India Company. In his posthumously published book *England's Treasure by Foreign Trade* (1664), Sir Thomas coined the term 'balance of trade' and set down the simple axiom that English trade policy should be to export more than it imports. To achieve this end, he proposed a number of measures including an import ban on goods that could be produced domestically; shipping on British ships only; a reduction on export duties; high tariffs; a ban on colonies trading with other countries; and state subsidies and aid for industries. One of the early and direct effects of mercantilism was the Navigation Acts. The first such Acts date back to 1381 and Richard II who decreed that 'no goods or merchandises shall be either exported or imported, but only in ships belonging to the king's subjects'. Restrictions added by the Tudors in the sixteenth century are credited with laying the foundations for the Royal Navy. In 1621 the Privy Council passed an order prohibiting the infant colony of Virginia from shipping tobacco to other countries. But it was not until 1651 under Cromwell that the first real Navigation Act came into force with the Act for Increase of

Shipping and Encouragement of this Nation. When Charles II was restored to the throne in 1660 the law was scrapped but restored just months later with additions extended the rights and restrictions of the Navigation Acts to British colonies. The 1660 Act opened the floodgates to more than a century of increasingly restrictive trade laws, which culminated in the Sugar Acts of 1764. It was not until 1849 that the free traders triumphed in British economic circles and the Navigation Acts were finally repealed.

England's strict adherence to the principles of mercantilism and its most infamous child (the Navigation Acts) was one of the principal reasons for the American Revolution. There were some positive effects from the mercantilist policy. One was that it spurred the growth of both the British Merchant and Royal Navy, and of course sea power became one of the central pillars of the British Empire. The American colonists benefitted from the shipbuilding boom (especially in New England) because American-built ships were classed as English products and were thus entitled to carry goods around the expanding British Empire. The Navigation Acts were also one of the reasons for the acquisition of the Dutch colony of New Amsterdam. The colonists soon discovered that if they traded with the Dutch colonials they could obtain a better deal than by sticking to the Navigation Acts. As London was more than 3,000 miles away, the British government found it difficult to stop the rampant smuggling operations, so it simply despatched a fleet, captured New Amsterdam and renamed it New York. However, the economic relationship soon came to be mirrored by the political. Under mercantilist rules the colonies were part of the British Empire but at the same time existed for the benefit of the mother country and were economically subservient to it. Politically, the colonists were 'freeborn Englishmen' entitled to all the rights and liberties of their relatives on the other side of the Atlantic such as those enshrined in Magna Carta and the Bill of Rights. But it became apparent that the political rights of the Americans were as subservient to the needs of England as trading rights.

The highly protective winner-takes-all mercantilist policies were a useful economic tool when Britain was establishing itself as an empire and industrial giant. However, once it had established itself as the workshop of the world, free trade became a more advantageous policy and in 1849 the Navigation Acts were repealed. Since then, the principles of free trade have dominated world economies and organisations such as the WTO have been set up to encourage it. That is not to say that mercantilism has disappeared from the economic lexicon. Developing economies are allowed greater leeway by the WTO in imposing tariffs because it is deemed that their infant industries require greater protection than those in the developed world. A revival of mercantilism is also seen in developed countries. Many economists believe that President Trump's America First policy, high tariffs, subsidies and emphasis on bringing American industry back to the States are little more than a renewed application of Sir Thomas Mun's seventeenth-century economic theories.

Corporate Anglo-America

Christopher Columbus nearly never left Europe. His plan to sail west to China had been rejected by the French, Portuguese, English and Spanish courts. It had just been dismissed again by King Ferdinand and Queen Isabella when the Spanish queen's confessor, one Juan Perez, persuaded the dual monarchy to change their minds and give it a go. The problem was money. There just wasn't enough of it around to risk it on an uncertain venture. Not a great deal of cash was required. Columbus wanted to build two ships and buy a third, the *Santa Maria*. They weren't big ships. The *Santa Maria* was only 100 tons and 75 feet long; about one-sixth the size of your average Russian oligarch's yacht. The total ship's complement for the *Pinta*, *Maria* and *Santa Maria* was only forty-five men. The amount of cash that was available was tied to a finite resource, which was in relatively short supply in fifteenth-century Europe. Coins were cast from either solid silver or gold and were carefully weighed by sceptical merchants before transactions were completed. The discoveries in America were about to provide a torrent of gold and silver that would shift the world's financial axis. But until Columbus returned, there was relatively little cash. The personal fortune of England's Henry VII, for instance, was restricted to an average-sized treasure chest in an unimpressive building called the Jewel House next to the Palace of Westminster. Today the Bank of England currently has 400,000 bars of gold in its vaults, and in a Manhattan basement the Federal Reserve Bank stores 6,200 tons.

As the size of the American treasure trove became apparent, so did the need for more money to exploit it. Some of it was paid for with the discoveries. But to extract the riches in the timeliest possible fashion, more cash was required. Europeans needed to speculate to accumulate and they developed the financial tools of banks, loans and equity investment to do just that. The English excelled at this new form of finance and their efforts laid the foundation for corporate America. Banking has been around in some form for at least 6,000 years. Babylonian merchants would deposit gold in ports which would be paid out when a shipment arrived. Promissory notes were being issued in India four thousand years ago, and the Chinese were using letters of credit around 200 BC. Loans with interest were commonplace in Ancient Greece and Rome, but they were usually made by individuals. But the nascent banking system took a severe knock with the introduction of Christianity and Islam. Both religions banned usury. One of the main reasons for Jewish domination of the banking industry was that Jews were exempt from the restrictions on charging interest for loans. During the Crusades, the Knights Templar acted as bankers to finance wars in the Middle East. The first recognisable modern banks started in the Italian city states to finance the Silk Road trade through Constantinople during the Renaissance. To circumvent the ban on usury, the bankers invented a number of legal fictions. For instance, a financier would charge an 'insurance premium' rather than interest on a loan.

The English acquired their banking skills from the Dutch. The latter controlled the lucrative spice trade in the seventeenth and eighteenth centuries through the Dutch East India Company (VOC) and for a time were England's main rival in the race for empire. They led the way in floating government-backed bonds for public infrastructure projects, introduced marine insurance and opened the Amsterdam Stock Exchange for equity finance. When the Dutch monarch William of Orange jointly assumed the English throne with his wife Mary in 1688, he brought with him the Dutch financial model, especially the structures related to public finance. Possibly the greatest Dutch contribution was shifting responsibility for payment of the public debt from the Crown to Parliament. The second was to amortise the debt through long-term bonds managed by the newly created Bank of England. The adoption of the Dutch model meant that English investments became a safe bet for the spice-generated Dutch investments and English banks started to accumulate capital.

In the early 1800s the US developed a variation of the bond market known as municipal, or muni, bonds. These were bonds sold by local and state authorities to raise money for infrastructure projects. In most cases the interest income received is tax deductible. One of the first municipal bond schemes was the building of the 363-mile Erie Canal between 1818 and 1824. The canal cost $7 million and 80 per cent of the money came from British investors. It paid off. The canal connected the untapped potential of the western plains to the markets of Europe. Tolls netted revenues of $121 million between 1824 and

1882 and freight traffic did not peak until 1951. The Erie Canal also established New York as America's premier port and the primary link between America and Europe. Municipal bonds have played a major role in building infrastructure elsewhere in America. The total number of capital assets built with muni finance is estimated at $4 trillion as of 2019.

The other big development was the creation of joint-stock companies, the forerunner of the modern corporation and equity-based finance. Equity – or shares – is a cheaper way of raising money for business ventures than a loan. The disadvantage of a loan is that you have to pay back the amount you borrowed plus interest and if the venture fails you can lose everything because you still have to repay the money. The advantage of a loan is that all the profit (minus the interest) goes into the borrower's pocket. With equity finance the risk is spread across a number of investors with each investor receiving a share of the profits based on the relative size of their investment. There is less risk but you have to share the profits. Equity investment is especially good if the business requires more capital than can be raised with a loan.

Like most financial systems, shareholdings have been around in one form or another for millennia. They were most commonly used in ancient times for maritime trade. Because of the threat of pirates, war or bad weather, shipping was a high-risk, high-reward business. Ship owners would club together with a group of merchants who would share the cost of the trade goods and the crew. When – or if – the ship returned to port they would split the profits. The onset of Europe's imperial age offered a new – and more dubious – opportunity for this ship-bound equity finance: privateering. Investors would buy shares in a warship which would be provided with what were called 'Letters of Marque' by a government which effectively legalised piracy against the enemy. The investors were allowed to keep any ship plus its cargo minus a cut for the government. Queen Elizabeth I was a big investor in English privateers. The English Sea Dogs, as they were known, set sail in 1560 and included such illustrious names as Sir John Hawkins, Sir Walter Raleigh and Sir Francis Drake. The Sea Dogs were effectively a private navy. The strategies they developed and the treasure they stole from Spanish galleons helped to establish the Royal Navy.

Privateers played a major role during the American Revolution. The colonial navy consisted of a mere sixty-five vessels, of which only eleven survived the war. In contrast, the various colonies issued 1,697 letters of marque whose holders were responsible for the sinking or capture of 2,208 British ships. Privateering remained an important part of the US naval economy until after the Civil War.

Joint-stock companies were also used to finance high-risk colonial settlements and trade monopolies. The first English joint-stock company was the Company of Merchant Adventurers to New Land, formed in 1553 to explore a route to China along the coast of Siberia. The crew froze to death. From the American point of view, the two most famous joint-stock companies were the Virginia Company of London (or the London Company) and the Plymouth Company. Both were given royal charters in 1606 for the exclusive right to settle and exploit territories in North America. The Virginia Company's slice extended extended between modern-day Cape Fear and Long Island Sound. The Plymouth Company was assigned territory which comprised modern-day New Jersey, New York, Pennsylvania and Delaware. To prevent clashes between the two colonies the settlements were separated by a 100-mile no-man's land. The Virginia Company struggled to survive in both physical and financial terms. Its royal charter was revised three times – in 1609, 1612 and 1621 – in a vain attempt to make the project more attractive to London investors. The development of the tobacco industry nearly saved the investors, but the English government's decision to block tobacco sales to the Dutch led to the dissolution of the company in 1624 and Virginia became a royal colony under the control of the Crown. The investors lost their money but founded the first English colony in North America. Investors in the Plymouth Colony suffered the same fate, only quicker. Its investors took fourteen years to send the Pilgrim Fathers across the ocean on the *Mayflower*, but the company was dissolved only four years later.

The failure of the Virginia and Plymouth companies did little to dampen the London craze for investing in joint-stock companies. Hundreds appeared and issued hand-written share certificates. The city's newly established network of coffee shops became a stock exchange trading floor. Fortunes were made overnight by dodgy underwriters and lost just as quickly. This unregulated financial chaos was peppered with rogues, leading to scandals such as the South Sea Bubble, which nearly sank the British economy in 1720. The unregulated chaos and the financial damage it wrought led to the British government banning the issue and sale of share certificates until the London Stock Exchange was created in 1825. This gave the US an opportunity to use the British experience to steal a march on the mother country by starting the first American stock exchange in Philadelphia in 1790. But the city of brotherly love was quickly overshadowed when the premier city on the eastern seaboard opened the New York Stock Exchange in 1817. As of February 2021, the New York Stock Exchange's market capitalisation of its listed companies was $25.6 trillion. The London Stock Exchange was capitalised at $4.6 trillion and together the two centres are the templates for a 24/7 global trading system.

The final piece in the jigsaw that established the modern financial system was the central bank. Up until the end of the seventeenth century the roles of the government and the monarch were indivisible. This gave the monarchs considerable political power but it also meant that they were personally liable for all debt and expenditure. As Europe became global, this personal liability became insupportable in both political and economic terms. What was required was a bank funded by the public and – in many cases – the government, which would act as the government's banker, lending it money against future revenues, issuing banknotes, minting coins, setting interest rates and overseeing the activities of other banks, controlling the money supply and ensuring financial stability for the benefit of the country as a whole. The first such central bank was Sweden's Riksbank, was founded in 1668 as joint-stock company. But the bank that set the standard for the rest of the world was the Bank of England, which opened its doors in 1699. The catalyst for the founding of the bank was the need for cash to pay for expensive wars in France and Ireland, as well as building up the Royal Navy and preventing the Stuarts' return to the English throne. The bank's original Royal Charter stated that it was created 'to promote the public good and benefit of our people', which is similar to the current mission statement: 'Promoting the good of the people of the United Kingdom by maintaining monetary and financial stability.'

During the colonial era, the Bank of England's remit extended across the Atlantic, but of course it stopped with independence. The need for a central bank for the new country quickly became a political hot potato. The Anglophile Federalists led by Alexander Hamilton wanted to recreate the centralised Bank of England on American territory and the Republican Party of Thomas Jefferson was opposed to any financial institution which took power away from the individual states. The Federalists won a temporary victory when George Washington reluctantly signed into law the bill creating the First Bank of the United States in 1791. But doubts over its role meant that its congressional charter was limited to twenty years. When the charter expired the bank was wound up. It was not until 1913 that the Federal Reserve Bank that performs the role of America's central bank was founded.

Despite being independent, the US was effectively an economic colony of the British Empire up to the start of the Civil War. This was best demonstrated by the Panic of 1837, which hit the economies on both sides of the Atlantic but was particularly damaging in America. In 1834 and 1835 Britain and America were booming, fuelled by British bank loans and America's westward expansion. The resultant cash surplus in the British banks led to increased and irresponsible speculation in American projects by the British and a run-down in the cash reserves at the Bank of England. At the same time, the improved British-financed transport links rebounded on the American cotton farmers as it meant they could move the crops to market faster, which led to a drop in cotton prices. Predicted cotton prices were used as collateral for British loans, which resulted in a widespread default on loans to British banks. At the same time, the American wheat crop of 1836/37 failed. The Bank of England reacted by raising interest rates to cover the cost of the defaults. British dominance of world money markets at the time meant that American banks were forced to follow suit. This led to another round of defaults among the cotton plantations. The crisis quickly spread to the rest of the country as cotton production at the time was the mainstay of the American economy. Out of 850 American banks, 343 were forced to close their doors. Unemployment soared to an estimated 25 per cent and hundreds of plantations went out of business. The American economy did not start to steadily grow again until the start of the California gold rush in 1848.

1776 and All That Cash

That was a big year. It was, of course, the year that the Declaration of Independence was written and signed by fifty-six American patriots. It was also the year that a Scottish philosopher and political economist named Adam Smith published his book *An Inquiry into the Nature and Causes of the Wealth of Nations*. It is arguable that Smith's work had as big an impact on the world of economics and finance as the Declaration of Independence did on politics. It put paid to the age of mercantilism and ushered in the principles of laissez-faire economics, capitalism, free enterprise, division of labour, free markets, wage competition and the 'invisible hand' of the market. The book was an immediate success. Within two years the government of Lord North was incorporating Smith's ideas in the British budget. But it was in America that the ideas of the Scottish economic philosopher found their most fertile ground. The concept of economic freedom was a perfect marriage with the struggle for political freedom as expressed in the Declaration of Independence. Laissez-faire capitalism became the economic watchword and guiding principle of nineteenth- and twentieth-century America and remains dominant to this day. It provided the philosophical impetus which spurred the country's growth and rapid industrialisation and transformed it from a colonial backwater into an economic super power. It is also blamed for generating monopolies and creating vast income disparities.

Adam Smith was born into an upper-class Scottish family. His father was a prominent lawyer and accountant and his mother was related to the powerful Douglas Clan. Two months after his parents' marriage, Smith's father died, leaving his widow to raise Adam on her own. Smith never married and remained close to his mother throughout his life. She died only four years before the political economist passed away in July 1790. Smith was educated at Glasgow and Oxford and decided on a career in academia. He first taught moral ethics and philosophy at the University of Edinburgh before setting up a permanent base at the rival Glasgow University. Smith wrote only two books. The first, *The Theory of Moral Sentiments*, was published in 1759 and dealt with the arcane subject of empathy and human relationships. It was well received and helped to fill his lectures. But as Smith career's progressed he discovered that his real interest and talent lay in developing the theory of political economics. Besides, people were more interested in making money than learning how to be empathetic.

In 1776, the prevailing economic system was still mercantilism. But it was on its way out under the pressures of expanding and increasingly complex economic structures. *The Wealth of Nations* helped kill it, nailed down the lid and buried it six feet deep. Mercantilism emerged from the lord/serf relationship with an emphasis on the possession of the physical trappings of wealth such as gold and silver. Markets were controlled by a political elite with the monarch at its apex. Adam Smith argued that the true source of wealth was labour and the organisation of its proper deployment. To ensure that labour achieved its full potential the 'invisible hand' of an unfettered market – or laissez-faire capitalism – was required. In practice this meant no tariffs, no protected industries, goods or markets, no Navigation Acts and the minimum of government regulation. Businesses would be set free to compete in an unregulated marketplace and allowed to succeed or fail in Darwinian fashion.

One of the key elements in Smith's thesis was the division of labour. He used the example of the manufacture of the modest pin to illustrate that it was more efficient for a worker to concentrate on what he did best, sell the products of his efforts and buy goods from other workers who were also focused on their best talents. At the very start of *Wealth of Nations*, Adam smith wrote:

I have seen a small manufactory of this kind where ten men only were employed, and where some of them consequently performed two or three distinct operations. But though they were very poor ... they could, when they exerted themselves, make among them about twelve pounds of pins in a day. Those ten persons, therefore, could make among them upwards of forty-eight thousand pins in a day. Each person, therefore, making a tenth part of forty-eight thousand pins, might be considered as making four thousand eight hundred pins in a day. But if they had all wrought separately and independently, and without any of them having been educated to this peculiar business, they certainly could not each of them have made twenty, perhaps not one pin in a day; that is, certainly, not the two hundred and fortieth, perhaps not the four thousand eight hundredth part of what they are at present capable of performing, in consequence of a proper division and combination of their different operations.

By switching to a system whereby each worker only performed one or two steps in the manufacturing process, productivity was increased by a factor of as much as fifty. The wealth created provided the owners with capital to hire more workers and produce more pins, which produced jobs and provided more cash for the workers to buy other goods and services. In short, it created wealth.

An example of how Adam Smith's pin metaphor had an impact in America is the story of Dr John Howe. Before 1840 almost all of the pins used in America were imported from Britain and produced by hand using the workers referred to in *The Wealth of Nations*. In 1832, Dr Samuel Howe took Smith's division of labour theory to its natural conclusion and invented a machine that could produce 24,000 pins a day without having to pay a labourer. By the 1870s the United States led the world in production of steel and iron pins, nails, rivets and spikes that held together everything from the tailor's clothes to the buildings and machines of America's fast-growing industrial revolution. Smith's division of labour theories spread across American industry and created assembly line industrialisation and mechanisation. In 1750, America's per capita level of industrialisation was just 4 per cent. In 1900 it was 69 per cent and poised to overtake Britain for the number one slot.

Adam Smith extended his division of labour theories to the global stage. He was the father of free trade and today would be called a globalist. One of the tenets of mercantilism was that everything – or at least as much as possible – had to be produced within the boundaries of the state. One of the reasons for tariffs and subsidies was to ensure that this was the case, as European countries were almost constantly at war and this created a fear of becoming dependent on another country's goods and then being cut off from them if war was declared. Smith argued that this was costly and inefficient. For example, if one country had more than enough coal to meet its energy needs and could extract and transport it to other countries at a reasonable price and a second country had access to inexpensive cotton and the factories to produce it, then the country with the coal should sell the black stuff to the country with the cotton and the country with the textiles should sell its product to the country with the coal. In both countries prices would be lowered, profits raised and the economies would grow. It was a win/win scenario. But it required an end to protective tariffs.

Smith also attacked the idea that a country's wealth should be measured in terms of the gold bullion it owned. Its true wealth, argued Smith, was measured in the productivity of its labour force. This thesis was taken up and expanded upon by David Ricardo, a big fan of Adam Smith and a wealthy financier turned political economist and politician. Ricardo's attack on the gold standard was prompted by the government's Bank Restriction Act of 1797. The reason was the Napoleonic Wars. Every time the French Emperor had a victory the British public would panic and rush to the bank to convert their paper money into secure and tangible gold. The consequence of these repeated panics was that the gold stocks which underwrote the economy were seriously depleted. Prime Minister William Pitt the Younger decided that the only way to deal with the problem was to ban the Bank of England from allowing the public to redeem their bank notes for gold. Effectively, Britain was taken off the gold standard for the first time. There was the inevitable public outcry, but Ricardo supported the government in his 1815 pamphlet *The High Price of Bullion*. The pamphlet contributed to Britain staying off the gold standard for another six years, but in 1821 it returned to it. The American Founding Fathers tied the dollar to silver, but later administrations moved it to gold. Economic crises in both countries forced periodic retreats from bullion-backed currencies and after the Second World War it was decided that gold payments would only be made between countries. Because of the strength of the US economy, most countries pegged their currencies to the value of the dollar, which in turn was pegged to gold at the price of $32 for one ounce of gold. But the cost of the Vietnam War and a run on gold reserves led President Nixon to stop international convertibility of the dollar in August 1971. The result was that the value of a country's currency became subject to Adam Smith's 'invisible hand' of the market. Gold remains an ultimate hedge for most countries and there are periodic demands from politicians on both sides of the Atlantic to tie their currencies to the metal.

Ricardo's most famous work was *Principles of Political Economy*, published in 1817, which introduced the theory of comparative advantage and completely destroyed the arguments of the proponents of high tariffs and mercantilists. Comparative advantage was the strongest argument advanced for the benefits of free trade. It was simple, said Ricardo: 'We should have no greater value if, by the discovery of new markets, we obtained double the quantity of foreign goods in exchange for a given quantity of ours.' Ironically, Ricardo's cogent argument in favour of free trade came two years after one of the most protectionist laws ever passed by British Parliament was enacted, and the battle for the repeal of the Corn Laws grew to represent a fight between those who wanted to retain tariffs as a last vestige of mercantilism and the followers of Adam Smith.

The Corn Laws were introduced when a sudden influx of foreign imports caused a drop in British corn prices at the end of the Napoleonic Wars in 1815. It should be made clear that in Britain corn did not refer to maize as in America, but included barley, rye and wheat. Protection of these basic staples was seen as essential for the stability of the British economy, especially by the wealthy aristocratic landowners who produced them. The tariffs, however, pushed up the price of bread and other staples to such an extent that workers in the newly industrialised manufacturing centres couldn't afford the basic foods required for their table. Ricardo argued that Britain's economic future lay not in agriculture but in its manufacturing industry and that the politically powerful landowners were being allowed to profit at the expense of the industrial workers. The starving workers agreed and rioted in support of free trade.

Ricardo died in 1823 while the Corn Laws were still very much in play. But his cause was taken up by Richard Cobden. In 1838 Cobden joined forces with political reformers known as the Chartists to create the Anti-Corn Law League, with Cobden at its head. The league became one of the world's first and most successful lobby organisations. Cobden toured the country making speeches and helped devise the penny post to create mass mailings against the legislation. There were, Cobden wrote, four good reasons for repealing the Corn Laws and moving to free trade:

> First, it would guarantee the prosperity of the manufacturer by affording him outlets for his products. Second, it would relieve the Condition of England question by cheapening the price of food and ensuring more regular employment. Third, it would make English agriculture more efficient by stimulating demand for its products in urban and industrial areas. Fourth, it would introduce through mutually advantageous international trade a new era of international fellowship and peace. The only barrier to these four beneficent solutions was the ignorant self-interest of the landlords, the bread-taxing oligarchy, unprincipled, unfeeling, rapacious and plundering.

Cobden's Anti-Corn Law League had its effect. But the final straw that broke the back of the corn camel was nature; 1845 was a bad year for British agriculture. The wheat harvest was savaged by a wet and cold July and August and a potato blight in Ireland brought starvation and forced migration. In January 1846 Prime Minister Sir Robert Peel was forced to publicly admit that Cobden was right about the Corn Laws and repealed them. The Corn Laws were the last hurrah of the mercantilists. By the 1850s – with Cobden's aid – free trade had spread to France, Belgium and the Netherlands. The end of protectionist tariffs in Europe created a vast market for America's farmers in the opening Midwest. By 1913, Britain imported 80 per cent of its wheat, most of it from the American breadbasket. Free trade between America and Britain, however, was largely one-way. The US shipped its agricultural products largely tariff-free but slapped high tariffs on Britain's industrial goods to protect its own developing industrial base. Between the end of the Civil War and the start of the First World War, American tariffs averaged about 45 per cent. By the turn of the twentieth century the US industrial base had grown to such an extent that it dominated world manufacturing. Its economic interests were now best served by embracing free trade and by 1920 tariffs had plummeted to just 18 per cent. But the allure of protectionism was still there and when the Great Depression hit, Congress retreated behind high tariff walls in the form of the 1930 Smoot-Hawley Tariff Act, which slapped a range of tariffs on 20,000 imports averaging 59 per cent. Smooth-Hawley was meant to protect American jobs, but most experts believe that it cost jobs and helped to create the economic conditions which led to the Second World War. The outcome was a determination to return to free trade in the post-war world in the form of the 1947 General

Agreement on Tariffs and Trade (GATT), which had the specific aim of establishing rules aimed at reducing and/or eliminating trade barriers. In April 1994 GATT spawned the World Trade Organisation. GATT was a set of rules. The WTO is a properly constituted inter-governmental organisation with a headquarters and staff who are charged with negotiating free trade agreements and resolving disputes between 164 member states.

Burn It, Invent It, Move It

England's green and pleasant land was created on top of pillars of coal. And not just any coal, but high-quality bituminous coal with a carbon content of 86 to 88 per cent, which means it gives a hot and efficient burn. There was also a reasonable quantity of anthracite, which has an even better carbon content of 95 per cent. Most of the coal is gone now. At its peak in 1913 the industry was extracting 187 million tons of the black stuff from mines that stretch far and deep under the North Sea. The switch to oil and non-fossil fuels plus the cost of deep mining versus cheap coal imports had pushed British coal production down to just 18 million tonnes by 2016. But there is no doubt that the former abundance of coal fuelled Britain's industrial revolution and spurred a string of inventions which laid the manufacturing base in Britain and America.

At the top of the invention list was the coal-powered steam engine. Credit for this invention usually goes to James Watt, after whom the unit of power is named. Watt's contribution was massive, but the first widely used steam engine was built by one Thomas Newcomen in 1712. His creation was in turn a variation on an engine built by the Anglo-French scientific duo Robert Boyle and Denis Papin. The Newcomen Engine, as it was called, used a cylinder filled with water, coal to heat the water and a piston that was forced up and down. The piston was attached to an arm which operated a vertical pump working in a straight up-and-down motion. The Newcomen Engine was an instant hit with mine owners who used it to pump water out of their flooded shafts. Hundreds were sold across Britain and Europe. One even turned up in Midlothian, Virginia (now a Richmond suburb) where America's first coal mines were opened. But because of its design, the potential of the Newcomen Engine was limited to the mining industry. James Watt took it to the next level. He realised that with some adaptations he could increase the efficiency, so introduced a separate condenser which dramatically cut the amount of energy required. His new steam engine was an even bigger hit with the mine owners than Newcomen's invention. But it was Watt's next adaptation that made his name almost synonymous with the industrial revolution. Watt formed a partnership with Matthew Boulton who provided the financial and marketing genius that drove Watt's inventions forward. Boulton suggested that the engine be adapted to power a rotational arm. It was, and Watt's steam engine would power the railways, steel presses, textile factories, steamships and a host of other machinery.

The advantages of moving freight and passengers in carriages sitting atop parallel lines had been discovered as early as the sixteenth century. Cart wheels became stuck in mud and ruts or their wheels flew off when they hit a rock. Tracks reduced friction and increased speed and efficiency. The first railway lines were made of wood and the carriages were drawn by horses. They were not very good. They splintered, cracked and broke. By 1750, Britain's industrial revolution had grown to the point where it was producing large quantities of pig iron. It was a small step from surplus production to replacing wooden rails with iron rails. But the carriages were still horse-drawn. The iron tracks and pit ponies became a regular feature in Britain's expanding coal mines, transporting the black stuff from the coal face to the bottom of the shaft to be hauled to the surface, first with a hand winch and later with Newcomen's engine and finally with James Watt's invention.

For railways to take off Watt's steam engine needed to be adapted. The problem was that the engine was stationary. It was designed to sit beside a mine shaft or on a factory floor and work machinery. To make it mobile required a transportable boiler with a separate condenser. Working with his Scottish engineer William Murdoch, Watt patented just such an invention in 1784. His work was expanded upon by Cornishman Richard Trevithick in 1804 with his *Catch Me Who Can* and *Puffing Devil* locomotives. Over the following twenty-one years there were numerous improvements by other engineers. Then along came George Stephenson with the *Rocket* and the first 25-mile railway from Stockton to Darlington. Stephenson's locomotive was aptly named. British railways took off like a rocket. In 1830 the first inter-city rail, from London to Manchester, was opened. Investors poured money into the new transport system. By 1870 Britain had 16,000 miles of railways. Almost every city, town and village was linked by tracks carrying 423 million passengers a year. A trip from London to Manchester was cut from five uncomfortable days in a horse-drawn carriage to under a day by rail. Britain shrank. It was not just the travelling public who benefitted. The railways connected markets across

Britain. Beef could be moved from Scotland to the south-east before it spoiled. The same with lamb and mutton from the hills of Cumbria and fruit from Kent. Tin, coal and manufactured products were quickly and efficiently transported to growing ports. Adam Smith's division of labour theory was realised on a national scale and a fast, efficient and extensive transport system turned the country into the workshop of the world. Between 1870 and 1900 output per head of population rose 500 per cent. At its height, Britain was producing a quarter of world's manufacturing output, financed by a growing banking sector and shipped around the world by the globe's largest merchant navy to the world's largest empire in history, protected by the world's largest naval defence force.

Just two years after Stephenson's *Rocket*, the US started to the lay the first track for the west-heading Baltimore and Ohio Railroad. By 1850 the US had 9,000 miles of track, most connecting the major towns and cities of the north-east to each other, and the cities to the ports of Boston, Baltimore and especially New York. Railway building in the South took off after the Civil War. By 1890 there were 29,000 miles of track in the South. In 1880 the US had 17,800 freight locomotives moving 23,600 tons of freight. The crucial moment in American railway history – in American commerce – came on 10 May 1869, when a golden spike was driven into a railway plate at Promontory Summit in the then Utah Territory. The 17.6 carat spike linked the Central Pacific and Union Pacific Railroads and the Pacific and Atlantic coasts. A 3,400-mile journey from New York to San Francisco which took a rambling wagon train four months or more to make could now be completed in as little as three days. Fruit and vegetables from southern California could be sold on New York market stalls. Cattle were driven to the railhead at Chicago, which grew to be America's second city. Grain was moved quicker and all year round to East Coast ports because the canals often froze in the winter. Reaching the Pacific coast, the railroad also opened a new Asian market to American goods.

There was, however, a railway problem in Britain, America and everywhere else when the first railways sprung into being. The tracks were made of iron, produced mainly in Britain and shipped across the oceans. Iron was cheap to produce and the British were good at shaping and pounding it into railway tracks. But it cracked and buckled under the weight of the heavy locomotives and carriages and the extremes of heat and cold. A new, more durable product was needed: steel. The tempered version of iron had been available as an expensive weapon of war since the sixth century BC, but until British inventor Henry Bessemer came along no one had figured out how to mass produce the product at an affordable price. Bessemer took the root product of cheap pig iron and simply blew air through it to remove the impurities. The problem of buckling rail tracks was solved overnight. But steel quickly found other uses in buildings, bridges, steamships, the skyscrapers of New York and eventually car production. Britain quickly took the lead in world steel production, jumping from 1 million tonnes in 1890 to 5 million by 1900. Production reached its peak in 1970 with 28 million tonnes a year. But British production was dwarfed by that of America thanks to the 1866 discovery of huge iron deposits in Minnesota's Mesabi range, plus the business genius of a British immigrant named Andrew Carnegie. Carnegie made his first million during the Civil War in the infant oil industry. He then invested that money bringing the Bessemer steel process to America. Carnegie established US steel, which became a monopoly controlling virtually of America's iron and steel production. From this base he turned the US into the world's largest iron and steel producer. In 1901, Carnegie became the richest man in the world when he sold his shares in the company for $303,450,000. He spent the last eighteen years of his life giving the money away to philanthropic projects in America and his native Scotland.

Goods could now traverse vast inland distances quickly and easily. But they still had to cross huge expanses of water to reach export markets. Robert Fulton's 1807 steamboat changed America's river traffic and inspired a young Samuel Langhorne Clemens to change his name to Mark Twain. American-born Fulton developed his ideas for a steam-driven boat during a twenty-year sojourn in Britain and France. During his travels he met James Watt and studied his steam engine. In 1806 he returned to America and the following year successfully sailed the steam-powered 'North River Steamboat' on a 150-mile Hudson River voyage from Albany to New York. Fulton's steamboat became a regular feature on American rivers carrying passengers and freight across country. But its design, limited range and heavy coal consumption made it impractical for ocean-going travel. For most of the nineteenth century sail remained supreme, and improved ship designs, such as the famous clipper ships, kept them at the forefront of trans-oceanic shipping. Here America played a major role in the building of the British fleet. The famous British oak forest that built the fleets of Drake and Nelson were severely depleted by the early nineteenth century. So the British navy turned to the virgin forests of New England for timber and most of the British ships sailed under the Red Ensign were built in American shipyards. In an unspoken tit for tat, the Royal Navy turned the Atlantic Ocean into a British lake to the mutual benefit of trade between both countries.

It wasn't until the end of the nineteenth century that steel-plated, steam-driven ships began to make a major impact on the world's oceans. There were outstanding exceptions such as Isambard Kingdom Brunel's *Great Western* and *Great Britain*. But long-distance steam ships were hampered by the need to carry a large amount of coal and/or stop frequently to take on fresh fuel supplies. Gradually, the great capacity of steam-driven ships plus improved efficiency chased the sailing vessels from the oceans. The final straw came with the substitution of oil for coal as the ships' fuel. Oil boilers were smaller. Oil-fired ships sailed faster. Oil did not require teams of stokers. Refuelling could be carried out at sea. In 1906 the Royal Navy launched its first oil-fired, steel-plated Dreadnought class ships and a naval armaments race began which ended with the First World War

Raising Taxes and Spending Them

Death and taxes are the only guarantees in life, as the well-worn adage goes. In fact, throughout history the two were inextricably linked. Taxes were most often levied by kings, queens, prime ministers, parliaments and presidents to wage war and inflict death. They were always unpopular whether they were the window tax that turned early British factories into airless hellholes, or Mrs Thatcher's poll tax that sparked riots in Trafalgar Square, or the stamp duty which ignited a revolution and created a nation. But perhaps the most unpopular tax of all time – and the one that has now become the accepted norm across the globe, and the biggest government money-raiser – is income tax.

The tax on income was the brainchild of Prime Minister William Pitt the Younger and was introduced in 1798 to relieve the pressure on the British exchequer brought about by the Napoleonic Wars so soon after the disastrous American Revolution. The first income tax was relatively tiny with a top rate of just 10 per cent. But it was hated, and in 1802–03 was quickly abolished, then promptly reimposed when fighting resumed before being dispensed with in 1816, a year after the Battle of Waterloo. Public opposition to a tax on income had as much to do with political philosophy as it did with the thought of parting with hard-earned cash. For the tax to be effectively levied, the taxpayer had to reveal details of his income. This was regarded at the time as an unacceptable attack on an Englishman's personal liberty. But income tax also made it easier for the government to budget, so in 1841 a tax on income was restored.

Disraeli and Gladstone, the two political giants of the second half of the nineteenth century, both promised an end to income tax, but they both failed to deliver and the tax continued, peaking at 98 per cent on unearned income in 1974. In 2019 the top rate of income tax was 40 per cent. In the financial year 2017/18, the UK government raised $237 billion in income tax and $172 billion in income-related National Insurance contributions. Together they represented over 40 per cent of government revenues.

Alexander Hamilton laid the foundations for America's tax system. The first Treasury Secretary avoided anything like an income tax and went for a system of duties on manufactured imports. Up until 1913, 90 per cent of America's tax revenues were derived from import duties and excise tax. Hamilton reckoned that this not only provided a useful source of revenue but also gave protection for American manufacturers to compete with their British counterparts. The policy was popular in the manufacturing North and unpopular in the agrarian South where farmers were forced to pay more for their British-produced textiles and iron products. Many historians regard the North–South battle over import tariffs as a major contributing cause to the Civil War. It wasn't until 1861 that the US followed the British example and introduced income tax, and then it was repealed in 1872. As in Britain, the tax on income was introduced to deal with the cost of war and, as in Britain, it started low, a top rate of just 5 per cent. One of the reasons for the opposition to a federal income tax was that it was regarded as an unacceptable infringement of states' rights and therefore unconstitutional. Congress eventually circumvented this problem by amending the Constitution. The sixteenth amendment reads: 'The Congress shall have power to lay and collect taxes on incomes, from whatever source derived, without apportionment among the several States, and without regard to any census or enumeration.' Again, the taxes started low, just 6 per cent at the top rate. But the exigencies of war meant that it jumped to 77 per cent in 1918. In 2018 the top rate for federal US income tax was 37 per cent. But then there was a variable state income tax on top of that, which ranged from California's 13.3 per cent to nothing in Texas and Florida. Income tax, however, had long since overtaken tariffs and excise as the major source of government revenues. In 2018 it provided about half of the government's money while import duties and excise tax made up only 4 per cent.

Having raised the money, the British and American governments found ways to spend it on things other than war. The rapid industrialisation of the nineteenth century in both countries provided opportunities to build capital infrastructures to sustain growth and social programmes to correct the consequences of unplanned development. Prior to the industrial revolution, the bulk of the British population lived in rural poverty. The machine age held out the prospect of a glamorous city life, but for many they just continued to struggle with low wages, insecure employment, unsanitary conditions and poor diet. On top of that they were squeezed into overcrowded housing and lost connections to supportive family and social structures. The US was not all that different, except that a large proportion of those crowding into American cities were European immigrants rather than American farm workers. Both governments were forced to address these problems in order to defuse growing social unrest.

Britain in the eighteenth century was undergoing a social transition from an agrarian society dominated by an aristocratic elite to an industrial one dominated by big business capital. The change started as early as Tudor times when a growing population and increased movement of people led to a large number of displaced vagabonds. This led to the poor laws and the dreaded Dickensian workhouses so vividly portrayed in novels such as *Oliver Twist* and which remained in existence until 1930. The Poor Law remained in existence until 1948. By the middle of the nineteenth century more Britons lived in the cities than the countryside and it had become painfully apparent that local government structures had to be created to cope with growing urban problems. These local governments became the channel through which social improvements were implemented, including sewers, clean water, sanitation projects and public hospitals. In 1870 free compulsory education was introduced throughout the country. In 1909 Winston Churchill (then a member of the Liberal Party and President of the Board of Trade) introduced old age pensions, which were followed in 1911 by the National Insurance Act to finance medical care. During the inter-war years Britain built its first public housing (or council houses) and started unemployment benefits. All of the above laid the groundwork for the British welfare state following the Labour Party's post-war landslide victory.

The blueprint for the 'cradle to grave' welfare state was written not by a Labour politician, but by a Liberal Party economist cum politician. William Beveridge's *Report to the Parliament on Social Insurance and Allied Services* was published in November 1942 and quickly renamed 'The Beveridge Plan'. It proposed that everyone of working age should pay a weekly national insurance which would finance benefits for unemployment, sickness and retirement. A big chunk of the money would also go to pay for the creation of a National Health Service to provide free medical care for all. The Beveridge Plan was fully implemented after the Labour Party victory with the addition of the nationalisation of key industries such as steel, coal, railways, electricity, water and telecommunications.

As the United States has a federal structure, the provision of social welfare programmes varied considerably from state to state, and still does. In colonial times and throughout most of the nineteenth century the Americans adopted the British Poor Laws. One thing that America had in abundance was land, and state and federal governments in the nineteenth century made free use of this resource to reward disabled war veterans. But most of the welfare programmes were administered by churches, philanthropists, businesses and family networks. This was partly because the average American standard of living was 30–50 per cent higher than in Britain and this meant there was more private money available for social improvements. Private money remains a major source for welfare programmes, but the problems created by the Great Depression of the 1930s underscored the need for federal aid and structures. The economy shrank by half during the depression years and unemployment soared to a quarter of the workforce. Federal government was forced to intervene because private and state organisations were unable to cope. The results included federal money for the 1932 Emergency Relief Act, the 1933 Civilian Conservation Act and the 1935 Social Security Act. The next big change to America's welfare spending came with Democratic President Lyndon B. Johnson's 'Great Society' of the 1960s. Unlike the Great Depression, Johnson's 'War on Poverty' was in response to almost unprecedented growth in the American economy and a desire to see increased wealth reflected in a more equitable division. In this respect, Britain's welfare state was often held up by American liberals as the example to follow. The result was a raft of legislation that improved civil rights, medical care, rural poverty, urban renewal and transport. The programmes faced opposition from conservative Republicans, but were expanded by presidents Richard Nixon and Gerald Ford.

However, the US fought shy of emulating Britain's National Health Service. For those who could afford it, America offered the best medical care in the world. But about 25 per cent of the population found the hefty private health insurance premiums beyond their means and suffered accordingly. Johnson's Great Society had the first stab at improving health service with Medicare and Medicaid. The former contributes to the medical costs of patients over sixty-five and some younger disabled people. Medicaid is a means-tested free health service used by about

25 per cent of the population. It is jointly funded by the federal and state governments and administered by the states. The quality of service varies considerably according to the political complexion of the state government. President Jimmy Carter, working with Senator Edward Kennedy, proposed the establishment of a universal healthcare system during his administration, but it never made it off the ground. It was shelved during the Reagan years and then revived during the Clinton administration with a proposal to force all employers to provide health insurance for their employees. First Lady Hillary Rodham Clinton was placed in charge of spearheading the Act through Congress and failed in the face of combined resistance from conservative Republicans, libertarians, pharmaceutical companies and insurance companies. It was left to President Barack Obama to eventually force through the 2010 Affordable Care Act. Obamacare, as it was quickly dubbed, cut the number of uninsured Americans in half by expanding the provisions of Medicare and Medicaid to force insurance companies to accept all applicants regardless of age, sex or pre-existing conditions, with federal subsidies for low-income patients. The Trump administration tried and failed several times to repeal Obamacare and replace it with a system more acceptable to Republican conservatives. President Joe Biden has promised to preserve and extend Obamacare.

The theoretical foundations of the welfare state were laid by British economist John Maynard Keynes, later Lord Keynes, arguably the most influential economist of the twentieth century. Keynes challenged the views of Smith and Ricardo that management of the economy was best left to the vagaries of market forces. He argued that the performance of the economy was dependent on overall spending and that it was largely irrelevant if the spending came from government or private business. In fact, Keynes wrote in his 1936 *General Theory of Employment, Interest and Money* that governments should intervene when the economy plummets. Keynesian economics dominated Anglo-American economic planning until the end of the 1970s when Milton Friedman at the University of Chicago joined forces with more conservative politics to produce what was called Thatcherism in Britain and Reaganism in America. Friedman promoted an alternative macroeconomic viewpoint known as monetarism and argued that a steady, small expansion of the money supply with strong links to private business was the preferred policy. Prime Minister Margaret Thatcher began the systematic dismantling of the Keynesian welfare state soon after taking office in 1979. Taxes were cut, free trade pursued, key industries privatised, government powers centralised, and the power of the unions was curtailed in order to encourage a more flexible labour force. Mrs Thatcher's policies were mirrored in the US after Ronald Reagan took the oath of office in January 1981. The one exception was the National Health Service. President Reagan was wholeheartedly opposed to 'socialised medicine' while Mrs Thatcher declared that 'the NHS is safe in our hands', although she did outsource the provision of many NHS services to private suppliers. The Reagan/Thatcher policies were continued by successive British and American administrations regardless of their political complexion right up to the 2008/09 banking crisis, which resulted in a return to Keynesian economics in the US and a long austerity programme in the UK.

One effect of Thatcherism was to open the British market to foreign capital. Keynesian economics did not work if key industries were owned by foreign capital. The political effect was either outright state ownership or a close relationship between the government and companies such as Imperial Chemical Industries and British Petroleum. BP, for instance, was a private company, but the government held a majority of its shares and thus had a major say in its policies. One of the first actions of Margaret Thatcher was to start the sale of the British government's stake in BP. Imperial Chemical Industries was gradually broken up and eventually completely sold in 2008 to the Dutch chemical company AkzoNobel. The 1970s and 1980s also saw a fire sale of British manufacturing assets and the development of North Sea oil and gas. Much of the investment capital raised was redirected to high-end service industries such as the legal and financial sectors and London re-emerged as a world financial capital. Support for free trade and the free movement of capital was one of the foundation stones of Thatcherism, which meant that British money was invested abroad and foreign capital was invested in British companies. By 2017 an estimated 37 per cent of the turnover of non-financial businesses came from foreign-owned companies. Half of the UK stock market is owned by foreign companies. Thatcherism coincided with the launch of the Worldwide Web and the consequent explosion of telecommunications and the globalist economy.

Another effect of Thatcherism was to tie the American and British economies closer together. At a Buckingham Palace banquet during President Trump's June 2019 state visit, Prime Minister Theresa May said that the Anglo-American trading relationship was worth $190 billion a year. President Trump replied that Britain and America have more than $1 trillion invested in each other's economies. In terms of recent foreign direct investment, the US was the number one investor in Britain with $450 billion in 2017. Britain invested a staggering $541 billion in the US in 2017 – 10 per cent of its total foreign investments. When the two leaders were speaking, British membership of the EU was up in the air and President Trump was promising to 'quadruple' Anglo-American trade if Britain opted for a 'No Deal' Brexit.

The two sides of the Atlantic, however, have started to diverge over free trade. Successive British governments since Mrs Thatcher have remained fully committed to the principle, but the Obama administration responded with a shift towards protectionist policies backed up with multilateral trade deals. But almost full-blown unilateralist mercantilism was enthusiastically embraced by President Trump, who saw American economic supremacy seriously challenged by the rise of China and the trading power of the European Union. Joe Biden is moving American trading policy back towards the Obama years.

10

Gun Control: Militia *vs* Tyranny

Tyranny Today

James Madison was the fourth president of the United States. He was also the author of the first ten amendments to the US Constitution, which are known as the Bill of Rights. He made it clear that the second amendment – the one that refers to the right to bear arms – was largely inspired by Britain's historical experience and the British Bill of Rights. The amendment was one of the least controversial when it was ratified in 1791. In fact, for almost 200 years gun control wasn't an issue in America and the second amendment was referred to as the 'Lost Amendment'. But times change. The second amendment is now a benchmark divide between American liberals and conservatives, between Republicans and Democrats. It has come to represent a threat to individual liberty for one side and a threat to life on the other. The amendment itself is only one short, simple and – one would have thought – easy to understand sentence: 'A well regulated militia, being necessary to the security of a free state, the right of the people to keep and bear arms, shall not be infringed.' What is clear is that the amendment has two parts. The first refers to the need for a 'well regulated militia, being necessary to the security of a free state'. The second half says that 'the right of the people to keep and bear arms, shall not be infringed'. Is this one amendment which should be read in its entirety with the second half contingent on the first? Or has the need for a citizen's militia become redundant in the modern age and therefore only the second half remains relevant?

The National Rifle Association (NRA) is in no doubt. Engraved on the wall of its entrance lobby are the words: 'The right of the people to keep and bear arms, shall not be infringed.' All references to militias are conspicuous by their absence. But why do American people need guns?

Conservatives say it is to protect themselves and their families from bad people with guns. Liberals reply: then take the guns away from the baddies as well as the goodies so no one can shoot. It is a policy that has worked in Britain, Australia and other developed countries. Conservatives retort that individual gun ownership is the ultimate deterrent against tyranny – the tyranny of anarchy and the tyranny of overbearing government.

The tyranny argument is being used increasingly by senior American politicians. Texan senator Ted Cruz used it in his campaign literature when he ran for the Republican presidential nomination:

> The second amendment isn't just for protecting hunting rights, and it's not only to safeguard your right to target practice. It's a constitutional right to protect your children, your family, your home, our lives, and to serve as the ultimate check against governmental tyranny – for the protection of liberty.

Senator Cruz is a significant beneficiary of the lobbying efforts of the NRA. In 2018 it was reported that Cruz received $77,450 from the right-wing blogger and broadcaster Erick Erickson, who justified the purchase of high-capacity semi-automatic weapons on the grounds that individual American citizens required protection from their own government. He wrote that the second amendment, 'contrary to much of today's conversation, has just as much to do with people protecting themselves from tyranny as it does burglars. Under the real purpose of the second amendment a 30-round magazine might be too small.'

President Trump became embroiled in the tyranny cause. During the 2016 presidential election he claimed that, if elected, Hillary Clinton would appoint a pro-gun control justice to the Supreme Court. He said: 'If she gets to pick her judges, nothing you can do folks.' He paused and added: 'Although the second amendment people – maybe there is, I don't know.' The Trump campaign team denied Democrat claims that Donald Trump had suggested gun violence to stop a pro-gun-control interpretation of the second amendment, but the seed had been planted.

Democratic politicians are not above using the tyranny argument and the threat of second amendment violence for their own political ends. New York congressman Tom Suozzi was criticised for suggesting in a town hall meeting that armed insurrection against President Trump could be necessary. He said: 'This is where the second amendment comes in quite frankly, because you know, what if the president wants to ignore the courts. What would you do? What would we do?' Congressman Suozzi was immediately and severely criticised by Democrats and Republicans. But again, the seed was planted.

Militia (and Some Tyranny) Yesterday

Most of the forty-seven descendants who have ruled England (and later Wales, Scotland and Ireland) were ruthless tyrants. They had to be to keep their crowns and the heads upon which they sat. Medieval Britain was a lawless place with very little in the way of effective communication, transport, political infrastructure or any of the other essential elements of a secure modern state.

The country was run along the lines of the feudal system which William I brought with him from Normandy. The feudal system was a complex web of oaths, loyalties and responsibilities up and down the social ladder. Since one of the main pastimes of the Middle Ages was waging war, a primary purpose of the feudal system was to provide a quick and easy method of assembling forces without the king or any of his subordinate lords being forced to deal with an expensive standing army, which threatened the additional danger that such an army could become an alternative political platform in its own right.

The significance of this political reality was that any laws involving weapons in early medieval England emphasised the importance of the formation of a militia. The first such law was Henry II's Act of Assizes in 1181. Henry had a good reason for strengthening the national militia. He was a compromise monarch who ascended the throne after a long and bitter war between his mother Empress Matilda and his uncle King Stephen. He needed a system to quickly raise an army to protect him from any other over-ambitious relatives with their eye on the throne, as well as building up what became known as the Angevin Empire in France, England, Ireland and Wales. The Act of Assizes provided him with the men and weapons to do the job. Every knight was required to own a helmet, lance, shield and mail shirt. Every freeman worth at least 16 marks had to have the same. Every freeman worth 10 marks needed a mail shirt, iron cap and lance. Every freeman, regardless of their financial standing, had to own at least a padded defensive jacket (a gambeson), iron cap and lance. Finally, Henry II required all the members of his militia to swear loyalty to him, thus short-circuiting the normal route through the feudal chain of command and strengthening the political power of the throne.

As the Middle Ages progressed, other laws requiring the ownership of weapons were added. Singled out for particular attention was the long bow – the cruise missile of the Middle Ages. Not only was almost every freeman, peasant and serf required to own a bow, they also had to spend their free time practising the art of archery. To make certain they did, laws were passed in England, Scotland and Wales banning the increasingly popular sports of golf and football because they interfered with archery practice. In fact, there is still a law on the English statute books requiring every adult male to practice archery for two hours a week. The stiff requirements paid off. English archers were feared throughout Europe and their deadly aim was responsible for decimating the flower of French chivalry at the battles of Crecy and Agincourt.

But even though everyone was required to own weapons and practise with them, there were still laws to control their use off the battlefield. For instance, most cities and towns prohibited the carrying of weapons such as lances, maces and swords inside the city limits. The only people allowed to carry such weapons were the sheriff's officers and the aldermen responsible for keeping the peace. If you were visiting a city you had to check your weapons at an approved tavern and collect them when you left. Such weapons were essential when travelling outside major cities and towns because the law of the land (or the local lord of the manor) was largely restricted to the urban or semi-urban areas. People who broke the law – 'outlaws' – were banished to live outside the manor.

The most important law regulating the control of weapons was the 1328 Statute of Northampton, which is still cited today in American and British cases involving gun control. The statute was decreed by Edward III in the wake of the overthrow of his father by his mother Isabella and her lover Roger Mortimer. In fact, the decree was actually orchestrated by Isabella because Edward III was only fourteen when he was crowned. With the possibility of a civil war looming, the Statue of Northampton declared:

> No man great nor small, of what condition soever he be, except the king's servants in his presence, and his ministers in executing of the king's precepts, or of their office, and such as be in their company assisting them, and also [upon a cry made for arms to keep the peace, and the same in such places where such acts happen] be so hardy to come before the King's justices, or other of the King's ministers doing their office, with force and arms, nor bring no force in affray of the peace, nor to go nor ride armed by night nor by day, in fairs, markets, nor in the presence of the justices or other ministers, nor in no part elsewhere, upon pain to forfeit their armour to the King, and their bodies to prison at the King's pleasure. And that the King's justices in

their presence, sheriffs, and other ministers in their bailiwicks, lords of franchises, and their bailiffs in the same, and mayors and bailiffs of cities and boroughs, within the same cities and boroughs, and borough-holders, constables, and wardens of the peace within their wards, shall have power to execute this act. And that the justices assigned, at their coming down into the country, shall have power to enquire how such officers and lords have exercised their offices in this case, and to punish them whom they find that have not done that which pertained to their office.

Then there were the sumptuary laws which were part of English life from the reign of Edward III in the fourteenth century. These laws dictated what clothes different classes of people were allowed to wear so that everyone knew at a glance exactly where a person stood on the social ladder. The practice continued well into the seventeenth century. In fact, in early Massachusetts, only people with a personal fortune of at least £200 were allowed to wear lace, gold thread and other finery. The sumptuary laws were the main reason for the world's first known gun control law. It dates from 1526 and prohibits anyone with a fortune of less than £100 from carrying a gun (or musket). The punishment was a fine and prison sentence. Guns, however, were becoming increasingly popular, and Henry VIII repealed the law in 1541.

The issue of tyranny mixed with gun control did not arise until England had a standing army and there was nothing that could be called a standing army until the seventeenth-century English Civil Wars. This was called the New Model Army because the Parliament-controlled army was 'remodelled' on a national rather than regional basis. Its members were banned from sitting in Parliament (an exception was made for Oliver Cromwell, the army's second-in-command).

The New Model Army proved a great military success. It went on to defeat the Royalists and later fought successful campaigns in Ireland, Scotland, Flanders and the Caribbean. Oliver Cromwell took complete control of it just before it sailed for its ruthless conquest of Ireland in 1649. The army was paid by Parliament but it quickly established itself as an independent and alternative political force. Cromwell was insistent that its officers and ranks were filled with devout Puritans chosen on the basis of merit and loyalty to him and the radical Republican Puritan cause. In some cases sections of the army went too far in developing independent political plans. The best known was a group called 'the Levellers' (see chapter 3). They were not a political party, more of a movement, but they were definitely way before their time.

Their demands, which were enumerated in their 1647 'Agreement of the People', included religious freedom an end to debtors' prisons, equality before the law, parliamentary elections every two years and the unheard of and completely radical idea of virtually universal male suffrage. All this was too much for Cromwell, whose political and social roots were with the landed gentry of East Anglia. In 1649 he brutally suppressed a series of three Levellers-inspired mutinies.

There were other problems between Parliament and the New Model Army. The biggest was Parliament's reluctance to actually pay the soldiers. The other was the legislators' refusal to remove Charles I from the throne. In 1648, Colonel Thomas Pride led a detachment from the army against Parliament and forcibly removed the non-Puritan members who were blocking the removal of the king. 'Pride's Purge' left what was called a Rump Parliament of radical Puritans who had no qualms with ordering the removal of the head of King Charles. Oliver Cromwell's name was third on the death warrant.

By this time the army was the recognised tool of Cromwell who made sure that they were paid well and on time. On top of that, many of them were rewarded with land grants after the conquest of Ireland, which, as discussed earlier, laid the seeds for the Irish Troubles of the twentieth century. In 1653, Parliament and Cromwell clashed over religious and other demands and the military commander sent in his musketeers to clear the Palace of Westminster of his opponents. The Rump Parliament was renamed the Barebones Parliament and became an irrelevancy. The New Model Army promptly proclaimed Oliver Cromwell Lord Protector on the then princely salary of £100,000 a year. Britain's first and only dictatorship had begun.

Cromwell was a religious fanatic backed by a religiously fanatical army. His rule from 1653 until his death in 1658 at the age of fifty-nine was noted as a joyless and brutal regime enforced with violence. He was a tyrant who created an army that repaid him by elevating him to the highest position in the land. Cromwell and the New Model Army are an historical example of the need to bear arms for protection against tyranny, and the memory of Oliver Cromwell and his army was still fresh in the minds of America's founding fathers when they were framing the Constitution.

Further Intolerable Acts

When Cromwell died, England nearly fell into a new civil war as the New Model Army broke into competing factions. The threat of the military was one of the reasons that a hastily reassembled Parliament decided to restore the monarchy in the form of Charles's son, Charles II, who is credited with the creation of England's first standing professional army, the main regiments of which were comprised primarily of soldiers from the New Model Army who were by now prepared to subjugate their radical political ideals to the security of a military career and regular pay.

The English army swore its loyalty to the monarch rather than to Parliament or the government and still does. But Parliament was now sovereign over the Crown, although just how sovereign took a few more decades to finally determine. Charles II had a relatively good relationship with Parliament and because of that the military abandoned its political ambitions and stuck to the job of defending the realm. But Charles was taking no chances. He managed to pack Parliament with his supporters and these Tories (as they were called) passed laws forcing gunsmiths to submit a weekly report to government officials of all gun sales. Parliament also passed a law requiring special licences for the importation of guns. Finally, in 1671, the Game Act took effect. This was ostensibly an anti-poaching law. But it also had the effect of depriving former members of Cromwell's army of their weapons. The Game Act prohibited the use of guns, bows and hunting dogs by anyone who did not own a large landed estate. As the landed estate owners were almost all keen monarchists, this gave the king and his supporters an opportunity to disarm everyone who wasn't.

The British public were prepared to put up with these and other restrictions because Charles II was a Protestant who represented the end of the dictatorship and the restoration of parliamentary sovereignty and a freer society. But the new king had no children with his Portuguese wife Catherine of Braganza, although he did have fourteen illegitimate children by seven mistresses. Charles II recognised all of his children and showered them with titles and land, but he could not give any of them the English throne. That was filled by his younger brother James II. In 1673, James II converted to the Roman Catholic Church. This was totally unacceptable to Parliament and the British public. The experience of the previous 150 years had given them a deep fear and hatred of Catholics. There was a widespread belief that a Catholic monarch would ban Anglicanism and take England back into the Catholic fold, and in doing so take away all the rights and liberties for which they had been fighting since the start of the seventeenth century.

Parliament responded to James II's conversion to Catholicism with an exclusion bill that banned Catholics from the English throne. Charles II, who was keen for his brother to succeed him, resolved the issue by marrying off James's daughter Mary to the Dutch Protestant William of Orange. This still failed to satisfy Parliament, so he dissolved it. In February 1685, Charles II died and was succeeded by his Catholic brother James who was almost immediately challenged for the throne by Charles II's son James, Duke of Monmouth. The latter was illegitimate, but anti-Catholic feeling was running so high that thousands of Protestants were prepared to overlook the circumstances of his birth and flocked to his banner when he landed at Lyme Regis on 10 June, 1688. The Monmouth Rebellion was defeated in just over a month and Monmouth was executed along with hundreds of supporters.

James II responded to the rebellion by increasing the size of his standing army, appointing Catholic generals to command key regiments, appointing Catholics to important public offices, attempting to pack Parliament with Catholic supporters, establishing diplomatic relations with the Vatican and trying to repeal laws discriminating against Catholics and preventing them from holding high office. British Protestants initially turned a blind eye because they believed that when James died he would be succeeded by his Protestant daughter Mary as he, like his brother, had no legitimate male heirs. Then on 10 June 1688, James II's devout Catholic wife Mary gave birth to a healthy boy and the situation changed overnight. Envoys were sent to the Netherlands to ask William of Orange if he would invade England on behalf of the Protestant cause and replace James along with his wife Mary.

William of Orange assembled an invasion force twice the size of the Spanish Armada, 40,000 men and 463 ships. After a false start he landed in Devon and started a slow march towards London. The now extremely unpopular James II suffered the disgrace of an evaporating army, and only a month after William's landing on 9 December, he sailed for France. The throne was vacant and waiting to be filled by his daughter Mary and her husband William. Most people in Britain thought they had been saved from a Catholic tyranny and hailed the accession of William and Mary as a 'Glorious Revolution'.

William wanted to be named co-monarch alongside his wife Mary who was in the natural line of succession to the throne. Parliament was at first unwilling to go along with this plan, but in the end it agreed in return for the monarchy's approval of the 1689 British Bill of Rights which established the principles of a constitutional monarchy in black and white. It also laid the first rules about a standing army, the quartering of British troops and the right to bear arms. The first section listed the ways in which James II attempted to 'subvert' the Protestant religion and the 'laws and liberties' of England. These included 'raising and keeping a standing army ... without the consent of Parliament' and 'causing good subjects ... to be disarmed'. The second half of the Bill of Rights laid down the remedies. Among them was a ban on a standing army 'in time of peace ... without the consent of Parliament' and a ban on the quartering of soldiers 'contrary to law'. Clause seven stipulated that Protestants 'may have arms for their defence suitable to their conditions, and as allowed by law'.

The British Bill of Rights was Parliament's reaction to the tyranny imposed by a Protestant-inspired standing army during the rule of Oliver Cromwell, and then, only half a century later, a second tyrannical government that threatened the restoration of a Catholic monarchy. It seemed that neither extreme could be trusted and therefore the only sure trustee of their liberty was the individual. Democracy and a constitutional monarchy at that time were unformed and untested political systems. They had the potential to work. But then they might fail. Until they had proven themselves, Parliament demanded that the people be allowed weapons to protect themselves.

The effects of the New Model Army, and the threat of Catholic James, were closely watched by colonial America. They also had a big impact on its development. There was a major influx of settlers to the loyalist-leaning Southern colonies during Cromwell's rule. Conversely, when the monarchy was restored, the North witnessed a population boom. American colonials were very aware of the tyranny *versus* guns debate and were directly affected by seventeenth-century English events and involved in them.

There was an immediate and obvious need for a citizen militia in colonial America, and because a militia is useless without weapons, there was no gun control. The earliest settlers were understandably faced with armed opposition from the existing occupants, the Native Americans. Less than two years after arriving in Jamestown, the English settlers were fighting a full-blown conflict known as Powhatan's War. This lasted until 1646. The Puritans and New England started their first major conflict with the natives in 1636. It lasted a year and was called the Pequot War. There were scores of other wars and skirmishes between colonialists and Native Americans including King Philip's War (1675–78) and Pontiac's Rebellion (1763–68). British and French settlers fought a series of running battles with the help of shifting Native American alliances from 1689 until the British conquest of French Canada in 1763. There were also a series of wars against the Dutch. The first one in 1664 resulted in the capture of New York and the second one led to New York's recapture by the Dutch, who then used it as a bargaining chip to secure their monopoly of the lucrative East Indies spice trade. Spain was a traditional British foe and the Southern colonies were in constant fear of Spanish attack in the early years. From 1739 to 1748, American militia were recruited by the British to fight Spain in South America. They included George Washington's older half-brother, Lawrence. The Southern plantation owners lived in constant fear of slave revolts and between 1739 and the Emancipation Proclamation of 1863 there were thirty-three uprisings by African Americans. Finally, there were a series of local revolts and rebellions against British colonial authority which had to be put down. These included Bacon's Rebellion (1676), Culpepper's Rebellion (1677), Leigler's Rebellion (1689–91), Coade's Rebellion (1689–92) and the Kent Island Rebellion (1637).

The settlers were left to their own devices to resolve these problems. Guns and a citizen militia were accepted as a necessary part of colonial life. In fact, gun ownership was positively encouraged by the colonial governments. As early as 1623, Virginia's colonials were prohibited from travelling outside of a settlement unless they were 'well-armed'. Massachusetts, from 1644, fined citizens who were not properly armed and in 1770 Georgia passed a law requiring citizens to take guns to church. There were exceptions to these laws. Slaves and Native Americans were denied the use of firearms in most colonies.

This started to change in the aftermath of the Seven Years War from 1756 to 1763, which, in America, was called the French and Indian War and lasted two years longer. The Seven Years War was the first global war and was fought in Europe, South America, the Caribbean, North America, India and the Philippines. In America, the battle was between France and Britain over who should be the dominant power in North America. It ended with British victory and possession of Canada and the Ohio River Valley. The other indirect consequence of the war and its aftermath was the American War of Independence. The issues of gun control, militias and government tyranny were prominent among the sparks that set it ablaze.

The Seven Years War caused the British national debt to nearly double from £75.6 million to over £132.6 million. Most of the expense was incurred in North America. Up until 1753, the American colonies were more or less an unmixed financial blessing which provided the raw materials that fuelled Britain's early industrial revolution. For this reason the colonists paid virtually no taxes. The British exchequer was keen not to upset the golden goose. At the same time, each colony's charter allowed for a large degree of self-government and protection of the rights and liberties enjoyed by all Englishmen. In 1763, Britain could no longer afford such disinterested generosity, especially as success in the war also increased the need for greater defence expenditure to protect a booming population from native Americans and a possible French Canadian rebellion.

The result was a series of taxes levied only on the thirteen American colonies. They included the 1765 Stamp Act and 1767 Townshend Tariffs. The previously untaxed colonists were outraged. This was a reversal of their previously enviable tax situation. It was also a complete denial of the long-standing English tradition that Parliament could only tax those that it represented. The colonists elected representatives to their individual colonial legislatures, but none to the British Parliament that had now decided to burden them with taxes. The cry went up: 'No Taxation Without Representation.' The final straw was the 1773 Tea Act. Bostonians responded by donning Native American costumes, boarding the tea ships and dumping the tea chests in Boston Harbor. This was too much for Prime Minister Lord North and George III. It was decided that an example had to be made of the rebellious Bostonians so that the other colonies would be coerced into proper behaviour. In Britain the laws were called the 'Coercive Acts'; in America they were called 'the Intolerable Acts'. The Boston Port Act closed the port of Boston until the city had paid compensation for the destroyed tea. The Massachusetts Government Act withdrew the colonial charter of Massachusetts and granted the royally appointed governor the power to appoint all public officials and restrict town hall meetings to one a year. The Administration Justice Act allowed the governor to order trials of public officials to be held in Britain and the Quartering Act allowed troops to be quartered in unoccupied buildings.

The Intolerable Acts had the opposite of the desired effect. Instead of being cowed into submission, the other colonies called a continental Congress to coordinate action. At the same time, local bodies started calling for the people to arm themselves. A prime example was issued by the denizens of Lancaster County in Pennsylvania: 'In the event of Great Britain attempting to force unjust laws upon us by the strength of arms, our case we leave to heaven and our rifles.' As the threat of armed rebellion grew, the British resorted to gun control. On 1 September 1774, a detachment of British soldiers sailed up the Mystic River and seized the Massachusetts colonial militia's gunpowder store. Governor Thomas Gage began warrantless searches for arms, ammunition and gunpowder and set up blockades to confiscate any arms being smuggled into Boston. The first shot of the Revolution, fired on 19 April 1775, was the result of British troops marching from Boston to Lexington and Concord to confiscate a cache of weapons.

As well as the continental Congress, each of the colonies set up their own representative governments separate from British authorities and many of them drew up a bill of rights based largely on the 1689 British Bill of Rights, setting down the each colony's guaranteed liberties. The Virginia Declaration of Rights, for example, included a clause stating that 'a well regulated militia, composed of the body of the people, trained to arms, is the proper natural and safe defense of a free state'. Similar pronouncements were made by the legislatures of Massachusetts, North Carolina, Pennsylvania and Vermont.

Guns and Tyranny in a Democracy

The war ended with the surrender of Lord Cornwallis at Yorktown on 19 October 1781. The cause that had united the thirteen American colonies was no longer and they immediately went their separate competing ways. There were Articles of Confederation which loosely tied the former colonies, but years of benign neglect by Britain, followed by taxes and war, had left Americans with a strong streak of libertarianism and a deep distrust of a federal government. The outcome was a national government with no power, especially military power, as each of the new states insisted on controlling their own defence with their own militia, which required their citizens to continue to bear arms.

The loose confederation led to increasing economic and inevitable political problems for the former colonies. They had been forced to borrow heavily to pay for the war and the British were demanding compensation for property confiscated during and after the revolution. American banks and merchants were being squeezed. Their remedy was to pass on the shortfall to the farmers who were then the backbone of the American economy. When they couldn't pay, the banks went to the courts and foreclosed on their properties. In 1786 a group of angry farmers from western Massachusetts rose up under the command of former Continental Army captain Daniel Shays, marched on the courts and destroyed the foreclosure documents. Shays' rebellion was eventually suppressed by the Massachusetts militia, but it was done in a ham-fisted way that convinced George Washington and others that a strong federal government was necessary, and in 1787 delegates were invited to a constitutional convention in Philadelphia to hammer out the framework of that government.

The Constitution that was agreed established the governmental mechanism for the former colonies. Almost immediately, a demand was made for amendments which set down the rights of American citizens.

The American Bill of Rights was codified as the first ten amendments to the US Constitution. James Madison's original draft of the second amendment was a sentence longer than what was eventually agreed. It read: 'The right of the people to keep and bear arms shall not be infringed; a well armed and well regulated militia being the best security of a free country; but no person religiously scrupulous of bearing arms shall be compelled to render military service in person.' What was referred to as the conscientious objector clause was a clear attempt to win support from the Pennsylvania delegation and its Quaker population. However, the other delegates were concerned that it created an opt-out for anyone who wanted to avoid serving in the citizens' militia, which the delegates saw as an essential duty.

The 'Lost Amendment' was rarely referred to in the courts for many years. This was mainly because America remained a frontier land where in many parts there was only limited law enforcement. Hostile Native Americans were part of daily life and guns were needed to put meat on the table as well as for protection. Indeed, guns were considered so important for protection that when gold was discovered in California, Congress passed a law providing free army weapons to the prospectors to protect them from bandits and claim jumpers. The exceptions to gun ownership remained African Americans and Native Americans. In fact, in 1857, the Supreme Court in the Dred Scott Case ruled that African Americans – freemen or slaves – were not entitled to the protection of the second amendment or any other part of the US Constitution. This changed with the Civil War, but after the Reconstruction, the Southern states again barred African Americans from gun ownership and the Supreme Court upheld the ban on the basis that the issue should be decided by the individual states.

Back in Britain the need for personal weaponry had substantially diminished. The democratic principles inherent in a constitutional monarchy were well established by the start of the nineteenth century, and the perceived threat of Catholic tyranny had vanished. In 1829, Parliament passed the Catholic Emancipation Bill, which restored full political rights to Catholics. Militias were also a thing of the past. A well-regulated police force handled law and order issues at home and a standing army and navy was fully deployed overseas in the service of the expanding British Empire. The need to carry guns as stipulated in the 1689 Bill of Rights was rapidly diminishing. In 1903, Parliament passed the first gun control law of modern times. The argument had shifted from militias for protection against tyranny to the restriction on weapon ownership for protection against gun-toting criminals.

The Pistol Act was followed by a series of increasingly restrictive laws on gun ownership passed in 1920, 1933, 1937 and 1968. Then came the Dunblane Massacre of 1996 when Thomas Hamilton tore through a primary school in Dunblane, Scotland, killing sixteen children and one teacher. The following year, pistols were banned.

Under current British law, shotguns, single-shot rifles and semi-automatic .22 calibre rifles are permitted. Everything else is banned. A licence has to be held by every weapons owner and they have to renew it every five years. Each application for a firearms certificate has to be made to the police, who must be satisfied that the owner has a 'good reason' to own the weapon and is 'without danger to the public safety or to the peace'. The police will also interview the owner, conduct a background check and make certain that the gun is safely stored in a locked cabinet. Finally, the owner must produce two character references before the licence is issued. If you own a gun, you can also expect to make friends with your local police, who will regularly inspect your home. The penalty for possession of any type of firearm without a certificate is up to fourteen years in prison and an unlimited fine. In 2017, eight people in England and Wales were murdered using a gun.

The American industrial revolution and consequent urbanisation led to similar shifts in attitude to gun ownership there, but with distinct differences. The rise in manufacturing coincided with the settlement of the West, and guns and militia were still needed for that settlement. Then there was the American Civil War in which state militias and gun ownership continued to play a major role. Although a standing army gradually grew in the nineteenth century to protect westward expansion, there were only 38,000 men in the entire US Army in 1880, compared to 422,000 in the German Army and about 250,000 in the British. The individual states also retained the right to maintain militias, which eventually morphed into the modern-day National Guard, and the Supreme Court regularly ruled that the individual states maintained a large measure of control over laws relating to gun ownership. To this day, gun control laws can vary dramatically from state to state.

Despite this, in the 1920s and 1930s the American public became increasingly focused on the rising number of gun murders brought about by gang warfare and turf battles during the Prohibition Era. In 1934, Congress moved to pass legislation banning the gangland weapon of choice, the sawn-off shotgun. It was successful, and partly because it had the support of the NRA. Karl Frederick, who was then president of the NRA, was called upon to testify. He told a congressional hearing: 'I have never believed in the general practice of carrying weapons. I seldom carry one ... I do not believe in the general promiscuousness of the toting of guns. I think it should be sharply restricted and only under licenses.' The law was passed and challenged by gun enthusiasts who took it to the Supreme Court on the back of the second amendment. In 1938 it was upheld. The Justices said that ownership of guns was protected only in the context of the need to maintain 'a well-regulated militia'. The Founding Fathers did not mean it to be a catch-all right for every individual.

The NRA had its roots in the militia argument and the aftermath of the Civil War. It was founded in 1871 by General Ambrose Burnside who had been shocked during the war at the poor level of marksmanship among the Union's conscripts. He was determined that if another war broke out the general population of men would know how to handle a gun and hit the side of a barn. The National Rifle Association was founded to teach marksmanship and gun safety – no other reason. It was not a founded as a lobby organisation for the gun industry and enthusiasts, and would not become one for more than a hundred years.

On 22 November 1963 President John F. Kennedy was assassinated in Dallas. The presidential assassination was followed on 4 April 1968 by the shooting of civil rights leader Martin Luther King Jr, followed only two months later by the gunning down of Bobby Kennedy on 6 June 1968. The calls for gun control were deafening. In October 1968 – after a tough battle against second amendment enthusiasts – the 1968 Gun Control Act was passed by Congress. It banned the mail-order sale of rifles and shotguns and prohibited convicted criminals, drug users and the mentally incompetent from gun ownership. It had NRA support. This was the last time that the National Rifle Association supported gun control legislation. The 1968 Gun Control Act was the start of a split between the traditionalists who wanted to continue the focus on gun safety, and activists who campaigned to promote the individual rights which they argued were guaranteed by the second amendment.

The latter group was led by Harlon Carter, who spent two years in prison for murder as a teenager after shooting a Mexican immigrant. Carter formed the NRA's political lobbying arm, the NRA Institute for Legislative Action. In 1977 he staged a coup, ousted the board of the NRA, took over as director and packed the organisation with his supporters. From that moment, the NRA shifted the primary focus of its activities to blocking any attempt at gun control whether at city, county, state or federal level. According to a CNN report, out of 535 members of the US Senate and House of Representatives, 307 have received financial support from the NRA. Possibly more important is public backing from the organisation. The exact number of NRA members is uncertain. The organisation said in 2018 that it was about 5 million but the Pew Research Centre estimated that it was as many as 14 million. Most of them join because the NRA backs the second amendment and opposes gun control. They receive from the organisation a regularly updated chart grading state and federal politicians on the basis of their position on gun control. A large proportion of the membership votes the way the NRA tells them. Political careers are made and broken by the NRA grading system.

The growing power of the NRA was forcibly demonstrated in the most recent Supreme Court decision on gun control and the second amendment – *DC* v. *Heller* in 2008. This 5-4 ruling was the first time that the court had addressed the issue of whether or not the second amendment allowed individuals to own weapons for self-defence. The city government of Washington, D.C. had passed a law banning handguns and requiring the owners of rifles and shotguns to keep their weapons unloaded, disassembled and in a locked cabinet. Security guard Dick Anthony Heller and five others challenged the law on the grounds that the second amendment guaranteed them the right to bear arms for self-defence. The Supreme Court agreed. As the narrow majority ruling said, the second amendment 'guarantees the individual right to possess and carry weapons in case of confrontation'.

Gun control is one of the great contrasts between Britain and America. The United States has more guns than people. In fact, it has the largest per capita gun numbers in the world. In 2016 there were about 11,000 gun-related homicides in the United States and more than 38,000 gun-related deaths, which include suicides and accidental shootings. In the same period in the UK there were twenty-six fatalities from gun-related crimes. That is equivalent to 130 because Britain's population is one-fifth the size of the US. Until 1791 the gun control policies of Britain and America worked in tandem. The experiences of medieval England, the English Civil Wars, Oliver Cromwell, James II and the British Bill of Rights were comparable to the requirements of frontier America. The countries started to diverge with the ratification of the Bill of Rights. The largely British experience led to the inclusion of the second amendment. But its subsequent interpretation and implementation is an American phenomenon.

Part of the reason for the divergence was the constitutional arrangements of the two countries. Britain had, and has, an unwritten constitution. British political figures have long been regarded as towering personalities with feet of clay. The constitution takes account of their fallibility by being based on precedent and the hodgepodge of laws that are under constant revision and reflect changing social circumstances. The gun control clause of the 1689 Bill of Rights reflects this. It allows individual Protestants to bear arms for protection against the threat of Catholic tyranny but then adds the get-out phrase 'as allowed by law'. The end of the Catholic threat, Catholic Emancipation, the acceptance of the need for a standing army, the success of democracy and the constitutional monarchy and urbanisation meant that the public's requirements shifted from the need for an armed militia for protection against tyranny to a well-regulated police force for protection against criminals.

America's Constitution is written, it is metaphorically chiselled in granite, and the men who did the chiselling have been granted god-like status. The Founding Fathers, who lived more than 200 years ago in an agrarian society without mass communication or transport and whose largest weapon was a muzzle-loading cannon, are to this day considered the ultimate source of legal and political wisdom. Political speeches and Supreme Court judgements constantly make reference to the 'intention' of the 'framers of the Constitution'. Their ankles are winged and their brows adorned with crowns of laurel leaves.

But even James Madison, the author of the second amendment, had doubts about gun control and the application of the second amendment. In 1787 he introduced a bill in the Virginia legislature to prevent out-of-season deer hunting and to penalise people who 'shall bear a gun out of his enclosed ground, unless whilst performing military duty'. Then in 1809, while Madison was president, there was the Rittenhouse Affair involving a dispute between the federal government and the Pennsylvania state government over the distribution of loot from a captured enemy ship. The US Supreme Court rejected the state government's case and ordered that it hand over its share of the prize money. They refused. Federal marshals were sent to collect the money. They were prevented from enforcing the ruling by armed members of the Pennsylvania state militia. The Pennsylvania Governor Simon Snyder appealed to President James Madison using the militia argument of guns against tyranny. Madison sided with the Supreme Court and said that the marshals were not agents of tyranny but rather representatives of the elected federal government. Snyder backed down.

Such an argument is unlikely to hold water with Wayne la Pierre, current chief executive of the NRA. In 1995, when he was executive vice president of the organisation, he wrote a six-page attack on pro-gun control legislators: 'It doesn't matter to them that the semi-auto ban gives jack-booted government thugs more power to take away our constitutional rights, break in our doors, seize our guns, destroy our property, and even injure or kill us ... Not too long ago, it was unthinkable for federal agents wearing Nazi bucket helmets and black storm trooper uniforms to attack law-abiding citizens.'

The problem with the defence-against-tyranny argument is that it raises the question of who determines whether or not they are the victim of government tyranny and what constitutes that tyranny. If an individual is allowed to bear arms than it should follow that the individual is allowed to determine whether or not they are the victim of a tyrannical act that justifies the use of a weapon. That is the argument of second amendment enthusiasts who have based themselves in the remoter parts of the American West, established heavily armed mini-states, declared themselves free of the restrictions of federal law and threatened with violence anyone who trespasses on their land. All in the name of the second amendment.

If taken to its logical conclusion, a strict adherence to the second amendment undermines not only law enforcement but also the Constitution itself. It justifies cherry picking the laws which individuals want to support, declaring tyrannical those that they oppose and defending their position with weapons allowed them by the very constitution which they are opposing. The tyranny argument held water when the tyrant was a puritanical dictator, a monarch driven by religious and political beliefs contrary to the wider public good or a government intent on taxing a populace without offering them parliamentary representation. A democratically elected government cannot – by its very nature – be a tyrannical one. If it is, then that democratic system is seriously flawed.

11

High Brow, Low Brow

Soft Power

People like to do business with people they like. They prefer to work with those they know and trust; someone with whom they share a common history, values and traditions. Kinship is often a powerful business motivator. Keep it in the family. A good dinner party guest is usually a good business partner. A shared knowledge of literature, music, films and the latest Netflix offerings is a useful icebreaker. Then there is humour. It may not always be understood, but it should at least be appreciated. A common language helps, or at least a something approaching a communal tongue.

In the complex, ever-changing world of global politics cultural common denominators have become an important element of what American political scientist Joseph Nye called 'soft power'. The idea of cultural links as a tool of international relations is a relatively recent phenomenon. Most past efforts would have been better described as 'hard power' in that if a state or ruler wanted something, they took it by force of arms. Other alternatives were marital alliances and trade agreements, the latter often imposed at the point of a gun. The advantage of 'hard power' is that it is swift and sure. The disadvantage, particularly in today's nuclear world, is that it could have disastrous consequences. Soft power is more complicated. It takes longer. But it is safer and its effects can be much longer-lasting.

Britain and the US are the world's two leading exponents of 'soft power' diplomacy according to most of the monitoring organisations. Both are helped by the language legacy of the British Empire which has left 25 per cent of the world speaking English. This has in turn created a huge market for Hollywood films. The language link has also established English as the world's lingua franca of contract law and international business. London is headquarters of four of the world's six largest law firms. Britain was the first country in the world to launch itself into the world of 'soft power diplomacy' in the 1930s, although the term was yet to be invented. In 1934 it founded what became the British Council to create a 'friendly knowledge and understanding of this country, of its philosophy and way of life, which will lead to a sympathetic appreciation of British foreign policy'. In 2019 there were 200 British Council offices in 100 countries. Two years before the start of the British Council, the BBC started broadcasts to the empire with what was then termed the BBC Empire Service. The BBC World Service now broadcasts news about Britain and the world in forty different languages. It is the largest broadcasting organisation in the world and reaches 210 million people a week.

America entered the world of organised soft power diplomacy in 1953 with the creation of the United States Information Agency (USIA). Closely modelled on the British experience, its main purpose was to counter Soviet efforts in Cold War propaganda. When setting up the USIA, President Eisenhower argued that the key to success was balance and credibility rather than propaganda. It also promoted the American way of life with structures similar to the British Council and operated a number of broadcasting outlets modelled on the BBC World Service, including Radio Free Europe, Voice of America, Radio and TV Marti, Radio Liberty and Radio Free Asia. Unfortunately, political pressures from Congress and the Central Intelligence Agency meant that the USIA strayed too often and too far into propaganda. The agency went out of business in 1999 and its responsibilities were split between the State Department's Under Secretary of State for Public Diplomacy and Public Affairs and the Broadcasting Board of Governors.

Perhaps America's most effective form of soft diplomacy was non-governmental – Hollywood. American films and television are regularly watched by an estimated one half of the world's population. They generally project an image of national prosperity and well-being with all-American action heroes fighting for truth, justice and the American way. British films and television have focused more on history and costume dramas. They reflect a reputation based on past glories while the US is a thrusting power in the here and now. The common language, historical links and the increasingly international audience and production links means that the films are Anglo-American, with British and American actors, crew and post-production units sometimes criss-crossing the Atlantic several times before release. This binational approach is in many ways a contemporary reflection of the cultural relationship that has existed between Britain and America since the first settlements in the seventeenth century and one of the main reasons American and British culture have a global reach.

Educating Uncle Sam and John Bull

The British have historically been world education leaders and their historic emphasis on book learning crossed the Atlantic so that since the late nineteenth century, Britain and America have led the world in literacy rates and first-rate universities. The world's oldest school was founded in AD 597 at Canterbury by St Augustine. It is still in existence as a top public (private) school and is known as King's College, Canterbury. Oxford University is the second oldest university in the world (after Bologna). They started teaching there in 1096. Cambridge came about after a group of Oxford students clashed with the local townsfolk, upped sticks and moved to the other side of the country to and set up shop there. Most of the schools in medieval England were set up to educate the younger sons of the aristocracy for jobs in the clergy, government or law. The elder sons were taught to be war leaders, which did not require knowledge of Latin grammar and Greek. The first attempt at something approaching universal education was the establishment of 'free grammar schools' in the mid-sixteenth century during the reign of Edward VI. In theory, the grammar schools were open to all. But in practice, working-class children from an early age were needed to work in England's predominantly agrarian economy. The wealthy middle classes paid to send their children to the growing number of private schools such as Winchester (founded 1394), Eton (founded 1441) and Harrow (founded 1572). The very wealthy hired tutors to educate their children at home. For the aspiring classes there were the 'dame schools' or 'village schools' where, for a nominal fee, your children could be taught the three r's of reading, writing and arithmetic. Dame schools were so called because lessons were held in the parlour of a local woman who had basic teaching skills.

Until relatively modern times, education in England was linked to the Church. Before the Reformation that meant the Roman Catholic Church. After the Reformation it meant the Church of England, and since the Anglican Church was the established State religion, the Church, the State and education became inextricably tied. In fact, until well into the nineteenth century university professors, fellows and most schoolmasters had to be ordained Church of England clergymen.

The link between the teaching profession and the Church was just as strong in America, especially in New England. However, the connection was not with the Anglican Church but with the dissenters who fled religious persecution. Almost all of the early teaching staffs of America's Ivy League universities were clergymen drawn from the Congregational or a related Protestant church. The Puritans placed a high premium on education, especially reading. Their lives revolved around the teachings of the Bible and to learn from the Bible one had to know how to read. The result was that the first school in American was the Boston Latin School, founded in 1636, only a dozen years after the landing at Plymouth Rock. Its curriculum was a carbon copy of that of the English schools and heavily based on teaching Latin and Greek. Latin remains a major part of the school's curriculum. The Puritans also founded America's first university, Harvard, in 1636, and named it after the English-born clergyman John Harvard, who bequeathed the university the then astonishing sum of £789 and the even more generous gift of 329 books. Harvard was modelled on its founder's alma mater, Cambridge University. In fact, it is no coincidence that Harvard is based outside of Boston in the town of Cambridge, Massachusetts. All of the colonial universities used their English counterparts as templates. The textbooks were imported from England, as were the teaching staff. Almost complete American dependence on British textbooks continued up to and beyond the Civil War. Most of the colonial students attended university to become clergymen. In the seventeenth and eighteenth centuries, most doctors and lawyers in both England and America were taught through apprenticeships, although some 117 American doctors from the colonial era were educated at Edinburgh University, including the American patriot Dr Benjamin Rush. At the time, Edinburgh was the world's predominant school of medicine.

Different social and economic circumstances meant that the South lagged behind the North when it came to education. Many of the planters were younger sons of English aristocrats sent to the colonies to make their fortunes in cotton and tobacco. Until slavery became established by the end of the seventeenth century the job of field hands was performed by illiterate indentured servants brought from England, Ireland and Scotland. Spending money on their education, or the education of their children, was considered a waste. The planters' children were taught basic numeracy and literacy at home by governesses or their mothers and then shipped off to England to finish their education. The only major colonial-era university in the South was the College of William and Mary in Williamsburg, Virginia. The South continued to lag behind in education after independence. In 1900, fourteen states did not have compulsory education. They were all in the South. Even as late as 1945, very few Southern children were educated beyond the age of thirteen.

As America expanded west the increasingly remote communities found it difficult to find enough teachers to educate their children. The solution was to replicate the dame and village schools that they had left behind in rural England. But these basic one-room schoolhouses still suffered from a shortage of teachers and so they adopted what was called the 'Monitorial System', which was developed by British educators Andrew Bell and Joseph Lancaster. This system involved the older children as helpers or 'monitors' to help the hard-pressed adult teachers with the younger children.

The few who did make it past high school and to university found themselves in carbon copies of the English seats of learning. Degree courses were three to four years. Classes were taught in Latin. The textbooks were imported from England, as were a large number of the professors. Church attendance was mandatory. Then in 1828 the president of Yale University, Jeremiah Day, introduced the guidelines for a four-year broad-based course that became known as the liberal arts education which now dominates American universities. During the first year – and sometimes two – students were required to study a wide variety of subjects. They started to specialise, or major, in the third year of their course. In contrast, British university students started specialising the moment they walked through the university doors and most of the degree courses were and are taken over three years. Other differences developed further down the education ladder. American children start formal education at between five and six (depending on the state). British children start at five. American education is geared towards continuous assessment while the British system is more exam-oriented. The debate rages as to which is the better system. The answer is probably dependent on the individual student. But generally speaking, educationalists agree that a British BA or BS degree is roughly equivalent to an American Masters.

Nation Shall Speak unto Nation

One of the main reasons education was able to advance so quickly in America was the English language. The common written and spoken word meant that Americans not only had links to a strong educational tradition but they could tap into a well-established market for textbooks and literature. Language also greased the wheels of trade and commerce. It was much easier for Americans to deal with English merchants – before and after independence – than to have to learn French and Spanish subjunctives. And as the British Empire expanded in the nineteenth century to encompass 25 per cent of the world's population, American business was able to ride on the British coat tails. But language is more than a tool for the teacher and the merchant. It is also a vehicle for national identity and nationalism. Throughout history, one of the first acts of the conqueror has often been to attempt to suppress the local language and replace it with his own. Conversely, in many former British colonies, one of the first acts following independence was to de-Anglicise place names and encourage the speaking and writing of the indigenous people. America was different. The new government in 1783 was descended from English settlers who spoke English, and economically the newly independent United States was still heavily dependent on trade with England. But at the same time, there were key literary and political figures that weaponised American English in the battle to forge a separate cultural and national identity. They were helped by a variety of non-English language sources and the separate evolution of the language back in Britain. Differences developed, but the practical advantages of working with what has become the closest thing that the world has to a universal language has kept the two sides of the Atlantic more or less linguistically united.

English is a mongrel language. Before the Romans arrived it was dominated by the Celts. The modern version of the Celtic language can be found in Welsh, Cornish, and Scottish and Irish Gaelic. The Romans, of course, gave us Latin which was the language of religion, government, law and education throughout medieval Europe and into the early modern age. Contemporary medical books and legal documents are a mix of the Roman and English words. And Latin's facility for splicing prefixes and suffixes is still used extensively in modern English. But the foundations of modern English are Germanic and were brought across the North Sea by two centuries of successive waves of Anglo-Saxons who invaded the country in the two centuries following the Roman withdrawal in AD 410. Mongrelisation did not, however, stop with the Anglo-Saxons. Next came the Vikings who occupied huge swathes of the north and eastern part of England. Several hundred old Norse words have survived into modern English including 'law', 'anger' and 'window'. After the Vikings there was 1066 and the Norman invasion. The Anglo-Saxon aristocrats were replaced by their Norman French counterparts and French became the language of the royal court. But Anglo-Saxon remained the everyday parlance of the common man and gradually overwhelmed the French invaders on the linguistic battlefield. By the fifteenth century the country was speaking what linguists have called Middle English, of which Geoffrey Chaucer's *Canterbury Tales* is an example. However, the language was spoken with different accents and dialects, which made it difficult for one part of the country to understand the other. And there was no uniform grammar or spelling. This changed dramatically with the introduction of the printing press in 1476. The mass production of books required standardised English and since the printing presses were mainly in London the dialect that was chosen was London-based and known as 'Chancery Standard'. It remains the basis for modern spelling, but not pronunciation.

By the start of the sixteenth century, the English language had moved from Middle English to Early Modern. This was the language of Shakespeare and the King James Bible. It was also the language of the first American colonials and the beginning of the linguistic divide. The differences centred on the pronunciation of the letter 'r' in what linguists call rho versus non-rho. In seventeenth-century English, the 'er' sound was pronounced with the involvement of the letter r as in 'ever' or 'Easter'. This was the pronunciation that the settlers took to America. But from the middle of the eighteenth century onwards the British aristocracy developed a non-rho pronunciation which replaced the 'er' sound with an 'ah'. Thus East-er became East-ah. The non-rho sound was also applied to the softening of vowels so that a soft 'a' became an 'ah'. Separated by 3,000 miles from daily exposure to these changes, the colonials carried on with the pronunciation of Shakespeare. What became the American pronunciation was reinforced by waves of Scottish and Irish immigrants who also spoke with a rho accent.

The other big difference was that from the very start the American colonials needed words to describe the new animals and plants they found in the New World. Words such as raccoon, moose and opossum were quickly assimilated from Native American. As a nation of immigrants, a variety of national cultures contributed to differentiating American English from the mother tongue: kindergarten (German), rodeo (Spanish), cookie (Dutch), levee (French) and chutzpah (Yiddish). There were also some seventeenth- and eighteenth-century English words which ceased to be used in Britain and are now considered typically American: fall for autumn, diaper for nappy and faucets for taps are a few examples. The African slaves contributed heavily to the Southern accent. Unused to the English language, they slowed down their speech and introduced West African sounds so that get became git, you became ya and then y'all.

African Americans also introduced and named new foods which they brought across the ocean such as peppers, okra and gumbo.

Despite the success of the printing press, there were no definitively agreed English spellings or word definitions until the middle of the eighteenth century. Spellings were based on pronunciation, dialects and accents. Chancery Standard was used by the London printers, but was read with difficulty outside the capital because people in other parts of the country simply did not speak the way the words were written. What was needed was a dictionary. There had been earlier attempts to produce one, but the results had been lacklustre. Then in 1746, a syndicate of printers resolved to solve the problem by asking Samuel Johnson to write what became, after eight years of research and writing, the *Dictionary of the English Language*. Johnson's work of 42,773 entries is considered a scholastic milestone and remained the standard reference work for the English language until the Oxford University Press set about producing a competitor 150 years later.

Johnson's dictionary was adopted as the gold standard on both sides of the Atlantic until Noah Webster came on the scene. Webster was a Connecticut politician and teacher who was determined to use language as a nationalist weapon to culturally break with Britain. In 1789 he declared that 'Great Britain, whose children we are, and whose language we speak, should no longer be our standard, for the task of her writers is already corrupted and her language on the decline'. America, maintained Webster, was superior to Britain and the rest of Europe 'because American values are superior'. Furthermore, he argued that American superiority needed its own language standard to replace British English and set about writing an American dictionary. His stated aim was to rescue American English from the influence of the British aristocracy and produce a dictionary steeped in the democratic principles of the common man. The first edition of *Webster's American Dictionary of the English Language* was published in 1806. The reference work was a political as much as a literary work. Webster deliberately changed the spelling of words in Johnson's dictionary. It was Webster, for instance, who dropped the letter 'u' from colour, labour and honour and replaced the letter 's' with a 'z' in words such as analyse. Webster focused on phonetic spellings, which he regarded as more democratic. His dictionary was also the first to list and adopt into English Native American words such as wigwam and moccasin. When Webster died in 1843 the rights to his dictionary were bought by George and Charles Merriam and the title of his reference work was changed to *The Merriam-Webster Dictionary*. It has remained the number one American English dictionary ever since.

Over the years Webster's dictionary has acted as a repository for new, American-originated words and phrases such as parking lot, merger, sidewalk, bottom line and downsize. British English has responded by either absorbing the American words into English and/or recognising that either usage is acceptable. For instance, many British publishers and editors now spell analyse with a 'z'. There is also a recognition that Webster's cultural democracy added colour (or color) to an otherwise dry and pedantic language and has made English more interesting. At the risk of disagreeing with Winston Churchill, it should be said that America and Britain speak from a shared root and the two countries remain linked – not divided – by their common language.

The Play's the Thing

Theatre is a fairly recent phenomenon in British cultural history. William Shakespeare is not only the leading playwright in the English language; he was also one of the first. Play-acting took a while to establish because the medieval Church regarded it as immoral. The exceptions were the religious mystery plays on themes such as Noah's ark, Cain and Abel or the raising of Lazarus. These were acceptable as a vehicle for teaching Biblical stories. The English Reformation loosened the moral apron strings and encouraged a swing to secular storytelling. And as most of the population was illiterate, the best way to tell a story that reached a wide audience was from the stage. This development was given added impetus by Elizabeth I, who was possibly Britain's greatest ever royal patron of the arts.

The Reformation also gave rise to a puritanical form of Christianity that was even louder in its condemnation of the immorality of theatre than the Catholic Church had been. In 1642 Parliament ordered the closure of all London theatres. The stage was attacked as 'lascivious' and actor were 'rogues'. By 1648 theatre seating was being demolished and anyone who dared to attend the handful of clandestine performances faced a hefty fine and possible prison sentence.

The Puritans who settled in New England transported their morality across the ocean. Plays were banned for many years and well into the nineteenth century performances were frowned upon. This was not the case in the South, especially Virginia, which attracted the aristocrats who had fled Oliver Cromwell's humourless England. After the restoration of the monarchy in 1660 the London theatres were reopened with a vibrancy that found its way to Virginia, slowly. The first American theatrical performances were staged in Williamsburg in 1716. The first purpose-built theatre was the Dock Theatre, which opened in Charleston, South Carolina, in 1736. The earliest known play was *Androboros*, written as a political satire in 1715 by Robert Hunter while he was governor of New Jersey. But it was not until the arrival of the British acting troupe of Lewis Hallam in 1752 that theatre started to blossom in America.

Hallam came from a British acting family and formed a company with his brother William. The company failed and the two men decided to try their luck in the colonies with a mainly Shakespearean repertoire. They started in Williamsburg and continued to struggle financially. Hallam is credited with the origin of the phrase 'ham actor' because he and the members of his acting troupe were forced to use pig fat to remove makeup because they could not afford the face cream they had used in London. Despite their financial difficulties, the company managed to perform in all thirteen colonies and laid the foundations for the New York theatre scene by building Manhattan's first theatre in 1754. Hallam, however, failed to overcome America's puritanical streak as colony after colony passed legislation banning the performance of plays. The first was Massachusetts, which barred theatre even before Hallam arrived (1750). It was followed by Pennsylvania (1759) and Rhode Island (1761). Theatre was banned throughout the colonies during the War of Independence. Some performances sneaked past the censors by disguising themselves as moral lectures, but they were few and far between. Hallam left the thirteen colonies for the more tolerant Jamaica, but the move proved damaging to his health and he died two years later. His widow Sarah and son Lewis Jr, however, returned to America. Sarah married William Douglass, with whom she formed the Old America Company in which she and her son were the leading actors. Lewis Hallam Jr is credited with giving the first performance of Hamlet on the American stage.

England's post-Cromwellian theatre kicked off three centuries of success. Charles II was a devotee of the theatre and the more risqué the play the better. For the first time in British history, women were allowed to perform on stage. The king's favourite mistress, Nell Gwyn, was an actress. The plays of the time reflected the national mood of relief that followed the dour days of the Commonwealth. A happy ending was crucial to the success of a performance, whether it was a tale of two lovers overcoming the odds or good triumphing over evil. The Restoration period also saw the emergence of the 'spectacular', the harbinger of today's special effects. These plays introduced features such as fireworks, shifting scenery, flying actors and trap doors. By the early nineteenth century British theatre included comic operas and melodramas based on contemporary life rather than the traditional historical fare. By the end of the century comic satire was dominating the British stage with playwrights such as Oscar Wilde and George Bernard Shaw, who attracted large audiences from the aristocracy and the growing and increasingly prosperous British middle classes. The working classes, however, were not forgotten. They were catered for by the musical hall. Victorian England was the heyday of British theatre. It was when London's West End was established as the world capital of the play with packed houses catering every night to a wide variety of tastes.

American theatre remained dominated by Britain, as the mother country was the source of most of the scripts and the acting talents. There were several travelling companies, but from the end of the American Revolution, the place to be was New York. Hotspots included Park Row, the Bowery Theatre, Niblo's Gardens, Palmo's Opera House and the Astor Opera House. Shakespeare was the most popular playwright and the most famous American-born Shakespearean actor was Edwin Booth, whose brother John Wilkes Booth assassinated Abraham Lincoln. Around 1850, rising rents forced American theatres out of downtown to midtown New York which was then mostly still farmland. 'Come and enjoy the fresh air,' suggested one theatre owner. Soon the theatres were gathering around Madison Square and dominating Broadway. After the Civil War they took the lead in developing musicals a medium in which America was to excel. The first was *The Elves*, which ran for fifty performances in 1870. Vaudeville debuted in 1881. About the same time the operettas of the British duo Gilbert and Sullivan became popular with New York audiences. During the Roaring Twenties the spectacular *Ziegfeld Follies* were all the rage, but also popular were a number of works by British playwrights including Shakespeare, Oscar Wilde and George Bernard Shaw. John Gielgud's performance of *Hamlet* in 1936 ran for a record 132 nights in New York. In the 1940s and 1950s Richard Rodgers and Oscar Hammerstein created the golden age of Broadway musicals with *Oklahoma*, *Carousel*, *State Fair*, *South Pacific* and *The King and I*.

Theatre in London and New York has faced fierce competition from cinema, but they are still the two most dominant centres of live theatre in the world and a major cultural expression of the English-speaking world. It is arguable that London has retained the edge with traditions stretching back to before Shakespeare and acting schools such as the Royal Academy of Dramatic Arts. It also has 230 theatres dotted around the city compared to just over 100 in New York. British performing arts contributed over $7 billion to the national economy in 2018, almost exactly the same as the contribution that Broadway makes to the US economy.

The Book Publishing World

Britain totally dominated the American literary scene up to the beginning of the twentieth century. In colonial America, most original American publishing was confined to New England sermons, though Benjamin Franklin's *Poor Richard's Almanac* was a great success. For textbooks, law books, plays, philosophy, science and the infant but growing market for fiction, Americans had to import everything from Britain. As Kathleen Burk wrote in *Old World, New World*: 'Britain was the English language hegemon.' At first this meant physically shipping the books across the ocean. But gradually, printing skills and presses crossed the Atlantic and English books were being reprinted on American presses. The first printing press arrived in America in 1636 and was used to print religious texts for the newly opened Harvard University. It was not until about 1715 that there were enough American print works to meet demand. Even then the American publishers decided against home-grown output and simply used their expanded capacity to print British works while refusing to pay royalties to the British writers or publishers.

The American copyright theft continued after independence and was to dominate the transatlantic publishing trade up to the end of the nineteenth century. In 1790 the law denied copyright protection to all but US citizens and duly recognised residents of the US. At the same time high tariffs were slapped on all literary works not printed in the US. American printers had only to meet the cost of paper, ink, advertising and distribution. There were attempts to circumvent the restrictions. Some British authors found American collaborators who would register the British books with the Library of Congress under the collaborator's name. But this meant anonymity and legal problems for both parties if discovered, so most ignored this route and swallowed the loss with loud complaints about thieving Americans. Charles Dickens was particularly loud about the inequity that meant that he never received a penny for the millions of his books sold in America.

The British responded with a tit-for-tat ban on copyright for American authors. There were very few Americans published in Britain for most of the nineteenth century, but those few had huge British audiences. They included James Fennimore Cooper, Washington Irving, Nathaniel Hawthorne, Mark Twain, Herman Melville and Henry Wadsworth Longfellow. Some of them managed to circumvent British copyright restrictions by moving to Britain at key times in their lives in order to qualify for British residency. Nathaniel Hawthorne, for instance, served as US Consul in Liverpool.

One of the results of the lack of copyright protection for British authors and publishers was that it stunted the growth of American literature. Why should American publishers pay royalties to home-grown authors when they could escape paying anyone? Besides, the British authors had already been tested in their own market before their works reached America. American publishers needed only to employ London agents who would read the reviews in the British press, perhaps collect a few months of sales figures and then report back to the offices in Boston, New York and Philadelphia with their recommendations and a copy of the book. There was the beginning of a change after the War of 1812, which led to a renewal of American patriotism and anti-British feeling. Among Americans there was a perception that the war was a great American victory. In Britain there was a bemused and somewhat patronising irritation at this American view. They regarded the war as a draw. The Americans invaded Canada and burned down York (later Toronto), but were repulsed. The British burned Washington but were stopped at Baltimore. As for the Battle of New Orleans, that was fought after the war ended.

But American authors and some publishers seized on the perceived victory by demanding that American culture break with the British and concentrate on developing its own identity and especially its own literature. The suggestion was treated with arrogant contempt by the British literary magazines and the ensuing exchange of insults has been referred to as 'The Paper Wars'. One of the most vitriolic exchanges was written in 1820 by the reviewer Sydney Smith in the influential *Edinburgh Review*:

In so far as we know, there is not such parallel to be produced from the whole annuals of this self-adulatory race. In the four quarters of the globe, who reads an American book? Or goes to an American play? Or looks at an American picture or statue? What does the world yet owe to American physicians or surgeons? What new substances have their chemists discovered? Or what old ones have they analysed? What new constellations have been discovered by the telescopes of Americans? What have they done in mathematics? Who drinks out of American glasses or eats from American plates, or wears American coats or gowns, or sleeps in American blankets? Finally, under which of the old tyrannical governments of Europe is every sixth man a slave, whom his fellow creatures may buy and sell and torture. When these questions are fairly and favourably answered, their laudatory epithets may be allowed, till that can be done, we would seriously advise them to keep clear of superlatives.

The post-war demands for a focus on home-grown authors fell on deaf ears. The fact is that at the time the American public was used to and preferred the well-established stable of British authors. Their preference was strengthened by the economic realities forced on the American publishing industry by the depression of 1837–43. Those few publishers who were able to stay in business during the depression years did so by resorting to the by then time-honoured and commercially established method of reprinting royalty-free British books only.

As the depression came to an end there was an attempt to negotiate an Anglo-American copyright agreement. There was another attempt in 1857. Both failed because success by now required the dismantling of the tariffs protecting the by now powerful American print lobby. The pendulum started to swing the other way after the Civil War, pushed by another renewal of cultural nationalism and a campaign led by Mark Twain. But the main catalyst for change came from the other side of the Atlantic at a conference in Berne, Switzerland, of diplomats, publishers and writers. The outcome was the first multinational international copyright agreement signed in in 1886 by an eclectic group: Britain, France, Germany, Italy, Belgium, Haiti, Liberia, Spain, Switzerland and Tunisia. The US sent observers to the conference but did not participate in the negotiations or sign the agreement. However, the treaty fed the growing realisation that the US was in danger of being left out in the publishing cold and faced the possibility of being swamped even more by foreign publishing houses unless it acted quickly. In 1891, Rhode Island senator Jonathan Chace successfully steered the International Copyright Act through Congress. This extended US copyright protection to a limited number of countries, the UK being key among them. The British responded with a reciprocal arrangement.

Regulating copyright laws led to an almost immediate increase in opportunities for American authors on both sides of the Atlantic. Writers such as F. Scott Fitzgerald, Raymond Chandler and Ernest Hemingway shot up the bestseller charts in both countries. But that did not mean their British counterparts were displaced. H. G. Wells, Agatha Christie, Dorothy L. Sayers and many others kept the British literary flag flying over America. There was now a more balanced literary Anglosphere which was able to sell not only in the two countries but across the growing English-speaking world. By the start of the twenty-first century the US was the world's second-largest publisher of books after China. Britain was the third-largest and streets ahead of every other country in number of books published per head of population (2,875 new titles a year per million inhabitants in 2013). British publishing also enjoyed the world's best export record: $1.5 billion a year in 2013 compared to $1 billion a year for American publishers. One of the main reasons for British success has been EU membership. A large number of European university courses are taught in English, especially the sciences and mathematics. This is partly because of the universality of English and because it is uneconomic for smaller European countries to print textbooks in the local languages. The tariff-free European Community trading zone has provided British publishing with access to this large and wealthy market. In 2021, American publishers were reported to be gearing up to grab a larger slice of the European book trade in the wake of British withdrawal from the EU. British publishers are said to be ready to respond by returning their focus to American readers.

Broadcasting

Television and radio are examples of inadvertent Anglo-American cooperation. The British invented it; the Americans figured out a way to make money from it by turning it into a vehicle for mass market communications. The two mediums grew out of each other's technology and experience and the British led the way in both. Radio was initially called 'wireless telegraphy' and its potential was first realised by the Scottish physicist James Clerk Maxwell in 1865 when he concluded that electromagnetic airwaves could be transmitted through air. But the big name in the history of radio was Guglielmo Marconi. He was an Italian-Irish inventor related to the wealthy Irish whisky Jameson dynasty. His knowledge of radio transmission was largely the result of self-taught studies and some time at Bologna University. He tried to interest the Italian government in his discoveries but they thought he was wide of the mark, so he went to England in 1896 at the age of twenty-one where he received a warm welcome. In 1901 Marconi sent the first transatlantic radio signal. By 1920 entertainment was being broadcast over the airwaves and in 1927 the BBC was granted its royal charter. Radio transmissions started almost simultaneously in the US. There were some attempts before the First World War to use telephone wires to broadcast news and entertainment, but these stopped with the onset of the war and were quickly overtaken by radio transmissions.

The British also take credit for the invention of television, but which Briton is open to discussion. The name most often linked to the first TV transmission is that of Scottish inventor John Logie Baird. He gave the first demonstration of a crude television broadcast on 25 March 1925 at Selfridge's on London's Oxford Street. But to make this first broadcast

Laird had to stand on the shoulders of engineers and investors dating back to the nineteenth century. In 1843, another Scot, Alexander Bain, invented a basic facsimile machine which was turned into a working model capable of transmitting crude images down telegraph lines. The British foundations were added to throughout the nineteenth and early twentieth centuries by scientists from France, Germany, Russia, Switzerland and Italy. But it was the BBC in 1936 that started making the world's first regular broadcasts with Baird's invention. Broadcasts were suspended at the start of the outbreak of the Second World War because the authorities were concerned that German planes could use the television signals to home in on targets. By 1939 the number of television sets had reached 15,000. Broadcasts resumed again in June 1947 and within six months there were 54,000 sets. The big boost, however, came with the 1953 coronation of Elizabeth II, which attracted 22 million viewers. The BBC had a monopoly on television broadcasting up until July 1954 when the Independent Television Act was passed and commercials made their debut on the small screen. But the basic parameters had been set by the BBC's public service ethos. The licences for the commercial channels were issued by the government and as part of their licence agreement the channels had to devote a proportion of their airtime to less commercially popular public service broadcasts and news programmes.

British broadcasting is known throughout the world for its adherence to certain principles concerning the dissemination of the 'right kind' of output. The credit for that belongs to one man: Sir John (later Lord) Reith, the first Director General of the BBC. He was a highly moralistic, some say prudish, Scotsman, who in 1922 was hired as general manager of the company which was to become the British Broadcasting Corporation. At the time, it produced only radio programmes, but the mission statement laid down by Reith became the guiding light for television and radio: 'To inform, educate and entertain.' The Reithian principles (as they become known) have been more or less adopted by public service broadcasters throughout the world, including America's National Public Radio (NPR) and Public Broadcasting Service (PBS). They have also set the benchmark for many commercial television channels. From the start, Lord Reith was determined that British broadcasting would avoid the pitfall of becoming a lowest-common-denominator commercial free-for-all a trap American radio arguably fell into. There would be no advertising. Instead, the broadcasting industry would be financed by a licence fee payable by all owners of radios (and later televisions). The fee would be set by the government but the broadcasters would be editorially independent. The BBC maintained its broadcasting monopoly until

1955 when commercial television was allowed on British screens. But even then Reithian principles were applied. The government granted the operating licences and the station owners had to agree to commit a large proportion of their airtime to public service broadcasting.

In contrast, American broadcasting was driven by the profit motive from the start. In fact, the US financial structure for broadcasters was dubbed 'the American Plan' as opposed to the public ethos of 'The British Plan'. There was an attempt by the US Federal Communications Commission to introduce a public service broadcasting commitment to television in 1947, but this had been largely dropped four years later. It was not until PBS was founded in 1969 and NPR in 1970 that the US had anything that could be described as a public broadcasting service. Both NPR and PBS are heavily dependent on British broadcasting for programming and there are a number of regular Anglo-American co-productions between the BBC and PBS.

The US lagged slightly behind Britain in launching its television industry. Its first experimental television station was launched in Schenectady, New York (W2XB, now WRGB). In 1948 there were still only 44,000 televisions in America. But shortly afterwards the demand for television grew so rapidly that the FCC had to freeze the issuing of new licences until 1952. By 1949 television stations were operated from New York to the Mississippi River and by 1951 they had reached California. In both America and Britain, commercial television became, in the words of Canadian-born British media mogul Lord Thomson, 'a licence to print money'. But by the 1980s the power and influence of terrestrial channels began to decline in the face of competition from cable, digital, satellite and internet TV. In the twenty-first century, broadcasts can be accessed via the internet from almost anywhere in the world. This exponential boom in the size of the world broadcast pie has made it increasingly difficult for traditional broadcasters to compete.

To remain commercially viable (in the case of American broadcasters) and to keep down the licence fee (in the case of the BBC), the broadcasters have turned increasingly to export sales of their productions and Anglo-American co-productions. In the financial year 2018/19, co-productions were worth $105 million. Total exports of British television broadcasts totalled a record-breaking $1.85 billion, of which $477 million went to the US. American commercial power, however, dominates global television content sales. The US sitcom series *Friends* stopped recording in 2004 and sixteen years later was still earning $1 billion a year in revenues, of which a major portion came from Britain. This was not always the case. In the early days of television all broadcasts were live and could only be broadcast within the national territories, or, at the very most, neighbouring countries capable of picking up British and American terrestrial signals. It was not until 1962 that the first live broadcast to Britain from the US was made via the Telstar satellite. These early transmission limitations meant that the two countries developed different programming, which reflected diverging cultures and interests and managed to keep programming fresh, interesting and different on both sides of the Atlantic.

Soothing the Savage Breast

Every Fourth of July there are patriotic parades in almost every city, town and village to celebrate America's independence from Britain. At the front of a large number of those parades are a drummer boy, a flag bearer and a bandaged flautist. All three are wearing dishevelled clothes and determined looks. They two men and the boy ignored the odds to take on and defeat the mightiest empire in the world. The song that they are playing and singing is 'Yankee Doodle Dandy', a ditty that some Americans might think twice about embracing if they knew its history. It started as an Anglo-Dutch harvest song before crossing the North Sea and English Channel to become a regular English feature. But it is the seventeenth-and eighteenth-century meaning of some of the lyrics that make it suspect. A doodle was a simpleton or village idiot. A dandy was someone who was sadly and unsuccessfully attempting to be fashionable. A macaroni was an extremely effeminate, probably homosexual, social climber. The feather in the headwear was the dandy's belief that a feathered cap would raise him to the status of a fashionable British aristocrat. In 1755 British army surgeon Dr Richard Shuckburgh introduced some anti-American lyrics while campaigning in upstate New York during the French-Indian Wars. He was disgusted by the disorganised and dishevelled colonial troops. It became popular with regular British troops who used it mock American colonials. During the War of Independence the British continued to march to 'Yankee Doodle Dandy', but the Americans decided they liked a bit of self-deprecation, and besides, it was a catchy tune. They kept the chorus and sang it right back to the British with some additional verses praising George Washington. When they won the war, the Americans just carried on singing.

'Yankee Doodle Dandy' is not the only patriotic American song. 'My Country 'Tis of Thee' is sung to the tune of the British national anthem. Baptist Seminary student Samuel Francis Smith was so inspired in 1831 by the patriotism the tune stirred in British breasts that he decided to steal the melody for American patriots. The result was an immediate success and the song was one of three regularly belted out at patriotic gatherings. But its links to the British national anthem probably helped to deny the song the ultimate accolade of becoming the American equivalent, when one was finally chosen in 1931. There were a number of other songs regarded as quintessentially American which had their origins in Britain. 'Amazing Grace' was written in 1779 as an abolitionist hymn by former British slave trader turned clergyman John Newton. It is a modern favourite of African American churches. Most of the traditional Christmas carols – with a few German exceptions – are British in origin. Almost all of the hymnals, especially those in the Episcopal church, are a straight lift from the English hymnal with some additions from the British founders of the Methodist church, John and Charles Wesley, who made extensive tours of America.

America has always been divided between North and South. And one of the main reasons for the division was the cultural differences laid at the start between New England's early Puritan settlers and the Virginian aristocrats. This is reflected in the different musical traditions which they both brought from England. The Puritans have a deserved reputation for being a dour lot: Christmas banned; church on Sunday mandatory; clothing restricted to plain black broadcloth; gambling banned, ditto smoking in public. Music and dancing were in a slightly different, almost schizoid, category. Fire-and-brimstone preachers such as Cotton and Increase Mather railed against the immorality of tuneful disorderly conduct, but failed to stop the New England colonists from bringing a rich musical tradition from England to the New World. From 1630 onwards ships' manifests reveal a regular flow of musical instruments from east to west. They were mainly string instruments such as violins and violas used to entertain customers in the newly opened taverns. They also provided musical accompaniment for dances, which were tolerated by the authorities as long as discretion was observed. It had to be restricted to private homes and mixed couples dancing was forbidden.

As expected, the Puritans' main contribution to American music was through religion. It started with the adoption of the Ainsworth Psalter, written by English Puritan Henry Ainsworth, in 1612. This was replaced in 1640 by the Bay Psalme Book, the first book published in America. A rare first edition copy of the book sold for more than $14 million. The Psalters are a collection of Old Testament psalms sung in church and at public meetings. The next step in New England's musical development came with the arrival from Britain of the Wesley brothers, who found fertile ground in New England for their extensive collection of hymns which became the musical mainstay of frontier camp meetings.

The South danced to a different tune. They sang, danced, gambled, grew and smoked tobacco, wore bright silks and did their best to enjoy life free of the restrictions of the Old World. The initial cultural capital of the South was Williamsburg, Virginia. A wide range of instruments were imported from England including the harp, harpsichord, clarinets, flutes and recorders. The piano did not make its first appearance until the middle of the eighteenth century. With the instruments came English folk tunes, which were frowned upon in New England but a major hit in the South. The song 'Barbara Allen' originated in England and the western folk tune 'The Streets of Laredo' is sung to the tune of the Irish ballad 'The Unfortunate Rake'. Another iconic song, 'Home, Home on the Range', draws its inspiration from unfavourably comparing British life to American. English folk music sank deep roots into the American South and West and laid the foundations for the contemporary country and western music scene.

Around 1700 the South's cultural capital shifted to Charleston, as money poured into the South Carolina port from the English-controlled slave trade. And with the African slaves came possibly the most unique and long-standing contribution to American – and eventually English – then European and world – music. Instruments such as the banjo have their antecedents in West Africa, along with the immersive approach to singing and the call and response song form so familiar in African American churches. Because the slaves were illiterate, songs provided them with a vehicle for transmitting an oral tradition. It also enabled them to retain a sense of identity and community. One song was a disguised instruction manual for runaway slaves seeking freedom in the North. 'The Gourd' urged slaves to follow the gourd-shaped star constellation, a way of describing the handle of the Big Dipper, which pointed north. African American music evolved into several streams which became America's greatest contribution to world music: jazz, blues, gospel, ragtime, swing, rock and roll, and hip hop. In the twentieth century American music influenced popular British musicians such as The Beatles, who modified the American offering with their own Merseybeat while re-conquering America along with other British artists such as the Rolling Stones and Elton John.

The Silver Screen

The film industry is one area in which the Americans have lorded it over the British almost from the start, and continue to do so. The first films, however, were neither British nor American. They were the creation of the French brothers Auguste and Louis Lumière, who organised the first public screening in Paris in 1895. It was an instant hit that within a year saw the brothers' success explode, with movie theatres (or cinemas) popping up across the globe. The American contribution was significantly aided by the involvement of Thomas A. Edison, who was as much a marketing genius as an inventor. He acquired the patents necessary for film making in the US, which meant that America's first film capital was conveniently located near Edison's Menlo Park base at Fort Lee, New Jersey, also convenient for Broadway actors eager to display their on-screen talents. In 1910 the director D. W. Griffith went on a scouting mission to California and stumbled on a friendly village a few miles north of Los Angeles. Prices were cheap and there was an abundance of sunshine. The village was called Hollywood. California had another advantage in that it was 2,500 miles away from Menlo Park and Edison's increasingly exorbitant fees. By 1930 almost the entire American film industry had moved from the east to the west coast and Hollywood was transformed from a sleepy village into the film capital of the world.

The weakness in the British film industry as compared to the American was apparent from the start. By 1910 nearly 70 per cent of the films shown in British cinemas were from the US. The British initially responded to the American challenge by taking the commercially easier route of using its imperial and European connections to become the international distribution base for American films, starting as early as 1906. But the biggest blow to the British and wider European film industry came in 1914 with the onset of war. With about half of the British GDP going to pay for the war effort, there was no money left over to make film entertainment. America moved to fill the vacuum and by 1920 it was churning out 800 feature films a year and had established an unassailable lead with a staggering 83 per cent share of the global market.

By 1925 the British government were concerned that British culture was being swamped by American films. In 1927 Parliament passed the British Cinematographic Films Act, which placed a quota on the number of foreign films that could be shown in British cinemas. In the immediate aftermath of the Second World War, an acute shortage of dollars led to a complete ban on the importation of American films. This was quickly rescinded in the face of public opposition and as a condition of the Marshall Plan. Up until 1980 there were several British government attempts to boost British film production by imposing quotas on American films shown in British cinemas. They all failed. Hollywood had a big English language home market, which meant more money to pay for better and more entertaining blockbusters they could sell to Britain and its empire. In 1980, the quotas were completely lifted. By the 1990s, 93 per cent of the films shown in Britain were made in America. In 2003, British-made films were only 5.7 per cent of the American market.

All of the above is not to say that Britain was uninvolved or did not contribute to the success of Hollywood. The fine print of the quota system exempted American-financed films that were partly produced in Britain. This led to American studios investing in and using British-based studios for at least part of their film production. In 1931 Warner Brothers acquired Teddington Studios to turn out what were termed 'quota quickies' in order to comply with British film restrictions. Other British-based studios have been – and still are – used by Hollywood, including Ealing, Elstree, Pinewood and Twickenham. The British studios have developed a reputation for post-production work and special effects. They are also a convenient technical and administrative base for American films shot on European and North African locations. Some of the best known and successful film franchises, such as James Bond, Star Wars and the Harry Potter series, were filmed at least in part at British studios. The financial capital, however, was provided by the US studios. This meant that the skills and jobs were created in the UK but the profits went to America.

Britain also provided story inspiration, acting and other creative talent. A shared history and literature meant that American audiences were as eager as the British to see UK-originated stories transferred from paper to screen. The tales of Charles Dickens, Shakespeare and Sir Walter Scott all found their way to Hollywood. In 1908, *A Christmas Carol* was possibly the first feature length film ever made, though in Chicago, not Hollywood. Britain's rich acting tradition provided some of Hollywood's most famous stars. Charlie Chaplin was an international star, a director and one of the founding members of the film studio United Artists. He is regarded as one of the most important figures in film history. Later major British actors from the golden age of Hollywood included Ronald Colman, Vivien Leigh and Cary Grant. In more recent years actors such as Emma Thompson, Judi Dench and Daniel Craig have continued the tradition of British acting talent drawing big audiences on both sides of the Atlantic. The UK film industry has also produced some of the greatest directing talent. Alfred Hitchcock was already established in Britain when David O. Selznick lured him to Hollywood in 1939. Over six decades, Hitchcock produced fifty films and was described by *Time* magazine as 'Britain's greatest export'. Other directors who have made their mark on Hollywood include David Lean, Carol Reed, Ken Loach, Sam Mendes and Alexander Korda. A number of Britons have made contributions as actors and directors, such as the Shakespearean actor Laurence Olivier.

It has become increasingly difficult in the globalised economy to talk about a British or American film industry. Writers, actors, directors and producers are scattered across the world and films are shot everywhere. However, the finance that keeps the wheels turning on the world film bus comes mainly from America and is channelled through offices in Hollywood. In 2019, the American film industry contributed $35.3 billion to the national economy. If you include television and video sales the figure climbs to a staggering $286 billion. The Hollywood-led creative industries sector accounts for about 3 per cent of the US economy. In comparison, the British television and film industry contributes about $4 billion to the UK GDP. The age of the independent Hollywood film makers is in fact drawing to a close. In May 2021, Amazon bought one of the few survivors, MGM, paying $8.45 billion for the film studio.

Sport

If one nation can lay claim to the title of the inventor of sport, it is Britain. Specific games may have started elsewhere. There is evidence that golf was played in the Netherlands before crossing the North Sea to Scotland; and children were kicking balls in ancient China, Greece and Rome centuries before football reached the streets of Manchester. But it was Georgian and Victorian Britain that set the rules that govern most of the world's sports. And those who make the rules control the game. Britain's sporting bodies set the rules for badminton, billiards, bowls, cricket, boxing, tennis, croquet, curling, rowing, football, motor racing, darts, golf, hockey, netball, rugby, table tennis, water polo and others. A number of American sports have their roots in British games. Cricket and rounders are the sporting antecedents of baseball. Basketball owes much to netball and gridiron football is a variation of rugby and association football. In 2019, America's professional sports industry was reported to be worth $70 billion a year. It is big business and that business owes much to the sportsmen of eighteenth- and nineteenth-century Britain.

Football (or soccer) is regarded as Britain's number one sport. It is played by 10 per cent of the population and watched by 46 per cent. Something resembling the modern game appeared in Britain in the twelfth century. An inflatable pig's bladder was kicked between two teams from opposing villages. There was no field as such and no set rules. The game could cover several square miles and result in serious injuries and, on occasion, death. The dangers of the game led to it being periodically banned, but by 1835 it found a home in Britain's upper-class public schools. British public schools placed a high premium on the manly pursuits, fair play and teamwork, qualities which have theoretically become the benchmark for world sports. Victorian England was the first time in modern history that a large class of people had sufficient leisure time to devote to sport, and railways provided transport so that school teams could travel from one game to another. It quickly became apparent that if the game was to continue, it needed a central administering body and a set of agreed rules. On 26 October 1863 officials from London football clubs met at the Freemason's Tavern in Holborn, London, to establish the Football Association and set up rules 'for the purpose of forming an association with the object of establishing a definite set of rules for the regulation of the game'. With an agreed rulebook under its belt, the game quickly spread throughout the British Empire, Europe and South America. The International Football Federation was founded in 1904 and the first World Cup was played in 1930. Soccer is the world's most popular sport with 3.5 billion fans and Britain's Premier League is the most closely followed football league on the planet. The game is played in every country in the world and only eight micro-states are not affiliated to FIFA.

The 1863 meeting that established the FA also led to a friendly split between the clubs that wanted to allow ball carrying and those who opposed. The ball carriers formed the nucleus of what became rugby and the main antecedent of American football. A version of football was played in American universities as early as 1823 and because of the violence of the game and a lack of any coherent rules it was often referred to as 'mob rule football'. Repeated injuries and fatalities led to the game being periodically suspended in the years before the Civil War, but it always managed to make a comeback. In 1862 Harvard introduced something that it called 'the Boston game', which involved an increased element of ball carrying. But the intercollegiate dispute over rules continued and is best illustrated by an 1874 match between Canada's McGill University and Harvard in which they used British rugby rules in the first half and 'Boston Game' rules in the second. The 'Father' of American football was Yale University's Walter Camp. He introduced blocking, the scrimmage line, and down and distance rules. Despite Camp's rules the game resulted in serious injuries every year. In 1905 there were eighteen fatalities, which led President Theodore Roosevelt to demand a meeting with the presidents of Harvard, Yale and Princeton at which he called for either a ban on the game or improved safety. The result was the creation of the

National Collegiate Athletic Association. Professional football entered the scene in 1922 with the formation of the National Football League, but college football dominated the sport until 1958 when television and a particularly exciting sudden-death championship game between the New York Giants and the Baltimore Colts catapulted the game into the American consciousness. Since then, the game has grown to become America's favourite sport with an average of 154 million television viewers a week. The sport is also growing internationally but still lags behind its British forebears. The 2020 Super Bowl managed to attract a global audience of 102 million. But this is nowhere near the 2019 Rugby World Cup Final viewing figures of 400 million; and both sports were dwarfed by the estimated 1 billion who tuned in to see the final match between Croatia and France in the 2018 Football (soccer) World Cup.

The Ponies

Horse racing is the world's oldest sport. Archaeologists have unearthed evidence that central Asian breeders were racing horses as early as 4,500 BC. It is this region of the world that has provided us with the thoroughbreds that compete on the world's race tracks. The sport was brought to Britain in the twelfth century by Crusaders eager to show off the speed of the Asian-bred mounts they acquired while fighting in the Middle East. The first British racetrack was built in Chester in north-west England. It still stands and is now the world's smallest race course. The first recorded horse race for prize money – £100 – was between horses owned by Lord Salisbury and Lord Buckingham in 1622. James I spent so much time with his horses at Newmarket that Parliament petitioned him to return to London and the business of running the country. The sport was so closely associated with the monarchy and the aristocracy that it was among the first things that Oliver Cromwell banned when he came to power. It was quickly restored with the Restoration in 1660. But it was not until the reign of Queen Anne that horse racing was recognised as a proper sport and it became the first to have a rule-setting governing body when the Jockey Club was formed in 1750.

In the colonies, horse racing was banned in Puritan New England and Quaker Pennsylvania. It was too closely associated with the upper classes and, more importantly, was closely associated with the evils of gambling. However, in New York and the South it was eagerly embraced. The first American racetrack was built on Long Island in 1665. In 1664 a quarter-mile racetrack was laid out in Henrico County, Virginia. In the same year the York County Court imposed a fine on a tailor who had the temerity to race his horse, 'it being contrary to the law for a labourer to make a race, it (horse racing) being a sport only for gentlemen'. Today and in the seventeenth century, horse racing was considered the sport of kings. That is because only kings and the upper classes could afford it. The lower classes were invited to the races to enjoy the thrills and spills and gamble their money, but no more than that.

The close association with gambling almost killed the sport in America. In Britain the gamblers were kept under control by the Jockey Club. It was not until 1894 that US equivalent, the American Jockey Club, was formed, by which time organised crime had made serious inroads into controlling the gambling and 314 racetracks. This was grist for the American anti-gambling lobby, which by 1906 had managed to force the closure of all but 25 of the nation's tracks. The American Jockey Club responded with the introduction of parimutuel betting, which sets aside up to 25 per cent of the money gambled to pay for operating costs and state and local taxes. American horse racing hosts probably the world's most popular race, the Kentucky Derby, but the sport is in decline. Only 1 per cent of Americans in 2018 said that following the horses was their favourite sport and there were only 112 operating tracks. But horse racing – using the same rules as those that govern the British sport – remains a key part of American sporting culture.

America's National Pastime

Baseball owes its existence to the British games of cricket and rounders. With cricket it was not so much the structure of the game as the mentality involved in hitting a ball with a bat. The first recorded game of cricket was in 1598, which means that it is almost certainly much older. In fact, many sport historians believe its origins may predate 1066. By the seventeenth century it was being played throughout Britain at village level and was one of the few sports tolerated during the Cromwell years. In the eighteenth century the sport had moved up to the county level, which remains the backbone of today's game. International cricket is the world's second most popular game.

The first recorded American cricket game was played in 1709 on the James River Estate and the sport quickly grew in popularity. The soldiers at Valley Forge organised regular matches whose players occasionally included George Washington. The world's first international cricket match was between Canada and the US in 1844 and English teams toured America in 1858, 1868 and 1872. For many years there was a battle for supremacy between the emerging game of baseball and cricket.

But in the aftermath of the Civil War baseball gradually won the upper hand. Cricket remained popular well into the 1930s, especially in the Philadelphia area, but the organisers' insistence on upper-crust amateur players couldn't compete with the exciting professionalism of baseball players such as Ty Cobb, Lou Gehrig and Babe Ruth. Today there are still over 1,000 cricket clubs and 25,000 players in the US, but they are mainly comprised of British and South Asian expats and rabid Anglophiles.

It was the British children's game of rounders that provided the basics for baseball. Like cricket, rounders has an ancient history. It is descended from the game of stoolball, which is still played in the southern English counties of Kent, Surrey and Sussex. The name base-ball was first mentioned in a children's book published in England in 1744. Author and publisher John Newbery wrote a rhyme for each letter of the alphabet. For 'B' he chose base-ball and then described rounders: 'The ball once struck off, away flies, the boy to the next destined post and then home with joy.' Rounders came to America via Canada and the first known American reference to it is in 1791 when the Pittsfield, Massachusetts, town fathers stopped it from being played near the town's new meeting house; presumably they were worried about broken windows. In 1828 the *Boy's Own Book* was published in London and devoted an entire chapter to the game and its rules. The following year a pirate copy of the book was published in Boston and the game took off. The rules of the game were simple. Each team had up to fifteen players who were either at bat or in the field. There were two innings and the teams did not change sides until all the batters were out. The bat was about a quarter of the size of a modern baseball bat and was usually swung with one hand. As soon as the batter hit the ball he set off to run around the three bases and return home to the fourth base. The bases were posts rather than flat bases as in baseball. A runner was out if his ball was caught in the air or if the post he was running to was touched by a fielder with the ball before he reached it. If a runner reached the second or third base his team was awarded half a point and if they made it all the way around the field they had achieved a rounder and were awarded one point.

The rules for rounders may have been set out in a book, but there was no official body to ensure that they were adhered to, with the result that different versions of the game were played in different parts of America. There were different names such as town ball, old cat, round town, goal ball, the New England game or Massachusetts baseball. The legend that the first proper game of baseball was organised by Abner Doubleday and played at Cooperstown, New York in 1839, is a myth devised by post-Civil War baseball authorities trying to Americanise the game by riding on the coat tails of Doubleday after he became a Civil War hero. The bulk of the credit should probably go to Alexander Cartwright, who in 1845 devised the Knickerbocker Rules, which were named after the newly formed Knickerbocker Baseball Club. The following year the first game under these rules was played in Hoboken, New Jersey, and by 1856 the New York newspapers were referring to baseball as 'America's national pastime'. The first professional baseball league, the National Association of Professional Base Ball Players, was not formed until 1871. It changed its to the National League in 1876. The American League was founded in 1901. The first World Series was played in 1903. It was called the 'World Series' not because it attracted international teams, but because it was sponsored by Joseph Pulitzer's *New York World* newspaper. Baseball has in fact spread internationally. The first game played beyond American borders was in 1871 in Cuba and that country and Japan have produced some of the world's best players outside the US. In 1969, Canada's Montreal Expos joined the National League and in 1977 the Toronto Blue Jays became affiliated to the American League. The game is played extensively in Japan, South Korea and the Philippines, as well as throughout most of Latin America. There is also a sprinkling of professional European clubs. In 2013 the World Baseball and Softball Confederation was formed and it promptly organised a sixteen-nation international championship called the Baseball Classic. The first championship title in 2013 was won by the Dominican Republic, but in 2017 it returned to its natural home in America. Britain has stuck with rounders and cricket, although softball is a popular game in the country's parks during the summer months.

In the Ring

The first evidence of boxing as a sport dates back to 4000 BC and ancient Egypt, from whence it travelled around the Mediterranean, eventually finding a place in the Greek Olympics in the seventh century BC. The ring was a circle of spectators and the fights lasted without a break until one of the boxers was too injured or exhausted to continue. Hands were protected with thin leather straps, which the Romans adapted for the deadly gladiator arena by adding copper and iron knuckles. With the collapse of the Roman Empire, boxing disappeared until 1681 when England's Duke of Albemarle put up a £100 purse for a boxing match between his butler and his butcher. The butcher won. Shortly afterwards matches were regularly being fought in London's Royal Theatre. The sport quickly spread across the city, which became the European capital for boxing. The fights were vicious, bare-knuckle affairs. There was no weight classification and no common rulebook. As in ancient Greece, the fights lasted until one of the fighters was either knocked out or too exhausted to continue.

In 1743 there was an attempt to introduce a semblance of order to the sport with the first code of rules devised by champion fighter Jack Broughton. Under Broughton's rules, if a man went down for thirty seconds he was out. Boxers could not hit below the waist or kick the opponent when he was down. Broughton also introduced primitive boxing gloves that he called mufflers. Broughton's rules were superseded in 1838 by London Prize Ring Rules which outlawed head butting, eye gouging, scratching, kicking, holding the ropes, using resin, biting, or holding stones or iron bars in the hands. In 1867 the Queensberry Rules, which form the basis of the modern game, were introduced. Boxers must wear padded gloves; each round lasts three minutes with a required one-minute break between each round; boxers can only use their hands; and if a boxer stays on the floor for ten seconds he has lost the fight. Weight classifications were also introduced.

By this time, the sport was firmly established on both sides of the Atlantic, but it was also running into trouble. Gambling had become an essential and corrupting element of boxing and was attracting criminal attention. At the same time, the British public were turning away from violent sports. In 1835 both bear-baiting and cockfighting were banned by the first Cruelty to Animals Act and in 1882 Britain's bare-knuckle fighters suffered a major setback when the courts ruled in *Rex* v. *Coney* that a bare-knuckle fight was an assault causing actual bodily harm even if the participants consented. This ended bare-knuckle boxing in England and shifted the centre of boxing across the Atlantic to America. There the boxing public were keen to see bare-knuckle fights and champion boxers such as John L. Sullivan regarded fighting with gloves as 'unmanly'. Another factor working in favour of the sport in America was the large number of poor European immigrants pouring into American cities. Boxing was a dangerous but quick route out of the slums to fame, fortune and glory. By 1915, the sport was dominated by the Irish, but they were joined by immigrant boxers from Scandinavia and Germany.

American boxing was also responsible for a wave of racism sparked off by the success of heavyweight fighter Jack Johnson. In 1908 Johnson became the first African American heavyweight champion of the world and the most famous black person in America and possibly the world. He held the championship title for seven years until 1915 against a series of white boxers and in doing so was regularly attacked by segregationist

America. Before one bout the *New York Times* wrote: 'If the black man wins, thousands and thousands of his ignorant brothers will misinterpret his victory as justifying claims to much more than mere physical equality with their white neighbours.' Johnson's most famous fight was in 1910 against undefeated former champion John L. Jeffries, who came out of retirement to take on Johnson as the 'Great White Hope'. Johnson beat him in the fifteenth round when Jeffries' corner threw in the towel. In the aftermath of the fight riots erupted in more than twenty-five states and fifty cities. African Americans celebrated, and disappointed whites fought back. At least twenty people were killed and hundreds more were injured. Johnson was perhaps America's first black power symbol and thus a target for the white Establishment inside and outside the ring. His hedonistic and extravagant personal life made it easy to attack him. For a start, he married three white women, which infuriated both black and white American society. In 1913 he was convicted by an all-white jury under the terms of the Mann Act of 'transporting women across state lines for immoral purposes'. Johnson fled first to Canada and then Europe with his wife Lucille rather than go to jail. He did not return to America until 1920 when he surrendered himself and spent ten months in prison. Johnson was pardoned by President Donald Trump in May 2018.

The experience of Jack Johnson led to the imposition of a colour bar on the sport after famous white fighters such as John L. Sullivan and Jack Dempsey refused to step into the ring with an African American. It was not until 1937 that another black fighter – Joe Louis – won the world heavyweight title again. Since then, African Americans have dominated the ring; the most famous being Muhammad Ali, who was surely the most significant and celebrated sports star of the twentieth century. British boxers such as Bob Fitzsimmons, Henry Cooper, Chris Eubank, Lennox Lewis and Anthony Joshua have ensured that the UK remains a force to be reckoned with on the world boxing circuit. But the United States has long since dominated the modern version of the sport that began in seventeenth-century Britain.

The Little White Ball

Golf is Scotland's contribution to the world of sport. Exactly when the Scots started hitting small balls across green expanses and into holes is unknown. But the game was popular enough in 1457 for Scotland's James II to ban the game because it was distracting his citizen army from archery practice. The ban was ignored and repealed forty years later as a lost cause. By the sixteenth century the game was being played at

St Andrews, which became the international home and rules-setter for the sport. Golf quickly became a popular sport with Scottish royals, and when Scotland's James VI moved south to become England's James I, he took his clubs with him. However, the game did not take off in England until the second half of the nineteenth century. In 1880 there were only sixty golf clubs in England. By 1900 the number had grown to 2,330.

Golf crossed the Atlantic about the same time it took off in England. The title of 'Father of American Golf' is generally bestowed upon Scots expat John Reid. In February 1888 Reid built a three-hole course in a Yonkers cow pasture and in November of that year formed the first American golf club, which he named St Andrew's in honour of the famous links course. The United States Golf Association (USGA) was founded just six years later and the first official US Open and Amateur Championship was held in 1895. By 1900 there were over 1,000 golf clubs in America.

Back in Britain, professional golf started to take off from the end of the nineteenth century. Men such as Harry Vardon, James Braid and J. H. Taylor dominated game, winning a succession of British and US Opens. But American golfers were determined to catch up. They imported hundreds of Scottish professionals to teach them the game and in 1911 the investment paid off with a US Open win by Johnny McDermott, the first home-born American to win the US Open. Of even greater importance for the American game was the stunning 1913 US Open win by twenty-year-old Francis Ouimet against a field of seasoned British golfers. Ouimet was a former caddy from a working-class family and his victory demonstrated that golf was no longer the preserve of the wealthy few.

Golf quickly spread across the globe, but the rivalry between the US and Britain remained at the heart of the sport. The world's four major golfing events are the Masters, the US PGA Championship, the US Open and British Open. Up until 1930 the balance of power lay with the British players. But Americans such as Bobby Jones reversed that position. After the Second World War, an increasingly wealthy US dominated the international sport, and between 1945 and 1970 the number of American golf courses more than doubled. American golfers continued to pay homage to the game's Scottish roots. The rules of the game in both countries have remained largely unchanged since they were set down by St Andrews in 1897, although in the first half of the twentieth century American clubs sometimes interpreted the rules differently. At a 1951 international conference the minor differences were ironed out and since then the USGA and St Andrews have met every four years for a review. *Decisions on the Rules* is now jointly published by the two golfing bodies.

Racquets and Wimbledon

Tennis originated in twelfth-century French medieval monasteries. In those days the monks batted a ball around the cloisters in a game they named *jeu de paume* (game of the palm). In the sixteenth century the racquet was introduced and an indoor version of the game known as 'real tennis' was born. The game was the exclusive preserve of the aristocracy and royalty and Henry VIII was a particularly keen player. His real tennis court at Hampton Court Palace can still be seen and occasional matches are still staged there. It is said that the king was playing on the court when Anne Boleyn was arrested and again when news was brought to him of her execution. Real tennis achieved a prominent place in French political history at the start of the French Revolution when the Third Estate adjourned to a tennis court after being thrown out of the Estates General. There they took the famous Tennis Court Oath 'not to separate, and to reassemble wherever circumstances require, until the constitution of the kingdom is established'. Real tennis, however, failed to achieve popularity beyond Europe's wealthy elite and started to die out. The British invention of lawn tennis filled the vacuum and democratised the game.

In the second half of the nineteenth century the most popular outdoor lawn game was croquet. In fact, the full name of the Wimbledon club is the All England Lawn Tennis and Croquet Club. British Army officer Walter Clopton Wingfield saw an opportunity to combine the neatly mowed grass of the croquet lawn with the net of real tennis and the bounce of the recently invented rubber ball, and thus invented the game of lawn tennis. His initial rules bear little resemblance to the game as played today; the net was much higher and the court was an hourglass shape. But Wingfield's contribution to the game was more as a marketer than as an inventor and rules-maker. In 1874 he started manufacturing tennis kits complete with racquets, balls, net, post, lawn markings and instruction manual. Lawn tennis was an instant sporting hit that swept the nation and quickly moved across the Atlantic. The first game of lawn tennis in America was played in the same year as the launch of Wingfield's tennis kits, at the Massachusetts estate of Colonel William Appleton. It was not until the following year that Wimbledon Croquet Club set aside one of its croquet lawns for lawn tennis players.

The first Wimbledon lawn tennis championship was played in 1877 to raise money for the financially strapped club. The first American national tournament was played in 1880 at Staten Island Cricket and Baseball Club. In 1881 the US Lawn Tennis Association was formed to standardise the rules of the game and the first US Tennis Open was held the same year. Grass courts were standard in both US and British tennis championships until 1975 when the US Open switched to clay courts and then eventually to a surface called pro deco turf, which is a hard court constructed of rubber, silica and acrylic on top of a concrete base. The Wimbledon tournament is the only one of the four major opens still played on grass. The Australian Open uses a similar surface called green set and the French Open is played on clay, a surface developed in 1880 by British brothers Willie and Ernest Renshaw while on holiday in the south of France.

The traditional early years of British ascendancy in sport were short-lived in the case of tennis. The British won almost all of the Wimbledon championships up to 1920, but the dominance of American players in the US Open was overwhelming from the first match in 1880. In 1900 the world's two leading tennis-playing countries held the inaugural Davis Cup match between competing teams from Britain and America. The UK won two and the US two before the field was expanded in 1905 to include Belgium, France, Australia, Austria and New Zealand. The Davis Cup is now the world's largest international team competition, with 143 nations competing for the prize in 2020. Tennis has expanded from its English roots to spread to every corner of the globe. But a tennis club on the outskirts of London remains the home, heart, soul and repository of the game's history and traditions. The same roles are performed by Wembley Stadium for football, Lords for Cricket, St Andrews for golf, Newmarket for horse racing, and Twickenham for rugby.

12

War and Diplomacy

The Greatest Empires

The British Empire was at its peak on the eve of the First World War. An island nation off the coast of north-west Europe with a population of 42.5 million held sway over a quarter of the world's population who lived on 24 per cent of the globe's total land area. It was the largest empire in history. The sea lanes that connected the British Empire were protected by a navy that was twice the size of its nearest rival, Germany. It was administered by a complex web of direct rule, protectorates, dominions, and alliances orchestrated from the colonial office in London's Whitehall. The ranks of the relatively small British Army were boosted by British-officered colonial forces who maintained order on the ground throughout the far-flung empire. Finally, there was invaluable support in the form of a first-class intelligence-gathering machine and diplomatic corps, colonial service and home civil service.

The British Empire is gone. But it is still regarded by many other countries with envy and sometimes anger, and in Britain with a mixture of pride and guilt over the methods required to build and maintain it. But as great as the British Empire was, it doesn't hold a candle to the reach and power of the United States and its position in the twenty-first-century post-imperial world. In 2018 the US spent $649 billion on defence. Its nearest rival was China at $250 billion. Its navy dominates every sea lane. Some 450,000 US military personnel were based overseas across every continent except Antarctica. Through the CIA, NSA and FBI, the US operates the world's largest intelligence-gathering machine. Underpinning this formidable structure are over 4,000 nuclear warheads capable of destroying the world several times over.

George Washington's 1796 farewell address warned against 'foreign entanglements'. He maintained that the scheming Europeans were not concerned with America's national interests. Their only goal was the exploitation of the fledgling nation for their own selfish ends. Britain was high on the perfidy list. The colonials had had to fight for independence to restore what they regarded as established British liberties. Washington's second administration was dogged by splits between pro-British Federalists and pro-French Republicans. Twenty years later British troops would burn down the White House. But Britain has stood at the crossroads of almost every major American foreign policy and military decision. Conflicts with European rivals were one of the main reasons that the American colonies came into being. And if the British weren't fighting European rivals over bits of America, they were fighting Americans over independence.

Throughout the nineteenth century British investment in the US meant that the Royal Navy's Atlantic fleet protected the young America from other European powers, thus enabling it to concentrate on westward expansion. By the end of the century, the US had achieved its continental ambitions and emerged as an economic rival to the mother country, albeit still a political and military dwarf. Its growing global trade links made it impossible to stay out of a world war that threatened both its underlying values and vital foreign markets. A rehash of Washington's isolationist message dragged post-war America back into it shell, but the threat of Hitler pulled it back out again. This second hot war was quickly followed by the Cold War, and the British worked hard to draw America into NATO and the Transatlantic Alliance to protect western Europe from the Soviet Union and help with the relatively successful winding up of its empire. This 'special relationship' has become one of the pillars of international relations. It is arguably one of the strongest, most stable, productive and long-lasting alliances on the global stage. Britain and America are inextricably linked at every level: trade and investment, political cooperation, nuclear policy, intelligence gathering and military cooperation.

Blame Spain

On 12 October 1492, Christopher Columbus landed in the Bahamas and changed the world forever. The political and economic axis of the world turned from China and Asia to western Europe, which, in 1492, was little more than a collection of struggling feudal states on the western edge of the Eurasian landmass. Columbus sailed west in the belief that he could take a short cut to the riches of the East. To his dying day he believed he had succeeded. In fact, he had failed. But in doing so he literally struck gold for Spain. And it was not long before New World gold was transforming Britain and driving it to found its own American colonies.

In a little over two decades the Spanish Conquistadors reached the mainland of South America and set out to rape, pillage, plunder and enslave the Native American civilizations. Treasures of gold and silver were melted down and shipped back to Spain in fleets of galleons. In Bolivia they discovered a mountain seemingly of solid silver and, with the help of the newly enslaved peoples, reduced it to a molehill.

Spain became the wealthiest country in the world, if not the wealthiest the world had ever seen. It is estimated that it shipped out close to $530 billion in silver bullion alone. Then there was the gold, the rice, indigo, tropical timber, precious jewels and other valuable products. Unfortunately for future Spanish generations, the Conquistadors failed to invest their new-found wealth wisely. Instead, they spent it. The crown took 25 per cent, which it spent on unproductive activities such as war, the Inquisition, fancy clothes, jewellery and church monuments. But the rest of Europe benefitted, including Britain, which made a fortune selling its wool to Spain and the Spanish Netherlands.

The English, however, were not satisfied with this bonus. They wanted a slice of the action. To do this they needed a *casus belli* to justify taking on the might of Spain. It came in the form of the Protestant Reformation. The devout Philip II of Spain took on the job of bringing England back into the Roman Catholic fold by force. The result was the Anglo-Spanish War from 1585 to 1604 and the expensive failure of the Spanish Armada.

Spain's invasion plan was just the excuse that Elizabeth I needed to attack the Spanish treasure ships. She dispatched Sir Francis Drake to South America where he sacked the towns of Santa Domingo and Cartagena and then went on to destroy 100 Spanish war ships in Cadiz. But it quickly became apparent to the English that the real money was not to be made in piracy but in stealing Spanish colonies and founding their own before the Spanish arrived.

One of the main reasons for the settlement of Jamestown in 1607 was Spanish interest in Virginia. They had sent an expeditionary team to the Chesapeake Bay in 1561, which led to a second expedition to establish a Catholic mission in Virginia. However, the local Native Americans rose up and killed everyone but a teenage boy. The Spanish decided Virginia was not worth the effort. They found no gold or silver and it was too far away from the centre of their operations in the Caribbean and South America. But the English were convinced that the only way to prevent Spanish northern expansion in the New World was to move into the region themselves. They did so in 1580 with the ill-fated Roanoke settlement and then finally with success at Jamestown. The fortifications raised by the Virginia settlement were primarily designed to thwart a Spanish attack. In fact, some historians believe that Spain planned just such an attack but was stopped by the Dutch destruction of the Spanish attacking fleet at Gibraltar.

If Virginia was too far north for the Spaniards, Florida was strategically vital for both London and Madrid. The original sixteenth-century Spanish colony stretched from the east coast of the Florida peninsula westwards to the Mississippi. Northwards it extended into Georgia and even, at times, parts of South Carolina. Florida was the northern shore of the Gulf of Mexico and the Caribbean Sea, which was Spain's strategic lake linking the gold mines of the New World to Europe. Britain needed to block Spanish expansion northwards, and in the seventeenth century bases were required in Florida to protect the Caribbean island colonies that Britain managed to wrest from Spanish control. In the eighteenth century, Spain attempted to destabilise the economies of the British southern colonies by offering freedom to runaway slaves. The first underground railway ran south. The result was that between discovery in 1513 and the end of the American Revolution in 1783, Florida bounced back and forth between British and Spanish hands, with the occasional French interlude. It was firmly in British hands when the War of Independence broke out, and Floridians were loud in their condemnation of the colonial rebels. Spain temporarily regained control of Florida with the 1783 Treaty of Paris, which ended the revolution, and a combination of Spanish control and loyalty to Britain meant that Florida didn't become part of the US until 1822.

By the start of the eighteenth century the Spanish Empire was beginning its long and painful decline. The British, on the other hand, were heading towards take-off. This meant that the Spanish War of Succession (or Queen Anne's War in America) was a disaster for Spain in Europe and America. The war was triggered by Spain's Charles II dying in November 1570 without an heir. His closest relatives were France's Bourbon dynasty and the Habsburgs of the Austro-Hungarian Empire. Both claimed the Spanish throne and its global empire. But the rest of Europe, led by Britain, was determined to prevent either royal house ascending the Spanish throne for fear that it would upset the European balance of power. The war that followed raged across Europe, the Atlantic, the Caribbean and North America. British colonists in the Carolinas and Georgia used the war as an excuse to invade Florida where they recaptured runaway slaves and nearly wiped out the local Native American population, who retreated to the Everglades, where they remain to this day. The Spanish were allied with the French, who used their base in Canada to attack New England. In February 1704, a combined force of French troops and Native Americans attacked the outpost of Deerfield in western Massachusetts; forty-seven English settlers were killed and 112 were carted off to captivity in Canada. The French also made unsuccessful incursions into Maine and attempted a grab for the rich fishing banks of New England and the lucrative fur trade in upstate New York. They failed at every turn. Britain began to emerge as the victor in North America and the original thirteen colonies started to take shape.

The war ended with the 1713 Treaty of Utrecht, which left Britain the dominant power in Europe and North America. France was forced to cede the Hudson Bay territory, Arcadia and Newfoundland. Spain was officially a spent force. It managed to retain its Caribbean and South American colonies, but was forced to relinquish its monopoly on the African slave trade to the British, who took it to new heights and dramatically changed the demography of the American colonies. The high cost of the war also led to the rapid decline of the Dutch East India Company and the end of the Dutch Golden Age.

Beavers, Spices and Tulips

The Dutch arrived to settle Manhattan Island, or what they called New Amsterdam, in July 1625. They were drawn across the Atlantic in part because the Netherlands was flush with money from the Spice Islands of the East and Dutch merchants were keen to invest in new projects. The Protestant Dutch also wanted to distract the Catholic Spanish, against whom they were fighting a war of independence that they would eventually win in 1648. And finally, the Dutch wanted to drive a wedge between the infant British colonies based in Virginia and Massachusetts Bay. The British had been instrumental in their fight against Spain, but by 1625 it was apparent that the Netherlands would be their next big rival. During the seventeenth century the two countries would fight three wars between 1652 and 1674 and Manhattan Island would change hands twice. Eventually it would be ceded to Britain and renamed New York, not because Britain won a war but as a consolation after losing a war.

Centuries of hard work reclaiming land from the sea combined with the burgeoning Protestant work ethic made the Dutch exemplary colonial settlers. They quickly built a solid pentagonal fort at the tip of Manhattan Island for protection against Native Americans and spread from their stronghold up the island and the Hudson River Valley. The settlement was financed and managed by the Dutch West India Company who had their eye on beaver pelts. The potential had been spotted in 1609 by English explorer Henry Hudson who sailed up his namesake river on a Dutch-financed expedition. Beaver pelts were big business in Europe; the pelts of the over-sized rodents have been estimated to be worth $300 each at today's prices. The main use of the fur was to supply a huge market for waterproof hats. In addition, castoreum, a product of beaver glands, was prized as a perfume and used in medicines. Families such as the Vanderbilts and the Roosevelts owe much to the humble beaver.

As profitable as the beaver trade was, it failed to come close to matching the value of the spice trade in the Dutch-controlled East Indies (now Indonesia). And the king of spices was the nutmeg. In the seventeenth century one nutmeg was said to be worth its equivalent weight in gold. The dockworkers that unloaded the spice in London and Amsterdam were forced to wear uniforms with the pockets sewn shut to prevent theft. The main reason for sky-high nutmeg prices was that the only place in the world where the nutmeg plant could grow was a chain of ten tiny volcanic outcrops called the Banda Islands, located on the opposite side of the world in the Indonesian archipelago. A particularly fruitful piece of real estate was called Run. It provided most of the world's nutmeg, even though it was only 1.8 miles long and half a mile wide. The Dutch East India Company had enjoyed a monopoly on the spice trade from Run and the Banda Islands since 1610. Then in 1616 the English muscled in with an expedition led by Captain Nathaniel Courthorpe, who occupied Run and started exporting nutmeg. The Dutch fought back, attacked the English post in 1620, killed Captain Courthorpe and re-established their total control over the priceless Spice Islands. The English were out, but they refused to relinquish their claim to Run.

In 1652, the Dutch decided to take advantage of England's preoccupation with its civil strife to gain the upper hand in the English Channel and North Sea. The result was the First Anglo-Dutch War, which lasted two years until 1654. The conflict was fought entirely at sea. Unfortunately for the Dutch, they miscalculated both the strength and determination of Cromwell's navy. It was a large, battle-hardened fleet that had been expanded during the Civil Wars to transport troops to Ireland and Scotland and blockade rebel ports. The outcome of the war was a limited victory for England, but it was far from a knock-out blow.

The Anglo-Dutch rivalry remained unresolved and the scene was set for the Second Anglo-Dutch War from 1665 to 1667.

When Charles II was restored to the English throne in 1660 many thought it would lead to England eclipsing the Netherlands on the world stage. But at the same time, France was posing problems and the new king found it difficult to decide whether to fight the Dutch or the French. The English capture of New Amsterdam on 27 August 1664 was one of the main causes for the outbreak of the Second Anglo-Dutch War. The Dutch colony was surrendered without a fight by Governor Peter Stuyvesant. In June 1665, New Amsterdam was reincorporated under English law and the colony's name was changed to New York in honour of the king's younger brother and heir to the English throne, the Duke of York. The Royal Navy went on to win the first major sea battle of the war off the English town of Lowestoft. Then things turned sour for Charles. The French sided with the Dutch, which led to the one of the longest naval engagements in history, 'the Four Days Battle'. The outcome was inconclusive, with both sides claiming victory, although the Dutch lost only four ships compared to the British loss of ten.

The English were running out of money. It was decided that to save cash, the Royal Navy's heavy ships would be laid up at the Chatham naval dockyard. With the English fleet substantially reduced, the Dutch pressed their advantage and sailed up the Medway River to inflict one of the worst defeats in English military history. Three of England's biggest fighting ships were completely destroyed. The largest, HMS *Royal Charles*, was captured without a shot being fired and was towed back to Amsterdam as a prize while another fifteen ships were sunk or scuttled. There were no Dutch losses. England lost the Second Anglo-Dutch War and was forced to sue for peace at the Treaty of Breda. Charles II had hoped that victory would give him Run and a firm foothold in the spice trade. This was now impossible. The English were forced to trade their claim on Run for the consolation prize of New York. There are those who think that Britain inadvertently secured the better deal. But Run Island continued to exclusively produce valuable nutmegs for another 153 years. Britain lost New York in 1776. It was not until 1810 that the Dutch monopoly was broken when the British spirited away trees for transplanting into similar hot and humid volcanic conditions elsewhere in the expanding British Empire.

There was one more Anglo-Dutch conflict, from 1672 to 1674. In July 1673, the Dutch briefly reoccupied New York, but in the Treaty of Westminster, which ended the third war, the Dutch relinquished all claims to their North American colony in return for the sugar plantations in

Suriname. By this time the Dutch had exhausted their treasury and their Golden Era was drawing to close. Britain, meanwhile, began its rapid rise. The only country standing between it and what eventually became history's largest empire was their old foe: the French.

The Old Foe

From 1066 until the end of the nineteenth century the British and the French were at loggerheads. The British learned to hate the French and the French came to despise the British. Then, in the end, a long shared history led to mutual respect and support in the two world wars of the twentieth century. Both sides claim a string of victories and defeats. The British talk about the Angevin Empire, the battles of Agincourt and Crecy, Blenheim, the Seven Years War, victory in India and, of course, the Napoleonic Wars and a few African skirmishes. On the other hand, Joan of Arc was canonised and quite rightly the French point out that they won the Hundred Years War (actually 116 years) and booted the English out of Calais. Under the Sun King, Louis XIV, they were the dominant European power, controlling South East Asia and Algeria, and gave the British a run for their money in Africa, the Middle East and North America. Without French support the United States would have found winning the War of Independence a lot harder. About Napoleon they are ambivalent. He was a military dictator who ostensibly espoused the French Revolution's ideals of liberty, equality and fraternity while conquering and oppressing Continental Europe. Britain was number one for most of their shared history and France was number two, striving to be number one.

It started with the Norman Conquest. Before William I defeated Harold at the Battle of Hastings, he was Duke of Normandy and had political footholds in neighbouring Brittany and Flanders. In fact, after conquering England, he spent much of his time back in France defending his interests there. William died in September 1087 fighting off encroachments by the French king, who in those days was little more than another French nobleman. An indication of William's perception of his lands on either side of the English Channel was that in his will he left his Continental possessions to his eldest son and the throne of England to his second son. To William the Conqueror, England was little more than a Norman colony. He removed most of the Anglo-Saxon nobility and replaced them with Norman knights, introduced the feudal structure and Norman laws and architecture, and for the next 300 years Norman French was the language of the English court. Technically, the King of England was a vassal of the King of France because Normandy owed suzerainty to the French throne and the King of England was a vassal of the Duke of Normandy. This remained the case until 1198 when Richard the Lionheart declared *Dieu et Mon Droit* (God and my right) and his independence from the French. Richard, it should be pointed out, spent only seven months of his ten-year reign in England. Richard ruled not only England but part of Ireland, a big chunk of Wales, Normandy, Aquitaine and Gascony. The Angevin Empire, as it was called, had been cobbled together through political marriages and conquest and stretched from the Scottish to the Spanish borders and occupied more than half of contemporary France.

By the time the Magna Carta was signed in 1215 there were signs that England's Norman aristocrats were beginning to identify more with the Anglo-Saxons they conquered than the Frenchmen they left behind. Their focus turned from France to subduing Wales and attempting to conquer Scotland, although the situation was complicated by the fact that what was becoming an 'English' aristocracy still held extensive lands in France, and they wanted to keep them. To do so they were forced to divide themselves between their French chateaux, English castles and crusades in the Holy land, using a communications system that moved at the walking pace of a shire horse. At the same time the French were beginning to distinguish between Anglo-Norman and French interests as their taxes and tithes disappeared across the Channel to England to absentee landlords who were increasingly Anglicised. The French king saw that the system was breaking down and decided to move on the Norman lands.

In May 1334 King Philippe IV offered refuge to David, the ten-year-old King of Scotland, England's other great medieval foe. Philippe then organised for the Bishop of Rouen to deliver a sermon in which he leaked that the French king was threatening to invade England. Britain's teenage king, Edward III, responded by claiming the French throne, so in 1337 the French launched a series of raids on English Channel ports. The Hundred Years War was underway.

From the English point of view, the Hundred Years War was marked by two of its greatest military victories. From the French point of view, it was defined by the fact that, despite losses at vital pitched battles, they won the war. Both of the English victories were a credit to the work of the longbow, a Welsh invention. An English archer could fire up to twenty arrows in a minute. In contrast, the French crossbow bolts could travel further and faster, but at the rate of one a minute. Medieval French battlefield tactics were to move their front line as close as possible to the enemy, then charge with mounted armoured knights who were drawn from the upper ranks of the aristocracy. Mopping-up exercises were conducted by the men-at-arms who were drawn from peasant stock. The French system relied on numerical strength and an arrogant belief in their superior code of chivalry. The British tactic was to kill as many of the enemy as possible with a mass troop of rapid-fire longbowmen and then stroll through the battlefield stealing armour and jewellery from the dead bodies. The British plans proved superior at the Battle of Crecy in August 1346, at the Battle of Poitiers in September 1356, and again at Agincourt in October 1415. At Crecy, 1,542 French noblemen were killed and 10,000 other ranks. British casualties were between 100 and 300. The French did not suffer massive casualties at Poitiers, but they did suffer the embarrassment of their king being captured. The English returned to the slaughter at Agincourt. It is estimated that the French lost another 6,000 men of which about 2,000 were the 'flower of the French nobility'. A further 1,500 Frenchmen were captured. British losses were estimated at 500.

One would have thought that these overwhelming British victories would have resulted in a final British success. But a combination of factors such as the Black Death and the inspirational leadership of a teenage French girl militated against such an outcome. Joan of Arc's charisma and unswerving belief in her God-appointed mission led to her gathering a large armed following who accompanied her to the French court. The king was persuaded to give her a shot at recovering the city of Orleans. Against the odds, Joan succeeded. But her success was seen by some as a threat to the throne despite her protestations of undying support. With the connivance of French noblemen, she was arrested and handed over to the English, who burned her at the stake because she was guilty – among other things – of the then capital crime of wearing men's clothes. The result was immediate martyrdom, which was embraced by the French court who had thrown her over. Joan's death acted as a catalyst which inspired the French to unite and throw out the English. It coalesced their thinking in a way that led to a shift from feudalism to nationalism. The peasants no longer owed their primary allegiance to hereditary nobility; the Anglo-Norman landlords had shown themselves unworthy of such allegiance by failing to protect them from 100 years of rape and pillage by English brigands they were supposed to control. At the same time, a middle class had been created to service war needs and this middle class prospered best under a clear national identity supported by a standing army that protected national territory and interests. English identity was partly forged in the face of the hatred of the French. By the end of the Hundred Years War, English had replaced French as the language of the court, most of the old Norman families had lost their lands in France and were concentrating on English, Scottish and Irish holdings, and the Anglo-French rivalry had become an integral part of the national identity of both countries. As the Age of Empire dawned it was only natural that this rivalry would cross the Atlantic and become a vital factor in the development of North America.

Both the French and the English were enraged at Pope Alexander VI's Treaty of Tordesillas, which divided much of the world between Portugal and Spain. Portugal was given control of non-Christian countries east of the Cape Verde islands (which meant Africa, Asia and Brazil) and Spain was presented with the rest of South America, the Caribbean, Central America and North America. The claims and interests of the rest of Europe weren't even mentioned. In Spanish and Portuguese eyes this meant they were excluded. In Dutch, French and British eyes it meant that they were not bound by the treaty, so it could be largely ignored and the Iberian empires were fair game for pirates, privateers and the occasional wars and land swaps. North America was a particularly attractive battleground. The French (and to a lesser extent the British) claimed that they had fishing fleets operating off the New England and Canadian coasts before 1492 and simply preferred to keep quiet about the source of their wealth and never set up permanent settlements.

The first official French visit to North America was led by the Italian explorer Giovanni de Verrazano, who in 1524 led an expedition which staked a French claim to the Atlantic coast stretching from the Carolinas to Newfoundland. The claim was confirmed by a voyage led by Jacques Cartier who banged out an iron plaque from a cooking plate, inscribed the French claim and planted it on North American soil with the French flag. However, they only settled the Canadian territory in 1535 and concentrated on that part of North America after Henri IV decreed that the French possessions would be restricted to the lands north of 40 degrees latitude and be called Canada. This still took a big chunk of what became the United States as 40 degrees latitude north ran through the future city of Philadelphia. This led to a series of clashes in the seventeenth and eighteenth centuries between the French and their Native American allies and the British New England settlers and their Native American allies. The other French chunk of North America was Louisiana, which stretched from the Great Lakes and took in the Ohio and Mississippi River Valleys all the way to New Orleans and the Gulf of Mexico. This massive territory was meant to provide another outlet to the sea for Canadian furs, and to act as a buffer against the Spanish in the west and – along with possessions centred on Montreal – as a launch pad for the eventual removal of the hated British from the Atlantic seaboard. Unfortunately for the French, it didn't work out quite like that.

France's first problem was the long reign of Louis XIV (1643–1715). Unfortunately for prospective French settlers, Louis's world was largely confined to the European mainland where he fought a series of wars to expand French territory and influence. He also spent a fortune building the Palace of Versailles. The few possessions that were successfully settled – Arcadia (later Nova Scotia) and Newfoundland – were ceded to Britain along with Hudson Bay by the 1713 Treaty of Utrecht because Louis was on the wrong side in Europe's Spanish War of Succession. The British exploited the relative lack of French interest to establish settlements faster in disputed territories in New England and in the southern colonies of Maryland, Virginia, North Carolina and Virginia. But after the death of the Sun King in 1715, French interest in building an overseas empire was renewed, not only in North America but also India. This led them into a series of conflicts with the British Empire including the Austrian War of Succession, King George's War, the War of Jenkins' Ear and finally the world's first global war, the Seven Years War (or the French and Indian Wars) in North America. The last war virtually wiped out the first French colonial empire.

By the middle of the eighteenth century, the French had woken up to the fact that they occupied valuable North American real estate and the British were becoming aware that they might not always hold the upper hand. On top of that, the British wanted to move into the American interior around the Ohio River Valley where the French dominated. A 1666 census of the population of what was called New France showed 3,215 inhabitants. By 1760, the population in Quebec province alone was estimated at 70,000. However, the Canadian population didn't come close to the estimated 2 million British colonists backed up by British naval superiority. So the British pressed their advantage and went on the offensive. America was their main theatre of operations but the Seven Years War was also fought in the Caribbean, South America, India and the Philippines. Britain successfully avoided a land war on European soil, where they would have faced France's large and powerful army, but declared war on France in May 1756. The British threw everything they had at the Canadian French. Two years later they captured Fort Louisburg, which controlled the entrance to the St Lawrence River, and in 1759 an Anglo-American force captured Quebec in a battle on the Fields of Abraham in which both the French and British commanders, the Marquis de Montcalm and General James Wolfe, were killed. The fighting in North America effectively ended in

1760, although it dragged on for another three years elsewhere in the world. In the end, the country with the deepest pockets won. It cost France an estimated $20 billion in gold at 2015 prices and Britain a staggering $100 billion.

In Britain, the cost of the war led to the collapse of William Pitt the Elder's government and set the political minds of the time thinking about how best to recover the cash. They concluded that the American colonists should pick up a large proportion of the tab; after all, British money and lives were expended to protect them from French invasion and that threat had now been completely eliminated. Furthermore, the amount of money to be raised and the way in which it could be raised was to be determined by Parliament in London without reference to the colonial assemblies. Not surprisingly, the formerly loyal colonists began to object to this attack by the mother country on their pocket books and the political liberties that they had enjoyed from the very start of the colonial experience. The colonists' complaints were ignored and a series of taxes were imposed, as described earlier. The colonists fought back by refusing to pay, throwing tea off ships and running tax collectors out of town. The British escalated the dispute by imposing a blockade on Boston – the heart of the opposition – and the situation spiralled out of control to the Battle of Bunker Hill, the Declaration of Independence and the American Revolution.

It is a matter of dispute as to whether the Americans won the War of Independence or if the French won it for them. Certainly the French were a decisive factor. They were still smarting from the loss of Canada, indulged in dreams of winning it back and really hated the British. Aware of the possible pivotal role of the French, the Continental Congress despatched first Silas Deane and then Benjamin Franklin to Paris to secure French backing for their cause. Deane had an early success in organising the covert supply of French gunpowder and weapons in early 1776 through a shell company called Rodrigue Hortalez Compagnie. It is estimated that munitions sent by the French government-financed company made up as much as 90 per cent of the colonists' munitions in the key Saratoga campaign in which Canadian and British forces led by General John Burgoyne planned to march through the Hudson River Valley to New York, effectively splitting New England and New York from the rest of the colonies. Burgoyne's mission failed miserably. At the Battle of Saratoga he was defeated by George Washington in October 1777 and forced to surrender the arms of his 5,895 British and Hessian troops. The colonials' victory persuaded the French to formally enter the war on the American side. During the course of the conflict the French committed 63,000 troops while the American strength averaged 40,000. British forces at their peak totalled 48,000 plus another 25,000 loyalist forces and 30,000 German mercenaries. The American navy peaked in 1779 with 5,000 sailors manning 53 frigates and sloops. The Royal Navy had 171,000 sailors on 94 ships-of-the-line, 104 frigates and 37 sloops. The French were able to offset the overwhelming British naval advantage with 146 ships-of-the-line. The French were also able to provide key leaders in the form of the young Marquis de Lafayette, Rear Admiral Comte de Grasse and the commander of the French Army forces in North America, Comte de Rochambeau. It was a combined force of Washington and Rochambeau's that surrounded Lord Cornwallis's army at Yorktown in September and October 1781, and de Grasse's fleet that cut off the British escape by sea. Cornwallis's surrender resulted in British Parliament voting to suspend all military operations in North America, and in 1783 the Treaty of Paris formally ended the war and recognised American independence.

Given the decisive impact of the French, they failed to gain much out of the Treaty of Paris. The war cost the French Treasury another $18 billion (at 2015 prices) and Canada remained firmly in British hands as the British had made a point of cultivating the original French colonial settlers and then, after 1780, allowed it to become a refuge for American loyalists. France's only territorial gains from the American Revolution were Tobago and Senegal. The Spanish, who provided nominal aid, regained control of east and west Florida and the island of Menorca. The United States gained not only its independence but all of the area east of the Mississippi River and south of the Great Lakes and St Lawrence River. Furthermore, France's crippling war debts, plus exposure in America to radical ideas about liberty and equality, played a major role in laying the groundwork for the French Revolution, the rise of Napoleon and the War of 1812.

The French Revolution, Bonaparte and 1812

The 1789 Declaration of the Rights of Man and the Citizen is to France what the Declaration of Independence is to America. It is also a Franco-American collaborative effort. Its two French authors were the hero of the American Revolution Marquis de Lafayette and the Catholic clergyman Abbé Sieyes. Both men consulted Thomas Jefferson, author of the Declaration of Independence, on every step of the way. Its French equivalent was heavily influenced by the doctrine of 'natural right', the firm belief that such rights are universal, the rights of all free individuals and protected by law. Today, these beliefs are an accepted part of the political fabric. In late eighteenth-century France, struggling with debt, an unpopular monarchy and an outdated feudal structure, they were truly radical. The result was an explosion that shook the political establishment on both sides of the Atlantic, split early American politics, launched America on a long period of neutrality, more than doubled the size of the United States, and pushed the young nation into another war with Britain.

The cost of two wars in America, the loss of an empire, a series of disastrous harvests, monarchical mismanagement and arrogance combined with the ideas of the Enlightenment to encourage the French people to revolt against the Ancien Régime. The American example – the first successful revolution of its kind – also played a significant role, although Thomas Jefferson probably overstated American influence when he said the French were 'awakened by our revolution'. The revolution started in May 1789 when Louis XVI was forced to convene the French parliament, the Estates General, for the first time since 1614. He needed their support to increase taxes. The Estates General were sick of an absolute monarchy underpinned by a feudal structure. In July the Bastille was stormed. In August the Declaration of the Rights of Man was published and the feudal rights and privileges of the Ancien Régime were abolished. France was in revolt against a corrupt and anachronistic system which was clinging to power by its fingernails with some help from frightened monarchies elsewhere in Europe.

Initially, the French Revolution was greeted in Britain with enthusiasm. Many saw it as proof that France was following the British example and abandoning absolute monarchism for the constitutional model. However, parliamentarians such as Edmund Burke warned early on of the dangers of revolution sliding into chaos and war and fairly quickly public opinion shifted away from support for the revolutionaries. In the US it was more complicated. France was the ally that had helped them to win independence. The French people were inspired by the American experience. The British were the enemy with whom there were still unresolved issues arising from the 1783 Treaty of Paris. But, on the other hand, Britain remained America's main investor and trading partner. They had a shared history and family ties with Britain, and France was decidedly unstable. The two different ways of viewing the French Revolution and the growing prospect of an Anglo-French conflict led to the formation of America's first political parties: the Federalists, who argued for closer relations with Britain and were led by John Adams and Alexander Hamilton; and the Republicans, led by Thomas Jefferson.

In 1792 the French started exporting their revolution to neighbouring countries. Britain and the Continental monarchies were worried, so much so that they declared war on France in January 1793. The US seriously considered coming to the aid of their revolutionary war ally, but on 21 January 1793 Louis XVI lost his head to Madame Guillotine and American public opinion shifted towards the pro-British Federalists.

The post-war of independence period was never pro-British. There were still bitter feelings about 30,000 American casualties (about 10,000 of whom died while British prisoners of war), concerns about the border with Canada (which would not be resolved until the early twentieth century), commercial debts, the continuing British military occupation of the Ohio Territory, and the uncomfortable realisation that, despite independence, the United States remained an economic colony of Britain. American exports to Britain rose by 300 per cent from 1785 to 1800. In the same period American exports to the British Empire averaged 45 per cent of all American exports. The British, for their part, adopted an arrogant and superior attitude towards America. Newspapers, pamphleteers and the occasional parliamentary speech called for a fresh war to reabsorb 'the colonies' back into the empire. If Britain had not become so absorbed with fighting the infection of the French Revolution it may have started another war with the United States. The war with France several times brought the US to the brink of open conflict with both Britain *and* France, as both countries regularly stopped and impounded American ships carrying goods to their enemy. Britain, however, came closest to blows simply because the larger Royal Navy attacked more American ships.

In 1790 the British had 195 ships-of-the-line. The French had sixty-three. The US had only fifteen. But if Britain ruled the waves, France dominated the land. By the time Napoleon marched on Moscow in 1812, the French Army had grown to 600,000 men compared to the British Army of 250,000. Artillery officer Napoleon was focused on dominance in continental Europe and the Mediterranean. For that he needed an army. He also needed the money to pay for an army. The defence budget in 1807 was 462 million francs, which soared to 817 million in 1813. To pay the bills, Napoleon confiscated the property of French 'enemies of the regime' and plundered the treasuries, art galleries and landholdings of the territories he conquered. But he never had enough, which is how in 1802 the US nearly doubled in size with the purchase of Louisiana from the financially stretched French emperor. Louisiana had been French until the Seven Years War when it was ceded to the Spanish in return for their support of the British cause. But Napoleon conquered Spain, which gave him the opportunity to hand over a tiny Italian kingdom in Tuscany for the return of 827,000 square miles of Louisiana. The deal was confirmed in 1800 in the secret Third Treaty of San Ildefonso. At the same time, President Thomas Jefferson, was trying to purchase New Orleans. The US had secured the lands east of the Mississippi but needed the port at the mouth of the river to secure navigation rights. He dispatched James Monroe and Robert Livingston to Paris to offer to buy the port city. Napoleon's response was: why would I want a river and its surrounding territory when the outlet to the sea is blocked? And besides, I need the money. Louisiana was thus purchased for $15 million as a direct consequence of a war between Britain and France.

In the end, the spark that started the second and last Anglo-American war was not attacks on US shipping but the British impressment of sailors off American ships. The British desperately needed sailors to man the ships needed for a blockade of European ports. Unable to find enough men in the British ports, the Royal Navy resorted to stopping American ships and dragging off sailors whom they thought were British-born, which was understandably a fair number of them given the trading connections between the countries. This, combined with the seizure of goods and a licensing system that forced British merchants to direct all of their Continental traffic through British ports, pushed President James Monroe to ask Congress to declare war on 18 June 1812.

The main target for the US was Canada. As Thomas Jefferson said at the time: 'Our aim is to drive Britain off the North American continent.' The US believed that the Canadians would welcome them as liberators bringing democracy and freedom to their northern neighbours. That was not, however, how the Canadians viewed the situation. The northern neighbour's population had swelled during and after the revolution with loyalists fleeing the US for the remaining branch of the British Empire on the North American continent. Being British, part of the British Empire and connected to the Crown was an essential part of the Canadian identity. This continues to be the case in the twenty-first century, even though there is no longer a British Empire. At the start of the war there were repeated attempts by America to invade Canada. Only one made any headway and then it withdrew. The only real success was twenty-seven-year-year-old Commodore Oliver Hazard Perry's defeat of the British naval forces on Lake Erie. They also managed to burn down the Canadian capital of York (present-day Toronto) on 27 April 1813, but failed to follow through. The US should have done better. They had the home ground advantage and for the first two years of the war the British Army was tied down in Spain fighting the Peninsular War against

Napoleon. After Napoleon's abdication on 11 April 1814 the British were able to throw more resources into the war against America and on 24 August 1814 burned Washington in retaliation for the attack on York. By this time, both sides were sick of war. The British had been fighting the French off and on since 1793. The treasury was drained. The American economy was suffering as well. The British naval blockade of the American seaboard forced down the value of American imports and exports from $192 million in 1811 to $31 million in 1814.

President Madison started seriously thinking about a negotiated peace in February 1813 when news reached Washington of the defeat of Napoleon's Grand Army in Russia. He realised from that moment that the British would defeat the French and then be able to throw the full weight of their army and navy against the US. John Quincy Adams, Albert Gallatin and James Bayard were despatched to London to negotiate a peace treaty, signed on Christmas Eve 1814. News of the peace deal failed to reach the US until after future president Andrew Jackson repulsed and soundly defeated a British attack on New Orleans. The timing of the battle and Jackson's overwhelming success in the Louisiana swamplands led Americans to claim victory in the War of 1812. In reality it was a draw, and only that because for most of the war the British were more concerned about the war in Europe than the sideshow in America.

Pax Britannica *versus* Manifest Destiny

Napoleon's defeat at Waterloo marked the beginning of a 100-year-long Pax Britannica and the realisation of America's continental Manifest Destiny. Armed with the world's largest navy, a burgeoning industrial base in search of markets and a humbled France, the British turned their backs on the old empire in America and established a massively bigger string of colonies in Africa, Asia and the Mediterranean. Some of them were prizes from the wars against France. British dominance in India had been established in the Seven Years War, nearly lost in the Indian Mutiny and then reaffirmed when the Subcontinent became a Crown colony in 1857. The British established a foothold in South Africa in 1806, drove the French out of Malta in 1813 and took over Ceylon in 1814. But it was not until Napoleon was despatched to his prison on the island of St Helena that the empire builders rolled up their sleeves in earnest as flag followed trade across the oceans. The British started the long process of a protectorate in the Persian Gulf in 1820. The Falklands were colonised in 1833, Singapore in 1819, Hong Kong in 1843 and New Zealand in 1840. Australia became a penal colony in 1788 – sorely needed, because before the American Revolution most of the British unwanted were despatched to the Southern colonies. It has been estimated that between 1815 and 1865, the British Empire grew at the rate of 100,000 square miles a year. Its foreign policy was to create a balance of power in Europe which left it free to grow its influence elsewhere.

While Britain was controlling the sea lanes to expand its global empire, the United States was creating a contiguous land-based empire. A coast-to-coast continental America had been a dream of the Founding Fathers and as the French and Spanish stumbled and Britain looked elsewhere, successive administrations saw their opportunity and took it. Illinois became a state in 1818, Alabama in 1819, Mississippi 1817, Missouri 1821, Texas 1845 and gold-rich California in 1850. The Americans, however, were not driven by the need for new markets. In the first half of the nineteenth century the US remained a predominantly agricultural nation with a narrow industrial base focused on the north-eastern states. The US was driven by an unswerving faith in their God-given Manifest Destiny to control North America and extend the fruits of democracy from sea to shining sea. The Native Americans who already occupied the territory were collateral damage sacrificed to the greater good.

That is not to say that Britain and America went their separate ways for the next 100 years. No, they were still inextricably bound together, and the British played a vital role in providing the cash that financed America's westward expansion, and the security that kept the other European powers at bay. Occasionally, they also clashed, as during the American Civil War, but gradually both sides came to the realisation that they needed each other and that their common heritage had linked them for better or worse. By 1850 half of all American exports went to Britain, mainly agricultural products. American imports of British manufactured goods in 1850 were 44 per cent of the total. British capital provided most of the cash to build America's infrastructure. When the railways started to take root in the 1850s, it was the British who supplied the steel as well as the investment capital. Between 1848 and 1852, British investment in American railways doubled from $60 million to $120 million, Land was another target for the British. By the end of the nineteenth century British aristocrats and land companies owned 25 million acres of the American West, an area equivalent to the state of Kentucky. And the British protected their investment. The Royal Navy's Atlantic Squadron blocked interference from the other European colonial powers and allowed the US to expend its efforts on expansion rather than building a large navy or army. As late as 1880, American military personnel totalled 36,000 compared to 248,000 in Britain and over half a million in France.

The two countries also found a common interest in the Latin American independence movement. Spain had been a spent colonial force for many years by the time Napoleon invaded the Iberian Peninsula. Bonaparte's move made the Spanish South American colonies fair game for the British who channelled guns and cash to revolutionaries in Argentina, Chile and Uruguay. After 1815 they went on to support the great South American liberator Simón Bolívar as he gained independence from Spain for Venezuela, Colombia, Bolivia, Ecuador, Peru and Panama in a series of wars. British support for Bolivar stemmed from the desire to keep Germany, France and Russia from carving up the crumbling Spanish empire. As British Foreign Secretary George Canning said: 'I created the New World to balance the Old World.' The three European countries were referred to as the 'Unholy Alliance'. Washington had the same interest. In 1823, Canning proposed that Britain and the US issue a joint declaration supporting the Latin American independence movement and opposing any further European colonisation of the region. President James Monroe thought this was the bones of a good idea but didn't want to share credit with the British, so in his 1823 State of the Union Address he proposed the Monroe Doctrine and a British idea became a pillar of American foreign policy.

Despite the heavy trade between the two countries, there were periodic clashes. Most of them concerned Canada and were a holdover from the War of Independence and the War of 1812. The British had hoped to maintain a foothold in the north-west territories south of the Great Lakes as well as naval superiority on the lakes. Gradually they realised that this was an untenable situation and they withdrew. In Maine in 1839 the Aroostook War broke out between American and Canadian lumberjacks over timber rights along the ill-defined border between Maine and Canada. The British, representing Canada, won that dispute. But they lost out on the border between Canada and the Oregon Territory. They wanted the boundary line drawn along the current border between Washington and Oregon. In the end the US–Canadian border became the 49th Parallel, with the exception that the British kept all of Vancouver Island and navigation rights on the Columbia River.

These disputes, however, were minor compared to the American Civil War where the two sides very nearly came into open conflict. The problem was the dependence of the British textile industry on cotton imports from the seceding American states. The British public were opposed to slavery, but as is so often the case in British history, money won out. On the ground, there were two main incidents which severely strained relations: the *Trent* Affair and the actions of the Confederate raiding ship the

Alabama. The *Trent* was carrying Confederate diplomats James Mason and John Slidell to London in November 1861 when it was stopped by USS *San Jacinto* and, in contravention of international law, removed the two men and carried them off to prison in Boston. Foreign Secretary Lord Russell demanded their immediate release and Prime Minister Lord Palmerston let it be known that he was considering sending the Royal Navy to set the Confederate agents free. President Lincoln concluded that British entry into the war would tip the balance to the Confederate side, backed down and released the men. The case of the *Alabama* was more complicated. International law allowed British firms to sell ships to both sides as long as the ships were not armed. The Confederate government ordered such a ship from a Liverpool dockyard. Washington demanded that the ship be detained. The British pointed out that it was unarmed. As soon as the *Alabama* was completed it raced to the Azores where it was equipped with the latest in ship's cannon. During her subsequent career she sank ten Union ships in the Atlantic and captured eighty-two merchant ships. The depredations of the British-built *Alabama* soured Anglo-American relations for six years after the war and were finally ended in 1871 when the British agreed to pay $15.5 million in compensation. In the end, pragmatism kept Britain out of the war and played a major role in saving the Union. The two turning points were the Union victory at the Battle of Gettysburg and the replacement of the confederacy by Egypt as the source of cotton for Britain's textile industry. Between 1861 and 1863, Egyptian cotton exports to Britain more than doubled. Unfortunately for the Egyptians, this also made it inevitable that they would end up as part of the British Empire.

The post-war period marked the beginning of the Anglo-American partnership, the rise of the United States as an industrial power and global player and the relative decline of Britain. The war created a transport and industrial infrastructure which provided a platform from which to leapfrog Britain in the industrial revolution stakes. America was increasingly viewed by successive British governments as a partner (albeit a junior one) in the Anglicisation of the world. The British provided practical support to the US in the 1898 Spanish-American War when the US entered the imperialist lists by mopping up the remnants of the Spanish Empire in the Caribbean as well as establishing itself as a Pacific power by taking over the Philippines. One of the most famous and jingoistic poems of the British imperial poet Rudyard Kipling is 'The White Man's Burden'. It was not, as many believe, a justification for the spread of the civilising influence of the British Empire. It was, in fact, aimed specifically at the US to urge them to conquer and 'civilise' the Philippines. The US, for its part, showed its gratitude for British support by being one of the few great powers to publicly back Britain in the Boer War.

At the same time, the rest of the world moved on. Britain had a long-standing foreign policy of creating a balance of power on continental Europe that prevented any of the European nations gaining a dominance that could be used as a platform to threaten its empire and trade routes. From 1815 to 1870 they were particularly successful in achieving this goal. Then came the rise of Prussia and the unification of Germany under the imperial banner of Kaiser Wilhelm II. The division of the German-speaking states was an important part of the balance of power that helped to maintain the peace in Europe for most of the nineteenth century. On the western edge of the Continent was France. In eastern Europe there was the Austro-Hungarian Empire. In the centre were thirty-nine German-speaking states loosely tied together in the German Confederation but unable to challenge either France or Austria, both of whom wanted to secure their positions by keeping Germany divided. This did not suit Prussia, the largest German state, who under Chancellor Otto von Bismarck and Kaiser Wilhelm set out to unite Germans under one government. To do this they needed to secure the acquiescence of both Austria and France. As neither country would willingly agree to the Kaiser's plans the Prussians went to war against Austria in 1866 and against France in 1870. They won both and in 1871 Kaiser Wilhelm II was proclaimed Emperor of the German Empire. With its political structure established, the German economy soared. Between 1890 and 1913 its exports trebled, putting it just behind Britain. Flush with cash, it beefed up both its navy and army. In 1880 the German navy totalled 88,000 tonnes; by 1914 it was 1.3 million tonnes. In 1884, Germany set out to acquire overseas colonies and in a few short years had established overseas colonial possessions in German East Africa (present-day Tanzania), German South-West Africa (present-day Namibia), Cameroon, Togo and Rwanda. In the Pacific it established colonies in Papua New Guinea, the northern Solomon Islands, the Marshall Islands, the Marianas and the Carolines. Germany's rapid industrialisation, massive increase in armed forces and scramble for colonies married to a new-found confidence and nationalism made it inevitable that it would eventually come into conflict with the British top dog. In doing so it would drag America into a war that would place the US on the political world stage, something successive American administrations had largely avoided since independence.

The War That Failed to End All Wars

George Washington is the closest thing that America has to a political deity. That is not surprising given that he led the country to independence against overwhelming odds and as its first president led it in the perilous first eight years of its existence. This reverence is why Washington's pronouncements on foreign policy are so important, and why they dictated America's relations with the rest of the world for so long and continue to have an impact today. The outline of those policies can be found in his September 1796 Farewell Address to his countrymen, published as he prepared to leave Washington for a well-earned retirement at Mount Vernon. Washington urged his fellow Americans to avoid what he called 'foreign entanglements'. He was especially opposed to any 'permanent alliances' with the European powers, who would always put their interests before that of the US. Instead, argued Washington, America should take advantage of its geographic isolation from the colonial powers to concentrate its efforts on establishing itself on the American continent. Washington rather immodestly wrote that he did not expect his advice to be heeded. He could not have been more wrong. The US did not enter into a permanent alliance until it joined NATO in 1949.

The fact is, however, that the United States could not have built its contiguous land empire without at least the tacit approval or at least acquiescence of Britain. Britain produced the technology for the American industrial revolution. It also provided a large chunk of the capital to build the necessary infrastructure that a modern industrial giant required. And finally, British foreign policy and the Royal Navy helped to keep other European powers out of the United States. America was no longer a member of the sprawling British Empire but it was quite happy to ride on its coat tails while occasionally asserting its independence by thumbing its nose at the mother country. The British were happy to go along with this because they were making tons of money out of the arrangement.

For most of the nineteenth century, Britain was the senior partner in this unspoken partnership. But after the United States sorted out its slavery and states' rights problems in its civil war, it surged forward. The shift in the economic relationship was inevitable. The US population grew from 4 million in 1800 to 75.9 million a hundred years later. Britain in the same period grew from 16 million to 41.1 million. The United States by the end of the nineteenth century was an economic superpower, but it was a political middleweight and a military flyweight. Its army in 1900 numbered a mere 96,000 men compared to 624,000 British soldiers.

A war was needed to move the US up the political and military ranks. It arrived in 1914 with the First World War, which also ended Britain's economic supremacy. As W. C. Sellar and R. J. Yeatman wrote in their satirical history of England, *1066 and All That*, at the end of the First World War, 'America was thus clearly top nation, and History came to a . (full stop).'

But when Britain entered the war on 4 August 1914, it was still the leader of the pack. The Royal Navy was the largest in the world with total warship tonnage at 2.7 million tonnes, more than twice that of Germany and three times the American fleet. Germany and her allies had between them 1.5 million soldiers at the outbreak of war while Britain, France and Russia could put just shy of 2.9 million into the field. From the start, President Woodrow Wilson realised that America's fortunes were tied to British success by trading links, finance, political values and – as most of the American establishment were of British stock – the kith and kin argument. But Washington's warnings were still echoing down through the years and blocking congressional and public support for American entry into the war. The Germans were fairly certain that America would eventually enter the conflict on the British side and that the country's large population and industrial power would spell disaster for the Kaiser's plans, however, so Berlin developed a military and political strategy aimed at knocking Britain out of the war before America could enter it.

Key to this strategy was the U-boat. Britain may have ruled the waves with the largest surface fleet, but Germany ruled under the waves and their submarines established a blockade around the British Isles and threatened to torpedo any ship that entered it. On 7 May 1915 a German U-boat torpedoed the Cunard luxury liner RMS *Lusitania* as it steamed from New York to Liverpool. In all, 1,128 people went to their deaths, including 128 Americans. Former President Theodore Roosevelt and a large slice of American public opinion demanded retaliation. But Woodrow Wilson was not ready to enter the war. He responded with a weak complaint. German U-boat attacks continued. Then, on 1 August 1915, the Germans sank another passenger ship, the SS *Arabic*. This time President Wilson said that if the Germans failed to stop unrestricted submarine warfare then the US would break diplomatic relations and enter the war on the British side. The Germans climbed down and the U-boats backed off and America, for the time being, remained neutral.

But by the end of 1916 Britain and Germany were on their knees. Both sides were bogged down in a costly trench war in Flanders fields. The British surface fleet's blockade of German ports was beginning to bite and German civilians were starting to suffer from malnutrition. The U-boat blockade excluded passenger ships but was still having an effect on food and other vital supplies into Britain. The German High Command convinced Kaiser Wilhelm II that if they were allowed to resume unrestricted submarine warfare than Britain would collapse before America had a chance to come to its rescue. On 9 January 1917, therefore, the ban on attacking passenger ships was lifted. On 3 February President Wilson suspended diplomatic relations with Germany. He said that America would not go to war over the U-boat activity on its own, but warned against other 'overt acts'. Then on 1 March came the most 'overt act' act possible. The British intercepted a telegram from German Foreign Minister Arthur Zimmerman to the Mexican government offering the return of former Mexican territories, now part of the US, in return for a military alliance with Germany. On 6 April 1917, Congress declared war on Germany.

Prime Minister Lloyd George expected that the US troops would simply be filtered into the depleted ranks of the British Army in the same way as Australians, South Africans, Canadians, Indians, and New Zealanders. He also expected cash-rich America to shoulder the costs of the war. President Wilson was having none of that. He wanted a seat at the top table when the peace was negotiated. To achieve that aim it was essential that American soldiers remain under US command and that the British economy remain in hock to the US. Wilson strengthened his bargaining position by refusing to formally join the alliance of the Entente powers. Instead the US was an 'associated power'. This meant that America did not participate in the divvying up of the German, Ottoman, Austro-Hungarian and Russian empires, but it also allowed Wilson to assume the moral high ground at the Versailles peace treaty negotiations.

Wilson had a fourteen-point plan which he laid out to Congress in January 1918. In his speech to a joint session he called for, among other things, self-determination for colonies, the end to secret treaties, free trade, disarmament, freedom of the seas in peace and war and 'a general association of nations' to provide 'mutual guarantees of political independence and territorial integrity to great and small nations alike'. The creation of the League of Nations in the aftermath of the First World War won Wilson the Nobel Peace Prize. Unfortunately for the world, it did not win the support of an isolationist US Congress. Opposition to American participation in the league was led by Idaho senator William Borah. In 1918 he declared that he wished 'this treacherous and treasonable scheme to be buried in hell'. Shortly after the Versailles negotiations started, Wilson's health began to fail. In 1919 he suffered a stroke. The president lacked the physical strength to win acceptance of the League of Nations. The war ended with the British Empire not only intact, but increased. The British were still perceived as the world's number one political and military power. But they were broke. Unable to invest because of its war debts, Britain's share of world manufacturing output by 1928 had shrunk to just 9.9 per cent while America's leapt to 39.3 per cent. The US was now the world's top superpower in economic terms, but determined to crawl back into its George Washington-inspired isolationist shell. For the time being, the US was prepared to let the British cousins remain on their political pedestal.

Britain not only paid its war bills, but that of most of its allies as well. Roughly 50 per cent of the country's GDP was diverted to war costs. When Lloyd George pressed Wilson to shoulder some of this burden he was doing so because Britain was on its financial knees. Wilson's refusal meant that Britain never financially recovered from the effects of the war, which contributed to the political instability that led to the Second World War. The US had, however, been willing to loan money to Britain right from the start of the war. In total, Britain owed the US a total of $4.3 billion in 1919. London offered to cancel its loans to other Allied countries, which totalled $7.8 billion, if the US would do the same with their British debt. Washington not only refused but insisted that Britain pay a higher rate of interest than any other debtor nation. Because of the high interest, the debt was still at $4 billion when Britain finally suspended payments in December 1933 at the height of the Great Depression.

Then there was the human cost of the war. Nearly a million British soldiers died in the First World War. These were young men cut off in their prime. Economic historians estimate the loss of so many lives cost the British economy eight years of growth. Then, as soon as the war ended, the world was struck by the Spanish flu pandemic. Fifty million people died worldwide, 228,000 of them in Britain. American losses in the First World War were 115,000. The US, however, did suffer more from the flu pandemic with an estimated 600,000 deaths.

Britain exited the war with its economic and political infrastructure intact, but the same could not be said for mainland Europe. Railways, roads, bridges, ports and merchant fleets were decimated. The centuries-old Ottoman and Austro-Hungarian empires disappeared. Dozens of new countries found their way onto the map or had their boundaries redrawn. In Russia, a half a millennium of Tsarist autocratic rule was replaced by a communist government dedicated to the overthrow of capitalist Britain and America. In Germany the political and economic dislocation, a feeling of betrayal by the German establishment, and racially inspired nationalism led to the rise of Adolf Hitler and the Nazi Party. The German (and Italian) experience was copied by the Japanese who invaded China in a bid to complete the colonial carve-up of the world's largest and once most powerful country. The old political establishment of landed aristocracy had led the world into the disaster of the First World War. Its methods were found lacking in the post-war world. Increasingly, Europeans drifted to the political extremes that offered easily identifiable scapegoats (filthy capitalists if you were a communist and money-grubbing Jews if you were a Nazi) and simplistic solutions.

The United States believed itself shielded from European and Asian upheavals. There was a Red Scare which dominated the American political scene in the immediate aftermath of the war. But the decade following the end of the war is best known as a period of unbridled prosperity with a dash of hedonism. It was also a tense period in Anglo-American relations as America moved to establish itself as a military power but without the responsibility that usually accompanies power. The tension focused on American attempts to seek naval parity with Britain. A large navy was seen as the best way to project power globally, and since the first half of the eighteenth century Britain had been the world's number one naval power. Washington felt that their changed economic circumstances meant that it was time for the US to assume the role, or at least achieve parity. Throughout the 1920s there were a series of negotiations to limit the relative size of the navies of the major powers. They also involved Italy, France and Japan, but were dominated by Britain and the US. British diplomats argued that their country's heavy reliance on imports dictated a greater need than America's for a navy to protect their merchant shipping. Washington, however, wanted to boost US naval presence in the Pacific to protect growing American interests in Asia and the Philippines and to counter British influence in the Caribbean and South America. In the end, economic realities prevailed and the US secured naval parity.

Isolationism No Longer an Option – Again

The 1930s were marked by the Great Depression, accompanying political instability, pronounced nationalism, extreme political views and regional conflicts that led inevitably to the Second World War. The depression started in America with the Wall Street Crash of 1929. By 1932 the US economy had shrunk by about a third and unemployment levels shot up to 25 per cent. Because the US was still producing about a third of the world's manufacturing output, the rest of the world followed suit.

Meanwhile, the Japanese invaded China in September 1931. Adolf Hitler came to power in March 1933. Italian dictator Benito Mussolini attacked Abyssinia (Ethiopia) in October 1935. Soviet dictator Joseph Stalin executed an estimated 750,000 people in the Great Purge between 1936 and 1938. Hitler annexed Austria in the Anschluss of March 1939 and Czechoslovakia's Sudetenland in September 1938. And finally, the Spanish Civil War from 1936 to 1939 led to the overthrow of the elected government by the fascist general Francisco Franco. The Spanish conflict was seen as a proxy war between Europe's two totalitarian political extremes: the Germans and Italians supported Franco and Moscow supported the Spanish socialists and communists. The democratic countries – Britain, the US and France – maintained a studied neutrality. They were determined to avoid another world war through the simple tactic of refusing to fight.

The tactic failed. The Germans and Soviets decided that their totalitarian structures and geopolitical considerations meant that more united them than divided them. On 23 August 1939, German Foreign Minister Joachim von Ribbentrop and his Soviet counterpart Vyacheslav Molotov signed the Molotov–Ribbentrop Pact, which committed both dictatorships to attacking Poland and dividing that country between them. A week later Hitler's army invaded the western half of Poland and annexed it. Britain, which had guaranteed Polish neutrality, declared war on Germany on 3 September.

The first eight months of the war were dubbed the Phoney War, with only limited fighting between the antagonists. Then, on 9 April, the Germans attacked Denmark and Norway. This was quickly followed by a blitzkrieg through Belgium and the Netherlands. In all, 338,000 members of the British Expeditionary Force were evacuated from Dunkirk between 26 May and 4 June. On 25 June 1940, France fell. Britain stood alone against the Axis powers of Germany and Italy.

In America, the isolationist lobby acted as a brake on the generally pro-British administration of Franklin Roosevelt and public opinion, helped by an active German immigrant community. There is evidence, however, that Roosevelt himself had decided as early as 1937 that Hitler's intention was to conquer the world, including the US, and that the Americans would have to work with Britain (and at that time France as well) to stop him. Washington at that time was also heavily focused on the Pacific where it envisaged an eventual war with the third Axis power, Japan. Roosevelt's instincts, however, were blocked by a reluctant Congress and America's Neutrality Act, which forbade the sale of weapons to the belligerents. Roosevelt persuaded Congress to allow weapons sales to the

British but only on a 'cash and carry' basis, which the financially strapped British could ill afford. Congress was reluctant to be more generous because they thought that Britain could fall at any time, a view which was vigorously peddled by Roosevelt's ambassador in London, Joseph Kennedy. Congressional and public opinion shifted when the RAF fended off a German invasion by driving the German Luftwaffe from British skies in the Battle of Britain in 1940. In September that year, Britain signed a deal giving America a series of ninety-nine-year leases on eight military bases stretching from Newfoundland to the Caribbean in return for fifty American destroyers. Then, in March 1941, the Lend-Lease Act was passed. Under its terms Britain received $34.1 billion in military aid in return for access to more bases and the transfer of valuable technology and scientific information concerning jet engines, rockets, radar, sonar, microwaves and nuclear weapons. In the post-war world, this technology allowed America to establish an early lead in the production of jet airliners and to become the first nuclear state. It led to the dropping of atomic bombs on Hiroshima and Nagasaki, and America's emergence from the war as the world's only superpower – for a time.

Throughout 1941, British and American military chiefs held secret talks in Washington on war strategy once the US found a way to officially enter the war. In August 1941, President Roosevelt and Prime Minister Winston Churchill met in Placenta Bay, Newfoundland, to hammer out what became known as the Atlantic Charter. During the three days of talks, Roosevelt sought to tie Churchill to the principle of self-determination for British colonies in a post-war world. Churchill argued for an American declaration of war against Germany and Italy. Both fell short of their goals, although the commitment in principle to self-determination in the charter can be viewed as the first step towards the end of the British Empire. Japan also regarded the Atlantic Charter as a hostile act by the United States, who had already cut Japan off from oil supplies because of its attacks on China. On 7 December 1941, the Japanese launched a pre-emptive strike against the American Pacific fleet at Pearl Harbor. The following day Congress declared war on Japan. Three days later Germany declared war on the US. Germany had already invaded the Soviet Union on 22 June 1941, so sides had been picked.

Once America joined the war and Germany found itself fighting a two-front conflict, the outcome was inevitable. With its industrial base protected by two oceans, the US was able to churn out a flood of weapons supplies. America produced 269,813 war planes between 1942 and 1945 compared to German production of 86,527. The United States put 16 million men into the army, navy and air force. The Allied forces overall totalled 81.2 million compared to 15 million in Germany and Japan. The numbers and capabilities of the Allied forces were so overwhelmingly in their favour that it is amazing that the Axis powers held out for as long as they did.

The Second World War is generally regarded as the start of the special Anglo-American relationship, although it is more accurate to say that the wartime experience was the flowering of a relationship whose roots were laid down centuries before. But it is true to say that the military and political coordination between London and Washington at this time was the closest in history and played a major part in the creation of the post-war world, and sustained the cooperation between the two countries across a wide range of disciplines. The war also confirmed the passing of the baton from Britain to America as the UK moved from the number one position to pursuing its national interests as the subordinate ally of the country it spawned.

The special relationship does not mean that problems between the two have ceased to exist. Countries are comprised of individuals with their own strengths, weaknesses and prejudices. There are many Americans who regard the British as arrogant, haughty, imperious, pompous and pretentious. Many British, for their part, think of the Americans as naïve, unsophisticated, crude, rude, and likely to shoot from the hip. But the crucible of war and a common heritage forged many close personal relationships that continued for years afterwards. The governments of both countries put their national interests first and sometimes this led to clashes, but they also both discovered that their national interests most often lay in their common interests.

13

Role Reversal

Junior Partner Becomes Senior Partner

Britain was a target of the communist movement before the ink was dry on the first edition of the *Communist Manifesto*. A stultifying class system, atrocious working and living conditions for the newly industrialised working class and a growing anti-colonial movement provided fertile ground for Karl Marx and Friedrich Engels' revolutionary rallying cry: 'Workers of the World unite! You have nothing to lose but your chains!' The British Establishment, however, was adept at fending off revolution through political evolution. Throughout the latter half of the nineteenth century and first half of the twentieth, those in power adapted and accommodated politically, economically and socially. They absorbed the democratically inclined Labour Party into their ranks as a left-wing counter to the communists, introduced social reforms and extended the electoral franchise. Russia's autocracy was more rigid and paid the price in 1917 with a communist revolution that declared itself the vanguard of an international revolt against world capitalism. In 1917, Britain and its empire were the main target. Number two was the fast-rising, freewheeling capitalist United States.

The capitalist countries, led by Britain and including the United States, responded with an expeditionary force aimed at throttling the Bolshevik Revolution in its cradle. The newly formed Soviet Union's reaction was to launch the Comintern to coordinate communist parties around the world to overthrow all capitalist governments. Throughout the 1920s and most of the 1930s, Britain's intelligence services regarded Soviet subversion as the major threat to British security. The US, encouraged by the British, took the same line and in the early 1920s there was a

Red Scare, with several bombs being set off by communist sympathisers, including one at the home of Attorney General Alexander Mitchell Palmer. The US refused to grant diplomatic recognition to the Soviet Union until the Roosevelt administration did so in November 1933. The more pragmatic British exchanged ambassadors in 1924, then withdrew diplomatic recognition in 1927 over a spy scandal before re-establishing relations in 1929.

It was not until Hitler became German Chancellor in March 1933 that Britain started to pay any attention to the threat of Nazism, and even then a large proportion of the British Establishment believed that the real danger lay in Moscow. The wartime alliance between Britain and the Soviet Union was as much an alliance of convenience as the Motolotov–Ribbentrop Pact that laid the groundwork for the invasion of Poland. Neither Stalin nor Churchill trusted each other. Roosevelt tried to mediate but when he died before the war's end on 12 April 1945 he was succeeded by novice Harry Truman who was not burdened with Roosevelt's Sovietophilia. At the 1945 Potsdam Conference it became clear that the Soviet Union would fight to keep their communist puppet government in Poland in power and that the rest of eastern Europe – and possibly western Europe – was also in danger.

Right from the start of the war, Roosevelt and Churchill agreed that the post-war world required international political and economic structures to preserve peace and encourage political stability. Roosevelt took the lead in reviving a variation of Woodrow Wilson's Fourteen Points with a difference. The League of Nations was to be replaced by the United Nations, backed up by a human rights charter and underwritten by security guarantees from the five most powerful countries – the United States, Soviet Union, China, France and Great Britain – who would be responsible for maintaining peace in their respective parts of the world. The US, for instance, was responsible for the western hemisphere, The Soviet Union for eastern Europe and Central Asia, China for Asia, France for parts of Africa and the Middle East and Britain for Africa, the Middle East and western Europe. China's role was quickly replaced by the Western powers after Mao Zedong's Chinese communists took power on 1 October 1949 and were blocked from UN membership by America. Britain took its role in the Middle East and Africa seriously but disappointed Washington by refusing to become involved in the formation of the forerunners of the European Economic Community. The UK eventually joined in 1973.

The post-war economic structures were hammered out at the Bretton Woods Conference in July 1944. The meeting provided economic stability by establishing fixed exchange rates tied to gold and the dollar. As the US at the time controlled two-thirds of the world's gold reserves, the system was heavily weighted in its favour. The Bretton Woods fixed exchange rate lasted until August 1971 when President Richard Nixon unilaterally terminated America's convertibility to gold. The dollar became a reserve currency and the pound was forced to float freely on currency exchange markets. Bretton Woods also established the World Bank and International Monetary Fund (IMF) – the brainchildren of British economic guru Lord Keynes. The IMF is designed to foster global economic cooperation, encourage financial stability, facilitate international trade, redress world poverty and promote sustainable growth. The World Bank underwrites IMF goals by offering loans to developing countries. The key element was that America controlled the post-war economic world almost from the moment the 1941 Lend-Lease Act was passed. This was a programme by which the US supplied weapons and materiel to the Allied countries. The sudden decision to cancel Lend-Lease at the end of the war on 21 August 1945 came as a major blow to the British who had been counting on its continuance until at least mid-1946, but the US government was determined that Lend-Lease would not be used for reconstruction purposes. The newly elected Labour government despatched Lord Keynes to Washington to negotiate an aid package. He successfully argued that Britain's wartime role deserved special treatment and walked away with a $6 billion grant in the form of the Anglo-American Finance Agreement. Repayments, however, were tied to the dollar, further increasing the American economic stranglehold on the British economy.

While aid packages were being negotiated the Soviet Union was consolidating its political stranglehold over eastern Europe and threatening Greece, Turkey and north-western Iran. In the closing days of the war Greece became embroiled in in a bitter civil war between communists and conservatives backed by Britain. At the same time, the Soviet Union applied diplomatic and military pressure on Turkey to gain unfettered access to the Mediterranean through the Dardanelles. Britain was responsible for the defence of the Aegean, but on 21 February 1947 British Foreign Secretary Ernest Bevin was told by Chancellor of the Exchequer Hugh Dalton that the parlous state of the British economy meant that Britain would have to stop all aid and withdraw its troops from Greece as of 31 March. Bevin immediately wrote to Under Secretary of State Dean Acheson to ask him to take up the baton. The Truman administration agreed and what became known as the 'Truman Doctrine' was laid before Congress by the president in a joint session on 12 March 1947. Nowhere in his speech did Truman mention the Soviet Union by name, but it was clear that the policy was directed against Moscow. The president summarised the situation in terms of fundamental ideological opposition and 'alternative ways of life' rather than great power politics; an opposition between 'free institutions, representative government, free elections ... individual liberty, freedom of speech and religion and (freedom) from political oppression' on one side and 'terror and oppression' on the other. He said that that when the latter are imposed on 'free peoples by direct or indirect aggression', international peace is undermined and the security of the United States is threatened. Bevin's initiative and Truman's speech set the US tone for the Cold War. It also resulted in $400 million in aid to Greece and Turkey, as well as military and civilian personnel to administer it.

The Truman Doctrine was followed by the Marshall Plan, an American effort to rebuild European economies so that they could withstand political and military aggression from the Soviet Union. It accelerated the split between East and West. The basic tenets of the plan were laid out by Acheson in a memorandum to President Truman. Acheson argued that Greece and Turkey were 'only part of a much larger problem growing out of the change in Great Britain's strength and circumstances'. The public first heard of the plan when Secretary of State George C. Marshall unveiled the bones of it at a Harvard commencement address on 4 June 1947. Marshall outlined in graphic detail the poverty found throughout Europe and offered American aid to alleviate 'hunger, poverty, desperation and chaos'. There was, however, a catch: before the US government would hand over any cash it required a jointly agreed plan by the European governments on how the aid would be used. Western Europe, led by British Foreign Secretary Ernest Bevin, had no problem with this. The Soviet Union, however, attacked the Marshall Plan as financial imperialism, refused to participate and blocked its new satellites in Eastern Europe from participation. Instead, in 1947 it set up the Communist Information Bureau (Cominform) as a political alternative to the Marshall Plan and then in 1949 established its economic equivalent, the Council for Mutual and Economic Cooperation (Comecon). Both were ineffective counters to the Marshall Plan.

Military as well as economic ties across the Atlantic were needed to demonstrate America's commitment to a democratic Europe. NATO, America's first permanent alliance, was the brainchild of British Foreign Secretary Ernest Bevin. After the 1945 Labour landslide, Prime Minister Clement Attlee had named Bevin as Foreign Secretary. As a left-wing trade unionist, Bevin had been a supporter and admirer of the Soviet Union before and during the war. However, as Moscow asserted its control over eastern Europe, the British Foreign Secretary became convinced that Stalin's Soviet Union was determined to undermine Western democracy and replace it with totalitarian communism. A prostrate Europe and penniless Britain were powerless to stop it. American help was required. He started by persuading the Truman administration to take over responsibility for the defence of Greece and Turkey, but soon concluded that this was insufficient. Working with the Canadians and French, he formulated a plan for a mutual defence pact. The US joined on 4 April 1949 and the North Atlantic Treaty Organisation was born. The Soviet response was the Warsaw Pact. The NATO treaty was completely successful in keeping Moscow at bay until the collapse of the Soviet Union.

Secrets

Information is power. Secret information is the most powerful of all. That is why governments spend billions gathering information and jealously guarding it. The extraordinarily close links between the American and British intelligence communities are unrivalled anywhere in the world. They are at the core of the special relationship which existed during the Second World War and survived the Cold War and the Trump Administration. Britain established the intelligence pattern for the US, provided Washington with vital German military secrets during the war, acted as advisers in helping to establish the Central Intelligence Agency (CIA) and National Security Agency (NSA), and has continued to work hand in glove with the US. Shortly before the start of the First World War, the British intelligence community split into two main branches: the Secret Intelligence Service (also known as SIS or MI6) was responsible for gathering foreign intelligence, while MI5 was responsible for counter-intelligence and, along with Scotland Yard's Special Branch, intelligence operations in the UK. In comparison, the US had virtually no intelligence organisations. Early in the war, British cryptographers managed to break the German military communications cipher known as the Enigma code. Enigma secrets were passed to the US from 1940 as part of an agreement between Churchill and Roosevelt. The exchange of information was formalised in May 1943 with the British United States Agreement (BRUSA) and reaffirmed for the Cold War period with the 1947 United Kingdom-United States (UKUSA) Agreement. UKUSA established the pooling of information between Britain's General

Communications Headquarters at Cheltenham (GCHQ) and America's newly created National Security Agency. Britain assumed responsibility for operations in Europe, Asia, the Middle East and Africa. The US had primary responsibility for the western hemisphere. UKUSA was quickly extended to include Britain's Commonwealth allies in Canada, New Zealand and Australia and became known as the 'Five Eyes Agreement'. The electronic intelligence gathered by all five countries is equally shared and the two main suppliers remain the NSA and GCHQ.

The CIA started life as the wartime Office of Strategic Services (OSS). After Pearl Harbor, President Roosevelt was seriously worried about the lack of American intelligence capability. Six months later, the OSS was created. Since May 1940, hundreds of British agents had been working out of the Rockefeller Center under the command of spymaster William Stephenson. They so impressed President Roosevelt that he asked Stephenson to work with William J. Donovan to set up an American equivalent, which was initially called the Office of Strategic Services and later, with continued British advice and support, became the post-war CIA. The two countries continued to share information and would conduct joint operations during the Korean War, the 1953 Iranian coup, operations in eastern Europe, support for Poland's Solidarity Movement, the fall of the Soviet Union, Operation Desert Storm, the Iraq War and the Syrian Civil War. The CIA London Bureau Chief attends weekly meetings of Britain's Joint Intelligence Committee and his British equivalent in Washington has access to US intelligence sources.

Nukes

The United States was the world's first nuclear power. But it was the British who provided the key scientific research required for the first mushroom cloud. Two Birmingham University scientists, Rudolf Peierls and Otto Fritsch, in March 1940, discovered the basic ingredient for an atomic bomb: nuclear fission in uranium. They took it to the British government who promptly launched an atomic bomb project codenamed Tube Alloys. The US became involved after a British scientific mission to the US in September 1940 as part of an information exchange to secure Lend-Lease. Up until that time, American atomic research was focused on peaceful uses. The British research plus an American scientific delegation led by Albert Einstein persuaded President Roosevelt that America needed to start work on an atomic weapon. Thus the Manhattan Project was born. Britain and America ran parallel projects for the next few years, but it became apparent to Churchill that Britain lacked the money, facilities and manpower to develop the bomb quickly enough to have an impact on the outcome of the war, so he authorised the full transfer of technology and British scientists to work in the States. From that moment the British project became American, so much so that at the end of the war, the Truman administration cut the British out of the project with the 1946 McMahon Act, which ended all technical cooperation and banned American allies from receiving any atomic weapon information. The British were furious. Hiroshima and Nagasaki made it painfully apparent that that possession of the atomic bomb ensured great power status in the post-war world; and Britain desperately wanted to remain a great power. However, as they had already transferred the technology to the US, the UK could do little more than protest. Without American support, the British were forced to relaunch Tube Alloys in July 1947 with the new codename of High Explosives Research. The first British atomic bomb was detonated on 3 October 1952 in the lagoon in the Monte Bello Islands off the coast of western Australia.

In the meantime, the Soviet Union exploded its first atomic bomb in Kazakhstan on 29 August 1949. The Soviets had been working on their own bomb since the early days of the war. In fact, Russian physicists made some of the early breakthroughs. Post-war, the Soviet effort was helped considerably by the British scientist Klaus Fuchs who had worked on the Manhattan Project. He provided Moscow with blueprints and early American research into the hydrogen bomb. Fuchs's key role in the development of the Soviet bomb confirmed American thinking as to the wisdom of locking Britain out of the atomic weapons research programme. Regardless, by 1952, the world had three nuclear powers.

It was soon apparent that the British would be an also-ran in the nuclear stakes. They had the scientists, they had the expertise, but they lacked the money. Between 1952 and 1956 the UK only managed to produce fourteen nuclear warheads. America took pity on them and under a programme codenamed Project E provided them the UK with warheads on the condition that they were assigned exclusively to the NATO command. They were not allowed to be part of an independent nuclear deterrent. The bombs were designed to be delivered by British planes called V bombers, which, by 1964, peaked at a roster of 159. But before that it was apparent that improvements in the Soviet air defence network meant that the plane-and-pilot delivery system was fast becoming obsolete. Missiles were needed. In 1955, the British government announced that a third of its defence budget for that year would be spent on nuclear weapons and the centrepiece was the land-based missile Blue

Streak with a range of 2,800 miles Unfortunately, Blue Streak became White Elephant. Between 1955 and 1960 a total of $182 million was spent on development, It was estimated that a further $1.7 billion was needed for launch. The British turned to America for help and it responded by repealing the McMahon Act and offering the Skybolt missile. But then in 1963 the US abandoned the Skybolt programme, leaving the British high and dry. The Skybolt crisis was resolved by an agreement between President John F. Kennedy and Prime Minister Harold Macmillan under which the US would provide Polaris submarines and missiles to Britain. When Polaris was decommissioned it was replaced by the Trident system, which is currently the mainstay of the British nuclear deterrent. The UK has four Trident submarines. Each carries up to eight missiles with a total of forty warheads and at least one submarine is on patrol at all times. The Trident is an independent nuclear deterrent in that the British Prime Minister makes the final decision pushing the button. The warheads are also British-made. But the missiles, the guidance system and a large part of the submarines are bought from the US and have to be serviced in the US, all of which brings into question just how independent Britain's nuclear deterrent actually is.

While Britain was struggling, America was forging ahead with its nuclear programme. Between 1945 and 1990 the US built 70,000 warheads. Like the British, they were initially bomber-led under the Strategic Air Command. But by 1960 the emphasis had switched to Intercontinental Ballistic Missiles (ICBMs) launched from fixed silos in the Midwest. These were largely replaced by submarine-launched ballistic missiles (SLBMs) which extended the range and reduced vulnerability. The next development was the Multiple Independently-targeted Re-entry Vehicle (MIRV) missile with several nuclear-tipped mini-missiles in each larger delivery rocket. Finally, there were the super-accurate cruise missiles. There were also tactical nuclear weapons based in Germany and from the 1960s intermediate-range nuclear missiles based in the UK and elsewhere in Europe.

The Soviets were able to match American developments missile for missile and warhead for warhead. The resultant nuclear arms race was expensive and raised the spectre of a nuclear Armageddon. In 1948 the US defence budget was $10.9 billion. Twenty years later it had grown to $80.7 billion. Over the same time period, Soviet defence expenditure grew from $13.1 billion to $85.4 billion. The British, in comparison, spent only $900 million in 1948 and $5.6 billion in 1968. By 1974 the nuclear arsenal of the United States had 2,233 missiles and the Soviets 3,830. Each side kept adding more and better systems in the hope their respective advances would deter an attack. By the early 1960s, the Kennedy Administration was espousing a policy of Mutual Assured Destruction as a means of preventing a nuclear war. MAD.

The first substantive moves towards limiting nuclear arsenals were begun by President Lyndon B. Johnson in January 1964 when he wrote to Soviet leader Nikita Khrushchev suggesting that the two sides scrap an equal number of obsolescent bombers. The diplomatic ball was thus set in motion for a series of complicated and protracted negotiations that resulted in a litany of treaties limiting the two sides' nuclear arsenals. They included the 1972 SALT I Treaty (Strategic Arms Limitations Treaty), 1972 ABM Treaty (Anti-Ballistic Missile Treaty), The 1979 SALT II Treaty, the 1987 INF Treaty (Intermediate-range Nuclear Forces Treaty) and the 1991 START I Treaty in which both sides agreed for the first time to reduce their arsenals. The last treaty was signed while the Soviet empire was in the throes of collapse, from the tearing down of the Berlin Wall on 9 November 1989 to the dissolution of the Soviet Union on 26 December 1991. The US-led NATO forces – including Britain – had won the Cold War.

Cold War Turns Hot

By 1950 the Iron Curtain had fallen in Europe and Asia's Bamboo Curtain was firmly in place. The boundaries were drawn, the arms race was on, and any pretence of continuing the wartime alliances was in the past. The scene was set for the war of words to turn into a war of guns and bombs, and it started to do just that in Korea. Up until the Second World War, Korea had been a well-kicked political football passed among Russia, China and Japan. In 1910 the country was annexed by Japan. During the Second World War, 4 million Koreans were forced into slave labour. About 400,000 Korean women became 'comfort women' for Japanese soldiers. At the Cairo, Tehran, Yalta and Potsdam conferences, the Allies agreed that Korea would be freed from Japanese rule and initially divided into Soviet and American zones along the 38th Parallel. Between 1945 and 1950 it would be administered as a joint trusteeship by Kuomintang China, the US, Soviet Union and Britain and then united after free elections. But corruption, Soviet ambitions, the victory of the Chinese communists, and the McCarthy witch hunts meant that the trusteeship ended in war rather than a peacefully united Korean Peninsula. It was a war which might have blown up into a wider conflict if not for pressure from British Prime Minister Clement Attlee on President Truman and American general Douglas MacArthur, the wildly ambitious and dangerously aggressive commander of the United Nations forces in Korea.

The Soviet Army invaded Korea just after midnight on 9 August, two days after the atomic bomb was dropped on Hiroshima and only hours before it fell on Nagasaki. Moscow had stayed out of the war in Asia to focus on the fight against Hitler. Fortunately for Stalin, the Japanese had no wish to fight on two fronts against the Americans and British in the east and the Soviets in the west. However, at the Tehran and Cairo conferences, the Soviet leader promised to join the fight against Japan as soon as Germany surrendered. The dropping of the bomb created the perfect opportunity for him to march unopposed into Korea, Manchuria and the Japanese Kurile islands. The US, sensing potential problems, occupied Korean territory below the 38th Parallel. Britain had no direct interest in northern Asia and left any dispute over the region to Washington and Moscow. The Soviets immediately threw their support behind veteran communist nationalist Kim Il-sung (grandfather of the current ruler Kim Jong-un) while the Americans supported avid anti-communist campaigner Syngman Rhee. Both were corrupt despots. Between 1945 and 1950 Rhee's government was responsible for the murder of 100,000 political opponents.

In theory, both the Soviet Union and US remained committed to the policy of a unified Korea. But the problem was that each had fixed ideas as to its political complexion and neither was prepared to compromise. In 1946 and 1947 the US pressed for national elections on both sides of the 38th Parallel and won United Nations' support for the proposal. The Soviets refused to cooperate. Therefore voting was conducted only in South Korea on 10 May 1948. After severely flawed and violent elections, Syngman Rhee was confirmed in power and shortly afterwards announced the formation of the Republic of Korea. The UN backed him as the head of the legitimately elected government on the peninsula. The Soviet Union responded by recognising Kim's People's Democratic Republic as the only lawful government. Both Syngman Rhee and Kim Il-sung claimed sovereignty over the entire peninsula. Washington and Moscow added to the tensions by providing military support to their respective client states. Then in January 1950 Secretary of State Dean Acheson made a speech in which he excluded South Korea from America's Asian defence perimeter. The Soviets interpreted this as the Americans throwing in the Korean towel. Six months later, the North Koreans, with Soviet support, invaded South Korea.

American troops had withdrawn in 1949 and the South Koreans were taken by surprise and quickly pushed back to the tip of the Korean peninsula. The attack was seen as the first test of the credibility of the UN, which had recognised the legitimacy of the south over the north, and the Security Council voted to send UN troops to repel the North Koreans. Two weeks later the first American forces arrived under the command of General MacArthur. They stopped the communist advance, launched a successful counter-attack behind their lines, pushed the North Koreans back across the 38th Parallel and finally forced them across the Yalu River, which marked the Chinese/North Korean border. During the fighting General MacArthur ignored presidential orders to avoid a meeting with Chiang Kai-shek, who had been forced by Mao Zedong's communist forces to flee mainland China for the island of Taiwan. MacArthur and Chiang met and plotted an American-supported attack across the Taiwan Strait to open a second front in the war in Asia. When the Chinese communists learned of the MacArthur-Chiang plan they attacked the UN forces across the Yalu River. The UN forces were pushed back. Truman responded with a claim that the US had 'no aggressive intentions towards China', but added the disturbing rider that the United States would use the atomic bomb if necessary.

Truman's atomic threat set alarm bells ringing in London. The British were the major contributor to UN forces after the US. A worried Attlee flew to Washington ten days after Truman's atomic bomb speech for four days of talks with the American president. He expressed concern that pressure from the McCarthy witch hunts would lead to an American attack on China, that such an attack would result in direct intervention by the Soviet Union, that a widening conflict in Asia would draw troops from the defence of Europe and leave it dangerously exposed, and that if Truman used the atomic bomb then the Soviets – who had recently tested their own weapon – would retaliate with a nuclear attack on Europe. Attlee was pushing on a door that was ajar, if not fully open. Truman's inclination was to contain rather than widen the Korean conflict. But he was under pressure from a conservative congress and a rebellious MacArthur. Attlee's intervention provided him with ammunition to dismiss MacArthur and keep a lid on the Korean War.

The Attlee government and Truman administration had markedly different perceptions of the nature of communism and the Chinese communists. The strongly held American belief was that the Chinese communists were operating within the grand design of a Soviet-controlled strategy. The British, on the other hand, viewed Chinese actions as a misinterpretation of a percived threat to their national interests and reaction to colonial exploitation. Attlee foresaw the possibility of the

Sino-Soviet Split and urged Truman to recognise communist China in order to be in a position to exploit historical differences between the two nations. The British were among the first to recognise Mao's government in January 1950. It was not until February 1972 that President Richard Nixon was persuaded of the wisdom of the British advice and visited Beijing.

Vietnam was the other major cold-turned-hot war, and the American failure there would leave a permanent scar on the American psyche. British actions did nothing to help that damaging legacy. British reluctance to become involved in the Vietnam War stemmed from their immediate post-war intervention in South East Asia at the end of the Second World War. They were called upon to occupy what had been French Indochina from September 1945 to June 1946 while the French colonial authorities sorted themselves out. British troops quickly found themselves fighting Ho Chi Minh's Viet Minh, who had been formed in 1940, first to oppose French colonial rule and later the Japanese. Ho had been a communist since his days as a Parisian waiter in the 1920s. But the British experience convinced them that the Viet Minh were not Moscow's puppets. They were nationalists rather than internationalists. Communist ideology was a tool for justifying their anti-colonial struggle against the French and gaining political and military support from the Soviets. But in the overheated atmosphere of the Cold War and following the Korean War, the Eisenhower administration was convinced that Vietnam was another Moscow-orchestrated 'domino' and supported the French with military and financial aid to fight the Viet Minh.

In 1953 the French decided to make a decisive stand against Ho's army at Dien Bien Phu. It was a military catastrophe. The French forces collapsed on 7 May 1954 and the country was divided into North and South Vietnam along the 17th Parallel. Before the French defeat, in March 1954, General Paul Ely, the French chief of Staff, flew to Washington to try to persuade America to commit troops. The Eisenhower administration considered unilateral intervention but decided it could only act in concert with London. British Foreign Secretary Anthony Eden, however, effectively vetoed British participation in what he judged to be an unwinnable war. Dien Bien Phu and the possibility of Anglo-American intervention coincided with the Geneva Conference on Indochina and Korea. To prevent an outright split between Washington and London, Eden proposed two treaties at the conference. The first was among the Western powers, China and the Soviet Union and guaranteed the neutrality of Laos, Cambodia and Vietnam. The second was a military alliance among the non-communist countries of South East Asia, which produced the South East Asia Treaty Organisation (SEATO). Vietnam was divided between the communist North and an increasingly corrupt South, the latter backed by the US with military, financial and intelligence support. The final decision to commit a large force of American troops was taken by President Lyndon B. Johnson in August 1964 following the Gulf of Tonkin incident. US troops fought in Vietnam until the fall of Saigon on 17 April 1975. More than 8.5 million Americans fought in the Vietnamese War; 58,000 died or were listed as missing in action. More than 300,000 were wounded. Throughout the war, the British stayed out of the conflict. In 1965, Labour Prime Minister Harold Wilson made moves towards contributing a token British force for the sake of Anglo-American relations, but this was blocked by a 1967 Labour Party conference which called on the Wilson government to completely disassociate itself from American policy in Vietnam. British refusal to become involved in the war in South East Asia was a major problem for Anglo-American relations in the 1960s and 1970s.

The End of Empire

From 1945 to 1956 an impoverished Britain clung to the remnants of an empire which it viewed as crucial to the maintenance of its claim to great power status. Then there was Suez. The 1956 Suez Crisis was the political/military watershed that confirmed the end of Britain as a world power, destroyed its lingering imperial pretensions, and undermined British influence in the Middle East. It distracted world attention from the simultaneous Soviet invasion of Hungary and created a dangerous strain in Anglo-American relations. It forced the resignation of British Prime Minister Anthony Eden and underscored Britain's weakness as an independent foreign policy maker. In short, it was a disaster for the United Kingdom and nearly put paid to the post-war special relationship.

The Suez Canal was to the British Empire what the Panama Canal was to the United States. It linked the factories of Britain to the markets and riches of Asia and the oil of Arabia. The company that controlled the canal was Anglo-French, and under a 1936 Anglo-Egyptian thirty-year treaty imposed by the British, the Canal Zone was occupied by British troops. In the immediate post-war years, the Egyptian government was pressured by nationalist and Islamic fundamentalist forces to renegotiate the 1936 treaty. A number of anti-British riots took place. The ensuing political instability was fertile ground for the coup that eventually brought to power Colonel Gamal Abdel Nasser. He was vehemently anti-British, anti-Israeli and a strong advocate of pan-Arabism. A primary goal for Nasser became the ownership of the Suez Canal and the withdrawal of British troops, and he moved closer to the Soviet Union to achieve that end. In 1955, British Prime Minister Anthony Eden became convinced that Nasser had to be overthrown in order to protect vital British and Western interests. His worst fears were confirmed when the Egyptian leader nationalised the Suez Canal Company on 26 July 1956.

Two days after the nationalisation of the canal, the British Treasury froze all Egyptian assets in Britain. France and the US quickly followed suit. Eden also ordered the mobilisation of 20,000 army reservists. The French threatened military action. US President Dwight Eisenhower organised a canal users' conference to try to force a settlement on Egypt. Nasser refused to attend. Then the US position shifted back towards its traditional anti-colonial position after Secretary of State John Foster Dulles announced that the US intended to play 'a somewhat independent role'. Dulles's pronouncement convinced Eden that war was inevitable and that it had to be won without American help. French Prime Minister Guy Mollet agreed and held secret talks in which he proposed that Israel would attack Egypt and in doing so provide Britain and France with a legal excuse to intervene and re-establish control of the canal. Each of the three countries had its own reason for attacking Nasser: Britain wanted to regain control of the Suez Canal, France wanted to eliminate a government that was supporting rebels in Algeria, and Israel wanted to gain access to the canal. The Eisenhower administration was kept completely in the dark.

The Israelis attacked on 29 October 1956. The next day the British and French governments issued an ultimatum to both sides to withdraw their forces, giving them twelve hours to reply. If no reply was received within the allotted time, then British and French troops would intervene to seize and protect the canal. The Israelis, of course, accepted the ultimatum. The Egyptians rejected it. British aircraft launched two days of air attacks that wiped out the Egyptian air force and British and French paratroopers were dropped at the northern end of the canal. In the intervening five days, Britain and France came under heavy political pressure to withdraw. The Soviet Union warned that the two European countries must bear the 'dangerous consequences' of taking 'the road of aggression'. But the most damaging opposition came from Washington, where Eisenhower described the attack as an action 'taken in error' and refused American support. He also warned Britain and France against using American weapons. Most importantly, Eisenhower withheld from the Eden government any credit while British troops remained in the Canal Zone, causing a run on the pound and threatening the collapse of the British economy. American anger with Britain was increased by Moscow's brutal suppression of the anti-Soviet Hungarian Revolution. At midnight on 3 November, an estimated 200,000 troops and 4,000 Soviet tanks invaded Budapest 'to help the Hungarian people crush the black forces of reaction and counter-revolution'. An estimated 50,000 Hungarians died. Many in the US administration claimed that the British and French action in Egypt provided the distraction and justification for crushing the first serious challenge to Soviet rule.

The Suez debacle underscored that the days of empire and imperial pretensions were fast fading, if not already gone. Britain faced a political tsunami pushing the cause of self-determination from within and without its empire. At the same time, the Soviets saw the demise of the empire as an opportunity to spread their ideology and establish socialism in the developing world. Imperialism, in the communist lexicon, was the international extension of capitalism. Colonies were exploited by capitalists in the same way as the workers were exploited in the imperial mother countries. In fact, the battle for the hearts and minds of the colonies was low-hanging fruit for Moscow, as socialist revolution could easily be coupled to the more acceptable cause of independence. The developing world thus became a battleground between the Soviets on one side and Britain and the US on the other, with the Soviets supporting left-wing anti-colonial movements, the British trying to wind down the empire in such a way as to ensure political stability that blunted the socialist cause, and the United States supporting British efforts by providing military and economic aid that the British could ill afford.

India was the first to win independence in 1947. It did so with a bloody partition along religious lines that split the country between India on the one hand and East and West Pakistan (later Pakistan and Bangladesh) on the other. Pakistan and India have teetered on the edge of conflict ever since and Moscow, Washington and Beijing have supported opposing sides, as well as being sucked into the Afghan quagmire. The problems started in the nineteenth century and the 'Great Game' between the British and Russian empires. The British lived in constant fear that the Russians would attack India through Afghanistan and the Russians were terrified that Britain would unseat them from their dominance in Central Asia. The invasion route for both sides ran through Afghanistan, which meant that Britain became involved in several disastrous wars to secure the mountainous Muslim kingdom. Moscow's invasion of Afghanistan in 1979 was a major factor in the collapse of the Soviet Union and the US has found it as perplexing, and continues to do so. The Soviets fared better in India following a 1955 visit to Moscow by Indian Prime Minister

Jawaharlal Nehru and a return visit to New Delhi by Nikita Khrushchev in the same year. The two countries formed close diplomatic, trade, political and military ties, which have continued into the post-Soviet period. In 2018, India was Russia's second-biggest market for weapons sales. President Trump's right-wing populism, however, found an Indian echo in the form of Hindu nationalist Prime Minister Narendra Modri. In response to Russian influence in India, the US – with British help – moved closer to Pakistan. This relationship has become both closer and more fraught with American involvement in Afghanistan.

The next major decolonisation move came in the Middle East with the independence of Israel and the creation of the Jewish state. The British were a major influence in the region from the early nineteenth century when it was perceived as a vital link to India. In fact, British interests in the region were largely administered by the India Office. Iran's importance grew exponentially when in 1908 British oil speculator William D'Arcy discovered massive oil deposits and established the forerunner of BP. His discovery coincided with the move from coal to oil as the preferred fuel for the navies. The British already had a strong presence in the Persian Gulf through protectorates in Oman, Kuwait, Bahrain and the United Arab Emirates. During the Second World War, Iran and neighbouring Azerbaijan became a route for the delivery of American Lend-Lease to the Soviets. To secure the link, Soviet troops were based in Iranian Azerbaijan and Moscow refused to withdraw them despite Iranian protests. By the end of 1947, Moscow had been forced out with the help of $30 million of US surplus military equipment. But Iran remained high on the State Department's and British Foreign Office's list of likely Soviet targets. It was fear of Soviet designs on Iran and its oilfields that led to an Anglo-American-orchestrated coup, which ousted left-wing and pro-Soviet Prime Minister Mohammed Mossadeq and replaced him with pro-Western Mohammad Reza Shah Pahlavi. The coup also broke Britain's monopoly of Iranian oil and opened the door to the US becoming increasingly involved in Iranian affairs. Before long, the US had replaced Britain as the pre-eminent foreign power in Iran and the main target of Iranian nationalists.

During the First World War, Britain and France agreed to divide the eastern Mediterranean between them in the Sykes–Picot Agreement, which gave France control of Lebanon and Syria and Britain control of Palestine, Jordan and Iraq. Saudi Arabia was considered a useless desert. This was a mistake which President Roosevelt exploited in 1945 when he negotiated American access to Saudi oil deposits – the world's largest. Roosevelt, however, failed to win the Saudis' support for a Jewish homeland in Palestine, which had been promised to world Jewry by British Foreign Secretary Arthur Balfour in 1917. The Balfour Declaration promised that the British government would

> ... view with favour the establishment in Palestine of a national home for the Jewish people, and will use their best endeavours to facilitate the achievement of this object, it being clearly understood that nothing shall be done which may prejudice the civil and religious rights of existing non-Jewish communities in Palestine.

The Balfour Declaration was followed by a flood of Jewish immigrants to British-administered Palestine in the 1920s and 1930s, riots by the Arabs already living there, and an increasingly untenable British position as they tried to keep the two communities apart. After the war Jewish numbers were swelled by Holocaust survivors and Jewish terrorist groups launched attacks against British forces as part of their demand for an independent Jewish state. By 1948, the British had had enough and precipitously withdrew. Hastily organised Jewish forces drove the Arabs out of their homes and into Gaza, Lebanon and Jordan. The US, pressured by America's powerful Jewish lobby, quickly recognised Israel and over the years has become the main support of the Jewish state, and its aid and protection remains the key component in America's Middle East policy today. The Soviet Union responded by supporting the Palestinians and their Arab backers, and the Arab-Israeli conflict became a major Cold War flashpoint.

In South East Asia Britain retained more direct control of the decolonisation process. A major focal point – and British Cold War success – was the Malayan Emergency from 1948 to 1960. The long guerrilla war was eventually won by the British with a combination of military pressure and a village resettlement programme. Malaysia achieved independence in September 1965. Singapore, at the tip of the Malay Peninsula, became independent in August 1965. Elsewhere in South East Asia, the Burmese and Sri Lankans were granted independence in 1948. Hong Kong was a special case. The island of Hong Kong became a British colony at the end of the First Opium War in 1842. It was the first of the unequal treaty ports which in the nineteenth century transformed China from Asian giant into a virtual colony of the Western powers. In 1898, Britain also took out a ninety-nine-year lease on the New Territories across Victoria Harbour in order to provide food and water for small and rocky Hong Kong. When the Chinese communists took power in October 1949, they closed all the treaty ports except Hong Kong and the

Portuguese enclave of Macau. Hong Kong became the only conduit for Western companies doing business with communist China and the British colony grew to become a major world financial centre. However, it was not sustainable without the New Territories, so Britain negotiated the return of the colony when the lease expired in 1997. As part of the agreement China agreed to sustain a legal approach of 'one country two systems' until 2047. Hong Kong would for fifty years remain a capitalist economy with the preservation of freedom of speech, religion and assembly. Its laws would be based on British law. The two systems, capitalist and communist, would gradually move closer towards each other and merge – peacefully – in 2047. However, the process of this merger has led to riots and demonstrations by young Hong Kong Chinese who fear that their liberties will abruptly disappear under a blanket of totalitarianism. As two of the biggest investors in Hong Kong's success, both Britain and America are carefully watching events but hamstrung by their inability to prevent 1.3 billion Chinese from doing more or less what they please.

On 15 November 1884, diplomats from fourteen European countries and the United States met in the Berlin residence of Germany's Chancellor Otto von Bismarck to sign the General Act of the Berlin Conference. The treaty had several results: the emergence of Germany as a colonial power; the regulation of trade on the African continent; and most important of all, the establishment of boundaries between the various European colonies, which would eventually become independent African states in their own rights. In some cases, the boundaries were drawn along natural geographic features such as rivers, but in most cases a straight edge ruler was used to draw a line from point A to B. In not a single instance did the European colonisers take into account the demographic and ethnic divisions involving about 3,000 tribes speaking 2,000 different languages. Neither did they consider the nomadic and semi-nomadic nature of most of the tribes or their existing political, social and economic structures. When it came time for decolonisation over sixty years later, the Europeans successfully argued that to change the boundaries would lead to destabilising political chaos. So they stayed in place, creating yet more chaos, confusion and instability.

Britain's African possessions were scattered and each had their own history, purpose and relationship with the UK. But they were all united in their desire for independence and their dislike of British racism and rule. In North Africa the British were in the aforementioned Egypt and neighbouring Sudan from the nineteenth century. They administered Libya and Eritrea during the war and immediately afterwards and had longstanding colonial interests in strategic British Somaliland and Aden on opposite sides of the entrance to the Red Sea. The two latter possessions became targets for the Soviet Union, and after independence Aden became the People's Republic of South Yemen, then in 1970 the People's Democratic Republic of Yemen and a base for Soviet submarines. British Somaliland was merged with Italian Somaliland and in 1960 became independent Somalia. In 1969 General Mohammed Siad Barre overthrew the elected government, started moving his country into Moscow's embrace and declared war on Ethiopia over the Ogaden region. The US, worried that pro-Soviet governments on opposite sides of the eastern end of the Red Sea would lead to Moscow's control of the strategic waterway, set about wooing Barre with British help. They were successful, but the Cold War legacy of the battle between Moscow and Washington for control of the Horn of Africa has been the major contributory factor to the continuing political turmoil in the two former British colonies.

Britain had been in West Africa since the seventeenth century when the region became the primary source of slaves for British colonies in the West Indies and America. Two of the colonies were governed by ex-slaves: Sierra Leone, led by former American slaves who fought with Britain in the American Revolution, and Liberia, which was an American colony created by the American Colonisation Society as an African home for freed American slaves. Both countries continue to be plagued by conflict between the descendants of the freed slaves and the indigenous populations. Britain also ruled Gambia and jointly administered Togo and Cameroon with France. Ghana, or the Gold Coast, was the first Black African country to achieve independence in 1957. US and British-educated Kwame Nkrumah set about projecting himself as leader of the pan-African independence movement and aligned himself with communist China. With Beijing's support he set up a Bureau of African Affairs, which trained guerrilla fighters to fight for independence elsewhere on the continent. Nkrumah's activities made him a target for CIA destabilisation attempts, prompting him to establish a one-party state. He was overthrown in 1966, but Ghana did not return to multi-party democracy until 1992.

Nigeria is an example of pre-colonial tribal divisions undermining prosperity. There are four main Nigerian ethnic groups: Hansa, Fulani, Igbo and Yoruba. Shortly after independence a civil war broke out after the Igbos attempted a military coup. The result was an attempt by the Igbos to secede from the rest of Nigeria and a civil war in which 3.5 million died, mainly from starvation. With a population of 191 million, Nigeria is Africa's most populous country. Large oil deposits also make it one of the richest. Corruption and political instability wrought by ethnic divisions ensure that Nigeria is also one of the most inequitable and corrupt societies. From 1966 it endured a series of dictatorships. It was not until 1998 that something approaching free and fair elections was re-established.

British East Africa was focused on Kenya, which was settled by British farmers – many of them the younger sons of the British aristocracy. They established a representative government that effectively left all political power in the hands of the white settlers and led to the dispossession of the dominant Kikuyu tribe from the sought-after fertile highlands. The treatment of the Kikuyu led to the post-war Mau Mau rebellion, from 1952 to 1956. The British ruthlessly responded with concentration camps and torture. Eventually, Kenya achieved independence in 1962 and the government of Jomo Kenyatta set about breaking up the white farms and distributing land to the Kikuyu. But despite the problems with the British, Kenyatta and his successors maintained a steadfast pro-western foreign policy.

To the west of Kenya, the British decided to rule Uganda through the dominant tribe, the Buganda, which became a problem when they tried to create a unified national state at independence. Tribal animosities eventually led to the rise of Idi Amin, one of the most ruthless and mercurial African dictators. Amin was eventually overthrown following a 1979 war with neighbouring Tanzania. Tanzania started life as German East Africa and after the First World War became part of the British Empire as Tanganyika. It became independent in 1961 under Julius Nyerere, who was a follower of Ghana's Nkrumah. Nyerere also forged close ties with communist China and set up a one-party socialist state because he believed that a multi-party democracy would exacerbate tribal differences. After Nyerere's death, the country moved towards a multi-party system, but still maintains close ties with China.

Julius Nyerere was also the first chairman of the Frontline States, which spearheaded opposition to white minority rule in southern Africa, in particular the two former British colonies of South Africa and Rhodesia, but also the Portuguese colonies of Angola and Mozambique and the South African-administered territory of Namibia (formerly Southwest Africa). The main focus in the region was South Africa, which was initially colonised by the Dutch starting in 1652 when they settled the area around the Cape of Good Hope. The British won control in 1805 via the Napoleonic Wars, but the Dutch-speaking settlers (the Boers or Afrikaners) bridled at British rule and trekked further inland to set up their own republic. When diamonds and gold were discovered they came under pressure again from the British, which led to two Anglo-Boer

Wars, British victory in 1902 and the union of South Africa. Legal racial segregation started in 1910 and was introduced by the British. But in 1948 the Afrikaner-dominated National Party came to power and entrenched and extended segregation and gave it a name – apartheid. The black majority (roughly 80 per cent of the population) were denied voting rights, allocated less than 10 per cent of the land, forced into slums and faced many other injustices. To combat this system, the black majority formed the African National Congress (ANC), Pan Africanist-Congress (PAC) and South African Communist Party (SACP). All of these organisations received weapons from the Soviet Union, and their leaders – those who were not imprisoned or executed – went to Moscow for political training.

Because of this Soviet support, and South Africa's strategic position at the tip of the continent, the US and Britain tacitly supported the apartheid government while publicly condemning its racial policies. The situation was complicated by the end of Portuguese rule in neighbouring Angola and Mozambique. The Portuguese had done little to train Africans to take over after independence so that their departure created a political vacuum, which was filled by the Soviet-supported MPLA in Angola, along with an estimated 36,000 Cuban troops. The opposing UNITA forces were supplied by the US and backed up with South African troops. The South Africans, however, failed to defeat the guerrillas and with the demise of white minority rule elsewhere in southern Africa they were faced with the possibility of a civil war or the peaceful transfer of power to the black majority. The collapse of the Berlin Wall and the end of the Cold War also meant that South Africa could no longer count on the support of the US and Britain as an anti-communist bulwark in Africa. In February 1990, ANC leader Nelson Mandela was released from jail. In 1991 apartheid was dismantled, and in 1994 Mandela was elected president and black majority rule was established in South Africa.

Another factor contributing to the end of apartheid was the collapse of white minority rule in South Africa's northern neighbour Rhodesia (later Zimbabwe). The country was founded by the fantastically wealthy British ultra-imperialist Cecil Rhodes. In 1888 he bought the land rights to present-day Zimbabwe and Zambia from the Ndebele's King Lobengula. The land was named Rhodesia after its imperialist founder and divided into Northern Rhodesia (later Zambia) and Southern Rhodesia (Zimbabwe). The colony became a major source of copper and attracted farmers who became rich growing tobacco, especially in Southern Rhodesia. But like the British settlers in Kenya, they refused to allow the indigenous African population political representation. By the early 1960s the British had accepted the political reality of what Prime Minister Harold Macmillan dubbed Africa's 'winds of change' and pressured the white minority in Rhodesia to accept black participation in the political process. In October 1964 Northern Rhodesia became independent under African prime minister Kenneth Kaunda. But Southern Rhodesia resisted British demands and in November 1965 declared itself unilaterally independent of Britain under the white minority government of Ian Smith. The British government regarded this as an act of rebellion but was unable to intervene militarily without the support of neighbouring South Africa, which threw its weight behind the Smith regime. The result was a fifteen-year-long civil war between Rhodesian forces supported by South Africa and a guerrilla army comprised of forces from ZANU, led by Robert Mugabe of the dominant Shona tribe, and ZAPU, led by Joshua Nkomo, whose Ndebele tribe made up 20 per cent of the black population. Both ZANU and ZAPU received finance and weapons from the Soviet Union. Without American and British support, Ian Smith was eventually forced to capitulate and in 1980 Rhodesia became officially independent under Robert Mugabe and changed its name to Zimbabwe.

The Fish and Ships War

Iceland is aptly named. If it weren't for the tail end of the Gulf Stream it would be as frozen as the misnamed Greenland, with the occasional volcano to warm your toes. Such an inhospitable climate makes it difficult for the 350,000 inhabitants to make a living. But the Icelanders are nothing if not inventive, and are also determined, proudly patriotic and extremely plucky. They have managed to carve out valuable niches in adventure tourism, geothermal energy, banking, aluminium smelting, and, most important of all, fishing. During the Cold War, Iceland was also a vital member of NATO. It provided nothing in the form of military hardware or personnel; the closest thing that Iceland had to a defence force was its Coast Guard. The island's strategic location, however, inflated the nation's importance out of all proportion to its population and resources. Iceland sits astride what is known as the Greenland–Iceland–UK Gap (GIUK), which guards the entrance to the North Atlantic from the Baltic and North Sea. This meant that any Soviet naval vessel moving into the North Atlantic was forced to sail right past Iceland. As a result, the US built a radar station and a state-of-the art naval air station at Keflavik outside the capital Reykjavik to monitor Soviet ship movements as well as provide a base for fighter interceptors and in-flight refuelling.

Iceland was a vital link in the American North Atlantic defensive chain. However, the waters around Iceland were rich in fish, especially cod, the favourite of British chip shops. British fishermen started fishing Icelandic cod in the fifteenth century and by the start of the Second World War their Icelandic fishing fleet was larger than all other national fishing fleets combined. After the war, the British fishing industry became dependent on Icelandic cod. But the Icelanders were also dependent on the cod for financial survival. From 1950 to 1980, as much as 90 per cent of the island's exports were fish at a time when overfishing by trawlers from both countries was decimating stocks. A clash between Britain and Iceland over king cod was inevitable and Iceland's strategic position played a determining role in the outcome. The US – and by extension the wider NATO alliance – was dependent on the base at Keflavik to provide vital intelligence. Cold War needs trumped historic British fishing rights and Iceland won. The British fishing fleet shrank to a shadow of its former self. And what became known as the Cod Wars became an example of how small, determined and desperate countries could drive a wedge between the two closest allies in NATO.

The first Cod War occurred between 1958 and 1961 when Iceland extended its territorial waters from 4 to 12 miles. Compared to the following conflicts it was a relatively low-key affair. But the Icelanders set a pattern by threatening to withdraw from NATO and expel the US from Keflavik. The result was that pressure was put on the British by Washington and NATO headquarters in Brussels and the British caved in. In the Second Cod War – 1972–73 – the Icelanders extended their territorial waters to 50 miles and introduced net cutters to deter British fishermen. Once cut, the steel cables would whip back across the trawler, slicing into anything on deck, including a trawlerman. Defence Secretary Lord Peter Carrington despatched several Royal Navy ships to protect British trawlers. The Icelandic *Althing* voted to withdraw from NATO, close Keflavik and expel the US forces. A last-minute intervention by the US resulted in Britain reluctantly accepting the extension to 50 miles. In 1975 the UN Law of the Sea Conference voted to extend sea-based special economic zones to up to 200 miles. Iceland took advantage of the ruling and extended its territorial waters to the absolute new limit. The move threatened to expel the British completely from the fishing grounds. The result was the third and final Cod War from 1975 to 1976. It was also the most dangerous. Twenty-two Royal Navy frigates were deployed to protect the British fishing fleet. Icelandic Coast Guard vessels again used net cutters and when that did not work they rammed British trawlers. Royal Navy frigates responded by ramming Icelandic Coast

Guard ships. Iceland retaliated by severing diplomatic relations with the UK. The British, however, refused to leave the fishing grounds. So the Icelanders again resorted to the tried and tested threat to leave NATO and expel US forces from Keflavik. This time the US secretly approached the Icelanders to stress their support. In January 1975, America's Deputy Chairman of the UN Law of the Sea Conference, John Morton Moore, approached Iceland's Ambassador to the UN, Haraldur Kroyer, and told him that the US supported Iceland's claim to a 200-mile economic zone and that 'the US had very strong sympathy with Iceland's cause and wanted to support it to the best of its ability'. This was all the Icelanders needed. They knew that with full American backing they couldn't fail. Again, the British were forced to cave in for the third and final time under pressure from Washington.

The British fishing industry never recovered from the final expulsion. It tried to replace Icelandic stock with fish stocks from British home waters but that route was blocked by the EU Common Fisheries Policy, which forced the UK to open its waters to trawlers from other EU member states. The British fishing lobby was one of the prime movers behind Brexit. Fishing remains an important part of the Icelandic economy and way of life. About 10 per cent of the population is involved in the industry. But diversification and declining fish stocks mean that fish now represent only 17 per cent of Icelandic export earnings. The big earner (42 per cent) is tourism. Keflavik Naval Air Station is no more. It was deemed redundant with the end of the Cold War and was closed in September 2005. The facilities are now part of the commercial Keflavik International Airport, a major stopover venue for flights across the Atlantic. All three countries have moved on and are again close allies, but the memory of the Cod Wars – and the destruction of the British fishing industry – remain a salient example of the sacrifices that Britain will make to preserve its relationship with America.

Gorby, Thatcher, Reagan

Throughout most of the Cold War, Britain was the junior partner in Anglo-American relations. However, the close and special relationship between President Ronald Reagan and Prime Minister Margaret Thatcher and a successful British interpretation of changes in the Soviet leadership played a major role in bringing an end to the Soviet Union. By the end of the 1970s, the Soviet leadership was an inept gerontocracy presiding over a corrupt and crumbling economy and power was maintained through oppression. For years, Western Sovietologists such as George Kennan had argued that the contradictions within the Soviet system meant that it would eventually collapse of its own accord. The West needed only to contain its expansionist tendencies until that day arrived. In May 1979, Margaret Thatcher was elected British Prime Minister and started to reap some of the harvest from the Soviet seeds of self-destruction.

Even before her election, Mrs Thatcher had established a reputation as a tough-talking anti-Soviet. In January 1976 she declared that Cuban and Soviet intervention in Angola proved that Moscow was 'bent on world domination' and called on NATO to strengthen its defences. In response, the official newspaper of the Soviet Ministry of Defence, *Krasnaya Zvezda*, dubbed Thatcher the 'Iron Lady'. The intended sarcasm backfired. Thatcher adopted the epithet happily as a compliment. The Soviet attack also grabbed the attention of Republican presidential candidate Ronald Reagan, who entered the White House in January 1982. The two leaders quickly established a common anti-Soviet bond that was cemented by a shared position on free market economics. The two leaders have been described as 'ideological soulmates' who turned the special relationship into the extra-special relationship.

The strengthening of the Anglo-American bond coincided with the collapse of the Soviet gerontocracy. In November 1982, Soviet leader Leonid Brezhnev died. He was succeeded in quick succession by two more members of the geriatric Soviet old guard: former KGB head Yuri Andropov, who lasted only fifteen months, and Konstantin Chernenko, who was in office for thirteen months before dying at the age of seventy-four. While the old guard were attempting to defy the grim reaper, British intelligence was hard at work trying to identify the next generation of Soviet leaders and, if possible, cultivate them. They decided that Mikhail Gorbachev, at that time the chief ideologue of the Communist Party, was the most likely candidate for General Secretary and that he was inclined towards economic and political reform. In December 1983 Gorbachev visited London as part of a Soviet delegation and Mrs Thatcher declared: 'I like Mr. Gorbachev. We can do business together.' She then went on to plead the future Soviet leader's cause to the US at a time when Washington was sceptical about his commitment to political and economic reform.

But while praising Gorbachev and his reforms, Thatcher also urged that the Western alliance take a cautious approach towards defence negotiations and security arrangements. She argued that Gorbachev's policies involved a strong element of risk for the Soviet leader, and that if he failed he could be replaced by a more hard-line communist figure who would take a tougher position on East–West relations.

Gorbachev's aim was to achieve political and economic reform while maintaining a one-party socialist system. He introduced two new concepts: *perestroika* (economic restructuring) and *glasnost* (political and social openness). His absolute priority was to improve the Soviet economy and place consumer goods on the shelves of Soviet shops. Failure to do so, he argued, undermined the socialist revolution at home and abroad. The need to improve the Soviet economy was given added impetus by projections indicating that Soviet oil reserves – which had financed large defence budgets and prestige industrial projects – were declining. The drop in oil revenues, plus economic mismanagement and corruption during the Brezhnev years, made it imperative that the industrial and service sectors of the economy were restructured before they were further undermined. This, in turn, meant decentralisation and incentive schemes for workers and managers. It also meant a relaxation of subsidised price structures.

The Soviet Union's economic problems meant that it could ill afford to continue the arms race. The result was the 1987 INF Treaty, the 1990 Conventional Forces in Europe Treaty and the 1991 Strategic Arms Reduction Treaty (START I). The Soviet leader also insisted that Moscow's satellite countries in eastern Europe and elsewhere introduce corresponding political and economic reforms, and he cut Soviet aid, which was keeping many of them afloat. The result was that the local communist puppet governments faltered and eventually fell. The most dramatic was the collapse of East Germany and the Berlin Wall in November 1989. In July 1991, the military arm of the Soviet Empire – the Warsaw Pact – was disbanded. The West, led by America and steadfastly backed by Britain in the number two slot, had won the Cold War.

9/11, Afghanistan, Iraq and Syria

On 11 September 2001, at 8.46 a.m., a hijacked American airliner crashed into the North Tower of New York's World Trade Center. Fourteen minutes later another airliner flew into the South Tower, and at 9.37 a.m. a third aircraft crashed into the western façade of the Pentagon in Arlington, Virginia. The suicide attacks were orchestrated by the Islamic Jihadist group Al-Qaeda and were the worst terrorist attack in human history. In all, 2,966 people were killed, 6,000 were injured and $10 billion of damage was done. In the coming years other Western countries or Western-linked targets became targets for the Islamist terrorists. The most dramatic attack on Britain came on 7 July 2005 when four separate suicide bombers on the London Underground and buses killed fifty-two and injured 700. The Cold War was over. The War on Terror was in full swing.

Al-Qaeda had its genesis in the 1979 Soviet invasion of Afghanistan when a twenty-two-year-old from the wealthy Saudi-based bin Laden family travelled to Afghanistan to help organise the struggle against the Russians. Osama bin Laden used his personal fortune and extensive financial connections to become the established conduit for money and weapons from the US and Saudi Arabia into Afghanistan. When the Soviets were finally defeated in 1989, Bin Laden was hailed throughout the Arab world – and in the corridors of the CIA – as the man who made it happen. Then came the August 1990 Iraqi invasion of Kuwait and the counter-attack by a US-led coalition that included Saudi Arabia and had the long-term consequence of US troops being based in the Saudi kingdom. The first Iraq War was unacceptable to bin Laden. He regarded the decadent US as the chief oppressor of the Arabs and Islam. To him, the thought that American soldiers would be based in the same country as Islam's two holiest places – Mecca and Medina – was repugnant in the extreme.

Meanwhile, back in Afghanistan, the country collapsed into civil war, and an Islamic fundamentalist party known as the Taliban emerged as the controlling power by 1998. The Taliban imposed strict Sharia law throughout Afghanistan and offered sanctuary to bin Laden and Al-Qaeda. In 1996, bin Laden declared war on the United States; in August of that year he launched his first attack, with simultaneous suicide bombings at the US embassies in Nairobi and Dar es Salaam. A total of 224 people were killed. Bin Laden was placed on the FBI's Most Wanted List and in December 2000, UN Security Council Resolution 1333 was passed condemning the use of Taliban territory for the training of terrorists and provision of a safe haven for Bin Laden.

The British had long experience of the region. Historic links gave them close ties with key figures in the political and business establishment, many of whom regarded London as their second home. Afghanistan bordered oil-rich Iran and the Middle East, giving Britain and the US a strong mutual interest in maintaining security in the area. To deal with this, the US provided the bulk of the financial and military muscle. Britain brought to the table political influence and historic legitimacy, and the two countries worked hand in glove throughout the region. In the 1990 Gulf War, the British had the second-largest Western military contingent after the US: 58,000 troops. When the World Trade Center was attacked, the British took the initiative in calling for NATO to support the invocation of Article Five of the NATO Treaty: the three musketeer clause, which calls on all NATO members to come to the aid of an attacked member of the alliance. This remains the only time in NATO's history that Article Five has been invoked. The result was an immediate attack on the Taliban when they refused to surrender Osama bin Laden. Within days, they had been pushed out of the Afghan capital of Kabul. The search for bin Laden continued until 2 May 2011 when he was tracked to a hideout in Pakistan and shot by US Navy Seals. The Taliban continued to fight against NATO forces, resulting in a drawn-out conflict in which Britain was again the second-largest military contingent after the US.

The closeness of Anglo-American operations in the Middle East and the British government's unquestioning support for US policy was most dramatically illustrated by the 2003 US-led invasion of Iraq. President George W. Bush was determined to topple Saddam Hussein, regarded as a major threat to stability in the Middle East. The Iraqi dictator had repeatedly threatened Israel, invaded Kuwait, launched a disastrous war against Iraq, used chemical weapons against his own Kurdish population, and was suspected of developing nuclear weapons. Since Desert Storm in 1990, successive US administrations had sought to force regime change with demands for weapons inspections, sanctions, the imposition of no-fly zones and political isolation. No one (outside of Iraq) liked Saddam; not the Arab states nor anyone in the West or the East. He was a dangerous loose cannon who threatened to set the Middle East powder keg alight. But disliking someone was insufficient grounds under international law for using military action to topple them. So Britain and America in concert set out to establish a *casus belli*. President Bush and Prime Minister Tony Blair argued that Iraq was developing weapons of mass destruction and had strong links with Al-Qaeda. Allies including France, Germany and Canada disagreed, as did the United Nations. But the British and American governments were determined to invade, did so, toppled Saddam, found no weapons of mass destruction or links to Al-Qaeda, and killed an estimated 460,000 Iraqis. The invasion and occupation also cost 4,691 American lives and 179 British. A subsequent British inquiry led by retired senior civil servant Sir John Chilcott condemned the preparation, illegality, justification and conduct of the war and the subsequent occupation of Iraq. The Iraq War was a huge blot on the legacies of both President Bush and Prime Minister Tony Blair, and led many British politicians to question the policy of blind support for American foreign policy.

London had little difficulty in supporting most of President Barack Obama's policies, although the US leader was more interested in building a relationship with Asia than maintaining close ties with Britain and Europe. His comment that Britain would go to the 'back of the queue' in any trade negotiations if it left the European Union was viewed by many as undue interference in British domestic policies and provided fuel for the anti-EU Brexit lobby. The June 2016 British public's vote to leave the European Union and Donald Trump's election as president led to a sea change in both British and American policies. It also raised the possibility of an even closer relationship between Britain and America. Withdrawal from the EU inevitably meant a reduction in trade across the English Channel. Britain needed to replace that trade with deals with other countries. It would also need to renegotiate free trade deals with seventy countries. The freedom to negotiate independent trade deals was one of the main reasons given for leaving the European Union; Brexiteers claimed that the difficulties involved in finding agreement among twenty-eight member countries was holding back British trade. Certainly this issue nearly scuppered an EU–Canada deal at the last minute when the Walloons in Belgium nearly blocked the deal because they feared the impact of Canadian beef and pork imports on their farmers. The British Remainers, on the other hand, said that being part of the world's largest trading bloc increased Britain's negotiating power.

From the 1990s, successive American administrations pursued a policy of negotiating bloc trade deals to encourage free trade and what they saw as the inevitability of globalisation. In 1994, the North America Free Trade Agreement (NAFTA) was signed and in 2016 the US and eleven other Pacific Rim countries signed the Trans Pacific Partnership (TTP). In 2013 negotiations were formally started between the US and EU for a free trade deal called the Transatlantic Trade and Investment Partnership (TTIP). President Trump was wholeheartedly opposed to free trade, negotiations with blocs, and globalisation, all of which he said were exporting American jobs overseas. He withdrew from the TPP, forced a renegotiation of NAFTA and withdrew from free trade talks with the European Union. He also imposed a wide range of tariffs on goods from China, South Korea, Canada, India, Mexico and the EU. In May 2019 he threatened Mexico with a blanket ban on imports if it failed to stop illegal immigration into the US. Trump's tariffs and opposition to free trade deals were central to his 'America First' Policy. He believed that large trading blocs encourage world growth at the expense of the United States and that America's interests were best served by weakening and breaking up regional blocs because they threatened America's dominant trading position as the world's largest economy. The EU and other regional trading blocs create a political and economic interdependence which encourages global political stability, but President Trump and his supporters believed that the economic price was too high. Brexit, therefore, was strongly encouraged by Trump, who offered Britain 'a great trade deal' to more than replace Britain's relationship with the EU. An Anglo-American trade deal became a cornerstone of post-Brexit plans for two successive Conservative prime ministers, Theresa May and Boris Johnson.

The 'great trade deal' was, however, jeopardised by the perpetual Irish problem and the election of Joe Biden as president in November 2020. An essential element of the Good Friday Agreement of 1998 was the open border between Ireland and Northern Ireland. This was possible as long as the UK was in the EU because there was already free movement of people, goods and services between all EU members. But with the UK (including Northern Ireland) out of the EU, that free movement ended and a dark cloud was cast over the Good Friday Agreement and the Irish peace that it underpinned. US Congress let it be known that it would reject any trade deal which undermined the Irish peace deal. The pledge was repeated by Joe Biden.

America had supplanted its parent as the world's major political and military power. Now it held the key to Britain's economic future. America was in a position to remake the country that made it.

Bibliography

Abraham, H. J., *Freedom and the Press*, NY, 1982.

Acheson, Dean, *Present at the Creation: My Years in the State Department*, NY, 1969.

Acton, Lord, *Essays on Liberty*, London, 1907.

Acton, Lord, *History of Freedom*, London, 1907.

Adams, Abigail, *The Adams-Jefferson Letters: The Complete Correspondence between Thomas Jefferson and Abigail Adams and John Adams*, Chapel Hill, NC., 1959.

Adams, John (ed. Charles Francis Adams), *The Works of John Adams, Second President of the United States with a Life of the Author*, Boston, 1850.

Adamson, Peter, *Medieval Philosophy Without Any Gaps*, Oxford 2019.

Admon, J., *Wilkes's Life and Correspondence*, London, 1805.

Ambrose, Stephen E., *Rise to Globalism: American Foreign Policy 1938-76*, Baltimore, Md., 1976

Andrews, Kenneth, *Trade, Planters and Settlement: Maritime Enterprise and the Genesis of the British Empire, 1480-1630*, Cambridge, UK, 1984.

Anonymous, *The Secret Barrister*, London 2018

Aristotle ed Stephen Everson), *The Politics and Constitution of Athens*, Cambridge, UK, 196.

Arms, Thomas, *Encyclopedia of the Cold War*, NY 1994.

Aspinall, A., *Politics and the Press, 1780-1850*, NY, 1959.

Ashton, R., *The Crown and the Money Market, 1603-1640*, Oxford, 1960.

Atiyah, P. S. and R. S. Summers, *Form and Substance in Anglo-American Law: A comparative Study of Legal Reasoning, Legal Theory and Legal Institutions*, Oxford 2002.

Aytorn, E., *The Penny Universities*, London, 1951.

Bablitz, Leanne, *Actors and Audience in the Roman Courtroom*, London 2007.

Bailyn, Bernard, *The Ideological Origins of the American Revolution*, Cambridge, Ma., 1967.

Baldwin, Peter, *The Copyright Wars: Three Centuries of Trans-Atlantic Battle*, Princeton, NJ, 1996.

Ball, W. W. Rouse, *A Short Account of the History of Mathematics*, NY, 1908.

Balmer, Ramdall, *The Making of Evangelicalism: From Revivalism to Politics and Beyond*, NY, 2010.

Bamford, James, *The Puzzle Palace*, Boston 1982.

Bar-Simon-Tov, Y., *Israel, the Superpowers and the War in the Middle East*, NY 1987.

Bastiat, Frederic, *The Law*, Paris, 1850.

Baus, K., *Handbook of Church History*, Oxford, 1965.

Bayliss, John (ed), *Documents in Contemporary History, Anglo-American Relations since 1939: The Enduring Alliance*, Manchester,UK, 1997.

Baxter, Robert, *The Magna Carta: Cornerstone of the Constitution*, Chicago, 2013.

Beak, David O., *In Pursuit of Purity: American Fundamentalism since 1850*, Greenville, S.C., 1986.

Beeman, Richard, *The Penguin Guide to the United States Constitution*, NY, 2010.

Benn, Carl, *The War of 1812*, Oxford, 2002.

Berlins, Marcel and Clare Dyer, *The Law Machine*, London 2000.

Billings, William, *Sir William Berkeley and the Forging of Colonial Virginia*, Baton Rouge, La., 2010.

Blackman, Douglas, *Slavery by Another Name: The Re-Enslavement of Black Americans from the Civil War to World War Two*, NY, 2009.

Boyle, Andrew, *The Climate of Treason*, London 1979.

Black, Edwin, *War Against the Weak: Eugenics and America's Campaign to Create a Master Race*, NY, 2003.

Black, J., *The English Press in the Eighteenth Century*, London, 1987.

Blackburn, Robin, *The Makings of New World Slavery*, NY, 1997.

Blackett, R.J.M., *Divided Hearts, Britain and the American Civil War*, Baton Rouge, La., 2001.

Blake, John W., *European Beginnings in West Africa, 1454-1578*, London. 1937.

Bleachley, H., *Wilkes: The Life*, London, 1917.

Bliss, Robert M., *Revolution and Empire: English Politics and American Politics in the 17th Century*, Manchester, UK, 1990.

Bolt, Christine, *Feminist Ferment: The Woman Question in the USA and England, 1870-1940*, London 1995.

Borkowski, Andrew and Paul Du Plessis, *A Textbook to Roman Law*, Oxford 1962.

Bourne, Kenneth, *Britain and the Balance of Power in North America, 1815-1908*, Berkeley, Ca., 1967.

Boxer, Charles R. *Coffee and Coffee Houses: The Origins of a Social Beverage n the Medieval Near East*, Seattle, Wa., 1985.

Brachey, Stuart, *The Wealth of Nations: An Economic History of the United States*, NY, 1988.

Braddick, Michael, *God's Fury, England's Fire, A New History of the English Civil Wars*, London, 2008.

Brands, H.W., *Cold Warriors*, NY 1988.

Brandon, Henry, *Special Relationships: A Foreign Correspondent's Memoirs from Roosevelt to Reagan*, London, 1988.

Brandon, P., *Life and Death of the Press Barons*, London, 1988.

Brandon, Ruth, *The Dollar Princesses: The American Invasion of the European Aristocracy, 1870-1914*, London, 1980.

Breckinridge, Scott, *The CIA and the US Intelligence System*, London, 2020.

Bremer, Francis, *John Winthrop: America's Forgotten Founding Father*, Oxford, 2003.

Briggs, Asa, *A Social History of England, 900-1200*, Cambridge, UK, 2011.

Brockliss, L. W. B., *The University of Oxford: A History*, Oxford, 2016.

Brown, Ian and Douwe Korf, *Digital Freedoms in International Law: Practical Steps to Protect Human Rights Online*, Washington DC., 2012.

Brown, John Russell, *The Oxford Illustrated History of Theatre*, Oxford, 2001.

Brundage, James, *Medieval Canon Law*, London 1995.

Burrows, Edwin G. and Mike Wallace, *Gotham: A History of New York City to 1898*, NY, 1999.

Bryant, Chris, *Parliament: The Biography (Vol 1): Ancestral Voices*, London 2014.

Bryant, Chris, *Parliament: The Biography (Vol 2): Reform*, London 2014.

Bulloch, James D., *The Secret Service of the Confederate States in Europe, or How the Confederate Cruisers Were Equipped*, NY, 1884.

Burk, Kathleen, *Britain, America and the Sinews of War, 1914-1918*, London, 1985.

Burk, Kathleen, *Old World, New World*, NY, 2007.

Burke, Edmund, (ed Issac Kramnick), The Portable Edmund Burke, London, 1999.

Butler, Jon, *The Revolution Before 1776*, Cambridge, Ma., 2000.

Butler, Jon, *Religion in Colonial America*, Oxford 2000.

Cameron, Watt D., *Succeeding John Bull: America in Britain's Place, 1900-1975*, Cambridge, 1984.

Bibliography

Campbell, Alastair, *The Blair Years: Extracts from the Alastair Campbell Diaries*, London 2007.

Campbell, Malcolm, *The Encyclopedia of Golf*, London, 1981.

Cardini, Franco, *Europe 1492: Portrait of a Continent 500 Years Ago*, NY, 1992.

Carlton, Charles, *Going to the Wars: The Experience of the English Civil Wars, 1638-1651*, London 1992.

Carnegie, Andrew and John Charles van Dyke, *The Autobiography of Andrew Carnegie*, Wooton Bassett, UK, 2018.

Carter, John, *The History of Horse Racing: First Past the Post: Champions, Thoroughbreds, Owners, Trainers and Jockeys*, London 2017.

Carwardine, Richard, *Transatlantic Revivalism: Popular Evangelism in Britain and America, 1790-1865*, Westport, Ct., 1978.

Chadwick, Owen, *The Victorian Church, Part One*, London 1966.

Christie, Ian R., and Benjamin Larabee, *Empire or Independence, 1760-1776: A British-American Dailogue on the Coming of the American Revolution*, NY, 1976.

Churchill, Winston, *A History of the English-Speaking Peoples (Vol. 2): The New World*, London, 1956.

Churchill, Winston, *A History of the English-Speaking Peoples (Vol 3): The Age of Revolution*, London, 1957.

Clapham, J. H., *The Bank of England, 1694-1797*, Cambridge, UK, 1944.

Clark, Ian and Nicholas J. Walters, *The British Origins of Nuclear Strategy, 1945-1955*, Oxford, 1989.

Coe, Lewis, *Wireless Radio: A History*, NY, 2006.

Coe, Neil M., Phillip F. Kell, *Economic Geogaphy: A Contemporary Introduction*, Oxford, 2017.

Coleman, D.C., *The Economic History of England, 1450-1750*, Oxford, 1970.

Collett, D., *A History of Taxes on Knowledge*, London 1906.

Conway, M. *The Life of Thomas Paine*, NY, 1892.

Conway, Stephen, *The Way of American Independence, 1775-1783*, London, 1995.

Court, W. H. B., *A Concise Economic History of Britain from 1750 to Present Times*, Cambridge, 1962.

Cousins, Mark, *The Story of Film: A Concise History of Film and an Odyssey of International Cinema*, London 2011.

Craig, Nelson, *Thomas Paine: Enlightenment, Revolution and the Birth of Modern Nations*, NY, 2006.

Cromwell, William C., *The United States and the European Pillar: The Strained Alliance*, NY 1992.

Crowley, Roger, *Conquerors: How Portugal Forged the First Global Empire*, London 2015.

Crystal, David, *The Cambridge Encyclopedia of the English Language*, Cambridge, UK, 1995.

Cummings, B., *The Origins of the Korean War*, Princeton 1981.

Darwin, Charles, *The Origin of Species by Means of Natural Selection, or the Preservation of Favoured Races in the Struggle for Life*, London, 1874.

Darwin, Charles (ed Francis Darwin), *The Life and Letters of Charles Darwin Including an Autobiographical Chapter*, London, 1887.

Davidson, Basil, *Africa in Modern History: The Search for a New Society*, NY 1978.

Dawkins, Richard, *The Greatest Show on Earth: The Evidence for Evolution*, London, 1979.

Day, Sebastian, *Intuitive Cognition According to John Duns Scotus*, London, 1943.

Deer, Ada, *Making a Difference, My Fight for Native Rights and Social Justice*, NY, 2019.

Dimbleby, David and David Reynolds, *An Ocean Apart*, London ,1988.

Dickens, A. G., *Martin Luther and the Reformation*, London, 1967.

Dollar, George W., *A History of Fundamentalism in America*, Greenville, S.C., 1973.

Donoghue, Bernard, *Prime Minister: The Conduct of Policy under Harold Wilson and James Callaghan*, London, 1987.

Douglas, Edward Leach, *Roots of Conflict: British Armed Forces and Colonial Americans*, Chapel Hill, NC, 1986.

Duncan, Raymond, *Soviet Policy in the Third World*, NY, 1980.

Donnelly, Desmond, *Struggle for the World*, NY, 1965.

Dunn, J., *The Political Thought of John Locke*, Cambridge, 1969.

Dupont, Jerry, *The Common Law Abroad: Constitutional and Legal Legacy of the British Empire*, London, 2001.

Edelhart, Michael, *The Virginians*, NY, 1982.

Edelstein, M., *Globalising Capital: A History of the International Monetary System*, Princeton, NJ, 1946.

Eden, Anthony, *The Suez Crisis of 1956*, Boston, 1966.

Eisenhower, Dwight, *The White House Years: Waging Peace, 1956-61*, London, 1961.

Eisenstein, Elizabeth L., *The Printing Press as an Agent of Change: Communications and Cultural Transformation in Early Modern Europe*, Cambridge, UK, 1979.

Evans, James, *Why the English Sailed to the New World*, London, 2010.

Falwell, Jerry, *Listen America!* NY, 1980.

Farmer, Alan, *Britain and the American Colonies*, London, 2008.

Fellows, Nicholas and Mike Wells, *Access to History: Civil Rights in the USA, 1865-1992*. Abingdon, UK.

Fener, Eric, *Reconstruction: America's Unfinished Revolution, 1863-1877*, NY, 2014.

Firth, C. H., *Oliver Cromwell and the Rule of the Puritans in England*, London, 1900.

Forbes, Esther, *Paul Revere and the World He Lived In*, Boston, 1942.

Francisco, Frank, *Evolution of the Game: A Chronicle of American Football*, NY, 2016.

Frank, J., T*he Beginnngs of the English Newspaper*, Cambridge, Ma., 1961.

Frankel, Joseph, *British Foreign Policy 1945-73*, NY, 1975

Frankopan, Peter, *Silk Roads: A New History of the World*, London 2015.

Fraser, Rebecca, *The Mayflower Generation: The Winslow Family and the Fight for the New World*, London, 2002.

Freedman, L., *Britain and Nuclear Weapons*, London, 1980.

Friedman, Milton, *Capitalism and Freedom*, Chicago, 1962.

Friedman, Thomas L., *The World is Flat: A Brief History of the 21st Century*, NY, 2006.

Friends, William J., *The Two Koreas in East Asian Affairs*, NY 1976

Furuya, Keiji, *Chiang Kai-shek: His Life and Times*, NY 1981.

Gant, Scott, *We're All Journalists Now: The Transformation of the Press and the Re-shaping of the Law in the Internet Age*, NY, 2007.

Garton Ash, Timothy, *Free Speech*, New Haven, 2016.

Geiter, M. K., and W. A. Speck, *Colonial America: From Jamestown to Yorktown*, London, 2002.

Gerhold, Dorian, *The Putney Debates 1647*, London, 2007.

Gilbert, David and David Matless, *Geographics of British Modernity*, Oxford, 2018.

Gilbert, Martin, *The First World War*, London 1994.

Gillmeister, Heiner, *Tennis and Cultural History*, London, 2017.

Gillon, Steven M., *The Pact: Bill Clinton, Newt Gingrich and the Rivalry that Defined a Generation*, Oxford, 2008.

Goldblatt, David, *The Game of Our Lives: The Meaning and Making of English Football*, London 2014.

Gordon, George Stuart, *Anglo-American Literary Relations*, Oxford, 1942.

Gowing, Margaret, *Britain and Atomic Energy*, London 1974.

Graham, Ian C. C., *Colonists from Scotland: Emigration to America, 1707-1783*, NY., 1956.

Gregg, P., *Freeborn John*, NY, 1961.

Gromyko, Andrei, *Memories*, NY, 1989

Grosser, Alfred, *The Western Alliance: European-American Relations since 1945*, NY, 1980.

Gujiral, M. L., *US Global Involvement: A Study of American Expansionism*, New Delhi, 1975.

Bibliography

Hallam, Elizabeth (ed), *The Plantagenet Chronicles*, London, 2002.

Halle, Lewis, *The Cold War as History*, NY, 1991.

Hamilton, Alexander (eds Harold C. Syrett and Jacob E. Cooke), *The Papers of Alexander Hamilton*, NY, 1987.

Hankins, Barry, *Francis Schaeffer and the Shaping of Evangelical America*, NY, 2008.

Hargreaves, Robert, *The First Freedom: A History of Free Speech*, Stroud, 2002.

Harper, John Lamberton, *American Machiavelli*, Cambridge, UK, 2004.

Hatton, T. J. and J.G. Williamson, *The Age of Mass Migration*, NY, 1998.

Hayek, F .A., *John Stuart Mill and Harriet Taylor*, London, 1951.

Hibbert, Christopher, *Charles I: A Life of Religion, War and Treason*, NY, 2007.

Hibbert, Christopher, *The English: A Social History, 1066-1945*, London, 1988.

Higgins, Trumbull, *Korea and the Fall of MacArthur: A Precis in Limited War*, NY, 1960.

Higgitt, David and Mark H. Lee, (eds), *Geomorphological Processes and Landscape, Britain in the last 1,000 Years*, London, 2012.

Hill, C., *Puritanism and Revolution*, Urbana, Il, 1958.

Hill, Christopher, *The World Turned Upside Down*, London, 1975.

Hitchens, C., *Blood, Class and Empire: The Enduring Anglo-American Relationship*, NY, 2004.

Hobbes, Thomas, *Leviathan*, London, 1651.

Hobsbawm, Eric, *Industry and Empire*, London, 1968.

Hofstader, Richard, *America at 1750: A Social Portrait*, NY, 1971.

Hogan, M.J., *The Marshall Plan*, NY, 1987.

Holland, R. F., *European Decolonisation, 1918-1981*, London, 1984.

Hope-Jones, A., *Income Tax in the Napoleonic Wars*, Cambridge, UK, 1959.

Hubbard, William Lines, *The American History and Encyclopedia of Music*, NY, 2015.

Jackson, Ashley, *Churchill*, London, 2011.

Jefferson, Thomas (ed Paul Leicester Ford), *The Writings of Thomas Jefferson*, NY, 1899.

Jenkins, Simon, *A Short History of England*, London, 2012.

Jenks, Leland, *The Migration of British Capital to 1875*, London, 1963.

Johnson, Boris, *The Churchill Factor: How One Man Made History*, London, 2014.

Johnsson, Albert, I*celand, NATO and the Keflavik Base*, Reykjavik, 1980.

Jones, J. R., *The Anglo-Dutch Wars of the 17th Century*, London, 1996.

Karnow, Stanley, *Vietnam: A History*, NY, 1983.

Keele, Ronato, *Ockham Explained*, Chicago, 2010.

Kennan, George, *The Fateful Alliance*, NY, 1984.

Kenin, Richard, *Return to Albion: Americans in England*, NY, 1979.

Kennedy, Paul, *The Rise and Fall of the Great Powers*, London, 1985.

Kurland, Philip B., and Ralph Lerner (eds), *The Founders' Constitution*, Chicago, 1987.

Lambert, Frank, *The Founding Fathers and the Place of Religion in America*, Princeton, 2003.

Lapierre, Wayne, *Guns, Crime and Freedom*, NY, 1994.

Levin, Yuval, *The Great Debate: Edmund Burke, Thomas Paine and the Birth of Right and Left*, NY, 2014.

Liddington, Jill and Jill Norris, *One hand Tied Behind Us: The Rise of the Women's Suffrage Movement*, London, 2000.

Locke, John, *Two Treatises of Government*, Warsaw, 2016.

Louis, William Roger and Hedley Bull, *The Special Relationship: Anglo-American Relations since 1945*, Oxford 1986.

Lowery, Malinda Maynor, *Lumbee Indians in the Jim Crow South: Identity and the Making of a Nation*, Chapel Hill, NC, 1990.

Maddicott, J. R., *The Origins of the English Parliament, 924-1327*, Oxford, 2012.

Maier, Pauline, *American Scripture: Making the Declaration of Independence*, NY, 1997.

Man, John, *The Gutenberg Revolution*, London, 2009.

Mannix, Daniel and Malcolm Cowley, *A History of the Atlantic Slave Trade*, London, 1966.

Manuel, Frank E., *A Portrait of Isaac Newton*, Cambridge, Ma., 1968.

Marshall, Tim, *Prisoners of Geography*, London, 2015.

Matusiak, John, *James I: Scotland's King of England*, Stroud, 2015.

Marr, Andrew, *A History of Modern Britain*, London, 2008.

Marx, Karl, *Capital*, NY, 1996.

McAllister, Ward, *Society as I have Found It*, NY, 1890.

McBrien, Richard P., *The Harper Collins Encyclopedia of Catholicism*, NY, 1995.

MacCulloch, Diarmaid, *Reformation Europe's House Divided, 1490-1700*, London, 2012.

MacCulloch, Diarmaid, *Tudor Church Militant*, London, 1990.

McCullough, David, *John Adams*, NY, 2002.

McCue, Jim, Edmund Burke and Our Present Discontents, London, 1997.

McCusher, J. J. and R. R. Menard, *The Economy of British America*, Chapel Hill, NC, 1985.

McDonald, Forest, *Novus Ordo Secbrum: The Intellectual Origins of the Constitution*, Appleton, Wi, 1985.

McFarlane, Anthony, *The British in the Americas, 1480-1815*, London, 1994.

McGrath, A., *In the Beginning: The Story of the King James Bible*, London, 2001.

Melzer, Scott, *Gun Crusaders: The NRA's Culture War*, NY, 2009.

Middleton, Richard, *Colonial America: A History, 1585-1776*, Oxford 1886.

Mill, John Stuart, *On Liberty*, London, 1859.

Milton, John, *Aeropagitica*, Oxford, 1644.

Mullan, H., B. Mee and M. Bozat, *The Ultimate Encyclopedia of Boxing*, London, 2013.

Newton, Sir Isaac, *Mathematical Principles of Natural Philosophy*, London, 1687.

Nixon, Richard, *R.N.: The Memoirs of Richard Nixon*, NY, 1978.

Nunnerley, David, *President Kennedy and Britain*, NY, 1972.

Nye, Joseph S., Jr., *Soft Power and the Means to Success in World Politics*, NY, 2004.

Ober, Josiah, *Political Dissent in Democratic Athens: Intellectual Critics and Democratic Rule*, Princeton, 1998.

Oliver, Neil, *The Story of the British Isles in 100 Places*, NY, 2018.

O'Rourke, Kevin H. and Jeffrey G. William, *Globalisation and History*, Cambridge, Ma., 1989.

Oshinsky, David, *Worse Than Slavery: Parchman Farm and the Ordeal of Jim Crow Justice*, NY, 1997.

O'Toole, G. J. A., *The Encyclopedia of American Intelligence and Espionage*, NY, 1988.

Paine, Thomas, *Common Sense*, Philadelphia, 1776.

Pankhurst, Sylvia, *The Suffragette: The History of the Women's Militant Suffrage Movement, 1905-1910*, NY, 1911.

Paul, Diane, *Darwin, Social Darwinism and Eugenics*, Cambridge, UK, 2006.

Penn, William, (eds Mary Maples Dunn and Richard S. Dunn), *The Papers of William Penn*, Philadelphia, 1983.

Philbrick, Nathaniel, *Mayflower: A Story of Courage, Community and War*, NY, 2006.

Philbrick, Nathaniel, *Mayflower: A Voyage to War*, NY, 2005.

Pimlott, Ben, *Harold Wilson*, London, 1992.

Pomeranz, Kenneth and Stephen Topik, *The World that Trade Created: Society, Culture and the World Economy*, NY, 2006.

Reid, D. G., R. D. Linder, B. L. Shelley and H. S. Sout, *Dictionary of Christianity in America*, Downers Grove, Il, 1990.

Rhodes, P. J., *Athenian Democracy*, Edinburgh, 2004.

Rhodes, Richard, *The Making of the Atomic Bomb*, NY, 1988.

Rutland, R. A., *The Birth of the Bill of Rights*, Raleigh, NC, 1955.

Sadler, Nigel, *The Legacy of Slavery in Britain*, Stroud, 2018.

Seitz, Raymond, *Over Here*, London, 1998.

Siebert, F., *Freedom of the Press in England 1476-1776*, Urbana, Il, 1965.

Smith, Harold, *The British Women's Suffrage Campaign, 1866-1928*, Abingdon, 2000.

Smith, R. B., *An International History of Vietnam*, NY, 1986.

Smith, Adam, *Wealth of Nations*, London, 1776.

Sommers, Michael, *The Right to Bear Arms*, NY, 2002.

Sopel, Jon, *If Only they didn't Speak: Notes from Trump's America*, London, 2018.

Spanier, J. W., *American Foreign Policy since World War Two*, Washington DC, 1988.

Spinney, Laura, *The Lost World of Doggerland*, National Geographic, December 2012.

Starkey, David, *Monarchy from the Middle Ages to Modernity*, London, 2006.

Steely, Mel, *The Gentleman from Georgia: The Biography of Newt Gingrich*, Mercer, Ga, 2000.

Steinbach, Susie, *Women in England, 1760-1914: A Social History*, London, 2003.

Steinberg, S., *500 Years of Printing*, London, 2017.

Stephen, James Fitzjames, *Liberty, Equality, Fraternity*, London, 1874.

Stowe, Harriet Beecher, *Life of Harriet Beecher Stowe*, NY, 1891.

Stowe, Harriet Beecher, *Uncle Tom's Cabin*, NY, 2015.

Street, Sarah, *Transatlantic Crossings: British Feature Films in the United States*, London, 2007.

Stuyvesant, William C. (ed), *Handbook of North American Indians*, Washington DC, 1978.

Taylor, Alan, *Colonial America*, Oxford, 2013.

Taylor, Derek J., *Who Do the English Think They Are?*, Stroud, 2017

Tidman, Evelyn, *One Small Candle: The Story of William Bradford and the Pilgrim Fathers*, London, 2013.

Tracy, James D. (ed), *The Rise of the Merchant Empires*, NY, 1990.

Tuchman, Barbara, *The Proud Tower, A Portrait of the World Before the War*, NY, 1966.

Tunstall, Jeremy and David Machin, *The Anglo-American Media Connection*, Oxford, 1999.

Ward, Geoffey, *Unforgivable Blackness: The Rise and Fall of Jack Johnson*, NY, 2014.

Wasring, John, *Indentured Migration and the Servant Trade from London to America, 1618-1718*, Oxford, 2017.

Washington, George (ed J. C. Fitzpatrick), *The Writings of George Washington from the Original Manuscript Sources, 1745-1799*, Washington DC, 1944.

Washburn, Wilcomb E., *The Indian in America*, NY, 1975.

Wecter, Dixon, *The Saga of American Society: A Record of Social Aspirationism*, London, 1937.

Weisbuch, Robert, *Atlantic Double-Cross: American Literature and the British Influence in the Age of Emerson*, Chicago, 1986.

Williams, Daniel K., 'Jerry Falwell's Sunbelt Politics: The Regional Origins of the Moral Majority', *Journal of Policy History*, Cambridge University, April 2010.

Williams, J. S., *The Supreme Court Speaks*, Austin, 1956.

Williams, P. *The Tudor Regime*, Oxford, 1979.

Williams, W. A., *The Roots of the Modern American Empire*, NY, 1969.

Wilson, A. N., *After the Victorians: The World Our Parents*, London, 2005

Wilson, A. N., *The Life of John Milton*, Oxford, 1983.

Wilson, Charles, *Profit and Power: A Study of England and the Dutch Wars*, London, 1957.

Wilson, Harold, *Memoirs: The Making of a Prime Minister, 1916-1964*, London, 1986

Wilson, Harold, *Final Term: The Labour Government, 1974-76*, London, 1979.

Wilson, Harold, *The Governance of Britain*, London, 1976.

Winkler, Adam, *Gunfight: The Battle Over the Right to Bear Arms in America*, NY, 2011.

Winship, Michael and Mark C. Carnes, *The Trial of Anne Hutchison: Liberty, Law and Intolerance in Puritan New England*, Boston, 2014.

Wolfley, Jeanette, 'Jim Crow Indian Style: The Disenfranchisement of Native Americans', *Indian Law Review*, 1990.

Woodruff, W., *America's Impact on the World: A Study of the Role of the United States in the World Economy 1750-1970*, NY, 1973.

Woodward, C. Van, *The Old World's New World*, Oxford, 1991.

Young, Alexander, *Chronicles of the Pilgrim Fathers of the Colony of Plymouth*, NY, 1841.

Zinn, Howard, *A People's History of the United States*, NY, 1980.

Index of People

Acheson, Dean 315-6, 322
Adams, John 78, 91, 97, 105, 107, 123-4, 171, 297, 300
Agricola 15
Airey, Sir George 25
Alexander the Great 39
Ali, Muhammad 279
Amish (Pennsylvania Dutch) 191
Annan, Kofi 26
Anselm of Canterbury 44-5
Anthony, Susan B. 111
Aristophanes 39
Aristotle 41-2, 48
Asquith, H. H. 103
Attlee, Clement 316, 321, 323
Bacon, Sir Francis 41, 63, 121
Bacon, Roger 44, 47-8
Baird, John Logie 264-5
Bentham, Jeremy 91-91, 97
Berners-Lee, Tim 129
Bessemer, Henry 223-4
Beveridge, William 227-8
Bevin, Ernest 315-7
Biden, Joseph 342
Bin Laden, Osama 339-40
Bismarck, Otto von 304, 330
Blackstone, Sir William 81-4
Blair, Tony 340
Bloomberg 26
Boleyn, Anne 156-7, 281
Booth, John Wilkes 122, 260
Boulton, Matthew 222
Brewster, William 160-161
Broughton, Jack 278

Bryan, William Jennings 177
Buckingham, Duke of 58-9
Burnside, Ambrose 246
Burke, Edmund 77-80, 97, 297
Cabot, John (Giovanni Cabot) 18
Callender, James 124
Calvert, George, Lord Baltimore 168-71
Calvin, John 158-9, 173, 175
Campbell-Bannerman, Henry 103
Canning, George 302
Carnegie, Andrew 194, 224
Carter, Haron 246
Cary, Anthony (Viscount Falkland) 74
Caxton, William 41-2
Charles I 50-51, 57, 59, 66-73
Charles II 72-4, 146, 166-7, 170, 187-9, 192, 209, 238-9, 259, 289
Charles V 136-7
Chaucer, Geoffrey 41, 256
Churchill, Jennie 197
Churchill, Winston 10-11, 69, 104, 132, 197, 200, 227, 258, 311, 314, 317, 319
Claiborne, William 168-9
Clinton, Hillary 106, 229, 233
Cobbett, Thomas 125
Cobden, Richard 219-220
Coke, Sir Edward 52-59
Constantine I, Emperor 40
Coolidge, Calvin 133

Cooper, Anthony Ashley, 1st Earl of Shaftesbury 63
Copernicus 41
Corbet, John 59
Cornwallis, Lord 22, 243, 296
Cranmer, Thomas 49, 158
Cromwell, Oliver 51-2, 57, 59, 61, 69-75, 98, 157, 169, 173, 184, 186-8, 194-5, 208, 236-8, 240, 247, 258-9, 274-5, 288
Cromwell, Thomas 157
Cruz, Ted 233
Da Gama, Vasco 17
Darnell, Thomas 59
Darrow, Clarence 177
Darwin, Charles 92-94, 216
Deane, Silas 295
De Athee, Gerard 32
De Beauvoir, Simone 41
Delane, John Thaddeus 125-6
De Montfort, Simon 36-7
Dempsey, Jack 279
Descartes, Rene 41, 45
De Soto, Hernando 19
De Valera, Carlos 136
Dias, Bartholomew 16
Dickens, Charles 10, 196, 227, 261, 271
Doubleday, Abner 276-7
Drake, Sir Francis 17, 137, 212, 224, 285
Dulles, John Foster 326
Edison, Thomas 270
Edward I 37
Edward III 155, 235-6, 291
Edward VI 157, 183, 252
Edwards, Jonathan 172-3

Bibliography

Elizabeth I 17, 37, 53, 66, 120, 135, 159, 182-3, 212, 258, 285

Engels, Friedrich 95-6, 313

Fairfax, Sir Thomas 70

Falwell, Jerry 177

Farage, Nigel 99

Fitzwalter, Lord Robert 31

Floyd, George 135

Ford, Gerald 228

Fox, George 166, 190-91

Franklin, Benjamin 33, 42, 78, 82, 122, 145, 261, 295

Fuchs, Klaus 319

Fuller, Nicholas 54

Fulton, Robert 224

Galileo 41

Galton, Francis 93

Garrison, William Lloyd 147-9

George III 21, 34, 62, 98, 104, 109, 193, 242

George V 103

Gilbert and Sullivan 260

Gilbert, Sir Humphrey 18

Gingrich, Newt 115-17

Glover, Reverend Jose 42

Godwinson, Harold 35

Goncalves, Antao 136

Gorbachev, Mikhail 337-8

Gorges, Sir Ferdinando 161-2

Gorsuch, Neil 86

Guttenberg, Johannes 40

Hamilton, Alexander 52, 92, 97, 105, 123-4, 194, 214, 226, 297

Hampden, John 68

Hampton, Edmund 59

Hancock, John 91

Hapsburgs 17, 58, 156

Haselrig, Arthur 68

Hawkins, Sir John 135, 137, 212

Hayes, Rutherford B. 108

Henry II 29, 234

Henry III 32, 36, 101

Henry VII 18, 48-9, 210

Henry VIII 37, 41, 49, 65, 103, 156-8, 183, 236, 281

Henry the Navigator, Prince 16

Henry, Patrick 27

Hitler, Adolf 94, 133, 200, 284, 309-10, 314, 322

Hobbes, Thomas 9, 52, 62, 63, 104

Holles, Denzil 68

Holmes, Sir Robert 140

Hope, Lord Chief Justice 122-3

Hopkins, Matthew 164

Hudson, Henry 18, 288

Huguenots 58, 150, 163, 185

Hume, David 41

Hussein, Saddam 340

Hyde, Anne 73

Innocent III, Pope 31-2

Jackson, Andrew 107, 147, 300

James I 33, 50, 53, 57, 66-7, 159-60, 168, 184, 274, 280

James II 64, 73-4, 78, 98, 140, 144, 166, 167, 170, 192-3, 238-9, 247, 279

James, Henry 197

Jefferson, Thomas 9, 21, 33, 35, 44, 52, 63, 81-2, 91, 97, 104-7, 123-4, 148, 176, 189, 214, 296-7, 299

Jeffreys, George Lord Chief Justice 192

Jeffries, John L. 279

John ap John 190

John, King 30-32, 35

John XII, Pope 47

Johnson, Boris 117, 342

Johnson, Jack 278-9

Johnson, President Lyndon B. 134, 228, 321, 325

Johnson, Samuel 257

Kavanaugh, Brett 86

Kennedy, President John F. 195, 229, 246, 320-21

Keynes, John Maynard 229-230, 315

King, Martin Luther Jr. 246

Knox, John 158

Lenin, Vladimir Ilich Ulayanov 80, 96

Lenthall, William 68

L'Estrange, Roger 64

Levellers, the 50-52, 70-71, 173, 236-7

Lilburne, John (Freeborn John) 50, 54

Lincoln, Abraham 57, 81, 122, 133, 135, 150, 260, 303

Lloyd George, David 99, 307-8

Locke, John 8-9, 41, 62-4, 82, 104

Lollards 155, 158, 181

Louis IV, Holy Roman Emperor 47

Louis XIII 58, 163

Louis XIV 290, 294

Louis XVI 297-8

Louis, Joe 279

Luther, Martin 48, 65, 134, 155 -6, 158, 173

McCarthy, Joseph 127-8, 321, 323

Macmillan, Harold 104, 320, 334

Madison, James 8, 44, 82, 104-5, 123, 148, 75, 232, 244, 248, 300

Marconi, Guglialmo 264

Maria, Henrietta (French Princess and Queen) 58, 67, 162, 168

Marshall, George C. 270, 316

Marshall, John, US Chief Justice 81

Marx, Karl 94-96, 313

Mather, Cotton 145, 268

Mather, Richard 184

May, Theresa 117, 230, 342

Mill, John Stuart 9, 97, 114-5, 132

Milton, John 8, 41, 51-, 64, 69, 229

Modena, Mary of 73

Monck, General William 72

Monmouth, Duke of 74, 139, 192, 239

Monroe, James 44, 148, 299, 302
Moret, Hannah 112
Mott, Lucretia 113
Mun, Sir Thomas 208
Murdoch, William 222
Napoleon Bonaparte 9, 14, 101, 218-9, 225, 290, 296, 298-300, 302, 332
Nasser, Gamal Abdel 325-6
Newton, Sir Isaac, 9, 61-62
Nicholas II, Tsar 96
Nixon, Richard 219, 228, 315, 324
Nkrumah, Kwama 331-2
Obama, Barack 134, 195, 229, 231, 340
Oglethorpe, James 171, 183
Orwell, George 40
Otis, James 121
Paine, Thomas 52, 77-81
Pankhurst, Sylvia 114
Penn, William 33, 76, 145, 164, 166-7, 191
Philip of Macedonia 39
Pitt, William the Elder 101, 295
Pitt, William the Younger 101, 218, 225
Pius V, Pope 158
Pizarro, Francisco 17
Plato 41-3, 48
Praise God Barebones 72
Pride, Colonel Thomas 71, 237
Prynne, William 50
Puritans 158-165
Putin, Vladimir 129, 205
Pym, John 68
Quakers 51, 97, 154, 165-167, 172-5, 190-191
Raleigh, Sir Walter 53, 212
Reagan, Ronald 177, 229-230, 336-7
Reid, John 280
Reith, Lord John 265-6
Ricardo, David 218-9
Richard I 30, 291

Richard II 155, 208
Rockefeller, John D. 19, 318
Rockingham, Marquis of 78
Rodgers and Hammerstein 260
'Roe, Jane', Norma McCorvey 177
Rosebery, Lord 70
Roosevelt, Franklin D. 10, 12, 310-14, 317-18, 328
Roosevelt, Theodore 273
Rousseau, Jean-Jacques 41, 52
Rupert, Prince 140
Russel, Lord, Foreign Secretary 126, 303
Russell, William 126
Sartre, Jean-Paul 41
Scotus, John Duns 45-8
Shakespeare, William 10, 256, 258-60, 271-2
Shaw, George Bernard 260
Smith, Adam 215-219, 223
Smith, Captain John 27
Sophocles 39
Spinoza, Baruch 41
Stanton, Elizabeth Cady 113
Stephenson, George 222-3, 318
Storey, William 126
Stowe, Harriet Beecher 149-50
Strickland, William 159
Strode, William 68
Sullivan, John L. 278-9
Sumner, William Graham 93
Suozzi, Tom 233
Tennent, Gilbert 172-3
Thompson, George 147-8
Thompson, William 112
Till, Emmett 134
Tizard, Henry 200
Trevithick, Richard 222
Tristos, Munto 136

Trump, Donald 86, 106, 116, 119, 131, 134-5, 151, 178, 205, 210, 229- 233, 279, 317, 328, 341-2
Twain, Mark 132, 173, 224, 261, 263
Victoria, Queen 55, 89, 260,, 272-3, 329
Walpole, Sir Robert 98
Washington, George 21-2, 25, 44, 81, 90, 105, 107-9, 144, 124, 188, 193, 214, 241, 243, 267, 275, 284, 295-6, 303, 305-6, 308
Watt, James 221-2, 224
Webster, Daniel 121
Webster, Noah 257-8
Wesley, Charles 171-2, 268
Wilberforce, William 111-12, 146-7
Wilde, Oscar 260
Wilhelm II, Kaiser 304, 307
Wilkes, John, MP 8, 38, 122
William I (William the Conqueror) 14, 29-30, 35, 45, 290
William of Ockham 45-7
William and Mary 74, 141, 170, 193, 239
Wilson, Harold 128, 325
Wilson, Woodrow 127, 133, 199, 306-8, 314
Wingfield, Walter Clopton 281
Winthrop, John 164-5, 184
Wolsey, Cardinal Thomas 49
Wollstonecraft, Mary 112
Wycliffe, John 48, 154-6, 158
Wynkyn de Worde 42
Yardley, George 138
Zenger, John Peter 122
Zuckerberg, Mark 130, 132